D0916347

Communication and Personality
Trait Perspectives

Accepting a trait explanation for communication does not eliminate or minimize the role that environmental and contextual variables play in determining communication behavior. In fact, when looking at a lone situation, the elements of the situation could often explain rather accurately the outcomes or the behaviors in the situation. Clearly, if someone points a gun at another person and tells that person to "shut up," only a very few of us would continue to talk. However, when attempting to explain (or predict) a person's communication behavior across situations, communication traits often offer a stronger indicator than environmental or contextual variables in providing an explanation for why people often communicate in a consistent manner, even though they are interacting in different situations with different people.

This book is divided into three sections. The first section includes four chapters devoted to the nature of trait research. The second section includes eight chapters that direct attention to individual communication-related traits. The final section includes only a single chapter. It is devoted to projecting the future of communication trait research.

In chapter 1, Daly and Bippus offer an introduction to the study of personality and communication. Daly and Bippus argue for the importance of communication traits in studying human communication. The chapters that follow make solid arguments for the genetic basis of communication traits. Recent research by Beatty and McCroskey (chapter 2), as well as by Horvath (chapter 3), supports the contention that the explanation for why people differ in their communication traits could be found by studying the genetics of individuals. Beatty and McCroskey propose a temperament approach to the study of communication traits. Horvath follows with evidence, based on research involving twins, that communicator style is genetically based. Drawing on Eysenck's biologically supported three-factor model of personality, Weaver, in chapter 4, argues that communication orientations are trait-based.

Let the reader be forewarned: What is being argued in these chapters, especially in Beatty and McCroskey's chapter, may be seen as controversial by some. If research continues to support the argument for temperament as the major root of one's personality, and thus how one communicates, the study of communication traits will be redirected. This new orientation for the study of communication has been dubbed the *communibiological paradigm* by Beatty and McCroskey. This potential paradigm shift has potentially very far-reaching implications that are addressed in the final section in chapter 13 by Beatty.

The chapters in Part II introduce and review some of the major current communication traits. The purpose of these chapters is not to provide an exhaustive literature review of the individual trait (in fact, the authors of the chapters reference other published works where such reviews can be found). The purpose instead is to introduce the communication trait to the reader with a focus on the role that the communication trait plays in the communication process. Rancer (chapter 7) gives an overview of argumentativeness, whereas Wigley (chapter 9) covers the destructive communication trait of verbal aggressiveness. McCroskey and Beatty (chapter 10) report on people's tendency to avoid communication in their chapter on communication apprehension. McCroskey and Richmond (chapter 5) report on peoples' tendency to approach communication in their chapter on willingness to communicate. Additionally, chapters are included concerning sociocommunicative style (Richmond & Martin, chapter 6), affective orientation (Booth-Butterfield & Booth-Butterfield, chapter 8), cognitive complexity (Burleson, chapter 11), and interpersonal communication motives (Rubin & Martin, chapter 12).

These chapters are included to provide representative, although certainly not exhaustive, illustrations of contemporary communication scholarship that stems from the trait perspective. Most of this work represents the trait research tradition based on the social-learning model. That model has dominated work in this area since the 1950s. It focuses mostly on the nature of the trait and its effects and generally presumes that the trait has been learned by the individual as a function of interacting with the environment from early childhood through adulthood. It is at this level that the social-learning and communibiological paradigms separate. Whether traits are developed by social-learning processes, are genetically determined, or represent an interaction of these two influences, the nature of the trait and the effects of the trait on communication behavior may be the same. Determining the source of the trait, however, may be critical in determining whether and how "positive" traits can be encouraged and "negative" traits can be controlled.

ACKNOWLEDGMENTS

We wish to acknowledge the major impact that the early work of Carl Hovland, Irving Janis, and Harold Kelley (commonly know as the Yale Group) has had on the research that led to this book. They served as a major positive influence on two generations of communication scholars. Their early book, *Communication and*

About the Contributors

Michael J. Beatty (Ph.D., Ohio State University) is a Professor of Communication at Cleveland State University.

Amy M. Bippus (M.A., Wake Forest University) is a Ph.D. student at the University of Texas.

Melanie Booth-Butterfield (Ph.D., University of Missouri) is a Professor of Communication Studies at West Virginia University.

Steve Booth-Butterfield (Ed.D., West Virginia University) is an Associate Professor of Communication Studies at West Virginia University.

Brant R. Burleson (Ph.D., University of Illinois) is a Professor in the Department of Communication at Purdue University.

Scott E. Caplan (M.S., University of Delaware) is a Ph.D. student in the Department of Communication at Purdue University.

John A. Daly (Ph.D., Purdue University) is the Amon Carter Professor of Communication and Professor of Management and Pharmacy at the University of Texas at Austin. He is currently President of the National Communication Association.

Cary W. Horvath (M.A., Kent State University) is an Instructor at Westminster college, New Wilmington, PA.

Matthew M. Martin (Ph.D., Kent State University) is an Assistant Professor of Communication Studies at West Virginia University.

James C. McCroskey (Ed.D., Penn State University) is a Professor of Communication Studies at West Virginia University.

Andrew S. Rancer (Ph.D., Kent State University) is a Professor in the School of Communication at the University of Akron.

Virginia P. Richmond (Ph.D., University of Nebraska) is a Professor of Communication Studies at West Virginia University.

Rebecca B. Rubin (Ph.D., University of Illinois) is a Professor of Communication Studies at Kent State University.

James B. Weaver, III (Ph.D., Indiana University) is an Associate Professor in the Department of Communication at Auburn University.

Charles J. Wigley, III (Ph.D., Kent State University) is a Chair and an Associate Professor in the Department of Communication at Canisius College.

Personality and Interpersonal Communication: Issues and Directions

John A. Daly
Amy M. Bippus
University of Texas

The purpose of this book is to summarize research and theory on personality and communication and place that research in perspective. Most of the chapters that follow deal with specific dispositions and their import for communication. This chapter, and the one that follows, attempt to frame much of the research that is summarized in later chapters by introducing a few important conceptual issues in the field of personality as they relate to communication scholars.

This chapter focuses on a limited number of topics. Many of the issues found in typical personality texts (e.g., psychodynamic theories, clinical assessment and modification of traits, phenomenological approaches to personality) are not examined for reasons of brevity as well as relevance. The topics that are examined are those that probably have the greatest importance to communication scholars. They include a brief overview of the core concepts of personality, perceptual approaches to traits, a survey of theory and research on the relationships among traits and behavior, a brief introduction to some of the methodological options and issues in personality research as they arise in typical communication projects, and a short discussion of the various roles that personality plays in communication.

THE TRAIT CONCEPT

The concept of a disposition entails an enduring tendency to behave, think, or feel in a certain way. A *trait* is, in Guilford's (1959) words, "any distinguishable, relatively enduring way in which one individual differs from others" (p. 6). Traits differ in a number of ways. Some are broad, some narrow in their focus. Some emphasize social characteristics, others highlight more cognitively oriented variables. Some are defined primarily by people's responses to questionnaires, others are more often recognized by their behavioral manifestations. Some are conceptualized as part of a larger scheme, whereas others stand alone. But whatever the differences, the underlying assumption is similar: People differ in systematic ways from one another. Traits attempt to define the meaningful ways in which people differ. Some researchers have attempted to distinguish between traits, as enduring dispositions, and states, as situationally specific responses. For instance, Zuckerman (1983) suggested that states and traits can be distinguished on four grounds: (a) traits have high retest reliabilities, whereas states do not; (b) a state should have a moderate correlation with its related trait, that is, a sampling of states over time should yield a summed score highly correlated with the related trait; (c) a trait should correlate more highly with other similar traits than with its related state, and the state response should correlate more highly with similar state responses than with the trait associated with it; and (d) traits should not be affected substantially by transient changes, whereas states may be so affected. The differences between trait and state are, in actuality, primarily differences of emphasis. Personality scholars tend to emphasize the trait over the state. In recent years, however, the distinction has become increasingly blurred. However, there is a recent trend in personality research to approach states and traits as complementary (Chaplin, John, & Goldberg, 1988), and to recognize and measure both the state and trait components of psychological attributes (Steyer, Ferring, & Schmitt, 1992).

One of the knottiest problems is defining a personality variable. Personality constructs seem to proliferate at an incredible pace. One can hardly avoid finding some aspiring new construct described in some journal each month. For the most part, these new constructs are unrelated to one another, created either because of some specific need of an investigator (e.g., a measure is created to serve as a covariate in an experiment) or because the researcher saw an unassessed individual difference in people and opted to create a construct and measure.

Although most of the traits found in typical studies of social behavior are conceptually independent, there have been some attempts to systematically categorize and determine central constructs. The dominant trend in trait research now is the Five-Factor Model (FFM), commonly referred to as the Big Five. The FFM of personality traits represents the resurgence of interest in the notion of broad dispositional traits. The most widely accepted form of the five factors—extraversion (E); neurotocism (N); openness to experience (O); agreeableness (A) and conscientiousness (C)—was proposed by Tupes and Christal (1961) and replicated by Norman (1963), but did not garner widespread attention until the 1980s. The FFM has developed as a response to the question regarding the basic dimensions of personality: What are the most important ways in which individuals differ in their enduring emotional, interpersonal, experiential, attitudinal, and motivational styles? The claim of FFM proponents is that these factors, singly or in combination, can be found in virtually all personality instruments (McCrae & John, 1992). The FFM originated in studies of natural language trait terms, such as the adjective checklist, using as its starting point the question, "How do lay people talk about traits?" The entering assumption was that language has evolved to reflect all aspects of personality. Given this, the presumption was that the process of distilling these trait terms into cohesive categories would tap the basic dimensions of personality. Thus far, the validity of the FFM has been supported in studies of other languages, including Spanish (Benet & Waller, 1995), German (Borkenau & Ostendorf, 1989), Estonian and Finnish (Pulver, Allik, Pulkkinen, & Hamalainen, 1995), and Dutch (Duijsens & Diekstra, 1995).

Although the FFM has enjoyed considerable popularity in the field of personality research, it is not without its detractors. There is no consensus as to the titles of the factors (although those noted here are the most widely accepted), and scholars disagree as to whether the FFM contains too many factors (e.g., Zuckerman, Kuhlman, & Camac, 1988) or too few (e.g., Digman & Takemoto-Chock, 1981; Jackson, Ashton, & Tomes, 1996). Many traits of interest in research contain elements of more than one dimension, leading to disagreement among some scholars as to how particular combinations of personality characteristics should be categorized within the FFM. The limitations of the FFM as a personality model have been argued by Block (1995), who contended that the lexical analysis methodology on which it is based is suspect, and that utility of the FFM as a factorial structure of traits across people is limited. Even its supporters admit that FFM is not a complete theory of personality; it does not explain unique individual characteristics, or the processes by which these characteristics manifest themselves in our interactions. Rather, the FFM simply provides a structure for the common dimensions of individual differences.

Despite its detractors, the FFM is firmly in place as a central construct of personality research. Researchers have now taken on the task of integrating existing trait measures within the FFM (e.g., de Raad & Hofstee, 1993; McCrae & Costa, 1994; Trapnell & Wiggins, 1990) and developing new measures to tap into it (Caprara, Barbaranelli, Borgogni, & Perugini, 1993; Duijsens & Diekstra, 1995). Theoretical development of the FFM has allowed it to be compared and tested against other measures of personality constructs not explicitly represented in common language. D. Buss (1992), for instance, provided an example of an interpersonal phenomenon (manipulation tactics) that can be linked to specific dimensions of the FFM. Communication scholars interested in personality need to be cognizant of the FFM and, more importantly, consider three possible implications. First, how do the variables studied by communication scholars fit within the FFM? Second, are there ways communication-related personality variables might be combined into something akin to the FFM? And finally, might communication scholars discover an integrative framework for the panoply of variables currently studied?

MEASURING TRAITS

Although there are a variety of techniques available to the communication scholar for assessing personality characteristics, the predominant approach is the *self-report*. Respondents complete a questionnaire composed of items conceptually and empirically related to the characteristic in question. Clearly, there are limitations to this technique. For instance, respondents may not answer accurately or truthfully, and in the case of most self-report tests used in communication research, there is no foolproof method for detecting such biased responses. People will often provide responses that place them in a favorable light (Daly & Street, 1980; Klein & Kunda, 1993).

Some self-reports are transparent in revealing what they measure. For example, measures of self-esteem that include items like "I like myself," or questionnaires on shyness that include items like "I am shy," conspicuously display the construct they are tapping. Other self-report techniques are less transparent. For instance, communication researchers interested in cognitive complexity often have subjects describe a person or event. The number of different constructs a subject comes up with is a measure of his or her complexity. This sort of assessment has less bias associated with it, at least in terms of the obviousness of what is being assessed. Daly, Bell, Glenn, and Lawrence (1985) offered another self-report technique for assessing individual differences in the way people represent conversations. They had subjects sort through a number of short conversational excerpts and judge them on the perceived similarity. The similarity judgments were then used in a multidimensional scaling that yielded two underlying dimensions: one that emphasized the surface features of the episodes, and the other emphasizing the underlying communication event that occurred in the episodes (e.g., politeness or disagreement). Subjects received scores on both dimensions. This indirect method for assessing a personality dimension avoided many of the potential biases common in self-reports. There are other techniques available (e.g., forced-choice measures and "bogus pipeline") that, although they are seldom used in communication studies, nevertheless offer ways for assessing personality dimensions while avoiding many of the problems often associated with self-reports. Some researchers have been critical of self-reports on the grounds that they are prone to error due to individuals' moods or prior beliefs about themselves (Locksley, Brill, & Neuner, 1984). Kolar, Funder, and Colvin (1996) found that in terms of predicting overt behavior, self-reports were less accurate as personality judgments than either single or aggregated reports from acquaintances. This finding suggests that combined scores of peers may be more accurate sources of personality scores than self-reports.

There are a number of methodological issues that are specifically relevant to the researcher conducting questionnaire research, including the middle category response tendency (Hasan, 1993) and the serial order of items effects (Steinberg, 1994). There has also been recent interest in the use of computerized surveys for the collection of self-report data. No substantial evidence has been found as yet that this computerized approach to data collection elicits different responses than conventional paper-and-pencil measures (Finegan & Allen, 1994; King & Miles, 1995).

An alternative to self-reports is observer ratings. In some investigations, people familiar with a person judge that person on some disposition. This technique also has limitations. Observers, for example, may be biased, may not observe certain acts (particularly private ones), or may have different perceptual definitions of dispositional characteristics than the observed individual. Traits may vary widely in the number of behavioral indicants or external manifestations that characterize them (Borkenau & Liebler, 1995). Despite these problems, there is evidence that observer ratings and self-reports of some behaviors are positively related (A. Buss & Plomin, 1984), although observers generally report lower frequencies than those offered by self-reports.

McCrae (1994) noted that the use of both self-report and observer ratings of personality can reduce the biases inherent in both types of data collection, and may yield richer information about the stability and consistency of personality attributes. Accuracy in personality judgments of individuals is a subject of continual concern for personality researchers. According to Funder and West (1993), three issues summarize concerns about accuracy: *consensus*, or the degree to which judgments by different observers of an individual agree with each other; *self-other agreement*, the extent to which observer's judgments of an individual agree with the individual's judgments of self; and *accuracy*, the degree to which personality judgments characterize actual attributes of the individual being judged. Attempting to simultaneously use both self-report and observer ratings of personality may provide a more conscientious approach for dealing with these issues.

Reliability in trait measurement is established by assessing internal consistency and consistency over time. Validity is typically established in three ways: first, by correlating the trait with other traits based on the expectation that similar traits should correlate highly and that dissimilar traits should have a more limited association (Campbell & Fiske, 1959); second, by comparing self-reports on the trait with observer reports of the individual's standing on the continuum represented by the trait; and third, by predicting and then observing behavioral correlates of the trait.

One limitation of most scaling techniques for personality variables is that scores are based on sample characteristics. The critical issue is the relative standing of individuals, and this emphasis does not permit judgments about a specific person. Although a person's absolute manifestation of a disposition may be constant, his or her relative standing can change due to changes in other members of the sample. Or the person's absolute manifestation of a disposition might change while his or her relative standing remains constant if all other members in the group change. This problem has led D. Buss and Craik (1984), among others, to suggest alternatives to traditional scales. They proposed an index of behavioral frequencies for a disposition.

Trait measures also reflect underlying assumptions about the units of personality. The vast majority of traits are dimensional variables thought to be possessed, to some degree, by all individuals. Thus, a continuous distribution is assumed. Alternatively, some personality variables may better be viewed as class variables, where differences are distributed into discrete classes (e.g., there are two classes of people) and a continuous distribution is not assumed (Gangestad & Snyder, 1985). Some recent research suggests that linear models of data analysis, such as factor analysis, may not be appropriate when used with dichotomous responses formats, and recommends the use of nonlinear models (Waller, Tellegen, McDonald, & Lykken, 1996).

PERCEIVING PERSONALITY

Although much of personality theory and research focuses on traits that distinguish people from one another, one strand of inquiry emphasizes instead the conceptions people hold about the personalities of others. Dweck, Hong, and Chiu (1993) suggested that individuals differ in the degree to which they perceive traits as stable and fixed. They argued for a distinction between entity theorists, who perceive traits as fixed and thus tend to draw global trait inferences from behavioral information, and incremental theorists, who tend to see traits as malleable qualities, and therefore use behavioral information to develop working hypotheses about traits, with these hypotheses being continually refined. Regardless of whether people actually have traitlike dispositions, to some degree most people seem to believe that they do. Two major topics fit within this area: implicit personality theory and trait attributions.

Implicit Personality Theory

Our language is filled with terms that are essentially descriptive of traits. Allport and Odbert (1936) found almost 18,000 trait words in English. Traits are part of the way people construe their social world. In the mid-1950s a major concern was how people form impressions of others. Following Asch's (1946) investigation, scholars attempted to determine the relationships that people perceive among trait terms. Under the rubric of implicit personality theory (Bruner & Tagiuri, 1954), a number of investigations were conducted to determine the underlying structure of people's beliefs about personality (e.g., Rosenberg & Sedlak, 1972; Wishner, 1960). Debates ensued about a variety of issues, including whether the structures people had for traits represented idealized versions of how people are or if they actually reflected the interrelationships of people's dispositions (Schneider, Hastorf, & Ellsworth, 1979). More recently, debates have emphasized the potential dialectic approach that most people have to making personality impressions (e.g., Lamiell, Foss, Trierweiler, & Leffel, 1983). A second issue was whether the interrelationships observed reflected mostly the semantic relations among behavior categories rather than the actual co-occurrence of behavioral traits (e.g., Shweder & D'Andrade, 1980; see also Romer & Revelle, 1985). In communication research, Norton (1980) and Sypher (1980) debated this issue. Neither concern has yet been resolved to the satisfaction of most.

A variant of implicit personality theory has been introduced by Cantor and Mischel (1979). They suggested that people may organize their trait perceptions into categories, labeled prototypes, that allow them to parsimoniously organize their impressions of others (Pryor, Kott, & Bovee, 1984). These categories are hierarchically organized. For example, within the prototype of extroversion may lie other traits (e.g., outgoing, talkative), as well as behavioral representations of the traits. As Chaplin et al. (1988) noted, state and trait components of prototypes are complementary schemas that people use to try to explain, predict, and control the behavior of others in social interactions. The memorability of traits and behaviors closely related to a particular prototype is generally greater than that of traits and behaviors that are incompatible with the prototype (Cantor & Mischel, 1977; see also Hastie & Kumar, 1979). Prototypes serve as guides for organizing knowledge about others. In judging others, people tend to rely on central or prototypical features (Mischel & Peake, 1982). Karylowski (1990) found evidence that oneself and familiar others are habitually used as cognitive prototypes against which information about others may be compared. Therefore, we find traits that are typical of us or our friends to be easier and faster to identify in others. Dunning, Perie, and Story (1991) noted that prototypes tend to be self-serving, as individuals tend to view those features they possess themselves as being central within desirable social categories. For example, people who write well are more likely to name writing skills as a feature of intelligence.

Trait Attribution

People often attempt to explain why individuals behave as they do when trying to determine "who they are." These attributions can be organized in a number of ways. A particularly important way of arranging attributions about others' behavior is by whether the observed behavior was due primarily to situation or to disposition. In many cases, people overemphasize the importance of dispositions and underemphasize the role of situational considerations in judging the behavior of others. On the other hand, when judging their own behavior, they often tend to highlight situational aspects and de-emphasize dispositional causes (Jones, 1979; Jones & Nisbett, 1971): "I do what I do because of the situation; you do what you do because that is the way you are." Prager and Cutler (1990) found that the tendency to make situational attributions about others increases as our acquaintance level with those individuals increases. Storms (1973) demonstrated this effect. Two people interacted while two others observed the conversation. The actual interactants made relatively more attributions to the situation than did the observers. The primary explanation for this pattern is familiarity: The person is more familiar with the self (and with the self in the particular setting) than the observers and thus makes more attributions to the situation and fewer attributions to the self. Furthermore, J. Johnson and Boyd (1995) found that an individual was more likely to regard subjective feelings and specific actions as indicative of his or her "true self," while deeming dispositional traits as more indicative of a friend's fundamental nature. When people are unfamiliar with a subject, they usually rely on traits (Jones & Nisbett, 1971). Some research has challenged this notion (e.g., Monson & Snyder, 1977; Monson, Tanke, & Lund, 1980), suggesting that greater familiarity should lead to stronger trait attributions. Kerber and Singleton (1984) attempted to resolve the conflict. They demonstrated that although there is a tendency for actors to make more situational attributions for their behavior than observers, there is no difference in the amount of trait attributions made by actors or observers.

      The tendency for observers to overemphasize trait explanations has often been used by critics of personality research. They suggest that personality scholars may themselves suffer from this tendency (labeled the *fundamental attribution error*) when they see personality as a meaningful way of understanding people. Shoda and Mischel (1993), however, suggested that individuals may make fairly sophisticated attributions, not relying simply on their perceptions of the global traits of others. They called for a consideration of how we perceive patterns of variability, based on the perceived expectancies, values, and goals of the observed individual. Such an approach recognizes the behavior of individuals as unique and complexly conditional, not simply a function of traits or situation. Shoda and Mischel noted that "conceptualizing personality in terms of cognitive social person variables involves discovering the underlying person variables that can reconcile and explain a potentially confusing pattern of if-then observations" (p. 577). This represents a move away from the fairly simplistic models of attribution based on global traits, toward a more sophisticated model incorporating concepts from cognitive social psychology. Many recent communication studies acknowledge the diverse variables and complex processes involved when people make attributions about their own and others' behavior (Manusov, 1990; Mongeau, Hale, & Alles, 1994; Weber & Vangelisti, 1991).

PERSONALITY AND BEHAVIOR

The relationship between disposition and behavior continues to be a source of debate in the field of personality. This concern, always present in the literature, was well enunciated in Mischel's (1968) text. In his review of personality and behavior, Mischel argued that the evidence for a link between dispositional tendencies and behavior is relatively weak. In the first place, people are not consistent across situations. One would anticipate that if there were true personality variables, they should be evidenced in a variety of situations. If a person was shy, one would expect to see shy behavior in a number of situations. Some communication scholars have also taken this position. Hewes and Haight (1979) sought to demonstrate that "predisposition to verbal behavior" (a personality dimension tapping people's tendencies to enjoy and engage in verbal activity) is not consistently reflected in a group of behaviors that should be evidence of that trait if cross-situational consistency is assumed. In later work, Mischel (Mischel & Peake, 1982; Peake & Mischel, 1984) drew a distinction between temporal stability (consistency over time) and *cross-situational consistency*, arguing that although temporal stability may be achieved, cross-situational consistency is generally weak (see also Conley, 1984). Second, Mischel observed that traits have poor predictability. He noted that the typical correlation between a personality variable and the individual behaviors purportedly related to that variable is weak, averaging around .30. The magnitude of this correlation is not impressive, accounting for less than 10% of the variance in prediction.

A bevy of responses followed and continue to this day. One was to suggest that Mischel's critique was too all-encompassing. First, such criticisms are best restricted to sociobehavioral variables because cognitive abilities and styles generally show cross-situational consistency. Second, there is good evidence for the long-term stability of many traits. Conley (1984, 1985) demonstrated high levels of stability across a number of traits for periods of up to 40 years. The most consistent were traits associated with intelligence. Personality traits had moderate consistency. Only self-opinion (e.g., morale) had low levels of consistency over long time periods. Moss and Susman (1980) demonstrated similar levels of consistency for traits, as has Block (1977). In his own defense, Mischel (1977) argued that most cases of consistency occur with judgmental or self-perception data, not with actual behavior.

Other responses to Mischel emphasized that low correlations were present only in undifferentiated cases. When characteristics of situations and people are considered together, correlations increase. A final reply focused on the nature of the behavioral criteria. Here, instead of emphasizing single behaviors in specific settings, a pattern of behavior across situations usually correlates well with dispositions and reveals good cross-situational consistency. The issues of situation, person, and behavior spawned by the Mischel critique are important, and each is reviewed briefly.

Situation

One of the primary issues in personality research that was highlighted by Mischel's critique concerns the role of situation in personality studies. The major issue—whether it is the situation or the person that best explains behavior—is one that dots the history of personality work (Snyder & Ickes, 1985). Some scholars have suggested that situations account for the vast majority of variability in behavioral prediction and that traits are relatively unimportant. They assume that behavioral differences are a function of the immediate environment rather than traitlike structures. Some proponents of this position argue that traits are really nonexistent in people; rather, they are part of the implicit belief systems of perceivers. Others suggest that situations are preeminent in behavior prediction; thus, although dispositions may exist, they are essentially irrelevant to behavior.

Although situations clearly play a major role in affecting behavior, a situationalist perspective has not received either strong empirical or conceptual support. First, systematic conceptualizations of situations are not well developed. Indeed, there are a virtually unlimited number of situational characteristics that could, directly or indirectly, affect behavior. Although some scholars have started to identify some of the major components of situations (e.g., Forgas, 1979, 1981, 1983; Fredricksen, 1972; Magnusson, 1982), much remains to be accomplished. Until that search is refined, little functional knowledge of the systematic impact of situations can be parsimoniously obtained. Second, when the role of situational variables is examined by itself, research suggests that these account for little more of the variation in behavior than traits. Funder and Ozer (1983) raised this concern. Taking a series of classic studies often used to demonstrate the importance of situational characteristics for behavioral prediction, they computed the magnitude of effect due to situation and found it to be only slightly larger than that associated with traits. The point of Funder and Ozer's (1983) study and others like it (e.g., Bowers, 1973; Golding, 1975; Sarason, Smith, & Diener, 1975) is that situational characteristics alone are not much better at predicting outcomes than are traits. Furthermore, situational characteristics and dispositions often make independent contributions to behavior prediction. The fact is that dispositions do account for some variation in behavior over and above situations, and to dismiss them is to reduce, unnecessarily, behavioral predictability.

Few scholars today argue that situation alone, in every setting, can account for the entire behavioral pattern of an individual. On the other hand, many scholars suggest that optimal predictability for behavior comes from focusing on the complex interrelationships among traits and situations. This can be demonstrated by comparing situations where personality traits are highly correlated with behavior and those where they are not. For instance, when people are placed in settings where they are highly self-focused, the correlation between disposition and behavior is much higher than when they are in settings where self-focusing is low. Pryor, Gibbons, Wicklund, Fazio, and Hood (1977) demonstrated this using sociability as the personality trait. Shoda, Mischel, and Wright (1993) also found evidence for the predictability of behavior in specific situations based on dispositions.

A second situational characteristic affecting the relation between traits and behavior may be the degree to which a situation constrains behavior (Snyder & Ickes, 1985). Some situations are highly constraining and thus require certain behaviors regardless of what an individual would prefer to do. Other settings are more open to people freely selecting their behavior. Behavior in a highly constrained setting is likely to be mostly a function of the setting's requirements. Thus, the correlation between disposition and behavior should be low. Alternatively, in less constrained settings the correlation should be more substantial. Various studies have supported this expectation (Mischel, 1977; Monson, Hesley, & Chernick, 1982). Several studies have found public versus private differences in trait manifestation (Lindeman & Verkasalo, 1995; Tice, 1992). Another characteristic may be the competency demands of the situation. Mischel (1984, 1985) described research with children, suggesting that greater behavioral consistency occurs when the situational requirements exceed children's competencies.

A related and more conceptually based approach that emphasizes the role of situations falls under the rubric of *interactionism* (Magnusson & Endler, 1977). The basic tenet of interactionism is that traits, by themselves, offer little predictability about behavior. When combined with situations, however, the interaction between a trait and situation can account for a sizable chunk of the behavioral variation. Interactionism is not a new idea (Endler, 1984; Endler & Edwards, 1986). It reflects Lewin's (1936) brief formula $B = f(P, E)$ which translates to: Behavior is a function of person and environment. Empirical evidence for the importance of an interactionist approach has been offered by Bowers (1973). He surveyed a group of studies that provided estimates of the relative contributions of situation, disposition, and their interaction on behavior and found that traits and situations each accounted for approximately 10% of the variation in prediction. The interaction of situation and disposition accounted for an additional 20% of the behavioral variance. Other studies (e.g., Argyle, Furnham, & Graham, 1991; Magnusson & Endler, 1977) offer further evidence supporting the substantial contribution made by disposition and situation together. Contradictory results have been reported by Sarason et al. (1975) in an extensive survey of personality studies and by Gifford (1981) in a study of sociability. Endler and Parker (1992) noted that, despite widespread endorsement of interactionism, it has not often been used in recent research.

Scholars interested in the relation between situation and disposition have also examined what may be labeled the *selection bias*. People often select situations that match or emphasize their traits (Emmons, Diener, & Larsen, 1986; Snyder & Ickes, 1985). For instance, extroverted individuals might place themselves in settings where extroversion is encouraged, whereas their introverted counterparts might choose situations requiring less social interaction (Diener, Larsen, & Emmons, 1984; Emmons, Diener, & Larson, 1985; Furnham, 1981). Daly and McCroskey (1975) found that high communication apprehensives anticipated selecting occupations having low communication requirements when contrasted with the occupations preferred by low apprehensives. Daly and Shamo (1978) demonstrated that same pattern for choices of academic majors based on writing apprehension. Snyder and Gangestad (1982) showed that high self-monitors preferred a group discussion setting that offered clearly defined normative expectations—a setting where they could easily adapt to the requirements of the situation. Alternatively, low self-monitors, who conceptually are less responsive to situations and guided more by their dispositional tendencies, preferred settings that permitted them to display their trait tendencies. These findings led to the conclusion that "individuals systematically choose to enter and to spend time in those social situations and interpersonal settings that are particularly conducive to enactment of their characteristic behavioral orientations" (Snyder & Gangestad, 1982, pp. 133-134). Kahle (1980) demonstrated a similar selection bias for locus of control, as has Zuckerman (1974) for sensation-seeking, Van Heck (1991) for temperament, and Diener et al. (1984) for the need for order. Emmons and Diener (1986) found that such self-selection of individuals to situations moderates response consistency and stability of behavior. Moreover, in some settings people may try to modify the situation so that it more closely matches what they would prefer in terms of their disposition. Thus, the extrovert, upon entering a quiet party, may become particularly boisterous, trying to change the social gathering's tenor into one with more social interaction—what he or she would prefer.

Person

One distinction that dots personality theory is that between ideographic and nomothetic approaches to the study of dispositions. A nomothetic approach seeks general laws of personality having wide applicability, whereas an ideographic approach emphasizes that people are different and that personality is organized in different ways for different individuals (e.g., Rushton, Jackson, & Paunonen, 1981). Each person may show a stable pattern of behavior across situations, but it is impossible to compare people because behavioral patterns may be unique to the individual. Although ideographic models are conceptually reasonable, they undermine attempts at generality. To say that everyone is different undercuts the basis of personality, which, by definition, seeks consistencies among people. A halfway point between the ideographic and nomothetic approaches is one that emphasizes that people differ in the degree to which they are consistent in their behavioral tendencies.

People differ in the degree to which they behave in accordance with their dispositions. Some people's behavior is highly consistent with their traits; others are far less consistent. For instance, the behavior of people who are high self-monitors should conceptually be less in accord with their traits than should the behavior of low self-monitors (Snyder, 1974). Snyder (1983) summarized research supporting this prediction. At the same time, Cheek (1982) demonstrated that the acting component of the self-monitoring scale is the primary contributor to greater consistency among low self-monitors in comparing peer reports and self-reports of traits. Another personality variable that may affect the relationship between traits and behavior is private self-consciousness (Fenigstein, Scheier, & Buss, 1975). A number of studies have found that highly private self-conscious individuals demonstrate far greater consistency between trait and behavior than less private self-conscious individuals (e.g., Scheier, Buss, & Buss, 1978; Underwood & Moore, 1981; see also Wymer & Penner, 1985).

Bem and Allen (1974) argued that people vary in their degree of behavior-trait consistency. For any personality trait, some people will be cross-situationally consistent, whereas others will not be. In one study they asked students how cross-situationally consistent they were on two traits (friendliness and conscientiousness). Using a variety of behavioral indices in various situations, Bem and Allen (1974) found that students who described themselves as cross-situationally consistent on a trait did indeed have more consistency in their behavior across situations (especially in friendliness) than students who said they were inconsistent. Mischel and Peake (1982) found that individuals classified as consistent on the basis of their own reports demonstrated more temporal stability in rated behaviors (but not actual behaviors) associated with conscientiousness than people who said they were not consistent. Kenrick and Springfield (1980) demonstrated a similar role for consistency (see also Rushton et al., 1981). Some recent evidence has cast doubt on Bem and Allen's findings on mathematical grounds (Tellegen, Kamp, & Watson, 1982) and empirical grounds (Chaplin & Goldberg, 1985; Paunonen & Jackson, 1985) even as other researchers (e.g., Diener & Larsen, 1984) found that some individuals are generally more consistent across situations than others. Beck, McCauley, Segal, and Hershey (1988) suggested that individual differences in the perception of prototypicality of trait categories should be taken into account when comparing cross-situational consistency with temporal consistency of behavior.

Another way of emphasizing the role of the person in traits is to highlight the importance of what have been labeled *self-schemata* (Markus, 1977). People who are involved in some dimension of personality (i.e., who feel the dimension important and/or hold extreme positions on the dimension) tend to have well-developed and highly organized schemata for that dimension. Having a strong schema for a disposition increases the likelihood that the disposition will be reflected in perceptions, memory, inferences, and behavior (Fiske & Taylor, 1984). Although potentially quite useful in understanding personality, there are conceptual and methodological problems unresolved at this time (Burke, Kraut, & Dworkin, 1984).

Zuckerman, Bernieri, Koestner, and Rosenthal (1989) stressed the importance of considering different moderating variables that explain this differential consistency in traits among people. They argued that researchers should consider as possible sources of this variation three types of moderating effects: *intraindividual,* to determine if the person may be consistent on some traits but not others; *interindividual,* to distinguish people who are generally consistent on traits from those who are not; and *inter trait,* which determine whether specific traits tend to have higher consistency than others across people. Common moderating variables, such as trait relevance or self-reported consistency, will vary in the degree to which they produce these three types of effects, and therefore may be tapping into different dimensions of consistency.

Behavior

One important trend in recent research and theory on personality has been a reconsideration of the nature of the behavioral indicants of personality. There have been two major strands of research in this area: multiple act criteria/aggregation and act frequency. Each emphasizes that single behaviors are not good representations of a disposition. Single behaviors in a single setting are too likely to be affected by the many situational factors present. Instead, a pattern of behavior across time, observers, and settings better represents a dispositional tendency. Proponents of these approaches suggest that the proper concern of scholars interested in personality is the general tendencies of individuals and not their specific behavior in specific situations.

Multiple Act Criteria/Aggregation. Research on the relation between attitude and behavior suggests that the two must be matched in their levels of generality if substantial correlations are to be obtained. Strong associations are observed between general attitudes and general behavioral patterns as well as between highly specific attitudes and behaviors. When the generality of behavior and attitude are not congruent, however, correlations are modest at best. The same pattern of matching should be true of personality traits and their behavioral indicants. A disposition is a general tendency to behave in some fashion and consequently should be predictive not of a single behavior but of a general pattern of behavior across various settings. Jaccard (1974) introduced the idea to personality, and Daly (1978) applied it to communication work. Consider Figure 1.1 as a model of the multiple act criteria.

Suppose we wanted to correlate shyness, as a disposition, with behavioral indicants of shyness. One dimension is composed of the different behaviors that might represent shyness (e.g., reduced talkativeness, fewer intimate disclosures, less argumentativeness); the other dimension is made up of the observation periods or settings (e.g., a classroom, a social conversation, or a job interview). The two dimensions, taken together, offer four different behavioral indices. The first (a single cell) is a single act in a single observational period (e.g., did the shy person demonstrate less talkativeness in a specific classroom setting on Monday, December 12?). The second (summing down a column) is a collection of different behaviors, all representative of the disposition in question, observed at one time (e.g., on Monday, December 12, in the classroom, did the shy person generally demonstrate less talkativeness, less argumentativeness, fewer intimate disclosures, and so on?). The third index sums across observation times for a single behavior (e.g., in classrooms, interviews, and social interactions, does the shy person demonstrate less talkativeness?). The fourth index incorporates different behaviors during different observation periods (in classrooms, interviews, social interactions, is the shy person less talkative, argumentative, and disclosive?).

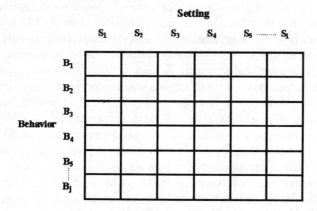

Figure 1.1. Multiple act criteria

With the latter three criteria, summing does not imply that the person must demonstrate every behavior (or in every observation period even display a behavior). Rather, the issue is one of preponderance: Shy people should show more of the behaviors more of the time than nonshy individuals. The multiple act criteria approach proposes that a general disposition will have its strongest correlation with multiple acts observed across a number of observational periods (the fourth indicant). The weakest correlation should be between the general disposition and a single behavior assessed (during one observational period. The point here is that when personality variables represent general tendencies the behavioral criteria should be as general as the disposition. When a very general disposition is correlated with a very specific indicant, one would expect a weak relationship.

Closely tied to the multiple act model is one emphasizing aggregation. This approach draws directly from test theory for its impetus. Test theory posits that the best indicator of an individual's performance is a highly reliable measure that has temporal stability. Epstein (1979, 1980, 1983), as well as others, argues that one would obtain larger reliabilities (i.e., greater consistency) for dispositions if the behavioral criterion was an aggregation of behaviors across time and setting. Just as one typically averages across subjects in an experiment for purposes of obtaining reliable estimates, so too by taking sample of behaviors across time and setting one can obtain a more reliable index of behavioral tendencies. Error of measurement is reduced and small inconsistencies tied to idiosyncratic aspects of the different situations are controlled through averaging. A number of scholars have demonstrated that when personality traits are correlated with an aggregated behavioral index, the correlation among the two is substantial (e.g., Woodruff, 1984). They also demonstrated that the aggregation of data across time results in much greater stability and consistency than the use of unaggregated data (Diener & Larsen, 1984; Small, Zeldin, & Savin-Williams, 1983). Cheek (1982) demonstrated that aggregation over raters and items yields stronger correlations between self-ratings and peer ratings. Aries, Gold, and Weigel (1983) found that dispositional dominance was strongly correlated with a collection of behaviors displayed during small group interactions. Individual behaviors had much weaker correlations with disposition. Moskowitz (1982) found temporal stability for dominance behaviors in children over an 8-week period. However, methodological issues have been raised about this approach (Day, Marshall, Hamilton, & Christy, 1983; Paunonen, 1984).

Although there is good supportive evidence for the multiple act/aggregation approaches, there are also certain problems that need to be addressed. For instance, in the typical study, behaviors are simply summed within and across observation periods. Treating each behavior as equal may be a questionable procedure. Moreover, the selection of behaviors and the choice of observation periods and settings have not receive sufficient attention. As a result, we may lose sight of the importance of understanding and predicting single behaviors in particular situations. The best measure that aggregation or multiple acts can provide is an average behavioral tendency, and although that may suffice in many cases, there are times when specific response predictions are needed. When summing across various characteristics of situations, one can forget that situations still play an important role in behavioral prediction.

Act Frequency Approach. In the act frequency approach (D. Buss & Craik, 1983, 1984), a disposition is represented by the frequency with which an individual engages, over time, in behaviors representative of that disposition. Acts can take a number of forms (e.g., physical actions, intentions, and stylistic tendencies), occur within differing contexts, and vary in the degree to which they represent the construct. In Buss and Craik's approach, representative acts for a disposition are obtained in a multistep sequence where various acts are nominated as indicators of a disposition, then rated for prototypicality, and sorted to assess the degree to which they represent more than one disposition. After obtaining a collection of acts, frequency estimations are obtained. A number of procedures are available, including self-report, observer ratings, and mechanical recordings. By emphasizing absolute frequencies and eschewing additional scaling methods, the net frequency approach permits comparisons that are not typically found in personality work. With most techniques, the only permissible comparisons are relative ones; people are compared vis-à-vis other people (Lamiell, 1981). In the act frequency approach, no reference to a group is necessary. Conceptually, there is a true zero point in the act frequency approach.

Frequency data allow the investigator to derive a number of different indicants. One might, for instance, collect frequency data on an individual for some disposition from two equal time periods. As the ratio of the two frequencies approaches unity, support emerges for an enduring tendency on the part of the subject. Computing a mean ratio across a group of people yields a *modal human tendency* with respect to the disposition. Frequency information allows comparisons among groups (e.g., cultures, age groups, generations, or societal categories) to examine whether there are group differences in the rate with which a given disposition appears. Children, for example, may have a larger rate of quarrelsome acts than adults. Moreover, different personality dimensions can be compared. Thus, one might discover that the rate of sociable acts is four times greater than the rate of aggressive acts in some population. Finally, the impact of different situational characteristics can be assessed (e.g., in public settings the rate of submissive behaviors is less than it is in private settings).

There are a number of similarities among the behavioral approaches. For instance, the act frequency approach emphasizes multiple act criteria insofar as a variety of behavioral indicants over time are tabulated to form a composite frequency estimate. As is the case with the multiple act approach, specific behavior predictions are not made; instead, predictions are made of general tendencies as evidenced by frequencies of a collection of acts representing the disposition. Additionally, in many constructs of personality an assumption is made that a trait is best represented by a group of highly correlated behaviors. Neither the multiple act approach nor the act frequency approach makes this assumption because it is conceivable that two people might engage in totally different behaviors, both of which are highly representative of the trait in question.

Recent Trends

Multiple act criteria and the act frequency approach attempt to address the problem inherent in the fact that many very disparate behaviors comprise a particular trait. Alternatively, some researchers have examined traits as goal-based categories (Read, Jones, & Miller, 1990; Read & Miller, 1989). From this perspective, traits are conceived of as stable, chronic configurations of four components: goals, plans designed to carry out those goals, the necessary resources for successful completion of those plans, and beliefs associated with the trait (Miller & Read, 1991). This perspective helps to explain how behaviors of varying prototypicality fit together into a cohesive conception of a trait, because those behaviors are seen as relevant to achieving the goals of the category. Read et al. (1990) found that the extent to which a behavior is related to the goals associated with a trait strongly predicted both the prototypicality of that behavior and the confidence with which people would make trait inferences from that behavior.

Kyl-Heku and Buss (1996), noting the emergence of goal-based approaches to personality research and the resurgence of traditional trait research with the FFM, proposed the concept of *tactics* as a link between the two trends. Tactics are defined by Kyl-Heku and Buss as the psychological and behavioral means through which personal goals, personal projects, and personal strivings are accomplished. People are assumed to be predisposed to the use of different patterns of tactics based on enduring tendencies and individual abilities. They assume that some goals are ubiquitous enough to be considered universal human goals, and that the different tactics that individuals use to achieve these goals may be linked to some underlying personality traits as proposed by traditional personality research. Kyl-Heku and Buss acknowledged that the tactic approach is preliminary, but stress its utility as a bridge between the Big Five and the goal-based trends in personality research.

A final trend in personality research that should be noted is the resurgence of attention to the biological foundations of personality (see chapter 2 also). D. Buss (1990) explained that several distinct lines of research fall under this umbrella, including evolutionary approaches and behavioral genetics. Evolutionary approaches focus on how personality attributes reflect adaptation and adjustments required by demands for reproduction and survival, and the essence of human nature as comprised of species-typical psychological mechanisms and the adaptive problems toward which they are directed. Behavioral genetics focuses on the heritability and genetic variation of personality traits. The influence of environment is a central concern of both approaches (Cipriani, 1996). This resurgence of interest in biological aspects of personality has informed research in areas such as courtship and mate selection (Baize & Schroeder, 1995; Kendrick, Sadalia, Groth, & Trost, 1990), altruism (Johnson, Danko, Darvill, & Nagoshi, 1992), Machiavellianism (Wilson, Near, & Miller, 1996), longitudinal personality change (Plomin & Nesselroade, 1990) and the FFM (MacDonald, 1995). The utility of biological perspectives of personality for communication researchers remains to be seen, but appear very promising. Graziano (1995) noted that evolutionary psychology is lacking strong theoretical groundwork for its application to interpersonal relationships. However, biological approaches offer fresh insight into a number of personality variables and constructs that are clearly of interest to communication scholars.

COMMUNICATION AND PERSONALITY

So far in this chapter, attention has been directed to certain major conceptual themes in personality. In this section, the different roles that personality plays in communication are described. Underlying this exposition is the basic question of why communication scholars should be interested in personality in the first place. What does personality research have to contribute to our understanding of communication? And, just as important, although less often considered, what does communication scholarship have to offer personality research and theory? Personality per se is the domain of psychologists. It should be the focus of communication scholars only insofar as it affects, or is affected by, communication.

The research summarized in the chapters that follow clearly indicates that personality and communication are inherently intertwined. Traits are correlated with communication-related variables in meaningful ways. They account for significant variation in communication behavior as well as communication-based perceptions. At the same time, communication plays an important role in the development and maintenance of dispositional tendencies. Psychological and sociological explanations of the etiology of many personality variables emphasize the critical role of communication. Self-concept theories inevitably posit the interactive nature of social interaction and the formation of self-valuing. Developmental models of shyness, assertiveness, gender role beliefs, altruism, locus of control, loneliness, and many other dispositions almost always incorporate aspects of social interaction in some form (e.g., reinforcement via communication, development of communication skills, or communication of norms) as major contributory correlates.

In communication scholarship, personality variables play a number of roles. First, they serve as useful covariates in some investigations. By statistically covarying certain dispositions, better evidence of the role of situational characteristics or experimental manipulations can be demonstrated. A communication scholar might, for instance, be interested in the degree to which certain situational characteristics affect talkativeness. Because communication apprehension (or some variant; see Daly & McCroskey, 1984) affects talkativeness (Daly & Stafford, 1984), the scholar may decide to assess participants' apprehension as part of data collection in studies where talk is considered, and then covary out the effect of apprehension. Statistically, covariance controls the effect of the personality variable. Any effects that remain after the disposition has been partialed out can reasonably be attributed to variables other than dispositional apprehension (although one needs to be cautious due to potential interactive effects of some trait and some situational or experimental manipulations).

A second, and related role that personality variables play in communication research is as predetermined factors in communication studies. To continue with the hypothetical study of talkativeness, apprehension could be built into the study as a component of the investigation. Subjects could be classified as high or low in communication apprehension, and the independent effect of apprehension — as well as the joint effect of apprehension and situation or experimental manipulation — could be probed. In contrast with covariance analysis, designing the study to incorporate a personality variable allows the investigator to examine the independent impact of that trait on talkativeness, as well as the interactive effects of apprehension and situation on talkativeness. One might find that under certain circumstances, apprehension is correlated with talkativeness, whereas in other settings there is no relationship (an interactionist position).

Daly and Diesel (1992) noted that numerous personality constructs have traditionally been of interest to communication researchers and are represented in a body of research or existing measures. Such self-related variables include self-esteem and self-concept, Machiavelliansim, locus of control, cognitive complexity, authoritarianism or dogmatism, and optimism. Socially oriented personality variables common in communication research include loneliness, self-monitoring, assertiveness, empathy, conversational sensitivity, and interaction involvement.

Communication researchers also develop and validate traits that have direct relevance to communication. These communication-oriented traits focus on dispositional tendencies to do (or not do) something related to communication. Thus, scholars in communication devise operationalizations of such constructs as communication apprehension and its many variants (McCroskey & Beatty, chapter 10, this volume; McCroskey & Richmond, chapter 5, this volume), communicator style (Horvath, chapter 3, this volume; Norton, 1983, 1988), argumentativeness (Infante & Rancer, 1996; Rancer, chapter 7, this volume) and verbal aggressiveness (Wigley, chapter 9, this volume). These scholars face all of the issues addressed so far in this chapter. One common step in projects focusing on the validation of a construct is correlating a particular disposition with others presumed to be relevant to the trait. Thus, we see studies where communication-oriented personality constructs such as communication apprehension (e.g., McCroskey, Daly, Richmond, & Falcione, 1977; McCroskey, Daly, & Sorensen, 1976) or loneliness (Bell & Daly, 1985) are correlated with other personality variables. Another variant of communication scholarship is the application of traits, devised both in other disciplines and communication, to communication-related concerns. This is probably the most common way in which communication scholars involve themselves in personality work. In some cases, investigators correlate a personality dimension (e.g., Machiavellianism, self-esteem, loneliness, assertiveness, gender role, or cognitive complexity) with some communication outcome (e.g., compliance-gaining strategies, affinity seeking, or persuasiveness). The focus is on the individual and the choices made as a function of disposition, or on how communication contributes to or reinforces the disposition. For instance, Segrin (1990, 1992) found support in measures of self-reports, observer ratings, and behavioral assessments for a link between depression and social skills deficit, which is itself a construct composed of several communication tendencies.

One recent personality construct that has gained prominence in communication research is attachment style, a construct reflecting a predisposition to form characteristic types of attachments with significant others based on the attachment style formed during infancy (Bartholomew & Horowitz, 1991). Attachment style has recently been explored as a correlate of intimacy and involvement (Guerrero, 1996), descriptions of romantic partners (Feeney & Noller, 1991), social support (Simpson, Rholes, & Nelligan, 1992) and relational maintenance strategies (Simon & Baxter, 1993).

Gender is another example of a commonly explored variable in communication research that is appropriate to regard as a personality construct. Gender has traditionally been measured by individuals' relative subscription to what were thought to be "feminine" versus "masculine" traits. Increasingly, researchers are regarding "expressiveness" and "instrumentality" as the dominant discriminating traits for gender (see Gill, Stockard, Johnson, & William, 1987; see also, Richmond & Martin, chapter 6, this volume).

An alternative approach is to focus on the relation among interactants as a function of their traits. Issues such as the complementarity of traits among interactants become highly relevant (e.g., the consequences of a highly cognitively complex individual interacting with either another highly complex person or a less complex one). One can argue with justification that this interactive approach is the proper domain for communication scholars interested in personality because the interaction among people is the central focus of this sort of work. How do two people, similar or different on some dimension of personality, mesh in a conversation? Does complementarity in personality dispositions enhance communication outcomes? Research of this type is only beginning to appear in the journals, but it certainly represents a fruitful direction for communication scholars. It is truly focused on communication.

DIRECTIONS FOR PERSONALITY IN COMMUNICATION SCHOLARSHIP

Communication research emphasizing personality has had no obvious structure or "master plan" associated with it. Each individual investigator selects her or his favorite trait and proceeds to explore the measurement, manifestations, or consequences of the disposition without much regard for how it fits within some larger domain of communication-related traits. Very simply, integrative models of communication-oriented traits have not been devised. Despite the prominence of the FFM in personality research, communication scholars have as yet largely failed to integrate the Big Five into their research, with few exceptions (e.g., Pollit, Lloyd, & Bloom, 1996). Although the measurement of personality constructs in communication is pervasive, perhaps the absence of a systematic or comprehensive integration of personality and communication research is due to the lack of recognition of these constructs as personality variables. Goal-based approaches to personality, another emerging trend in the field, is also quite promising as a possible integrating framework (Miller, Cody, & McLaughlin, 1994). This approach may provide a useful framework for unifying the countless "strategies," "types," "roles," "tactics," "styles," and other concepts that populate the communication literature, representing behavioral, situational, and trait-based variables that have often been overlooked as aspects of personality.

Even more important than a conceptual model for the structure of communication-related personality variables are well-developed theoretical formulations for the place of personality in communication research. How, when, and why do dispositions affect the ways in which people communicate? It is not sufficient simply to suggest that shy people talk less because they are shy, or to argue that lonely people are less happy because they have less than the desired number of interactions. In each case, the reason for the effect is identical to the definition of the trait. For example, Daly, Vangelisti, and Weber (1995) suggested that people high in speech anxiety tend to perform worse in public speaking situations than their less anxious counterparts because they are more self-focused and less attentive to preparation. The trait of speech anxiety in this way is linked to specific and meaningful behavior and cognitions that directly impact communicative performance. This is one example of the kind of explanatory models that need to be posited to describe conceptually the manner in which communication and personality are related. More broadly, it is important to identify the places and situations in which personality plays a vital role in communication. Why do dispositions appear important in some settings and unimportant in others? In short, what are the conceptual boundaries for personality scholarship in communication?

One trend in contemporary personality scholarship is the identification of specific behavioral indicants of different dispositions. In the various behavior approaches to personality reviewed earlier (e.g., multiple act, aggregation, and act frequency), it is critical that the investigator identify a group of behaviors that have some relevance to a trait. Communication scholars need to consider which communication behaviors are most representative of the traits they wish to explore. However, the field of communication has spent a lot of time devising trait measures but comparatively little time conceptually and empirically developing behavioral indicants of those traits. This is especially problematic because generally when trait measures fail to correlate adequately with behaviors, investigators rush to indict the trait, forgetting that many times the trait has significantly stronger conceptual and empirical bases than the behaviors involved in the study.

Behavioral indicants can vary in their level of specificity, ranging from broad communication characteristics (e.g., shy people show less involvement) to highly specific behaviors (e.g., shy people engage in fewer head nods while listening). In recent years, one tendency in communication research has been to focus more on the actual behaviors exhibited when people communicate. Under a variety of labels (e.g., conversational analysis, dominance, and compliance-gaining), research has begun to identify behavioral measures for dispositional tendencies related to dominance and influence, affinity, and social integration, among others. Not only is it important to discover reliable and valid behaviors as correlates for trait measures, but newer conceptualizations of traits, such as act frequency, demand added emphasis on the specification of behaviors related to trails. It may be that by focusing more on the behavioral displays of traits, many of the concerns associated with self-report measures will be of less critical importance.

An alternative trend, but just as important, is the increasing concern by communication scholars regarding the cognitive aspects of communication and personality. It may be that people have communication-related cognitive dispositions. The search for ways of measuring these dispositions and of identifying their correlates has only recently begun. One approach has been to examine individual differences in the ways people organize information about conversations. Daly et al. (1985) devised two measures to assess what they termed *conversational complexity*. In one procedure, subjects completed a sorting task that produced measures of the degree to which they construed underlying structural aspects of conversation, as well as the extent to which they focused on surface features of conversations. Not surprisingly, people who represented conversations in deeper ways (focusing on underlying features) demonstrated a high degree of involvement in and enjoyment for social interaction. A second procedure, mimicking research on cognitive complexity, assessed the differentiation that subjects had for the concept of conversation. Those with greater differentiation were more conversationally involved and less apprehensive. Another line of inquiry involves individual differences in cognitive capacity to process such messages. The work of Greene and his colleagues (Greene, Lindsay, & Hawn, 1990; Greene, McDaniel, Buksa, & Ravizza, 1993) suggests that when people are attempting to construct messages to achieve multiple social goals, numerous features of their speech reflect these more complex cognitive processes and greater cognitive load.

Miller et al. (1994) argued persuasively that the communication field must develop a greater understanding of situational factors and how they are perceived by interactants, including the role relationships involved, the setting of the interaction, and the nature of the joint activity. They emphasized the utility of a common set of units for understanding how situation is interwoven with persons, relationships, and interactions, and endorse Miller and Read's (1991) goal-based approach as a possible framework. This type of integrative approach is necessary in the field to span the myriad factors that produce specific message choices.

Future scholarship also needs to focus more on the links between communication and the development and maintenance of dispositions. Even though there is evidence for strong hereditary bases for basic temperaments (A. Buss & Plomin, 1984), communication in the child's social environment is likely to have substantial and long-lasting effects on disposition. Very little work within the communication discipline has emphasized the ways in which communication-related traits develop, it is a fertile area for future pursuits.

REFERENCES

Allport, G. W., & Odbert, H. W. (1936). Trait names: A psycholexical study. *Psychological Monographs, 47*(1, Whole No. 211).

Argyle, M., Furnham, A., & Graham, J. A. (1981). *Social situations.* Cambridge: Cambridge University Press.

Aries, E., Gold, C., & Weigel, R. (1983). Dispositional and situational influences on dominance behavior in small groups. *Journal of Personality and Social Psychology, 44,* 779-786.

Asch, S. P. (1946). Forming impressions of personality. *Journal of Abnormal and Social Psychology, 41,* 25 8-290.

Baize, H. R., & Schroeder, J. E. (1995). Personality and mate selection in personal ads: Evolutionary preferences in a public mate selection process. *Journal of Social Behavior and Personality, 10,* 517-536.

Bartholomew, K., & Horowitz, L. M. (1991). Attachment styles among young adults: A test of the four-category model. *Journal of Personality and Social Psychology, 61,* 226-244.

Beck, L., McCauley, C., Segal, M., & Hershey, L. (1988). Individual differences in prototypicality judgments about trait categories. *Journal of Personality & Social Psychology, 55,* 286-292.

Bell, R., & Daly, J. A. (1985). Some communicator correlates of loneliness. *Southern Speech Communication Journal, 50,* 121-142.

Bem, D. J., & Allen, A. (1974). On predicting some of the people some of the time: The search for cross-situational consistencies In behavior. *Psychological Review, 81,* 506-520.

Benet, V., & Waller, N. G. (1995). The Big Seven factor model of personality description: Evidence for its cross-cultural generality in a Spanish sample. *Journal of Personality & Social Psychology, 69,* 701-718.

Block, J. (1977). Advancing the psychology of personality: Paradigmatic shift or improving the quality of research? In D. Magnusson & N. S. Endler (Eds.), *Personality at the crossroads* (pp. 37-63). Hillsdale, NJ: Erlbaum.

Block, J. (1995). A contrarian view of the five-factor approach to personality description. *Psychological Bulletin, 117,* 187-215.

Borkenau, P., & Liebler, A. (1995). Observable attributes as manifestations and cues of personality and intelligence. *Journal of Personality, 63,* 1-25.

Borkenau, P., & Ostendorf, F. (1989). Investigations of the five-factor model of personality and its assessment. *Zeitschrift fur Differentielle und Diagnostische Psychologie, 10,* 239-251.

Bowers, K. S. (1973). Situationism in psychology: An analysis and critique. *Psychological Review, 80,* 307-336.

Bruner, J. S., & Tagiuri, R. (1954). Person perception. In G. Lindzey (Ed.), *Handbook of social psychology* (Vol.2, pp. 634-654). Reading, MA: Addison-Wesley.

Burke, P. A., Kraut, R. E., & Dworkin, R. H. (1984). Traits, consistency, and self-schemata: What do our methods measure? *Journal of Personality and Social Psychology, 47,* 568-579.

Buss, A., & Plomin, R. (1984). *Temperament: Early developing personality traits.* Hillsdale, NJ: Erlbaum.

Buss, D. M. (1990). Toward a biologically informed psychology of personality. Special Issue: Biological foundations of personality: Evolution, behavioral genetics, and psychophysiology. *Journal of Personality, 58,* 1-16.

Buss, D. M. (1992). Manipulation in close relationships: Five personality factors in interactional context. Special Issue: The five-factor model: Issues and applications. *Journal of Personality, 60,* 477-499.

Buss, D. M., & Craik, K. H. (1983). The dispositional analysis of everyday conduct. *Journal of Personality, 51,* 393-412.

Buss, D. M., & Craik, K. H. (1984). Acts, dispositions, and personality. In B. Maher & W. Maher (Eds.), *Progress in experimental personality research* (Vol. 13, pp. 242-301). New York: Academic Press.

Campbell, D., & Fiske, D. (1959). Convergent and discriminant validation by the multitrait-multimethod matrix. *Psychological Bulletin, 56,* 81-105.

Cantor, N., & Mischel, W. (1977). Traits as prototypes: Effects on recognition memory. *Journal of Personality and Social Psychology, 35,* 38-48.

Cantor, N., & Mischel, W. (1979). Prototypes in person perception. In L. Berkowitz (Ed.), *Advances in experimental social psychology* (Vol. 12, pp. 3-52). New York: Academic Press.

Caprara, G. V., Barbaranelli, C., Borgogni, L., & Perugini, M. (1993). The "Big Five Questionnaire": A new questionnaire to assess the Five Factor Model. *Personality & Individual Differences, 15,* 281-288.

Chaplin, W., John, O., & Goldberg, L. (1988). Conceptions of states and traits: Dimensional attributes with ideals as prototypes. *Journal of Personality and Social Psychology, 54,* 541-557.

Chaplin, W. F., & Goldberg, L. R. (1985). A failure to replicate the Bem and Allen study of individual differences in cross-situational consistency. *Journal of Personality and Social Psychology, 47,* 1074-1090.

Cheek, J. M. (1982). Aggregation, moderator variables, and the validity of personality tests: A peer-rating study. *Journal of Personality and Social Psychology, 43,* 1254-1269.

Cipriani, D. C. (1996). Stability and change in personality across the life span: Behavioral-genetic versus evolutionary approaches. *Genetic, Social and General Psychology Monographs, 122,* 55-74.

Conley, J. J. (1984). The hierarchy of consistency: A review and model of longitudinal findings on adult individual differences in intelligence, personality, and self-opinion. *Personality and Individual Differences, 5,* 11-25.

Conley, J. J. (1985). Longitudinal stability of personality traits: A multitrait-multioccasion analysis. *Journal of Personality and Social Psychology, 49,* 1266-1282.

Daly, J. A. (1978). Communication apprehension and behavior: Applying multiple act criteria. *Human Communication Research, 4,* 208-216.

Daly, J. A., Bell, R., Glenn, P., & Lawrence, S. (1985). Conceptualizing conversational complexity. *Human Communication Research, 12,* 30-53.

Daly, J. A., & Diesel, C. A. (1992). Measures of communication-related personality variables communication research reports. *Communication Education, 41,* 405-414.

Daly, J. A., & McCroskey, J. C. (1975). Occupational desirability and choice as a function of communication apprehension. *Journal of Counseling Psychology, 22,* 309-313.

Daly, J. A., & McCroskey, J. C. (Eds.). (1984). *Avoiding communication: Shyness, reticence, and communication apprehension.* Beverly Hills, CA: Sage.

Daly, J. A., & Shamo, W. (1978). Academic decisions as a function of writing apprehension. *Research in the Teaching of English, 12,* 119-126.

Daly, J. A., & Stafford, L. (1984). Correlates and consequences of social-communicative anxiety. In J. Daly & J. McCroskey (Eds.), *Avoiding communication: Shyness, reticence, and communication apprehension* (pp. 125-144). Beverly Hills, CA: Sage.

Daly, J. A., & Street, R. (1980). Measuring social-communicative anxiety: Social desirability and the fakability of scale responses. *Human Communication Research, 6,* 185-189.

Daly, J. A., Vangelisti, A. L., & Weber, D.J. (1995). Speech anxiety affects how people prepare speeches: A protocol analysis of the preparation processes of speakers. *Communication Monographs, 62,* 383-397.

Day, H. D., Marshall, D., Hamilton, B., & Christy, J. (1983). Some cautionary notes regarding the use of aggregated scores as a measure of behavioral stability. *Journal of Research in Personality, 17,* 97-109.

de Raad, B., & Hofstee, W. K. (1993). A circumplex approach to the Five Factor model: A facet structure of trait adjectives supplemented by trait verbs. *Personality & Individual Differences, 15,* 493-505.

Diener, E., & Larsen, R. J. (1984). Temporal stability and cross-situational consistency of affective, behavioral, and cognitive responses. *Journal of Personality and Social Psychology, 47*, 871-883.

Diener, E., Larsen, R., & Emmons, R. (1984). Person X situation interactions: Choice of situations and congruence response models. *Journal of Personality and Social Psychology, 47*, 580-592.

Digman, J. M., & Takemoto-Chock, N. K. (1981). Factors in the natural language of personality: Re-analysis, comparison, and interpretation of six major studies. *Multivariate Behavioral Research, 16*, 149-170.

Duijsens, I. J., & Diekstra, R. F. W. (1995). The 23BB5: A new Bipolar Big Five questionnaire. *Personality & Individual Differences, 19*, 753-755.

Dunning, D., Perie, M., & Story, A. L. (1991). Self-serving prototypes of social categories. *Journal of Personality and Social Psychology, 61*, 957-968.

Dweck, C. S., Hong, Y., & Chiu, C. (1993). Implicit theories: Individual differences in the likelihood and meaning of dispositional inference. Special Issue: On inferring personal dispositions from behavior. *Personality & Social Psychology Bulletin, 19*, 644-656.

Emmons, R. A., & Diener, E. (1986). Situation selection as a moderator of response consistency and stability. *Journal of Personality & Social Psychology, 51*, 1013-1019.

Emmons, R. A., Diener, E., & Larsen, R. (1985). Choice of situations and congruence models of interactionism. *Personality and Individual Differences, 6*, 693-702.

Emmons, R. A., Diener, E., & Larsen, R. J. (1986). Choice and avoidance of everyday situations and affect congruence: Two models of reciprocal interactionism. *Journal of Personality & Social Psychology, 51*, 815-826.

Endler, N. S. (1984). Interactionism. In N. S. Endler & J. M. Hunt (Eds.), *Personality and the behavioral disorders* (Vol. 1, pp. 183-219). New York: Wiley.

Endler, N.S., & Edwards, J. M. (1986). Interactionism in personality in the twentieth century. *Personality & Individual Differences, 7*, 379-384.

Endler, N. S., & Parker, J. D. (1992). Interactionism revisited: Reflections on the continuing crisis in the personality area. *European Journal of Personality, 6*, 177-198.

Epstein, S. (1979). The stability of behavior: I. On predicting most of the people much of the time. *Journal of Personality and Social Psychology, 37*, 1097-1126.

Epstein, S. (1980). The stability of behavior: II. Implications for psychological research. *American Psychologist, 35*, 790-806.

Epstein, S. (1983). Aggregation and beyond: Some basic issues in the prediction of behavior. *Journal of Personality, 51*, 360-392.

Feeney, J. A., & Noller, P. (1991). Attachment style and verbal descriptions of romantic partners. *Journal of Social & Personal Relationships, 8*, 187-215.

Fenigstein, A., Scheier, M. F., & Buss, A. A. (1975). Public and private self-consciousness: Assessment and theory. *Journal of Consulting and Clinical Psychology, 43*, 522-527.

Finegan, J. E., & Allen, N. J. (1994). Computerized and written questionnaires: Are they equivalent?. *Computers in Human Behavior, 10*, 483-496.

Fiske, S. T., & Taylor, S. E. (1984). *Social cognition.* Reading, MA: Addison-Wesley.

Forgas, J. P. (1979). *Social episodes: The study of interaction routines.* London: Academic Press.

Forgas, J. P. (1981). Affective and emotional influences on episode representations. In J. P. Forgas (Ed.), *Social cognition: Perspectives on everyday understanding.* London: Academic Press.

Forgas, J. P. (1983). Episode cognition and personality: A Multidimensional analysis. *Journal of Personality, 51*, 34-48.

Fredricksen, N. (1972). Toward a taxonomy of situations. *American Psychologist, 27*, 114-123.

Funder, D. C., & Ozer, D. J. (1983). Behavior as a function of the situation. *Journal of Personality and Social Psychology, 44*, 107 - 112.

Funder, D. C., & West, S.G. (1993). Consensus, self-other agreement, and accuracy in personality judgment: An introduction. *Journal of Personality, 61*, 457-476.

Furnham, A. (1981). Personality and activity preference. *British Journal of Social and Clinical Psychology, 20*, 57-68.

Gangestad, S., & Snyder, M. (1985). "To carve nature at its joints": On the existence of discrete classes in personality. *Psychological Review, 92*, 317-349.

Gifford, R. (1981). Sociability: Traits, settings, and interactions. *Journal of Personality and Social Psychology, 41*, 340-347.

Gill, S., Stockard, J., Johnson, M., & Williams, S. (1987). Measuring gender differences: The expressive dimension and critique of androgyny scales. *Sex Roles, 17*, 375-400.

Golding, S. L. (1975). Flies in the ointment: Methodological problems in the analysis of percentage of variance due to person and situations. *Psychological Bulletin, 82*, 278-288.

Graziano, W. G . (1995). Evolutionary psychology: Old music, but now on CDS? *Psychological Inquiry, 6*, 41-44.

Greene, J. O., Lindsey, A. E., & Hawn, J. J. (1990). Social goals and speech production: Effects of multiple goals on pausal phenomena. *Journal of Language & Social Psychology, 9*, 119-134.

Greene, J. O., McDaniel, T. L., Buksa, K., & Ravizza, S. M. (1993). Cognitive processes in the production of multiple-goal messages: Evidence from the temporal characteristics of speech. *Western Journal of Communication, 57*, 65-86.

Guerrero, L. K. (1996). Attachment-style differences in intimacy and involvement: A test of the four category model. *Communication Monographs, 63*, 269-291.

Guilford, J. P. (1959). *Personality*. New York: McGraw-Hill.

Hasan, B. (1993). The middle category response style: Does it exist? *Journal of Personality & Clinical Studies, 9*, 47-53.

Hastie, R., & Kumar, P. A. (1979). Person memory: Personality traits as organizing principles in memory for behavior. *Journal of Personality and Social Psychology, 37*, 25-38.

Hewes, D. E., & Haight, L. (1979). The cross-situational consistency of communicative behaviors. *Communication Research, 6*, 243-270.

Infante, D. A., & Rancer, A.S. (1996). Argumentativeness and verbal aggressiveness: A review of recent theory and research. In B. Burleson (Ed.), *Communication yearbook* (Vol. 19, pp. 319-351). Thousand Oaks, CA: Sage.

Jaccard, J. J. (1974). Predicting social behavior from personality tests. *Journal of Research in Personality, 7*, 358-367.

Jackson, D. N., Ashton, M. C., & Tomes, J. L. (1996). The six factor model of personality: The facets from the Big Five. *Personality and Individual Differences, 21*, 391-402.

Johnson, J. T., & Boyd, K. R. (1995). Dispositional traits versus the content of experience: actor/observer differences in judgments of the "authentic self." *Personality and Social Psychology Bulletin, 21*, 375-383.

Johnson, R. C., Danko, G. P., Darvill, T. J., & Nagoshi, C. T. (1992). "Docility" versus reciprocity as an explanation for evolutionary selection for altruistic behavior. *Personality & Individual Differences, 13*, 263-267.

Jones, E. E. (1979). The rocky road from acts to dispositions. *American Psychologist, 34*, 107-117.

Jones, E. E., & Nisbett, R. E. (1971). The actor and the observer: Divergent perceptions of the causes of behavior. In E. E. Jones, D. E. Kanouse, H. H. Kelley, R. E. Nisbett, S. Valins, & B. Weiner (Eds.), *Attribution: Perceiving the causes of behavior* (pp. 79-94). Morristown, NJ: General Learning Press.

Kahle, L. R. (1980). Stimulus condition self-selection by males in the interaction of locus of control and skill-chance situations. *Journal of Personality and Social Psychology, 38*, 50-56.

Karylowski, J. J. (1990). Social reference points and accessibility of trait-related information in self-other similarity judgments. *Journal of Personality and Social Psychology, 58*, 975-983.

Kendrick, D.T., Sadalla, E. K., Groth, G., & Trost, M. R. (1990). Evolution, traits, and the stages of human courtship: Qualifying the parental investment model. Special Issue: Biological foundations of personality: Evolution, behavioral genetics, and psychophysiology. *Journal of Personality, 58*, 97-116.

Kenrick, D. T., & Springfield, D. O. (1980). Personality traits and the eye of the beholder: Crossing some traditional philosophical boundaries in the search for consistency in all of the people. *Psychological Review, 87*, 88-104.

Kerber, K. W., & Singleton, R. (1984). Trait and situations, attributions in a naturalistic setting: Familiarity, liking, and attribution validity. *Journal of Personality, 52*, 205-219.

King, W.C., & Miles, E. W. (1995). A quasi-experimental assessment of the effect of computerizing noncognitive paper-and-pencil measurements: A test of measurement equivalence. *Journal of Applied Psychology, 80*, 643-651.

Klein, W. M., & Kunda, Z. (1993). Maintaining self-serving social comparisons: Biased reconstruction of one's past behaviors. *Personality & Social Psychology Bulletin, 19*, 732-739.

Kolar, D. W., Funder, D. C., & Colvin, C.R. (1996). Comparing the accuracy of personality judgments of the self and knowledgeable others. *Journal of Personality, 64*, 311-337.

Kyl-Heku, L. M., & Buss, D. M. (1996). Tactics as units of analysis in personality psychology: An illustration using tactics of hierarchy negotiation. *Personality and Individual Differences, 21*, 497-517.

Lamiell, J. T. (1981). Toward an idiothetic psychology of personality. *American Psychologist, 36*, 276-289.

Lamiell, J. T., Foss, M. A., Trierweiler, S. J., & Leffel, G. M. (1983). Toward a further understanding of the intuitive personologist: Some preliminary evidence for the dialectical quality of subjective personality impressions. *Journal of Personality, 51*, 213-235.

Lewin, K. (1936). *Principles of topological psychology.* New York: McGraw-Hill.

Lindeman, M., & Verkasalo, M. (1995). Personality, situation, and positive-negative asymmetry in socially desirable responding. *European Journal of Personality, 9*, 125-134.

Locksley, A., Brill, G., & Neuner, R. (1984). The conceptual similarity effect: A source of error in self-reports of personality traits. *Journal of Research in Personality, 18,* 442-450.

MacDonald, K. (1995). Evolution, the five-factor model, and levels of personality. Special Issue: Levels and domains in personality. *Journal of Personality, 63,* 525-567.

Magnusson, D. (1982). Situational effects in empirical personality research. In A. Kossakowski & K. Obuchowski (Eds.), *Progress in psychology of personality* (pp. 116-123). Amsterdam: North-Holland.

Magnusson, D., & Endler, N. S. (Eds.). (1977). *Personality at the crossroads. Current issues in interactional psychology.* Hillsdale, NJ: Erlbaum.

Manusov, V. (1990). An application of attribution principles to nonverbal behavior in romantic dyads. *Communication Monographs, 57,* 104-118.

Markus, H. (1977). Self-schemata and processing information about self. *Journal of Personality and Social Psychology, 35,* 63-78.

McCrae, R. R. (1994). The counterpoint of personality assessment: Self-reports and observer ratings. *Assessment, 1,* 159-172.

McCrae, R. R., & Costa, P. T. (1994). Does Lorr's Interpersonal Style Inventory measure the five-factor model? *Personality & Individual Differences, 16,* 195-197.

McCrae, R. R., & John, O. P. (1992) An introduction to the Five-Factor Model and its applications. *Journal of Personality, 60,* 175-216.

McCroskey, J. C., Daly, J. A., Richmond, V. P., & Falcione, R. (1977). Studies of the relationship between communication apprehension and self-esteem. *Human Communication Research, 3,* 269-277.

McCroskey, J. C., Daly, J. A., & Sorensen, G. (1976). Personality correlates of communication apprehension: A research note. *Human Communication Research, 2,* 376-380.

Miller, L.C., Cody, M. J., & McLaughlin, M. L. (1994). Situations and goals as fundamental constructs in interpersonal communication research. In M. L. Knapp & G. R. Miller (Eds.), *Handbook of interpersonal communication* (2nd ed., pp. 162-198). Thousand Oaks, CA: Sage.

Miller, L. C., & Read, S. J. (1991). Inter-personalism: Understanding persons in relationships. In W. H. Jones & D. Perlman (Eds.), *Advances in personal relationships: A research annual* (Vol. 2, pp. 233-267). London: Jessica Kingsley Publishers.

Mischel, W. (1968). *Personality and assessment.* New York: Wiley.

Mischel, W. (1977). The interaction of person and situation. In D. Magnusson & N. S. Endler (Eds.), *Personality at the crossroads:*

Current issues in interactional psychology (pp. 333-352). Hillsdale, NJ: Erlbaum.

Mischel, W. (1984). Convergences and challenges in the search for consistency. *American Psychologist, 39,* 351-364.

Mischel, W. (1985, August). *Personality: Lost or found? Identifying when individual differences make a difference.* Paper presented at the annual meeting of the American Psychological Association, Los Angeles.

Mischel, W., & Peake, P. K. (1982). Beyond deja vu in the search for cross-situational consistency. *Psychological Review, 89,* 730-755.

Mongeau, P. A., Hale, J. L., & Alles, M. (1994). An experimental investigation of accounts and attributions following sexual infidelity. *Communication Monographs, 61,* 326-344.

Monson, T. C., Hesley, J. W., & Chernick, L. (1982). Specifying when personality traits can and cannot predict: An alternative to abandoning the attempt to predict single-act criteria. *Journal of Personality and Social Psychology, 43,* 385-399.

Monson, T. C., & Snyder, M. (1977). Actors, observers, and the attribution process: Towards a reconceptualization. *Journal of Experimental Social Psychology, 13,* 89-111.

Monson, T. C., Tanke, E. D., & Lund, J. (1980). Determinants of social perceptions in a naturalistic setting. *Journal of Research in Personality, 14,* 104-120.

Moskowitz, D. S. (1982). Coherence and cross-situational generality in personality: A new analysis of old problems. *Journal of Personality and Social Psychology, 43,* 754-768.

Moss, H. A., & Susman, E. J. (1980). Longitudinal study of personality development. In O. G. Brim & J. Kagan (Eds.), *Constancy and change in human development* (pp. 530-595). Cambridge, MA: Harvard University Press.

Norman, W. T. (1963). Toward an adequate taxonomy of personality attributes: Replicated factor structure in peer nomination personality ratings. *Journal of Abnormal and Social Psychology, 66,* 574-583.

Norton, R. (1980). The illusion of systematic distortion. *Human Communication Research, 7,* 88-96.

Norton, R. W. (1983). *Communicator style.* Beverly Hills, CA: Sage.

Norton, R. W. (1988). Communicator style theory in marital interaction: Persistent challenges. In S. Duck, D. F. Hay, S. E. Hobfoll, W. Ickes, & B. M. Montgomery (Eds.), *Handbook of personal relationships: Theory, research and interventions* (pp. 307-324). Chichester, UK: Wiley.

Paunonen, S. V. (1984). The reliability of aggregated measurement: Lessons to be learned from psychometric theory. *Journal of Research in Personality, 18*, 383-394.

Paunonen, S. V., & Jackson, D. N. (1985). Ideographic measurement strategies for personality and prediction: Some unredeemed promissory notes. *Psychological Review, 92*, 486-511.

Peake, P. K., & Mischel, W. (1984). Getting lost in the search for large coefficients: Reply to Conley. *Psychological Review, 91*, 491-501.

Plomin, R., & Nesselroade, J. R. (1990). Behavioral genetics and personality change. Special Issue: Biological foundations of personality: Evolution, behavioral genetics, and psychophysiology. *Journal of Personality, 58*, 191-220.

Pollit, B., Lloyd, K., & Bloom, V. L. (1996, November). *Attributional analysis and the Big-Five personality correlates of communication apprehension and talkativeness.* Paper presented at the 82nd annual convention of the Speech Communication Association, San Diego, CA.

Prager, I.G., & Cutler, B. L. (1990). Attributing traits to oneself and to others: The role of acquaintance level. *Personality and Social Psychology Bulletin, 16*, 309-319.

Pryor, J.B., Gibbons, F.X., Wicklund, R.A., Fazio, R.H., & Hood, R. (1977). Self-focused attention and self-report validity. *Journal of Personality, 45*, 514-527.

Pryor, J. B., Kott, T. L., & Bovee, G. R. (1984). The influence of information redundancy upon the use of traits and persons as organizing categories. *Journal of Experimental Social Psychology, 20*, 246-262.

Pulver, A., Allik, J., Pulkkinen, L., & Hamalainen, M. (1995). A Big Five personality inventory in two non-Indo-European languages. *European Journal of Personality, 9*, 109-124.

Read, S.J., Jones, D. K., & Miller, L.C. (1990). Traits as goal-based categories: The importance of goals in the coherence of dispositional categories. *Journal of Personality and Social Psychology, 58*, 1048-1061.

Read, S. J., & Miller, L. C. (1989). Inter-personalism: Toward a goal-based theory of persons in relationships. In L. A. Pervin (Ed.), *Goal concepts in personality and social psychology* (pp. 413-472). Hillsdale, NJ: Erlbaum.

Romer, D., & Revelle, W. (1985). Personality traits: Fact or fiction? A critique of the Sweder and D'Andrade systematic distortion hypothesis. *Journal of Personality and Social Psychology, 47*,1028-1042.

Rosenberg, S., & Sedlak, A. (1972). Structural representations of implicit personality theory. In L. Berkowitz (Ed.), *Advances in experimental social psychology* (Vol. 6, pp. 235-297). New York: Academic Press.

Rushton, J. P., Jackson, D. N., & Paunonen, S. V. (1981). Personality: Nomothetic or ideographic? A response to Kenrick and Springfield. *Psychological Review, 88,* 582-589.

Sarason, I. G., Smith, R. B., & Diener, E. (1975). Personality research: Components of variance attributable to the person and the situation. *Journal of Personality and Social Psychology, 32,* 199-204.

Scheier, M. G., Buss, A. H., & Buss, D. M. (1978). Self-consciousness, self-report of aggressiveness, and aggression. *Journal of Research in Personality, 12,* 133-140.

Schneider, D. J., Hastorf, A. H., & Ellsworth, P. C. (1979). *Person perception.* Reading, MA: Addison-Wesley.

Segrin, C. (1990). A meta-analytic review of social skill deficits in depression. *Communication Monographs, 57,* 292-308.

Segrin, C. (1992). Specifying the nature of social skill deficits associated with depression. *Human Communication Research, 19,* 89-123.

Shoda, Y., & Mischel, W. (1993). Cognitive social approach to dispositional inferences: What if the perceiver is a cognitive social theorist? *Personality and Social Psychology Bulletin, 19,* 574-585.

Shoda, Y., Mischel, W., & Wright, J. C. (1993). Links between personality judgments and contextualized behavior patterns: Situation-behavior profiles of personality prototypes. *Social Cognition, 11,* 399-429.

Shweder, R. A., & D'Andrade, R. G. (1980). The systematic distortion hypothesis. In R. Shweder (Ed.), *New directions for methodology of social and behavioral science* (Vol. 4, pp. 37-58). San Francisco: Jossey-Bass.

Simon, E. P., & Baxter, L.A. (1993). Attachment-style differences in relationship maintenance strategies. *Western Journal of Communication, 57,* 416 - 430.

Simpson, J. A., Rholes, W. S., & Nelligan, J. S. (1992). Support seeking and support giving within couples in an anxiety-provoking situation: The role of attachment styles. *Journal of Personality & Social Psychology, 62,* 434-446.

Small, S., Zeldin, R. S., & Savin-William, R. C. (1983). In search of personality traits; A multimethod analysis of naturally occurring prosocial and dominance behavior. *Journal of Personality, 51,* 1-16.

Snyder, M. (1974). The self-monitoring of expressive behavior. *Journal of Personality and Social Psychology, 30,* 526-537.

Snyder, M. (1983). The influence of individuals on situations: Implications for understanding the links between personality and social behavior. *Journal of Personality, 51,* 491-516.

Snyder, M., & Gangestad, S. (1982). Choosing social situations: Two investigations of self-monitoring processes. *Journal of Personality and Social Psychology, 43,* 123-135.

Snyder, M., & Ickes, W. (1985). Personality and social behavior. In G. Lindzey & E. Aronson (Eds.), *Handbook of social psychology* (pp. 883-948). New York: Random House.

Steinberg, L. (1994). Context and serial-order effects in personality measurement: Limits on the generality of measuring changes the measure. *Journal of Personality & Social Psychology, 66,* 341-349.

Steyer, R., Ferring, D., & Schmitt, M. J. (1992). States and traits in psychological assessment. *European Journal of Psychological Assessment, 8,* 79-98.

Storms, M. D. (1973). Videotape and the attribution process: Revising actors' and observers' points of view. *Journal of Personality and Social Psychology, 27,* 165-175.

Sypher, H. E. (1980). Illusory correlation in communication research. *Human Communication Research, 7,* 83-87.

Tellegen, A., Kamp, J., & Watson, D. (1982). Recognizing individual differences in predictive structure. *Psychological Review, 89,* 95-105.

Tice, D. M . (1992). Self-concept change and self-presentation: The looking glass self is also a magnifying glass. *Journal of Personality & Social Psychology, 63,* 435-451.

Trapnell, P. D., & Wiggins, J. S. (1990). Extension of the Interpersonal Adjective Scales to include the Big Five dimensions of personality (IASR-B5). *Journal of Personality and Social Psychology., 59,* 781-790.

Tupes, E. C., & Christal, R . E. (1961). *Recurrent personality factors based on trait ratings* (USAF ASD Tech. Rep. No. 61-97). Lackland Air Force Base, TX: U.S. Air Force.

Underwood, B., & Moore, B. S. (1981). Sources of behavioral consistency. *Journal of Personality and Social Psychology, 40,*780-785.

Van Heck, G. L . (1991). Temperament and the person-situation debate. In J. Strelau & A. Angleitner (Eds.), *Explorations in temperament: International perspectives on theory and measurement. Perspectives on individual differences* (pp. 163-175). New York: Plenum.

Waller, N. G, Tellegen, A., McDonald, R. P., & Lykken, D.T. (1996). Exploring nonlinear models in personality assessment: Development and preliminary validation of a negative emotionality scale. *Journal of Personality, 64*, 545-576.

Weber, D. J., & Vangelisti, A. L. (1991). "Because I love you . . .": The tactical use of attributional expressions in conversation. *Human Communication Research, 17,* 606-624.

Wilson, D. S., Near, D., & Miller, R.R. (1996). Machiavellianism: A synthesis of the evolutionary and psychological literatures. *Psychological Bulletin, 119,* 285-299.

Wishner, J. (1960). Reanalysis of "Impressions of personality." *Psychological Review, 67,* 96-112.

Woodruff, C. (1984). The consistency of presented personality: Additional evidence from aggregation. *Journal of Personality, 52,* 308-317.

Wymer, W. E., & Penner, L. A. (1985). Moderator Variables and different types of predictability: Do you have a match? *Journal of Personality and Social Psychology, 49,* 1002-1015.

Zuckerman, M. (1974). The sensation seeking motive. In B. Maher (Ed.), *Progress in experimental personality research* (pp. 79-148). New York: Academic Press.

Zuckerman, M. (1983). The distinction between trait and state settles is not arbitrary: Comments on Allen and Potkay's "On the arbitrary distinction between traits and states." *Journal of Personality and Social Psychology, 44,* 1083-1086.

Zuckerman, M., Bernieri, F., Koestner, R., & Rosenthal, R. (1989). To predict some of the people some of the time: In search of moderators. *Journal of Personality and Social Psychology, 57,* 279-293.

Zuckerman, M., Kuhlman, D. M., & Camac, C. (1988). What lies beyond E and N? Factor analyses of scales believed to measure basic dimensions of personality. *Journal of Personality and Social Psychology, 54,* 96-107.

2

Interpersonal Communication as Temperamental Expression: A Communibiological Paradigm

Michael J. Beatty
Cleveland State University
James C. McCroskey
West Virginia University

A robust account, or theory, of how and why people interact as they do stands as the ultimate justification for the time and energy communication scholars have dedicated to research. Although numerous functions and desirable characteristics are often mentioned in discussions of theory construction (e.g., description, control, parsimony, abstractness; Reynolds, 1971), prediction and explanation, considered essential functions of theory, have traditionally attracted by far the greatest amount of attention in philosophical treatments of social theory (Achinstein, 1971; Blalock, 1969; Borger & Cioffi, 1970; Reynolds, 1971; Rudner, 1966; Taylor, 1964; Toulmin, 1969; von Wright, 1971; Zetterberg, 1965). Numerous ideologically based debates regarding proper modes of theory construction have appeared in the communication literature for about two decades, however, communication scholars working from diverse epistemological perspectives also have emphasized prediction and explanation (for summaries see, Infante, Rancer, & Womack, 1993; Littlejohn, 1983).

Although prediction and explanation are conceptually separate, they function interdependently in the formulation of powerful theories. Accurate predictions are vital. Unless findings generated by methodologically rigorous inquiry confirm predictions implicated by a theory, the explanations represented by the predictions must be questioned, if not rejected, regardless of intuitive appeal of the explanations. As an illustration, recall the evolving conception of our solar system, which we probably first learned in elementary school (for a review see, Hawking, 1988). Aristotle, known in the field of interpersonal communication principally for his thinking about rhetorical matters, also claimed that the earth was stationary and that the sun, moon, stars, and other planets rotated around it, a depiction that was appealing on an ideological plane at the time. It was not until 1514 that Copernicus suggested that the earth and other bodies orbited around the sun. Because the notion that the earth was not the center of the universe was considered heretical by the church, Copernicus spent the remainder of his life under house arrest. Using the newly invented telescope, Galileo suspected that everything might not be orbiting directly around the earth as Copernicus suggested. With each improvement, predicted locations of the moon, planets, and stars were closer to observations. However, observations did not perfectly match predictions until Kepler modified Copernicus' theory, proposing that planets moved in elliptical rather than circular orbits (circles were aesthetically preferable even to Kepler).

The physicists attempting to describe the solar system did not accept partially accurate predictions. Fortunately, models were reformulated until they achieved perfect fit between predictions and observations. Extending this work ethic to our efforts to explain interpersonal communication, scholars should be motivated to seriously reevaluate theories when research findings provide only meager support for predictions (small statistical effects). Noted methodologist Cohen (1990) emphasized the importance of effects relative to statistical significance concluding that "the primary product of research inquiry is one or more measures of effect size, not p values" (p. 1310). In a very real sense, favoring a theory because it casts interpersonal communication in an intuitively appealing light even though its predictive power is slight and rejecting a theory that yields accurate predictions because of perspective bias is analogous to advocating Aristotle's belief over Copernican thinking about the center of the solar system and preferring circular planetary orbits over ellipses. Theorists must follow the path that leads to improved fit between prediction and observation.

At the same time, Blalock (1969) reminded us that "facts do not speak for themselves" (p.2), underscoring the importance of explanation as a context for interpreting observation. In short, prediction describes "how" variables should be statistically related, whereas explanation addresses "why" such statistical relationships should be expected. Our task as interpersonal scholars, should we choose to accept it, is to devise theories that lead to accurate predictions regarding communicators' thoughts, feelings, and actions; and comprehensive explanations that enhance our understanding of why communicators think, feel, and act in the manner observed. Surely, Lewin (1945) had such theories in mind when he remarked that "nothing is as practical as a good theory" (p. 129).

SIGNIFICANCE OF TRAITS TO "GOOD" INTERPERSONAL COMMUNICATION THEORY

Conceptualization of Communicator Traits

Noticing that people differ from one another requires very little perceptiveness. Indeed, casual observers would note that people are not alike in the ways they react to stimuli. When people can be reliably differentiated on the basis of their responses, social scientists use trait labels, to refer to prototypical responses to a stimulus or class of stimuli. As an illustration, the term communication apprehension was coined (McCroskey, 1970) as the trait label for individuals' avoidance and anxiety reactions (response) to communication (stimulus). Decades of research have documented the utility of trait constructs within the context of communication inquiry and theory construction.

Communicator Traits and Predictive Power

With the premise in mind that different people respond differently to stimuli, we argue that any theory of interpersonal communication that is inattentive to communicator traits is necessarily and substantially incomplete. This incompleteness is manifest most conspicuously in weak predictive power, a tell-tale sign of inadequate explanation when sound research methodology is employed. One response to the problem of low predictive power has been the redefinition of effect sizes. Guilford (1956) advanced a scheme in which, for example, correlation coefficients in the .40 to .70 range were considered moderate. The minimum correlation coefficient considered "high" was .70. This category system for assigning verbal labels to correlation coefficients was based on the relative predictive accuracy afforded within each range of coefficients. Subsequently, however, Cohen (1988) adopted a normatively based rationale, revising the statistical criteria for various effect sizes (i.e., after considering the magnitude of effects typically observed in social science research, Cohen posited correlation coefficients of .3 as "medium" and .5 as "large").

A major drawback to redefining effect sizes is that theorists become complacent, satisfied with inaccurate predictions although the latest statistical jargon might supply aid and comfort to the weak hypothesis. Although accounting for 25% percent of the variance may be substantial against the backdrop of lesser models, we cannot overlook the 75% that remains unexplained. If we do overlook the considerable misfit between predictions and observations indicated by large residual terms, our theories will be considerably less "practical." Despite the benchmark criteria suggested in his text, Cohen (1990) recently made a similar point, underscoring the fundamental importance of predictive accuracy as a criterion for research findings. Ultimately, accepting theories that yield inaccurate predictions and then justifying them on normative grounds appears an admission of weakness, at least when compared to the physical sciences. Regardless of how redefining small, medium, and large effects makes us feel about our theoretical progress, revising our interpretations of variance explained does not improve the actual predictive power of the theory.

Instead of engaging in empirical hexing of anticipated results, we should seriously consider the possibility that a large chunk of the residual represents trait differences among individuals. Although a great many missing variables can always be suspected, we contend that communicator characteristics, or traits, constitute the most parsimonious set. Although trait approaches are not without critics, our position is that the critics are wrong. Indeed, we maintain that when predictive power is considered, traits are at the center of the interpersonal universe. We address the specific complaints lodged against trait conceptualizations in the development of this chapter. As an overview, however, perhaps the most glaring oversight of trait critics is their inattentiveness to the huge body of neurobiological research that has accumulated over the past decade.

Contributions from Psychobiological Research

In recent years psychobiologists, working mostly under the rubric of temperament, have made impressive advances in the understanding of human behavior, especially in social contexts (Aggleton & Mishkin, 1986; Bates & Wachs, 1994; Bouchard, 1993; Buss, 1989; Buss & Plomin, 1975, 1984; Calkins & Fox, 1992; Collins & Depue, 1992; Davidson, Ekman, Saron, Senulis, & Friesen, 1990; Davis, 1992; Depue & Achene, 1989; Eaton, 1983; Eysenck, 1991; Eysenck & Eysenck, 1985; Farb, Aoki, Milner, Kaneko, & LeDoux, 1992; Fowles, 1980; Fox, 1989, 1991; Fox, Bell, & Jones, 1992; Gray, 1982, 1987, 1990, 1991; Grillon, Ameli, Woods, Merikangas, & Davis, 1991; Gunnar, 1990; Kagan, 1992; Kagan, Reznick, & Snidman, 1988; Kagan & Snidman, 1991; LeDoux, 1986; LeDoux, Cicchetti, Xagoraris, & Romanski, 1990; Lykken & Telligen, 1996; Myers & Dierer, 1995; Reiman, Fusselman, Fox, Raichle, 1989; Reiman, Raichle, Butler, Herscovitch, & Robins, 1984; Rolls, 1990; Rothbart, 1989; Rothbart, Derryberry, & Posner, 1994; Rushton, Fulker, Neal, Nias, & Eysenck, 1986; Sears & Steinmetz, 1990; Smith & DeVito, 1984; Steinmetz, 1994; Steinmetz & Thompson, 1991; Stelmack, 1990; Stelmack & Geen, 1992; Strelau, 1994; Thomas & Chess, 1977; Wachs, 1992; Zuckerman, 1991a, 1991b, 1995; Zuckerman, Kuhlman, & Camac, 1988). According to Bates (1989), *temperament* refers to "biologically-rooted individual differences in behavioral tendencies across various kinds of situations and over the course of time" (p. 4). In addition to providing strong evidence for the biological basis of traits, much of the behavior studied by psychobiologists is easily recognizable as what scholars in our field consider interpersonal communication. As shown later in this chapter, shyness, extraversion, communicator style, agressiveness, assertiveness, and empathy, just to name a few, all have been strongly linked to inherited neurobiological processes. We maintain that no theory of human interaction can be taken seriously unless it is informed by the massive body of research literature that has already established strong effects for inborn, individual differences in neurobiological processes that underlie major dimensions of social behavior. In this chapter, we stake out five neuobiologically based, theoretic propositions that must be addressed in the formulation of interpersonal communication theory; describe three basic neurobiological systems that are directly relevant to interpersonal communication theory; consider the meaning of the five propositions within the context of broader laws of physics; and examine implications of the paradigm advanced in this chapter.

THE CENTRAL PROPOSITIONS OF COMMUNIBIOLOGY

Although the five propositions delineated here represent a radical departure from current thinking about human communication, they are widely accepted among psychobiologists (e.g., Strelau, 1994). In a very real sense, we are proposing a paradigm shift. Parallel to psychobiology and social biology, the following propositions provide the framework for a communibiological paradigm.

Proposition 1: All psychological processes—including cognitive, affective, and motor—involved in social interaction depend on brain activity, making necessary a neurobiology of interpersonal communication

Simply stated, theoretical speculation about thinking, feeling, and behaving during human interaction must be consistent with knowledge regarding brain and brain related functioning. Although the interpersonal communication literature is replete with constructs positing processes that hint at neurobiological activity of some sort (e.g., assembling, differentiation, selecting), communication scholars have not yet specified the neurological activity expected to underlie the supposed processes, nor have they validated the constructs against appropriate neurological criteria. Put bluntly, we do not know whether cognitive or affective processes inferred by scholars from the behavior of communicators exist within neurobiological reality. Major construct validity problems would arise, for example, if activity levels of the neurological structures responsible for complex versus simplistic data processing failed to differentiate people along the cognitive complexity continuum as they composed responses to the experimental stimulus. Conceptual labels, whether referring to processes or traits, are merely metaphoric surrogates for complex neurobiological systems. As such, most of the constructs in our field represent starting points, requiring further elaboration. Part of the elaboration process consists of linking proposed constructs to specific neurobiological operations.

Although communication scholars have posited more and more constructs and processes presumed to be going on in the heads of people anticipating or engaged in interaction, usually by asking people to recall previous interpersonal episodes, psychobiologists have been making considerable headway mapping the neurobiological circuitry associated with psychological processes. Although the neurobiological functions are not completely understood, much is now known about extraverted social behavior

(Eysenck & Eysenck, 1985; Stelmack, 1990; Stelmack & Geen, 1992), shyness (Buss, 1989; Kagan, et al., 1988; Kagan & Snidman, 1991), hostility and aggression (Adams & Victor, 1993; Marieb & Mallatt, 1992; Panksepp, 1982, 1986; Rushton et al., 1986; Spoont, 1992; Zuckerman, 1995), self-imposed constraint in social situations (Bouchard, 1993), impulsivity (Zuckerman, 1994) approach and avoidance behavior (Fowles, 1980; Gray, 1982, 1987, 1990, 1991) and selective attention, focus (Derryberry & Rothbart, 1988; Macleod & Mathews, 1988; Nelson, 1994; Posner, 1990; Posner & Peterson, 1990; Posner & Presti, 1987; Vogt, Finch, & Olsen, 1992), and memory (Brown & Kulik, 1979; Davis, 1992; Squire, 1987). As mentioned, these constructs overlap with scholarly interest in interpersonal communication behavior. Indeed, the relevance of neurobiological analyses of communication behavior is quite evident in Bates' (1989) observation that "there is general agreement that temperament is manifest largely in the context of social interaction" (p. 4).

By comparison, our field has fallen behind in the quest to understand and explain the complex processes underlying social behavior. Although a few interpersonal communication scholars have recognized the potential contribution of neurobiology to our understanding of social interaction (e.g., Cappella, 1991, 1993; Horvath, 1995; Knapp, Miller, & Fudge, 1994), the bulk of work in interpersonal communication has proceeded as though communicators were not biological organisms. However, simply scanning a recent issue of *Psychological Science* should convince any serious scholar interested in interpersonal communication that we will lag even further behind if we continue ducking our obligation to show that metaphoric, hypothetical explanations are at least neurologically plausible.

Proposition 2: Brain activity precedes psychological experience

Scholars addressing issues regarding the nature of the relationship between brain activity and subjective experience, termed the *mind-brain* problem (Popper & Eccles, 1977), have taken one of three stances. *Physical reductionism* holds that all psychological experience is a product of brain functioning. For reductionists, subjective experience is like the images seen during a motion picture, illusory consequences of the film and the operations of the projector. In stark contrast, *mentalism* posits the existence of a nonbiological form of consciousness that directs brain activity in efforts to carry out its will. Thus, for mentalists, subjective experience may precede brain functions. A third stance, *interactionism,* is anchored by the assumption that both reductionists and mentalists are partly correct. According to interactionists, some psychological experience is triggered by automatic brain activity (e.g., reflexive blinking) but some brain activity is initiated by conscious intent (e.g., intentional blinking).

Our position is decidedly reductionistic, although we remain receptive to axioms that are mentalistic or interactionistic. However, if scholars insist that psychological processes underlying communicative behavior are subject to autonomous control, they must describe the mechanisms making such processes possible. Certainly, scholars taking a mentalist or interactionist position on the mind-brain problem take on the obligation to describe the circuitry that allows an extraphysical mind to orchestrate changes in the physical brain. Regarding this issue, it is noteworthy that mentalist and interactionist philosophies emerged at a time and in a culture in which church and state were not separate and such positions were often required to make room for religious convictions in the concepts of "spirit" and "free will." Although it would be inaccurate to suggest that neurobiological research unequivocally supports reductionism, the preponderance of evidence certainly points in that direction. Moreover, as psychobiologists make continued progress, the case for reductionism is likely to become only stronger.

Proposition 3: The neurobiological structures underlying temperament traits and individual differences are mostly inherited

As discussed earlier, traits are labels used by theorists to describe collective samples of cognition, affect, or behavior. As such, traits are not inherited but the neurobiological structures are mostly due to heredity. Recent studies of identical twins have produced strong evidence for this position regarding a wide range of socially significant traits. Zuckerman (1994) remarked that "There is little difference between the correlations for identical twins who were raised apart and those who were raised together, which indicates that shared environment is of little importance for these traits" (p. 245). The list for which the best predictor of a person's trait level is that of his or her twin, whether raised apart or together, includes altruism, empathy, nurturance, aggressiveness, assertiveness (Rushton et al., 1986), constraint (opposite of impulsivity; Bouchard, 1993), and general happiness (Lykken & Tellegen, 1996). Especially important for interpersonal communication theorists are the findings of Horvath's (1995) study of twins, which indicated strong hereditary components to the relaxed, open, dominant, and communicator images dimensions of Norton's (1978) communicator style construct. The variance attributable to heredity for these four elements of style ranged from 50 to 78%.

Although Lykken and Tellegen (1996) accounted for nearly 80% of the variance in happiness, most studies of twins have accounted for somewhat less. The average variance explained is around 50%, however. Clearly, critics might point out that heredity fails to account for all of a particular trait, opening the door for an environmental or situational argument. Three considerations are important, however. First, as with all social science research, a variety of methodological imperfections attenuate the observed effects. For instance, the measures employed as dependent variables always introduce error into the study in a variety of ways. Improving the psychometric properties of trait measures would likely increase the magnitude of the associations discovered in studies of twins. Second, there are biological influences (such as nutrition, prenatal drug or alcohol use) on neurobiological structures other than heredity, that might produce a discrepancy in trait scores as a function of altered neurobiological structures. Third, regardless of whose definition of effect sizes is embraced, the impact of heredity of interpersonally significant behavior patterns is sizable, both normatively and objectively. Considering that a single construct, common biology, accounts for one half or more of the variance in behavior patterns, the criterion of parsimony clearly favors a communibiological model.

This proposition lays out a two fold epistemological consideration for interpreting research findings: first, correlations between parents' personality characteristics or behaviors and children's personalities and behaviors should not be attributed to learning processes unless variance due to common biology is first removed. Second, when findings based on self-report data conflict with biological principles, the presumption must rest with biology. With respect to the first point, studies linking college age males' behavior with the parenting styles of their fathers (e.g., Brook, Brook, Whiteman, & Gordon, 1983) have been interpreted as evidence of a learning effect (e.g., Beatty, Burant, Dobos, & Rudd, 1996). However, it is not only possible but probable, given the evidence cited earlier that much of the sons' characteristics are due to heredity. Likewise, the second point draws our attention to the interpretation of research findings. In her study of twins, Horvath (1995), for example, found small correlations between communicator style variables for some variables. Although it is tempting to conclude that some traits are genetic, whereas others are learned, we might view the findings as revelatory about the composite of items presumed to measure a trait. Perhaps these factors merely represent artifactual phenomena, not measuring traits or anything else of interpersonal significance. Whether one assumes that (a) biology is the criterion against which self-reports are validated or (b) self-report scales are the criterion against which biological hypotheses are tested, depends on the scholar's axiology. In this chapter, we consistently argue for a biological criterion. As much as any other feature of communibiology, our position on heredity clearly outlines a paradigm quite different from current thinking among interpersonal scholars.

Proposition 4: Environment or "situation" has only a negligible effect on interpersonal behavior

Reviewing the research focused on well-being, Lykken and Tellegen (1996) concluded that:

> No one doubts that making the team, being promoted at work, or winning the lottery tends to bring about an increment in happiness, just as flunking out, being laid off, or a disastrous investment would be likely to diminish one's feelings of well-being . . . however, the effects of these events appear to be transitory fluctuations about a stable temperamental set point or trait that is characteristic of the individual. (p. 189)

The principle that boundaries of individual reactions to environmental stimuli are defined by individual temperament is embedded in the concept of temperamental set points. In the case of communication apprehension, for instance, the specific response to the demand for social interaction is difficult to predict in a particular circumstance, but the class of responses can be predicted with substantial accuracy (Beatty, 1987).

Although expressions of temperament are stimulated within the context of environments or situations, extending our analysis to view interpersonal communication as an expression of temperament means diminishing the role of environmental stimuli or situations in our explanation of social behavior. Rather, environment is seen as a set of potential inputs that are selectively processed in accord with individual temperament, resulting in a set of responses or outputs. In this way, all interpersonally relevant stimuli are mediated through neurobiologically based temperament structures. Researchers have made considerable progress mapping the neurobiological circuitry involved in selective perception (Posner, 1990; Posner & Peterson, 1990; Posner & Presti, 1987; Vogt, Finch, & Olsen, 1992).

Anatomically, the anterior attention network that drives selective perception consists of the amygdala, the cortex, the midprefrontal cortex, and the anterior cingulate gyrus. In general, this neurobiological circuit functions in a manner consistent with an individual's overall temperament. For instance, compared to nonanxious people, the anterior attention networks of anxious people are more sensitive to threatening and negative stimuli (Mathews, 1990). Numerous studies demonstrate a strong correspondence between social anxiety, for example, and interpretation of situational cues (see Beatty & McCroskey, 1996a), suggesting that situational information is filtered through individual traits.

One of the more promising insights, however, regarding the role of situation or context in affecting behavior that can be gleaned from a temperament perspective pertains to the *goodness or poorness of fit* between temperament and environment (Chess & Thomas, 1989; Greenspan, 1981; Keogh, 1982; Martin, Nagle, & Paget, 1983; Pullis & Cadwell, 1982; Strelau, 1983; Thomas & Chess, 1977; Thomas, Chess, & Birch, 1968). According to Thomas et al., accurate predictions of human behavior require attentiveness to "the characteristics of the individual, the demands of the environment, and the 'fit' between them" (p. 137). Regardless of the context, a good fit exists between a person and the social environment when the situational demands or the characteristics of others in the environment, either by chance or strategy, complement the salient features of the person's temperament. Of course, goodness or poorness of fit is always a matter of degree. When the fit is good, acting in accord with temperamental urges is generally perceived as appropriate behavior. For instance, a good fit exists for students who are apprehensive about communication and classes that do not require presentations or oral participation. A poor fit, on the other hand, arises when the demands of the environment are incongruous with a person's temperament. Requiring apprehensive students to make oral presentations or requiring a verbally aggressive person to engage in passive behavior when aggravated by another are examples of poor fit. Faced with poor fit, the individual can behave as inclined by temperament and endure social sanctions or suppress temperamental urges and experience stress. Whether one acts inappropriately or suppresses urges depends on the extent to which competing neurobiological systems controlling approach and avoidance activity are triggered by the environment. If the stress produced through suppression exceeds the individual's capacity to tolerate pressure, we might expect a dramatic temperamental display (e.g., rage in response to what appears to others as a minor interpersonal transgression).

Proposition 5: Differences in interpersonal behavior are principally due to individual differences in neurobiological functioning

Summarizing the connection between neurobiology and behavior, Steinmetz (1994) stated that at the core of temperament "is a set of temperament-related brain structures that are responsible for generating and maintaining temperament-related behavior patterns" (p. 18). For decades, temperament scholars have been describing neurobiological structures that underlie clusters of various social behaviors. For example, Gray (1982, 1987, 1990, 1991) proposed the most detailed model of the neurobiology of temperament. Gray integrated neurobiological structures into three interconnected behavior systems, the *behavior activation system* (BAS), the *behavior inhibition system* (BIS), and the *fight or flight system* (FFS). The BAS describes the neurobiological structure that energizes goal-directed behavior. Anatomically, the BAS includes the basal nuclei, the neocortical regions connected to it, the dopaminergic fibers that extend from the midbrain, and the thalamic nuclei (Gray, 1991). In contrast to the BAS, activation of the BIS—through the perception of novel stimuli or those associated with anticipated punishment or termination of reward—produces increased arousal as a function of its connection with the limbic system, increased attentional focus on threatening stimuli due to anterior attention network involvement, and cessation of contemporaneous behavior. The BIS circuitry links the hippocampus, the subiculum, and the septum with the limbic system, which consists of the medial wall of the limbic lobe, the olfactory cortex, the cingulate and subcallosal gyri, and the subcortical areas of the amygdala, hypothalamus, epithalamus, anterior thalamic nuclei and part of the basal nuclei (Gray, 1991). Finally, the FFS controls the instigation of aggressive behavior and the onset of active withdrawal. The set of neurological circuits interconnects the basolateral and centomedial nuclei of the amygdala, the ventromedial nucleus of the hypothalamus, the central gray region of the midbrain, and the somatic and motor nuclei of the lower brain stem (Gray, 1991). Other scholars have described similar systems in their analyses of "rage" (Adams & Victor, 1993; Marieb & Mallatt, 1992; Panksepp, 1982, 1986).

Although humans share in common the anatomic features of the three systems described by Gray, individual differences in the reactivity of these structures produce individual differences in observable behavior. As Gray (1991) stated "temperament reflects parameter values" and "the major dimensions of personality . . . are created by individual differences in such parameter values" (p. 23).

Extending Gray's thinking, Strelau (1994) pointed out that individual differences in parameter values can take the form of "sensitivity to neurons' postsynaptic receptors or sensitivity in their synaptic transmission, the amount of neurotransmitters being released, the activity of the neural structures (including receptors) to different kinds of stimuli, all taking part in the determination of individual differences in traits" (p. 135).

Research indicates that impulsive individuals, neurotic extraverts (Gray, 1991), and psychopaths (Arnett, Howland, Smith, & Newman, 1993) tend to possess low thresholds for BAS activation, whereas anxiety prone-individuals tend to possess low thresholds for BIS stimulation (Gray, 1991). Panksepp (1986) showed that prosocial behavior such as friendliness, bonding, and comforting behavior depends on suppression of the FFS. Although these studies link personality and behavioral clusters with individual neurobiological subsystems, specific behavior in particular situations is a function of the relative reactivity of all three systems. For instance, elsewhere we have conceptualized communication apprehension in terms of reactive BIS relative to BAS (Beatty, McCroskey & Heisel, in press) and we have proposed that trait verbal aggressiveness represents reactive FFS and BAS relative to BIS functioning (Beatty & McCroskey, in press). Similarly, passive - aggressive individuals could be thought of as those whose BAS, FFS, and BIS are all easily stimulated. In this way, aggression circuits are turned on and amplified by BAS circuitry but the simultaneous activation of the inhibition system deters passive - aggressive individuals from deploying confrontational tactics.

Critics of trait conceptualizations of interpersonal communication have missed the importance of competing subsystems in their analysis. For instance, when communication apprehensives are asked to make public presentations, we can reliably predict avoidance and withdrawal unless another offsetting neurobiological subsystem is triggered. Students can be both apprehensive about communication and highly motivated to achieve academically (Beatty, Forst, & Stewart, 1986). Thus, when presentation grades are important to the overall course grade in a required public speaking course, both BAS and BIS systems are activated amounting to a classic approach-avoidance conflict. The use of a single trait measure to predict behavior is inadequate in such cases. Moreover, casting doubt on the validity of the trait in question or the trait perspective in general from the results of such a study applies a simplistic criterion for falsification where a more complex one is required. During social interaction, more than one trait is often salient for participants. Underlying these traits are neurobiological structures, the reactivity of which varies across individuals. Interpersonal communication scholars must not continue to ignore these biological features of human interaction.

COMMUNIBIOLOGY WITHIN A BROADER PERSPECTIVE: THE PHYSICAL LAWS OF THE UNIVERSE

Rationale for a Physics of Communibiology

The neurobiological, reductionist paradigm developed in this chapter naturally and logically necessitates theoretic attention to the broader context within which communibiological functioning takes place, the physical laws of the universe. Viewing communibiological functioning as embedded within physics provides a three-tiered foundation for understanding interpersonal communication, especially from a trait perspective. First, at the most basic level, because we are composed of matter we are subject to physical laws in a manner identical to all other objects: An ethnomethodologist who leaps from a 20-story building will fall at the same rate as a sack of unpublishable scientific manuscripts dropped from the same height, even though the latter may constitute the greater loss to the scientific literature. Second, physics proposes that measurable properties of objects (weight) vary according to characteristics of surrounding space (e.g., gravitational force), but the relative values of such properties of two objects remains constant. Thus, if A weighs more than B on earth, A will weigh more than B on the moon, although A will weigh less on the moon than on earth. A parallel case applies to properties of communicator traits. For instance, if A's level of trait verbal aggressiveness is higher than B's in one circumstance, A's level will also be higher than B's in other circumstances, although verbal aggressiveness might be inhibited or facilitated in various interpersonal stimuli. Third, we are neurobiologically structured to understand experience in terms of physical laws. It is our unique predisposition to comprehend physical laws that has made human survival and much technological advancement possible. Consider, for example, that until Einstein's remarkable insights, astronomers were unable to predict the orbit of mercury (for a crisp treatment, see Friedman, 1991). Einstein reasoned that the mass of the sun produced a gravitational force sufficient to warp both space and time, distorting our observations of Mercury. In the end, Einstein's calculations were shown to be correct. However, the essential point is that Einstein's accomplishment did not require that he travel to

Mercury to conduct field research. Rather, like Copernicus, Galileo, Newton, and Kepler before him, Einstein inferred specific physical laws from a broader, in-born, intuitive sense of the universe.

Implications of A Paradigm Grounded in Physics

A paradigm of interpersonal communication set within the context of physics has three main implications for the study of human relationships. First, rather than searching inductively for models of human relationships, we propose that communication scholars attempt to fit data pertaining to aspects of social interaction to extant physics equations. The primary task of such an endeavor consists of defining the terms. For example, interpersonal attraction could be conceptualized as interpersonal gravity. The common expression "falling in love," which references giving way to gravity does not represent a random or capricious selection of words. Instead, language choices and inferences pertaining to human relationships originate in the brain along with those about physical laws. Perceptions and judgment are distorted when people are emotionally involved with others just as the mass of a planet warps time and space. The stress experienced during relational termination might be compared to the stress induced by attempts to escape the gravitational pull of the earth. Although such examples do not provide powerful evidence for a gravitational model of attraction, they are consistent with our notion that we comprehend and talk about the universe (interpersonal relationships included) along the lines of physics.

An empirical test of the model would, among other things, require conceptual and operational definitions of interpersonal mass. Researchers could follow Saltiel and Woelfel's (1975) lead, defining *mass* as the aggregate of favorable information about the object person. Incidentally, in their analysis of attitudes and attitude change, Saltiel and Woelfel referred to *inertia* and *acceleration,* concepts borrowed from physics. Saltiel and Woelfel's thinking was profound, especially for its time. Our position, however, is literal rather than metaphoric. Bluntly stated, we contend that interpersonal communication is the physics of human relationships.

Second, a physics-driven paradigm provides a framework for understanding "unpredictable" communicative behavior. It is common knowledge among physicists that the most profound challenge to Einstein's version of the universe came from quantum mechanics. In particular, physicists conducted experiments that suggested that activity at the atomic level may be random, upsetting Einstein's fundamental axiom regarding an orderly universe.

Einstein's response to this feature of quantum mechanics was (a) that the observed activity only appeared random, meaning that the governing principle had not yet been discovered; and (b) even if no law emerged, observations of randomness were confined to small and rather trivial activity of electrons. Similarly, we propose that major, important interpersonal functioning follows systematic principles. Accordingly, social interaction appears unpredictable when our analysis is incomplete or when environmental demands are insufficient to activate communicators' dominant neurobiological systems.

Third, it is also common knowledge that Einstein envisioned a unified theory of the universe, often proclaiming that the important task was to discover the physical laws because all else will be forgotten. Given his personal style and views about human relationships, Einstein must have known at some level that human activity must be explained by a unified theory. Although it is tempting to distinguish human behavior from the functioning of other objects, we might note that such assumptions may be unwarranted to the extent that consciousness resides in the building blocks of all matter. In his discussion of photons, the indivisible light particle, Zukav (1978) concluded:

> We have little choice but to acknowledge that photons, which are energy, do appear to process information and to act accordingly, and therefore, strange as it may sound, they seem to be organic. Since we are also organic, there is a possibility that by studying photons (and other energy quanta) we may learn something about us. (pp. 63-64)

In addition to raising questions about the distinction between humans and other configurations of matter often perpetuated in the social and behavioral sciences, Zukav stated that consciousness may reside within the energy quanta of which our neurobiological systems are composed. Because consciousness originates from neurobiological operations, the indivisible units of analysis for interpersonal scholars interested in goal-oriented communication are probably quantas, not dyads. Indeed, we might learn something fundamental about human interaction by studying physics.

From the perspective of theory construction, we must also acknowledge that parsimony and empirical relevance are important features of "good" theory. Parsimony, of course, relates to the simplicity of a theory. Empirical relevance requires that theoretical claims are consistent with extant knowledge. Earlier in this chapter we emphasized the importance of consistency between claims made by communication scholars and neurobiological principles. We further contend that both parsimony and empirical relevance are enhanced by anchoring a theory of interpersonal communication in a paradigm that consists of principles derived from physics as well as biology. If we work from a paradigm, however, that requires a separate set of principles a unified theory becomes impossible, and we alienate ourselves from the rest of the universe. A unified theory of the universe ultimately must include a parallel conceptualization of human functioning.

In our view, arguments based in ideological beliefs about differences in humans and physical objects is insufficient to warrant rejection of an attempt at a unified theory, especially if the arguments are made by scholars who are not fully competent in biology and physics. Clearly, competent and convincing refutation requires full comprehension of that which is rejected. The history of physics and philosophy have always run parallel, one informing the other: Virtually all philosophers have written about nature and physicists have made assumptions and comments of a philosophical nature. Why should interpersonal scholars be less rigorous in their efforts to formulate sound theory? Bearing in mind that Aristotle's absurd notions about the solar system were kept buoyant by ideological biases rather than empirical data, our task is to submit hypotheses based on physics principles to rigorous empirical tests. We should search for a separate set of principles to explain human interaction only after those that lead to accurate predictions about the rest of the universe have been shown to be inadequate. This perspective, of course, underscores the importance of methodological competence, especially regarding quantitative analysis. As history reveals, advances the understanding of space and time have almost always required increased mathematical sophistication (Hawking, 1988). Similarly, the complexity of the quantitative analysis of communication must parallel the complexity of the communication processes under study.

IMPLICATIONS OF A COMMUNIBIOLOGICAL PARADIGM

Generally speaking, temperament can be thought of as the repertoire of reaction patterns to external stimuli demonstrated by infants when they enter the world (Chess & Thomas, 1989). Underlying neurobiological structures or circuitry are "responsible for generating and maintaining temperament-related behavior patterns" (Steinmetz, 1994, p. 18). Although there is consensus regarding the vast majority of issues, research and theory have progressed along diverse lines. The empirical foci of temperament inquiry ranges from analysis of narrowly defined features of temperament (e.g., attention span) to broader personality traits (e.g., extraversion) and types (e.g., difficult child) consisting of various combinations of traits and features. Although we have emphasized neurobiological dimensions of temperament, the viability of each approach depends on the level of abstraction at which interpersonal scholars focus their work. Indeed, the entire spectrum of temperament-related qualities of individuals potentially contributes to our understanding of social interaction.

Although communication scholars have only recently begun to seriously discuss the value of biology to interpersonal communication studies, social biologists and psychobiologists have dedicated more than a decade of research effort to temperament. Furthermore, the relevance of temperament to interpersonal communication has not escaped their theorizing. In fact, Bates (1989) remarked that among temperament scholars "there is general agreement that temperament is manifest largely in the context of social interaction" (p. 4). Along these same lines, Steinmetz (1994) observed that in addition to being responsible for interpersonal behavior, neurobiological systems are triggered by stimuli that "might be expected during social interaction in which the entire context of the experience might be necessary to activate temperament-related brain structures" (p. 19).

As we view it, the communibiological perspective outlined in this chapter has five main implications for trait conceptualizations of interpersonal communication. First, the identification of neurobiological structures that are linked to particular patterns of behavior strongly supports trait perspectives in so far as neurobiological systems are relatively immutable features of individuals. Unless a person's biology changes, we expect reasonably consistent forms of responses. This is not to say that any single trait determines a particular response. Rather, we propose that (a) neurological structures define an individual's repertoire of responses, (b) traits serve as conceptual labels or short-hand for response repertoires, and (c) multiple neurological structures may be activated during social interaction because interpersonal communication takes place within complex and stimuli-rich environments. Therefore, although attempts at falsification are critical to any scientific enterprise, studies designed to test trait conceptualizations must adhere to realistic expectations for trait constructs. In particular, critics have overlooked the point that any single trait may represent only one of many neurobiological subsystems that may be operative in any interaction.

Second, scholars interested in pursuing a communibiological paradigm must begin to explicate the neurobiological structures underlying particular behavior patterns and explain the nexus between communication-related stimuli and activation of the relevant structures. In many cases, the major circuitries such as those described in this chapter serve as useful starting points. In other cases, communicative functions related to perceptual and interpretive activity probably require unique neurobiological analyses.

Third, interpersonal communication researchers are invited to conduct direct tests of many of the propositions advanced in this chapter. It is possible to operationally define many of the neurobiological processes without boring holes in participants' heads, conducting MRI tests, or examining cadavers. A careful survey of the literature reveals many self-report type instruments and observational techniques that have already been validated against brain functioning (Bates & Wachs, 1994). One area that requires no surgical activity but is nonetheless potentially profitable to interpersonal scholars, for example, concerns the consequences of goodness and badness of fit. Because temperamental behavior patterns are neurobiologically driven, environments that suppress trait responses should produce high stress levels. As discussed earlier, research tends to support this effect regarding fit between students and teacher styles. With only a modicum of ingenuity, the consequences of temperament-environment fit can be examined across a wide range of interpersonal contexts. If suppression of individuals' temperamental responses results in high levels of stress, the observation that some individuals act out of character with their traits can hardly be taken as evidence against the significance of the traits.

Fourth, the communibiological perspective acknowledges that communicators are first and foremost biological entities. We do not somehow transcend our brain structures when we interact. Neurobiological composition limits and restricts our range of responses just as our genetic profile limits our maximum height or ability to understand complex mathematics. From this vantage point, research findings are interpreted from a biological frame of reference. Thus, when research findings conflict with biological principles, we favor the biological explanation. Accordingly, attentiveness to biology is not merely an alternative or supplemental analysis, it is fundamental to the concept of traits and to the development of "useful" theories of interpersonal communication.

Finally, we have set the communibiological paradigm within the context of physics, further emphasizing a reductionistic approach to human interaction. Traits, which we view as biologically driven mechanisms, can be thought of as physical properties such as mass and inertia. Such a perspective will probably annoy scholars who wish to believe that humans are somehow much more in charge of their actions than depicted in our analysis. However, in Copernicus' time, many wished to believe that the earth was the center of the universe because the earth is where they resided. Unfortunately for Copernicus, thinking was dominated by an inflated sense of human importance and fueled by ideology and wishful thinking. Our position is that good theories of interpersonal communication should be empirically based rather than anchored in wishful thinking about human nature. Like the physicists before us, we should not accept models that only partially fit observation. We believe that predictions and observations will never quite match without serious consideration of neurobiologically based communicator traits.

ACKNOWLEDGEMENTS

We are indebted to Sally Vogl-Bauer, University of Wisconsin, Whitewater; Patricia Burant, West Virginia University; Jill Rudd, Cleveland State University; and Kristin Valencic, Cleveland State University, for their support and assistance during the preparation of this chapter.

REFERENCES

Achinstein, P. (1971). *Law and explanation.* Oxford, UK: Clarendon Press.

Adams, R. D., & Victor, M. (1993). *Principles of neurology* (5th ed.). New York, McGraw-Hill.

Aggleton, J. P., & Mishkin, M. (1986). The amygdala: Sensory gateway to the emotions. In E. Plutchik & H. Kellerman (Eds.), *Emotion: Theory, research, and experience: Vol. 3 Biological foundations of emotion* (pp. 281-299). San Diego, CA: Academic press.

Arnett, P. A., Howland, E. W., Smith, S. S., & Newman, J. P. (1993). Automatic responsivity during passive avoidance in incarcerated psychopaths. *Personality and Individual Differences, 14,* 173-184.

Bates, J. E. (1987). Temperament in infancy. In J. D. Osofsky (Ed.), *Handbook of infant development* (2nd ed., pp. 1101-1149). New York: Wiley.

Bates, J. E. (1989). Concepts and measures of temperament. In G. A. Kohnstamm, J. E. Bates, & M. K. Rothbart (Eds.), *Temperament in childhood* (pp. 3-26). New York: Wiley.

Bates, J. E., & Wachs, T. D. (Eds.). (1994). *Temperament: Individual differences at the interface of biology and behavior.* Washington, DC: American Psychological Association.

Beatty, M. J. (1987). Communication apprehension as a determinant of avoidance, withdrawal, and performance anxiety. *Communication Quarterly, 35,* 202-217.

Beatty, M. J., Burant, P. A., Dobos, J. A., & Rudd, J. E. (1996). Trait verbal aggressiveness and the appropriateness and effectiveness of fathers' interaction plans. *Communication Quarterly, 44,* 1-15.

Beatty, M. J., Forst, E. C., & Stewart, R. A. (1986). Communication apprehension and motivation as predictors of public speaking duration. *Communication Education, 35,* 143-146.

Beatty, M. J., & McCroskey, J. C. (in press). It's in our nature: Verbal agressiveness as temperamental expression. *Communication Quarterly.*

Beatty, M. J., & McCroskey, J. C., & Heisel, A. D. (in press). Communication apprehension as temperamental expression: A communibiological paradigm. *Communication Monographs.*

Blalock, H. M. (1969). *Theory construction: From verbal to mathematical formulations.* Englewood Cliffs, NJ: Prentice-Hall.

Borger, R., & Cioffi, F. (Eds.). (1970). *Explanation in the behavioral sciences: Confrontations.* Cambridge, UK: Cambridge University Press.

Bouchard, T. J. (1993). Genetic and environmental influence on adult personality: Evaluating the evidence. In J. Hettema & I. J. Deary (Eds.), *Foundations of personality* (pp. 15-44). Norwell, MA: Kluwer Academic.

Brook, J. S., Brook, D., Whiteman, M., & Gordon, A. S. (1983). Depressive mood in male college students: Father-son interaction patterns. *Archives of General Psychiatry, 40,* 665-669.

Brown, R., & Kulik, J. (1979). Flashbulb memories. *Cognition, 5,* 73-99.

Buss, A. H. (1989). Temperament as personality traits. In G.A. Kohnstamm, J. E. Bates, & M. K. Rothbart (Eds.), *Temperament in childhood* (pp. 49-58). New York: Wiley.

Buss, A. H., & Plomin, R. (1975). *A temperament theory of personality.* New York: Wiley.

Buss, A. H., & Plomin, R. (1984). *Temperament: Early developing personality traits.* Hillsdale, NJ: Lawrence Erlbaum Associates.

Calkins, S. D., & Fox, N. A. (1992). The relation among infant temperament, attachment, and behavioral inhibition at 24 months. *Child Development, 63,* 1456-1472.

Cappella, J. N. (1991). The biological origins of automated patterns of human interaction. *Communication Theory, 1,* 4-35.

Cappella, J. N. (1993). The facial feedback hypothesis in human interaction: Review and speculation. *Journal of Language and Social Psychology, 12,* 3-13.

Chess, S., & Thomas, A. (1989). Temperament and its functional significance. In S. I. Greenspan & G. H. Pollack (Eds.), *The course of life: Early childhood* (Vol. 2, 2nd ed., pp. 163-228). Madison, CT: International Universities press.

Cohen, J. (1988). *Statistical power analysis for the behavioral sciences* (2nd ed.). Hillsdale, NJ: Lawrence Erlbaum Associates.

Cohen, J. (1990). Things I have learned (so far). *American Psychologist, 45,* 1304-1312.

Collins, P. F., & Depue, R. A. (1992). A neurobehavioral systems approach to developmental psychopathology: Implications for disorders of affect. In D. Cicchetti (Ed.), *Rochester symposia on developmental psychopathology: Vol. 4. Developmental perspectives on depression* (pp. 29-101). Rochester, NY: University of Rochester Press.

Davidson, R. J., Ekman, P., Saron, C. D., Senulis, J., & Friesen, W. (1990). Approach/withdrawal and cerebral asymmetry: Emotional expression and brain physiology I. *Journal of Personality and Social Psychology, 58,* 330-334.

Davis, M. (1992). The role of the amygdala in fear and anxiety. *Annual Review of Neuroscience, 15,* 353-375.

Depue, R. A., & Achene, W. G. (1989). Neurobehavioral aspects of affective disorders. *Annual Review of Psychology, 40,* 457-492.

Derryberry, D., & Rothbart, M. K. (1988). Arousal, affect, and attention as components of temperament. *Journal of Personality and Social Psychology, 55,* 958-966.

Eaton, W.O. (1983). Measuring activity level with actometers: Reliability, validity, and arm length. *Child Development, 54,* 720-726.

Eysenck, H. J. (1991). Biological dimensions of personality. In L. A. Pervin (Ed.), *Handbook of personality* (pp. 244-276). New York: Guilford Press.

Eysenck, H. J., & Eysenck, M. W. (1985). *Personality and individual differences: A natural science approach.* New York: Plenum.

Farb, C., Aoki, C., Milner, T., Kaneko, T., & LeDoux, J. (1992). Glutamate immunoreactive terminals in the lateral amygdaloid nucleus: A possible substrate for emotional memory. *Brain Research, 593,* 145-158.

Fowles, D. C. (1980). The three arousal model: Implications of Gray's two-factor learning theory for heart rate, electrodermal activity, and psychopathy. *Psychophysiology, 17*, 87-104.

Fox, N. A. (1989). Psychophysiological correlates of emotional reactivity during the first year of life. *Developmental Psychology, 25*, 364-372.

Fox, N. A. (1991). If it's not left, it's right: Electroencephalogram asymmetry and the development of emotion. *American Psychologist, 46*, 863-872.

Fox, N. A., Bell, M. A., & Jones, N. A. (1992). Individual differences in response to stress and the development of emotion. *Developmental Neuropsychology, 8*, 161-184.

Friedman, J. (1991). Gravitation. In R. G. Lerner & G. L. Trigg (Eds.), *Encyclopedia of physics* (2nd ed., pp. 449-455). New York: VCH Publishers.

Gray, J. A. (1982). *The neuropsychology of anxiety*. New York: Oxford University Press.

Gray, J. A. (1987). Perspectives on anxiety and impulsivity: A commentary. *Journal of Research in Personality, 21*, 493-509.

Gray, J. A. (1990). Brain systems that mediate both emotion and cognition. *Cognition and Emotion, 4*, 269-288.

Gray, J. A. (1991). The neuropsychology of temperament. In J. Strelau & A. Angleitner (Eds.), *Explorations in temperament* (pp. 105-128). New York: Plenum.

Greenspan, S. I. (1981). *Psychopathology and adaptation in infancy and early childhood*. New York: International University Press.

Grillon, C., Ameli, R., Woods, S. W., Merikangas, K., & Davis, M. (1991). Fear-potentiated startle in humans: Effects of anticipatory anxiety on the acoustic blink reflex. *Psychophysiology, 28*, 588-595.

Guilford, J. P., (1956). *Fundamental statistics in psychology and education*. New York: McGraw-Hill.

Gunnar, M. R. (1990). The psychobiology of infant temperament. In J. Colombo & J. Fagan (Eds.), *Individual differences in infancy: Reliability, stability, prediction* (pp. 387-409). Hillsdale, NJ: Lawrence Erlbaum Associates.

Hawking, S. (1988). *A brief history of time and space*. New York: Bantam.

Horvath, C. W. (1995). Biological origins of communicator style. *Communication Quarterly, 43*, 394-407.

Infante, D. A., Rancer, A. S., & Womack, D. F. (1993). *Building communication theory* (2nd ed.). Prospect Heights, IL: Waveland.

Kagan, J. (1992). Temperamental contributions to emotion and social behavior. In M. S. Clark (Ed.), *Emotion and social behavior* (pp. 99-118). Newbury Park, CA: Sage.

Kagan, J., Reznick, J. S., & Snidman, N. (1988). Biological bases of childhood shyness. *Science, 240*, 167-171.

Kagan, J., & Snidman, N. (1991). Infant predictors of inhibited and uninhibited profiles. *Psychological Science, 2*, 40-44.

Keogh, B. K. (1982). Children's temperament and teachers' decisions. In R. Porter & G. M. Collins (Eds.), *Temperamental differences in infants and young children* (pp. 269-285). London: Pitman.

Knapp, M. L., Miller, G. R., & Fudge, K. (1994). Background and current trends in the study of interpersonal communication. In M. L. Knapp & G. R. Miller (Eds.), *Handbook of interpersonal communication* (2nd ed., pp. 3-20). Thousand Oaks, CA: Sage.

LeDoux, J. E. (1986). The neurobiology of emotion. In J. E. LeDoux & W. Hirst (Eds.), *Mind and brain: Dialogues in cognitive neuroscience* (pp. 301-354). New York: Cambridge University Press.

LeDoux, J. E., Cicchetti, P., Xagoraris, A., & Romanski, L. M. (1990). The lateral amygdaloid nucleus: Sensory interface of the amygdala in fear conditioning. *Journal of Neuroscience, 10*, 1062-1069.

Lewin, K. (1945). The research center for group dynamics at Massachusetts Institute of Technology. *Sociometry, 2*, 126-136.

Littlejohn, S. W. (1983). *Theories of human communication* (3rd ed.). Belmont, CA: Wadsworth.

Lykken, D., & Tellegen, A. (1996). Happiness is a stochastic phenomenon. *Psychological Science, 7*, 186-189.

MacLeod, C., & Mathews, A. (1988). Anxiety and the allocation of attention. *Quarterly Journal of Experimental Psychology, 40*, 653-670.

Marieb, E. N., & Mallatt, J. (1992). *Human anatomy*. Redwood City, CA: Benjamin Cummings.

Martin, R. P., Nagle, R., & Paget, K. (1983). Relationships between temperament and classroom behavior, teacher attitudes, and academic achievement. *Journal of Psychoeducational Assessment, 1*, 377-386.

Mathews, A. (1990). The cognitive function of anxiety. *Behavioral Research and Therapy, 28*, 455-468.

McCroskey, J. C. (1970). Communication-bound measures of anxiety. *Speech Monographs, 37*, 269-277.

Myers, D. G., & Dierer, F. (1995). Who is happy? *Psychological Science, 6*, 10-19.

Nelson, C. A. (1994). Neural basis of infant temperament. In J. E. Bates & T. D. Wachs (Eds.). *Temperament: Individual differences at the interface of biology and behavior* (pp. 47-82). Washington, DC: American Psychological Association.

Norton, R. (1978). Foundation of a communicator style construct. *Human Communication Research, 4,* 99-112.

Panksepp, J. (1982). Toward a general psychobiology of emotions. *Behavioral and Brain Research, 5,* 407-467.

Panksepp, J. (1986). The anatomy of emotions. In R. Plutchik & H. Kellerman (Eds.), *Emotion: Theory research and experience: Biological foundations of emotions* (Vol. 3, pp. 91-124). San Diego, CA: Academic Press.

Popper, K. R., & Eccles, J. C. (1977). *The self and its brain.* New York: Springer.

Posner, M. I. (1990). Hierarchical distributed networks in the neuropsychology of selective attention. In A. Carramaza (Ed.), *Cognitive neuropsychology and neurolinguistics: Advances in models of cognitive function and impairment* (pp. 187-210). New York: Plenum.

Posner, M. I., & Peterson, S. E. (1990). The attention system of the human brain. *Annual Review of Neuroscience, 13,* 24-42.

Posner, M. I., & Presti, D. (1987). Selective attention and cognitive control. *Trends in Neuroscience, 10,* 12-17.

Pullis, M., & Cadwell, J. (1982). The influence of children's temperamental characteristics on teachers' decision strategies. *American Educational Research, 19,* 165-181.

Reiman, E. M., Fusselman, M. J., Fox, P. T., & Raichle, M. E. (1989). Neuroanatomical correlates of anticipatory anxiety. *Science, 243,* 1071-1074.

Reiman, E. M., Raichle, M. E., Butler, F. K., Herscovitch, P., & Robins, E. (1984). A focal brain abnormality in panic disorder, a severe form of anxiety. *Nature, 310,* 683-685.

Reynolds, P. D. (1971). *A primer in theory construction.* Indianapolis: Bobbs-Merrill.

Rolls, E. T. (1990). A theory of emotion, and its application to understanding the neural basis of emotion. *Cognition and Emotion, 4,* 161-190.

Rothbart, M. K. (1989). Temperament and development. In G. A. Kohnstamm, J. E. Bates, & M. K. Rothbart (Eds.), *Temperament in childhood* (pp. 187-247). New York: Wiley.

Rothbart, M K., Derryberry, D., & Posner, M. I. (1994). A psychobiological approach to the development of temperament. In J. E. Bates & T. D. Wachs (Eds.), *Temperament: Individual differences at the interface of biology and behavior* (pp. 83-116). Washington, DC: American Psychological Association.

Rudner, R. S. (1966). *Philosophy of social science.* Englewood Cliffs, NJ: Prentice-Hall.

Rushton, J. P., Fulker, D. W., Neal, M. C., Nias, D. K. B., & Eysenck, H. J. (1986). Altruism and aggression: The heritability of individual differences. *Journal of Personality and Social Psychology, 50,* 1192-1198.

Saltiel, J., & Woelfel, J. (1975). Inertia in cognitive processes: The role of accumulated information in attitude change. *Human Communication Research, 1,* 331-344.

Sears, L. L., & Steinmetz, J. E. (1990). Acquisition of classically conditioned-related activity in the hippocampus is affected by lesions of the cerebellar interpositus nucleus. *Behavioral Neuroscience, 104,* 681-692.

Smith, O., & DeVito, J. (1984). Central nervous integration for the control of autonomic responses associated with emotion. *Annual Review of Neuroscience, 7,* 43-65.

Spoont, M. R. (1992). Modulatory role of serotonin in neural information processing: Implications for human psychopathology. *Psychological Bulletin, 112,* 330-350.

Squire, L. R. (1987). *Memory and brain.* New York: Oxford University Press.

Steinmetz, J. E. (1994). Brain substrates of emotion and temperament. In J. E. Bates & T. D. Wachs (Eds.), *Temperament: Individual differences at the interface of biology and behavior* (pp. 17-46). Washington, DC: American Psychological Association.

Steinmetz, J. E., & Thompson, R. F. (1991). Brain substrates of aversive classical conditioning. In J. Madden IV (Ed.). *Neurobiology of learning, emotion, and affect* (pp. 97-120). New York: Raven Press.

Stelmack, R. M. (1990). Biological bases of extraversion: Psychophysiological evidence. *Journal of Personality, 58,* 293-311.

Stelmack, R. M., & Geen, R. G. (1992). The psychophysiology of extraversion. In A. Gale & M. W. Eysenck (Eds.), *Handbook of individual differences: Biological perspectives* (pp. 227-254). New York: Wiley.

Strelau, J. (1983). *Temperament, personality, activity.* San Diego, CA: Academic Press.

Strelau, J. (1994). The concepts of arousal and arousability as used in temperament studies. In J. E. Bates & T. D. Wachs (Eds.), *Temperament: Individual differences at the interface with biology and behavior* (pp. 117-141). Washington, DC: American Psychological Association.

Taylor, C. (1964). *The explanation of behavior.* New York: Humanities Press.

Thomas, A., & Chess, S. (1977). *Temperament and development.* New York: Brunner/Mazel.

Thomas, A., Chess, S., & Birch, H. (1968). *Temperament and behavior disorders in children.* New York: University Press.

Toulmin, S. (1969). Concepts and the explanation of human behavior. In T. Mischel (Ed.), *Human action* (pp. 71-104). New York: Academic Press.

Vogt, B. A., Finch, D. M., & Olsen, C. R. (1992). Functional heterogeneity in cingulate cortex: The anterior executive and posterior evaluative regions. *Cerebral Cortex, 6,* 435-443.

von Wright, G. H. (1971). *Explanation and understanding.* Ithaca, NY: Cornell University Press.

Wachs, T. D. (1992). The nature of nurture. Newbury Park, CA: Sage.

Zetterberg, H. (1965). *On theory and verification in sociology.* New York: Bedminister Press.

Zuckerman, M. (1991a). Biotypes for basic personality dimensions? "The Twilight Zone" between genotype and social prototype. In J. Strelau & A. Angleitner (Eds.), *Explorations in temperament* (pp. 129-146). New York: Plenum.

Zuckerman, M. (1991b). *Psychobiology of personality.* Cambridge, MA: Cambridge University Press.

Zuckerman, M. (1994). Impulsive unsocialized sensation seeking: Biological dimension of a basic dimension of personality. In J. E. Bates & T. D. Wachs (Eds.), *Temperament: Individual differences at the interface of biology and behavior* (pp. 219-255). Washington, DC: American Psychological Association.

Zuckerman, M. (1995). Good and bad humors: Biochemical bases of personality and its disorders. *Psychological Science, 6,* 325-332.

Zuckerman, M., Kuhlman, D. M., & Camac, C. (1988). What lies beyond E and N? Factor analysis of scales believed to measure basic dimensions of personality. *Journal of Personality and Social Psychology, 54,* 96-107.

Zukav, G. (1979). *The dancing Wu Li masters: An overview of the new physics.* New York: Bantam.

3

Biological Origins
of Communicator Style

Cary Wecht Horvath
Kent State University

Infant babbling is the same worldwide, regardless of the language ability of parents or native culture (Lenneberg, 1967). Girls are typically ahead of boys in the development of language skills, saying their first words sooner, and using more articulate and complex language at earlier ages (Schlesinger & Groves, 1976). Identical 30-year-old twin men who were reared apart explain their extreme promptness and cleanliness as resulting from either learning from a "perfectly ordered" mother, or rebelling against a mother who was an "absolute slob" (Neubauer & Neubauer, 1990, p. 21). Each of these examples points to the potential importance of biological influences on communication behavior. Most people, however do not like to think much about this possibility. According to Neubauer and Neubauer "people generally accept the gene's role in physical appearance, but they (we, all of us) tend to attribute everything else to experience" (p. 19).

Of course, the idea that genes predispose social behavior is not new. Charles Darwin (1859) was one of the first scientists to suggest that genetic factors contribute to physical and mental traits through processes of heredity, variation, and selection. Mendel (1866) advanced the concepts of *phenotype* (outward appearance), *genotype* (genetic makeup), *segregation* (that each parent contributes to a genotype), and *dominant* and *recessive genes*. In recent years, those genes have been found to contribute to psychological traits and maladies such as Alzheimer's disease, alcoholism, schizophrenia, anorexia nervosa, extroversion, delinquency, and reading disability (DeFries & Gillis, 1993; Plomin, 1990). In the field of psychology, the nature - nurture debate has been virtually synonymous with questions about heredity and IQ, and "has been resolved for the vast majority of psychologists," with genetics being a clear contributing factor (McGue, Bouchard, Iacono, & Lykken, 1993, p. 59). Although scholars in other disciplines have acknowledged biology's critical role in behavior, communication scholars have been reticent to do so.

Biology is an important and largely ignored influence on personality. Cappella (1991) proposed five important reasons why communication researchers should study potential biological bases for human communication. First, because the communication discipline is rooted in social psychology, researchers have had a natural tendency to assume that communicative behaviors may be explained by social or psychological forces (i.e., by situational influences on an individual). Cappella argued that researchers should consider competing explanations to maintain theoretical balance. Second, Cappella thought it myopic to study only social factors while completely ignoring the fact that humans are biological organisms, complete with animal reflexes and genetic material. These reflexes and genes may greatly affect or determine human behavior.

Third, according to Cappella (1991), communication has focused on individual differences (e.g., gender, personality, situation, culture). Attention to biological origins in communication would provide a means for studying human similarities. Fourth, discovery of biological origins would not be easily dismissed as cultural or socialization artifact. Information about genetic influence on communication could serve as fundamental knowledge for researchers, knowledge that is common rather than idiosyncratic to the human experience.

Fifth, Cappella (1991) proposed that "scientific" knowledge must satisfy three criteria. It must be stable, pancultural, and ahistorical. Scientific methods in communication study do not always satisfy these criteria. That is, knowledge about communicative behavior is seldom able to be generalized to various situations, cultures, and time periods. If the communication discipline is to be respected for scientific inquiry, it must produce this type of basic knowledge. Study of biological origins of human communication has potential to yield knowledge that is more broadly able to be generalized.

A study of communicator style designed and conducted from a biological perspective is discussed here. Communicator style was chosen for study because it is a global construct in human communication, and like personality or temperament, was thought to likely be inherited. It is an important communication construct because it impacts individuals' perceived attractiveness and communication effectiveness.

COMMUNICATOR STYLE

Communicator style, as defined by Norton (1978), is "the way one verbally, nonverbally, and paraverbally interacts to signal how literal meaning should be taken, filtered, or understood" (p. 99). According to Norton (1983), style "gives form to content" (p. 11). It is a meta-message and is often redundant with the literal message. However, when style and literal messages conflict, the style component is valued as more meaningful.

Similar to temperament or personality, style typifies the way an individual might be characterized. Style is a trait construct, a construct that describes a central tendency of behavior. "At least one enduring or habitual pattern that defines a norm or norm deviation" exists for each individual (Norton, 1983, p. 45). Norton stated that an individual's style is multifaceted, multicollinear (style variables are not independent), and variable, but sufficiently patterned. Therefore, the style construct assumes that although behavior may vary slightly from situation to situation, it remains relatively consistent overall. Certain facets that make up a communicator's style are more prominent in some individuals. For example, dominance and contentiousness might be pronounced in some people, but not in others.

Norton (1978, 1983) proposed 10 style variables that, in different combinations, make up people's multifaceted styles: dominant, dramatic, contentious, animated, relaxed, impression-leaving, attentive, friendly, open, and precise. These 10 are conceptualized as independent variables that intermix with different intensities in each person. Together, they predict an individual's communicator image (the self-image about communication).

Much research has shown that communicator style affects how attractive and effective people are. For example, Norton and Pettegrew (1977) found that dominance best predicted a person's attractiveness, followed by styles that were attentive, friendly, and relaxed. Depending on an individual's role, certain styles are also more effective than others. For example, teachers are less effective if they have a dominant or contentious style (Andersen, Norton, & Nussbaum, 1981; Norton, 1977; Rubin & Feezel, 1986). It might follow that if communicator style has an inherited dimension, some people have a natural tendency to be more or less attractive and effective.

ORIGINS OF COMMUNICATOR STYLE

Research has rarely addressed the origins of communicator style. Scholars have concentrated on the way individuals are, and not on why they are that way. The minimal attention paid to the why of the matter has centered on the belief that communicator style is learned.

Social Learning Theory

Norton (1983) stated that style is an accumulated set of behaviors, influenced by cultural or role expectations, impromptu expectations, and by idiosyncrasies (e.g. the gossip monger). Thus, Norton conceptualized communicator style as a set of learned behaviors. This conceptualization concurs with the situation/state/nurture/ environment position in the ongoing trait-state debate. By stating that communication behaviors are learned, Norton (1983) would agree that an individual's environment will largely determine resulting behavior. Likewise, McCroskey and Richmond (1987) favored a social learning theory explanation of communication apprehension. They believed that the development of positive or negative expectations guides communication behavior (but see McCroskey & Beatty, chapter 10, this volume).

Many theorists have agreed with this situationist perspective, viewing the newborn baby as a "blank slate," on which the environment will make its mark. Some dramatic examples of environmental influence involve children who have been raised in isolation or in the wild, who have only partial success with attempted social rehabilitation (Itard, 1807; Singh & Zingg, 1942). In his advancement of social behavior theory, Mischel (1968) wrote that "behavior depends on the exact stimulus conditions in the evoking situation and on the individual's history with similar stimuli" (p. 191). To Mischel, cognition was an effect of behavior, not a predictor. For example, if a dog bites a child, the child then develops a fear of dogs. Therefore, individual differences are explained by specific, observable stimuli that elicit behavior, rather than intrapsychic predispositions.

In a similar vein, Dollard and Miller (1950) believed that behavior is a response to reinforcement from society. Innate drives such as hunger and avoidance of pain or learned drives, such as the desire to succeed are signaled by environmental cues like a traffic light or a 5 o'clock whistle. Dollard and Miller explained traitlike behavior as stimulus generalization. That is, stimuli may be generalized to other similar stimuli. For example, if a person fears public speaking because of a bad experience, a fear of all communication might follow.

In all, social learning theory maintains that a person's experiences meld together to create unity in personality (Rotter, 1964). As people grow older and experience more, personality becomes more consistent and stable. Even then, expectancies of positive or negative reinforcement still determine behavior. Researchers who accept this theory must pay attention to people's personal histories if there is any hope of understanding their behavior. Although this theory is seductive in its simplicity and generalizability, there is scant research in the field of communication to indicate that it has a meaningful level of predictive power with regard to human communication behavior.

Personality Theory

A competing theoretical approach to the origin of behavior is trait-oriented. The philosophy guiding this research orientation is that people have internally based predispositions that result in relatively stable personality characteristics. Cattell (1946) cited nervousness, sensitivity, intelligence, energy, excitability, constraint, and memory as examples of inherited traits. Although Infante (1987) acknowledged that the situation may inhibit or influence communication behavior, he conceptualized verbal aggressiveness as a multidimensional trait. He argued that cognitive structures that mediate personality "have their genesis in instinct" (p. 160).

This view is consistent with common experience, which tells us that people often remain the same throughout life. Indeed, intuitive evidence for traits seems to exist. Through home movies, pictures, or memories, we remember family and friends who display the same characteristics and mannerisms over many years. According to Neubauer and Neubauer (1990), grandparents and other extended family members are valuable because they often remind us of family-oriented traits, pointing out a long line of musical talent, intelligence, or quickness to anger. Additional intuitive evidence for inborn personality traits lies in the case of child prodigies, or children who have unusual intelligence or talent without training. Also, a trait approach answers why siblings who are raised in the same environment turn out differently, or why "the same fire that melts the butter, hardens the egg" (Allport, 1937, p. 102).

In addition to this intuitive evidence is empirical evidence for inborn personality traits. In general, research following this theory seeks to answer the question: " How much of a person's phenotype can be explained by genotype, and how much by environment?" (Stern, 1949).

Most of the research supporting a personality approach employs a twins design. Researchers using the twins method generally observe identical and fraternal twins, or ask for the twins' self-report on questionnaires. Identical, or monozygotic (MZ), twins are the result of one egg fertilized by one sperm. The zygote then separates into two independent systems that are identical in terms of genetic structure. Naturally, all MZ twins are of the same gender. Fraternal, or dizygotic (DZ), twins result from fertilization of two eggs by two sperm. Genetically, these offspring are no more alike than normal siblings (Stern, 1949). So, a twins design allows researchers to compare people who differ in amounts of genetic similarity, but who are raised in the same environments. According to Matthews and Krantz (1976), using twins to study the heritability of personality characteristics follows this rationale:

> This . . . method relies on the fact that monozygotic twins are identical genetically, whereas dizygotic (fraternal) twins have, on the average, only half of their genes in common, as do siblings born at different times. If monozygotic twins are significantly more alike than dizygotic twins and provided relevant environmental experiences do not differ for monozygotic and dizygotic twins, it follows that the characteristic has an inherited component. (p. 141)

Twin study has revealed important personality differences in MZ and DZ twins. First, there is evidence that infants differ in temperament. Even from the first moments of birth, individual personalities exist. According to Torgersen and Kringlen (1979), babies show different behavioral characteristics immediately after birth. They used a twins design for the reasons just mentioned, and also to control for any possible intrauterine, or early postnatal environmental, influences on the babies. They found that MZ babies were more alike than DZ babies in behavioral regularity, threshold of responsiveness, and intensity at 2 months of age, and in all temperamental variables at 9 months.

Buss and Plomin's (1984) studies of twins' temperament also yielded evidence for the trait perspective. They concluded that no broad evidence for environmental influences for personality differences existed. For example, types of childrearing did not seem to be related to temperament. However, they did feel confident that temperament has an inherited component. Specifically, Buss and Plomin (1984) found that activity, emotionality, and sociability have a genetic component. Correlations between MZ twins were substantially higher on these variables than they were for DZ twins. They also found that children tend to resemble their parents in temperamental disposition. Although Buss and Plomin believed that temperament originates in genetics, they also felt that the final outcome may be mediated by environmental influences.

Buss and Plomin (1975) stated that "it is in the stylistic aspect of behavior that temperament makes its major contribution" (p.33). For example, a door can be opened several ways. It can be nudged, kicked, or pushed gently. The content or the goal of the action remains the same: The door is opened. However, the way that the door is opened relates to temperament (in this case, activity). Because communicator style involves the "way" one paraverbally behaves, the heritability of temperament gives credence to the possible heritability of communicator style.

Because of Buss and Plomin's (1984) genetic link to sociability, McCroskey and Richmond (1987) suggested that the communication apprehension construct might have its roots in genetics. However, they said that no hereditary research has involved the measurement of communication apprehension (CA), "so the question of the impact of heredity on CA must remain open" (p. 145).

Thoday and Parkes (1968) argued that a genetic link to communication is not so speculative. From their analysis of the results of 10 twins studies, they rank-ordered the relative importance of heredity for seven abilities (verbal, word fluency, perceptual speed, spatial, memory, number ability, and reasoning). Verbal and word fluency skills topped the list.

Lykken (1982) said that considerable evidence exists to suggest that conservatism, leadership, persuasive power, dominance, and positive affect (happiness) are influenced by genetics. For Lykken, researchers can recognize highly heritable traits when they "compute intra-class correlations as measures of within-pair similarity and they expect DZ twins to be at least half as similar as the MZ twins" (p. 365). (In twin research, correlation coefficients are treated as ratio data.)

According to Magnusson and Endler (1977), there are basically four ways to conceptualize behavior. The first two are the trait model and the psychodynamic model. These models are similar because they both focus on personality as the mechanism of behavior. They differ, however, in methodology and treatment of data. The third model is situationism, which explains behavior by environmental forces on the individual. In the 1960s and 1970s a fourth model emerged, called interactionism, that integrated the previous models. It is this approach that is investigated here.

Interactionism

The interactionist approach has gained increased acceptance because it takes both contextual and personality variables into account. Thus, it is a more realistic interpretation of the complexity of communication. To interactionists, "overt behavior is a function of the continuous feedback/interaction between the person and the situation" (Cody & McLaughlin, 1985, p. 263). According to Kimble (1993), popular logic in psychology is as follows: "Behavior is the consequence of relatively enduring potentials for, and relatively more temporary instigations to, performance" (p. 14). In other words, genetics give us individual potential for behavior that may be stimulated by various environmental influences. According to Plomin, Loehlin, and DeFries (1985), there is a reluctance among situationists to accept the idea of genetic influences on behavior. However, to understand fully how behaviors develop, an interactionist orientation is imperative.

Although the interactionist viewpoint has only recently gained popularity, Allport (1937) stressed the idea in the late 1930s. He believed that "personality develops continually from the stage of infancy until death, and throughout this span it persists even though it changes" (p. 102). Thus, the idea of change, yet stability is inherent in this perspective. The doctrine of genetic determination might help to clarify this idea. It "does not state that personality is inherited, but rather that no feature of personality is devoid of hereditary influences" (p. 105).

For Allport (1937), it was impossible to untangle the influences of personality from environment and heredity. Every personality characteristic receives simultaneous influence from heredity and environment. He expressed this idea in the equation:

$$\text{Personality} = f \text{ (heredity) X (environment)}$$

The factors in this equation are not additive, but multiplied. Therefore, if either were zero, personality would not exist. Allport felt that either heredity or environment could hold more influence regarding individual cases. However, as a rule, the "raw materials of personality," being the physique, endowment of intelligence, and temperament are genetically determined and largely fixed. Heredity's force maintains primacy.

Other researchers believe that it is possible to untangle the influences of heredity and environment. Using adoptive and nonadoptive families, Plomin, Loehlin, and DeFries (1985) found that 50% of correlations between environment and infant development could be explained through genetic factors, and the remaining 50% could be explained by purely environmental influence. Plomin et al. (1985) also noted that labeling a measure environmental does not make it exclusively so. A heredity factor is always part of the participant's response. Plomin et al.'s (1985) use of the adoptive and nonadoptive child design is an accepted but unusual method of nature-nurture research (because of the difficulty in finding adoptive families due to confidentiality). By far, the "use of the twins design has been critical for identifying pure environmental factors that are linked to personality characteristics" (Baker & Daniels, 1990, p. 110).

In summary, it seems that the role of genetic influence on behavior has been underestimated (Plomin et al., 1985). According to Clausen (1973), "we need to become more knowledgeable about the nature of man as an organism" (p. 15). The trait literature summarized here consistently reveals that there are inherited dimensions of intensity, activity, emotionality, sociability, and dominance. From an interactionist position, the following two research questions emerge with reference to communicator style:

1. What is the relation between communicator style and temperament for identical and fraternal twins?
2. Will pairs of identical twins' scores on communicator style be more strongly related to one another than fraternal twins' scores on communicator style?

The first research question tests the assumption that communicator style is like temperament, in that both constructs represent behavioral personality. It should follow that if results indicate that temperament has an inherited dimension, so should communicator style, and vice versa. Answers to the second research question will indicate the heritability of communicator style. In short, the goal of data analysis is to determine whether communicator style, like temperament, is inherited.

The study that I conducted employed the twins design that compares MZ pairs to same-gender DZ pairs (for a detailed report of this study see Horvath, 1995). This method has important advantages. It is the most effective and available means of studying human heredity and environment (Stern, 1949). Also, Lykken (1982) suggested that twins are usually easy to recruit, cooperative, and even willing to participate in multiple or longitudinal studies. They are typically representative of the population as well. According to Rutter, Korn, and Birch (1963), the comparison of same-gender MZ and DZ twins is regarded as a natural experiment, with the expectancy that MZ twins will be more alike than DZ twins, and that MZ pairs should have no large differences. One potential problem with this design is commonly asserted—presumably MZ twins are raised to be more alike (Rutter et al., 1963). Many believe twins are often dressed and treated in identical ways, which implies learned, not inherited ways of behavior.

Not so, said Loehlin and Nichols (1976) in a book based on their ambitious study of 850 sets of twins. They argued that MZ twins typically have more experiences in common than DZ twins. However, MZ twins raised together have no tendency to be more alike than those reared apart. This might be explained by the effects of competition and contrast between MZ twins reared together, leading them to perceive themselves as more different from one another. Rutter et al. (1963) also noted the tendency for parents of MZ twins to exaggerate small differences between the two. Therefore, MZ twins are not necessarily raised to be more alike and, in fact, are often encouraged to be different.

A second concern with the design is the ability to generalize from a twins sample. Koch (1966) addressed this idea, concluding that twins are different from the general public in two ways. Twins tend to score lower in tests of intelligence than nontwins, and twins tend to be physically smaller than nontwins. However, there is no difference between twins and nontwins in ability, personality, or interests. Because my study focused on personality, and no differences exist between twin and nontwin populations on this variable, it appears that the results can safely be extended to the nontwin population.

I attended the Twinsburg, Ohio, Twins Festival in August 1991, at which time I solicited the names and addresses of approximately 200 sets of twins. The twins were a mixture of identical and same-gender fraternal pairs (male and female). Festival participants ranged from about ages 11 to age 75, and were from 20 U.S. states.

Lykken (1982) pointed out that DZ twins are half as likely as MZ twins to volunteer for study. I found that this was true for those attending the Twins Festival as well. Because there was a disproportional number of MZ to DZ twins in my sample, I also contacted mothers-of-twins organizations to recruit additional DZ twin participants. The goal was to have about 100 MZ sets, and 100 DZ sets as subjects for the final analysis in order to achieve statistical power at .80 when interpreting correlations.

The fact that my sample was not random, but drawn mostly from the Twins Festival might be perceived as another possible problem because of self - selection. It is possible that the pairs attending might be more positive and enthusiastic about being twins, and therefore, more likely to be similar. For example, Lykken (1982) wrote that DZ pairs who volunteer as participants are probably more likely to be similar than other DZ pairs. On closer inspection, it is clear that this is not a problem, but an advantage of the design. If DZ twins identify more with each other, think of themselves as more alike, and still report more dissimilarity than MZ twins, the results implying heritability are strengthened. The tests conducted in this study, therefore, should be viewed as ones that will provide conservative evidence for heritability.

I mailed questionnaires to 247 sets of twins (approximately 125 MZ pairs and 125 same-gender DZ pairs), with each twin receiving an individual questionnaire. The surveys were mailed in August, 1992, and initial response from the twins was disappointing. I received less than 30% of the questionnaires within the 2 week deadline, and only a few more in the 2 weeks that followed. Confounding the low response was the fact that for a questionnaire to be viable, it had to have a match (twin). So, in September, I again mailed questionnaires, but only to those twins who failed to respond the first time. The final total of returned questionnaires was 261, or 52.8% of the 494 packets. Kerlinger's (1986) estimation of the typical 50% rate of return was on target. Of the final questionnaires, 53 were twinless twins—that is, they responded but their twin never did. The remaining 208 questionnaires were used for analysis.

Of the 208 packets, 124 were identical twins (62 pairs), and 84 were fraternal twins (42 pairs). Of the identical twins, 34 (27.4%) were male and 90 (72.6%) were female. Age was fairly evenly distributed, and ranged from 11 to 76 (M = 35.36, Md = 33, SD = 17.42). In age groups, 21% were age 20 or under, 44% were between 21 and 40, 24% were between 41 and 60, and 11% were 61 or over. On the average, respondents reported middle-class economic status (M = 2.86, Md = 3, SD = .911, where 3 represented middle class and 2 represented middle-upper class).

Of the fraternal twins, 22 (26.2%) were male, and 62 (73.8%) were female. Unlike the identical pairs, age was somewhat unevenly distributed, ranging from 12 to 67 (M = 29.12, Md = 24.5, SD = 14.54). When grouping by age, 33% were age 20 or under, 48% were between 21 and 40, 14% were between 41 and 60, and 5% were 61 or over. The majority of fraternal twins also reported middle-class status (M = 2.97, Md = 3, SD = .57). In general, more identical pairs and more females responded to the questionnaires.

The questionnaire packet contained a cover page on university letterhead that explained the purpose of the study and emphasized that the twins should respond separately to the measurement scales. I also noted that the code number on each questionnaire was only for the purpose of matching the twins and would be in no way connected to the participants' names. Furthermore, I pointed out that an associate would open the returned envelopes, giving me only the anonymous questionnaires. In this way, the participants could be sure that their names would not be associated with their answers. In addition to the cover letter, the packet contained the measurement scales and a self-addressed stamped envelope.

Two measures were included in the questionnaire packet. The first instrument was Norton's (1983) communicator style measure. Norton (1978) argued that given the small number of items and short scale range, reliabilities are acceptable for all but the "friendly" subconstruct: friendly (.37), animated (.56), attentive (.57), contentious (.65), dramatic (.68), impression-leaving (.69), open (.69), relaxed (.71), communicator image (.72), and dominant (.82). (The precise subconstruct was added later, with no reported alphas.)

Although the subconstructs are intercorrelated, attempts to determine dimensionality embedded in the structure of intercorrelations was relatively unsuccessful (Norton, 1978). However, cluster analysis and smallest space analysis have indicated that the subconstructs tend to band together in two ways; activity versus inactivity, and directive versus nondirective communication (Norton, 1978). Later, Norton (1983) advised against factor-analyzing the communicator style measure because, he argued, it tends to "brutalize" [sic] the data.

The second measure was Buss and Plomin's (1984) EAS Temperament Survey for adults. I included this scale to determine if the inherited categories of sociability, activity, and emotionality are correlated with any of the communicator style elements. This would help answer the first research question asked earlier.

The EAS measure has five reliable subscales (Buss & Plomin, 1984): activity (.81), sociability (.85), and three dimensions of emotionality—distress (.82), fearfulness (.75), and anger (.85). The subscales also show good distributional properties through factor analysis. The distress and fearfulness subscales, however, are moderately correlated ($r = .58$, $p < .01$), as are the distress and anger subscales ($r = .33$, $p < .01$). These emotionality subscales tend to factor together.

In addition, I included a few demographic questions asking about gender, age, occupation, U.S. state of residency, and economic status, used to describe the sample. A measure of zygosity was also included by one question that identified twins as identical or fraternal.

A matched-pairs design guided the study. The independent variables were twin zygosity (MZ or DZ), and the dependent variables were scores on the different personality measures. The design was repeated for each of the personality measures (the EAS and communicator style subscales).

Cronbach alpha was used to determine the reliability of the Communicator Style and EAS subscales. Also, the EAS was factor-analyzed to determine whether the measure maintained structural stability in this study. Cronbach alphas were computed on each of the 11 subscales, and mean scores were substituted for missing data.

To answer the first research question—What is the relationship between communicator style and temperament for identical and fraternal twins?—Pearson correlation coefficients were computed for the combined group MZ and DZ twins on the communicator style and EAS subscales. Descriptive statistics were also calculated for all variables.

To answer the second question—Will pairs of identical twins' scores on communicator style be more strongly related to one another than fraternal twins' scores on communicator style?—two separate analyses were completed. First, I applied Loehlin and Nichols' (1976) formula to estimate the "heritability" of twin data:

$$2 \, (rI - rF)$$
$$(or) \, (MZr - DZr) \, X \, 2$$

Translated, the difference between mean MZ/I (identical) and DZ/F (fraternal) Pearson correlations is multiplied by 2 to produce a percentage of the variance that can be accounted for by genetics. For example, if the average MZ correlation is .50 and the average DZ correlation is .30, genes could account for 40% variation in the measure:

$$2 \, (50 - 30) = 2 \, (20) = 40 \, (\%)$$

A second analysis complied with Lykken's (1982) assertion that for a trait to be inherited, MZ (average) Pearson correlations must be twice the magnitude of DZ correlations. So, two sets of criteria were used to estimate the heritability of communicator style and temperament traits. These two analyses allowed me to answer the second question.

Analyses of the twin data revealed predictable relationships between the communicator style and EAS subscales. In addition, MZ pairs' scores were more strongly related than DZ pairs' on nearly all subscales of the EAS and communicator style measures. Strikingly strong relationships existed between MZ pairs in all dimensions of the EAS, and in the open, dominant, relaxed, and communicator image dimensions of the communicator style measure. The latter characteristics were found to have strong genetic influence.

RELIABILITY

To determine the internal reliability of the communicator style and EAS subscales, Cronbach alphas were computed for each. Alphas were acceptable for some of the communicator style subscales in this study, but weak for others. Subscales with acceptable (.60 and above) alpha levels were impression leaving (.82), relaxed (.80), contentious (.77), dramatic (.73), open (.75), and dominant (.79). Those with less than impressive alpha levels were friendly (.54), precise (.54), attentive (.41), animated (.56), and communicator image (.28). Associations for these subconstructs, therefore, are very conservative estimates of what might be true relationships.

For the most part, all alpha levels were surprisingly high for the communicator style subscales. Many of the alphas for the first (high) group of variables were substantially higher than Norton's (1978) alphas. Even some of the alpha levels in the second (low) group of variables were much improved from Norton's reported alphas. Norton (1978) stated that alphas as low as .56 are good for this measure given the small number of items and the short scale range. However, I was hesitant to accept the internal reliability of these variables, so I performed additional item analyses. Item analysis revealed two items contributing to low alphas on the animated subscale (Item 53), and the communicator image subscale (Item 55). When the two items were removed, reliability improved somewhat for the animated (.58) subscale, and improved a great deal for the communicator image (.73) subscale. So in the final analysis, the reliabilities of 4 out of the 11 subscales (friendly, attentive, precise, and animated) were questionable.

Unlike communicator style, the internal reliability of most of the EAS subscales was acceptable. Although Buss and Plomin (1984) reported subscale alphas ranging from .75 to .85, the alphas in this study were somewhat lower. The levels for activity (.69), fearfulness (.65), anger (.64), and distress (.82) were all in the acceptable range, but the first three were somewhat low. Eliminating items did not improve the internal consistency of the subscales.

Factor analysis was used to determine whether the EAS maintained structural stability. The 20 items were subjected to principal components analysis with varimax rotation. The criteria for a factor to be retained were an eigenvalue greater than 1.0 and at least two primary factor loadings of at least .55 with no secondary loadings over .40.

The solution identified six factors that accounted for 64.2% of the total variance. However, Factors 5 and 6 failed the criteria to be retained because only one item in each factor loaded cleanly. The remaining four factors accounted for 53.4% of the total variance, and consisted of 16 items.

Factor 1, fear/distress (eigenvalue=4.59), accounted for 23% of the total variance. All but one of the items from the fearfulness and distress subscales collapsed to make up this factor. This factor reflected frequent feelings of upset, insecurity, or panic. Factor 2, activity (eigenvalue=2.70), accounted for 13.5% of the total variance, and was comprised of the items from the activity subscale. (One item from this subscale also loaded on Factor 6.) This factor represented the tendency to live a fast-paced, hurried lifestyle. Factor 3, anger (eigenvalue=1.78), accounted for 8.9% of the total variance, and was made up of three anger subscale items. (One item also loaded on Factor 1.) This factor represented the tendency to be quick-tempered. Factor 4, sociability (eigenvalue=1.59), accounted for 8.% of the total variance, and included the two sociability items that referred to a desire to be alone or with others.

The fact that the fearfulness and distress scales factored together was not surprising, given that Buss and Plomin (1984) warned that these scales were moderately correlated, and have a tendency to factor together. Because the factor analysis of the EAS instrument indicated that the subscales are stable structures, and because the subscales were sufficiently reliable, the original EAS subscales were used in remaining analyses.

MAJOR FINDINGS

Correlations Between Subscales

To answer the first question, two-tailed Pearson correlations were computed between EAS and communicator style subscales (see Horvath, 1995). This analysis helped us understand how communicator style is related to temperament. The first concern was the three EAS emotionality dimensions of fearfulness, distress, and anger, and their relationships to the communicator style dimensions.

The fearfulness ($r = -.35$, $p < .01$) and distress ($r = -.31$, $p < .01$) subscales were negatively related to the relaxed communicator style dimension. This makes sense, considering that relaxation is an opposite emotion to fear or distress. The EAS anger variable correlated with many of the style variables. It was related to precise ($r = .31$, $p < .01$), dramatic ($r = .35$, $p < .01$), and dominant ($r = .34$, $p < .01$), and more strongly related to contentiousness ($r = .59$, $p < .01$). Again, it makes sense that an angry person would display these characteristics.

The other EAS dimensions were also correlated with the communicator style subscales, however, correlations with the EAS activity dimension were very low (less than .30). This was surprising, because the animated, friendly, open, dramatic, and dominant communicator style dimensions certainly seem to contain an element of activity. Although these variables were positively related to activity, correlations were low.

The EAS sociability subscale was positively related to being friendly ($r = .33$, $p < .01$), open ($r = .40$, $p < .01$), dominant ($r = .32$, $p < .01$), and also having a positive communicator image ($r = .33$, $p < .01$). Again, these correlations are no surprise. Sociable people are generally friendly, open, and confident.

It seems clear from this analysis that close relationships exist between the communicator style construct and the temperament construct. Therefore, elements of the communicator style measure also seem to measure how fearful, distressed, angry, and sociable people are. It follows that if temperament is inherited, some elements of communicator style might be as well.

Within-Twin Pairs

To answer question 2, Pearson correlations were computed within twin pairs for each of the communicator style and EAS subscales. The correlations for identical and fraternal pairs were used in

Loehlin and Nichols (1976) formula: 2 (rI - rF). According to Loehlin and Nichols, the resulting value from that formula (for each of the subscales) would represent a percentage of variance that could be accounted for by genetics.

Strong support emerged for Buss and Plomin's (1984) assertion that temperament has an inherited component. Correlations were substantially higher for all of the EAS subscales for identical twin pairs, and lower for fraternal pairs. According to this formula, genetics accounts for approximately 74% of the variance in sociability, 98% in activity, 94% in distress, 60% in fearfulness, and 56% in anger. Therefore, by this analysis, it can be argued that genetics has a great influence on a person's temperament.

Results were somewhat similar for the communicator style subscales. Correlations between identical twins were always higher than those of fraternal twins, with the exception of the attentive and animated variables. However, using the Loehlin and Nichols (1976) formula, the friendly, impression-leaving, attentive, and animated dimensions of communicator style were affected by genetics very little, or not at all.

Contentiousness was slightly influenced by heredity, with 12% of the variance accounted for by genetics. Dramatic and precise characteristics were more moderately influenced by heredity, with 22% of the variance in dramatic behavior, and 24% of the variance in precise behavior accounted for by genetics.

The strongest evidence for heredity's influence on communicator style is in the last group of variables. An impressive 62% of the variance in the relaxed dimension, 78% in the open dimension, 50% in the dominant dimension, and 66% in the communicator image dimension was accounted for by genetics. Therefore, although some of the communicator style elements had little genetic influence, according to the Loehlin and Nichols (1976) formula, others had a great deal of genetic influence.

Because demographic characteristics differed for the MZ and DZ groups, partial correlations were used to control for age and gender. Although slight differences in correlation coefficients resulted, there were no significant differences.

The second analysis followed Lykken's (1982) assertion that for a trait to be inherited, identical twin correlations should be twice as strong as fraternal correlations. All of the temperament variables passed this test with the exception of anger. That is, all of the identical twin correlations on the EAS subscales were twice the magnitude (or close, in the case of the anger dimension) of the fraternal twin correlations. Three out of the 11 communicator style dimensions clearly passed this test: relaxed, open, and communicator image. Although the dominant variable did not pass this test, it was very close. According to Lykken, these traits are highly heritable. So, by virtue of two separate analyses, results show that the communicator style elements of relaxed, open, dominant, and communicator image have an inherited dimension.

In short, analysis of the twin data revealed that the EAS and communicator style subscales were reliable, with the exceptions of friendly, attentive, precise, animated, and sociability. Additionally, factor analysis supported the dimensions of the EAS measure. Correlation coefficients revealed predictable relations between EAS and communicator style subscales, and more importantly, on most subscales, MZ twin scores were more closely related than DZ twin scores. Specifically, results showed that the variables that are most likely inherited are: relaxed, open, dominant, communicator image, and all of the EAS temperament variables (sociability, activity, fearfulness, distress, and anger).

DISCUSSION

The role of genetic influence on behavior has been largely ignored by communication scholars and underestimated by most others (Plomin et al., 1985). Cappella (1991) wrote that it is important for communication scholars to consider biology as an alternative explanation for behavior, rather than continuing the dogmatic acceptance of social learning theory. New information concerning genetic influence on communication behavior could provide a means for studying human similarities and commonalties among people rather than their differences, to produce knowledge that is stable, pancultural, and ahistorical.

Adopting that sentiment, I explored the possibility of a hereditary influence on communication characteristics. Specifically, the similarity of communicator style traits of identical and fraternal twins were compared to determine the existence of a genetic contribution. Additionally, temperament variables, known to have genetic influence, were compared to communicator style dimensions.

The first research question concerned the relation between communicator style and temperament for identical and fraternal twins. Results showed that the two constructs have subscales that are correlated. Much of the communicator style measure taps the temperament variables of fearfulness, distress, anger, sociability, and activity. So, with the knowledge that temperament has a strong history of heritability (Buss & Plomin, 1984), and that the temperament and communicator style subscales are related, elements of communicator style also seem to be influenced by heredity.

The second research question asked whether of identical twins' scores on communicator style will be more strongly related to one another than fraternal twins' scores. The data indicated they were. This was true for the temperament variables as well. Nearly all (82% of the communicator style correlations, and 100% of the temperament correlations) of the identical twin correlations in the analyses were higher than those of fraternal twins.

To examine further the second research question, two sets of analyses were used to determine the heritability of each of the communicator style and temperament variables. All the temperament variables passed both tests with the exception of anger, which very nearly passed the second test. That is, heredity accounted for a portion of the variance in all of the temperament subscales, and almost all of the identical twin correlations doubled the fraternal twin correlations. The subscales of activity and distress were most profoundly influenced by heredity, and the sociability, fearfulness, and anger subscales were also greatly affected.

Only some of the communicator style variables could pass both tests. Those variables for which heredity accounted for a portion of the variance, and in which identical twin correlations doubled fraternal twin correlations, were relaxed, open, communicator image and (closely) dominant. (The friendly, impression-leaving, contentious, precise, and dramatic subscales passed the first analysis, but not the second.) Genetics accounted for at least half of the variance for these subscales. For the open subscale, heredity accounted for as much as 78% of the variance.

Because temperament is inherited (Buss & Plomin, 1984) and because temperament and communicator style had related components, I anticipated that communicator style might be inherited as well. This was true for 4 of the 11 dimensions of the communicator style measure, but it was true for all of the temperament variables. Therefore, communicator style and temperament are similar, but are not the same.

However, it is important to remember that this is a conservative estimate, because additional communicator style elements passed one analysis that determines heritability, but not the other. If I chose to use only Loehlin and Nichols' (1976) criteria for determining heritability, 9 out of 11 communicator style variables would have passed. It is also quite possible that some of the communicator style variables would have passed both tests if their alpha levels were higher. The observed low reliabilities substantially reduced the statistical power of the analyses in this research, contributing to much lower effect estimates than would likely be found if more reliable instruments were employed.

My research was designed to employ two separate analyses in order to establish concurrent validity. In all, I have confidence in the results concerning the four most heritable style variables, because their alpha levels reached a decent range (from .73 to .80). This was not the case for all of the style variables. It seems clear that the dimensions indicating a relaxed, open, confident, and dominant style clearly have a genetic component.

Why are these communicator style elements most affected by genetics? What is common among these variables? The common theme of these four style variables is a sense of *confidence*. To be a dominant communicator, one must take charge and be perceived as assertive (Norton, 1978, 1983; Norton & Pettegrew, 1977). A relaxed communicator exudes confidence (Norton, 1978, 1983). It also takes self-confidence to disclose personal information to others, as open communicators do. Finally, people with positive self-assessments of their communicative ability (communicator image) surely have self-confidence (Norton, 1983). Inspection of the items that represent these four style variables, one could argue that they not only describe confidence, but also communicative arrogance (see Horvath, 1995).

A sense of confidence is not necessarily present in the remaining style variables. Dramatic, contentious, animated, impression-leaving, attentive, friendly, and precise communicators do not necessarily have as great self-admiration as displayed in the previously mentioned items. In fact, some of these behaviors might even be construed as submissive. For example, the rigid posture and frequent eye contact of the attentive listener is negatively related to dominance (Norton, 1978, 1983).

So, if communicative confidence is largely inherited, how might this affect a person's life? Because style variables affect attractiveness and effectiveness, an innate tendency to be (or not be) relaxed, open, dominant, and have a positive communicator image could influence the way people are perceived and evaluated by others.

For example, if a person's sense of being relaxed when communicating is inherited, important ramifications exist. This could mean that some people are "born" to be comfortable with communication, whereas others are sentenced to suffer from communication anxiety throughout their lives. According to McCroskey and Richmond (1987), people who suffer from trait communication apprehension are perceived more negatively at work, at home, and at school than people who are more willing to communicate. The impact of willingness to communicate can extend to a person's choice of spouse, place of residence, and career. Also, the idea of an inherited sense of relaxation or apprehension would have special meaning for communication instructors, who teach that effective public speaking and interpersonal communication is a simple matter of mastering fundamental skills, and that anyone can do it well with enough practice. That probably just is not so.

Communicative effectiveness in school and work environments has often included open and relaxed characteristics (Andersen et al., 1981; Brandt, 1979; Buller & Buller, 1987; Glauser & Tullar, 1985; Hansford & Hattie, 1989; Honeycutt & Worobey, 1987; Infante & Gorden, 1987, 1989; Norton & Nussbaum, 1980; Rubin & Feezel, 1986). Additionally, a dominant/open style has been shown to be most socially attractive, along with being relaxed (Norton & Pettegrew, 1977). If people are more or less genetically predisposed to be open, dominant, or have a positive communicator image, it could follow that they would be more or less likely to be socially attractive or effective.

However, communicator style variables are only partially inherited. Consistent with the interactionist perspective, these data indicate that the environment still plays an important part in the evolution of communicative personality. Allport's (1937) idea that personality can persist even though it changes should remind us that genetics does not hopelessly lock us in to a predetermined set of traits.

Andersen (1987) noted that communicator style is a predisposition, which is a "close relative" of the personality trait. A predisposition is limited to a set of behaviors, and is not the basis of the individual's entire personality. So, whereas communicative tendencies might be inherited, they are only part of the human personality. Influence from the environment, and from oneself can also shape an individual. Following this logic, a person might inherit a tendency to feel communication apprehension (lack of relaxation); but when forced to interact frequently with others, the anxiety decreases. So for this individual, the tendency to feel anxious when communicating is always there, but is manageable in familiar contexts.

According to Rowe (1993), we must think of genetic determinism as "probabilistic causation." That is, if a particular trait is heritable, it increases the likelihood of the manifestation of that trait. For example, 13% of the children of schizophrenics develop the illness themselves. Assessment of the probability of one child's future is uncertain, but the fact that 130 out of 1,000 children will develop the condition is highly certain. Therefore, "probabilistic causation does not imply that all outcomes are improbable" (p. 193).

This study was a first effort in exploring heredity and communication. There were several limitations. For example, the response rate was lower than desired (although acceptable), which reduced the statistical power of the study. Also, some of the demographics were skewed. For example, the participants were more often identical twins, and more often female. In addition, some of the measures of internal reliability were too low to be meaningful (especially for the sociability, friendly, attentive, precise, and animated subscales). It is appropriate here to echo the views of many who have used the communicator style instrument previously—better measures of these subconstructs need to be developed and used in place of the current instrument.

Future researchers might consider attempting some other techniques in studying personality and heredity, such as the comparison of adopted or stepchildren with biological and adoptive parents. For example, it would be interesting to study communicator style using a technique other than the twin design. The latter is an excellent design, but obtaining sufficient, representative, sets of twins for such research is no simple task.

Additionally, other communication constructs that have been considered to be personality traits should be the focus of future research in this area. Andersen (1987) listed the following communicative predispositions: communication apprehension, perceived communication competence, communicator style, extroversion, predispositions toward verbal behavior, rhetorical sensitivity, reticence, self-disclosiveness, shyness, singing apprehension, touch avoidance, unwillingness to communicate, and writing apprehension. Andersen also listed trait communication behaviors, which are consistent and observable patterns of overt behavior, such as speaking time, gaze, smiling, and body movement. Any of these could be promising areas of future research about genetic influence on communication.

What knowledge has emerged from these data that could be considered stable, pancultural, and ahistorical? Matthews and Krantz (1976) stated that "if monozygotic twins are significantly more alike than dizygotic twins and provided relevant environmental experiences do not differ for monozygotic and dizygotic twins, it follows that the characteristic has an inherited component" (p. 141). From this logic, it can be argued that regardless of context, culture, or time, genetics contributes to a communicator's style and temperament. Some aspects of communicator style are more or less influenced by heredity, but the existence of heredity's influence can no longer be denied or ignored by serious communication scholars.

REFERENCES

Allport, G. W. (1937). *Personality: A psychological interpretation.* New York: Holt.

Andersen, P. A. (1987). The trait debate: A critical examination of the individual differences paradigm in interpersonal communication. *Progress in Communication Sciences, 8,* 47-82.

Andersen, J. F., Norton, R. W., & Nussbaum, J. F. (1981). Three investigations exploring the relationship between perceived teacher communication behaviors and student learning. *Communication Education, 30,* 378-392.

Baker, L. A., & Daniels, D. (1990). Non-shared environmental influences and personality differences in adult twins. *Journal of Personality and Social Psychology, 58,* 103-110.

Brandt, D. R. (1979). On linking social performance with social competence: Some relations between communicative style and attributions of interpersonal attractiveness and effectiveness. *Human Communication Research, 5,* 223-237.

Buller, M. K., & Buller, D. B. (1987). Physicians' communication style and patient satisfaction. *Journal of Health and Social Behavior, 28,* 375-388.

Buss, A. H., & Plomin, R. (1975). *A temperament theory of personality development.* New York: Wiley.

Buss, A. H., & Plomin, R. (1984). *Temperament: Early developing personality traits.* Hillsdale, NJ: Lawrence Erlbaum Associates.

Cappella, J. N. (1991). The biological origins of automated patterns of human interaction. *Communication Theory, 1,* 4-35.

Cattell, R. B. (1946). *Description and measurement of personality.* New York: World.

Clausen, J. A. (1973). The organism and socialization. In S. Scarr-Salapatek & P. Salapatek (Eds.), *Socialization* (pp. 3-17). Columbus, OH: Merrill.

Cody, M. J., & McLaughlin, M. L. (1985). The situation as a construct in interpersonal communication research. In M. L. Knapp & G. R. Miller (Eds.), *Handbook of interpersonal communication* (pp. 263-312). Beverly Hills: Sage.

Darwin, C. (1859). *On the origin of species by means of natural selection or the preservation of favoured races in the struggle for life.* New York, NY: Appleton.

DeFries, J. C., & Gillis, J. J. (1993). Genetics of reading disability. In R. Plomin & G. E. McClearn (Eds.), *Nature, nurture, & psychology* (pp. 121-145). Washington, DC: American Psychological Association.

Dollard, J., & Miller, N. E. (Eds.). (1950). *Personality and psychotherapy: An analysis of terms of learning, thinking, and culture*. New York: McGraw-Hill.

Glauser, M. J., & Tullar, W. L. (1985). Communicator style of police officers and citizen satisfaction with officer/citizen telephone conversations. *Journal of Police Science and Administration, 13*, 70-77.

Hansford, B., & Hattie, J. (1989). Perceptions of communicator style and educational environments. *Australian Journal of Education, 33*, 53-67.

Honeycutt, J. M., & Worobey, J. L. (1987). Impressions about communication styles and competence in nursing relationships. *Communication Education, 36*, 217-227.

Horvath, C. W. (1995). Biological origins of communicator style. *Communication Quarterly, 43*, 394-407.

Infante, D. A. (1987). Aggressiveness. In J. C. McCroskey & J. A. Daly (Eds.), *Personality and interpersonal communication* (pp. 157-192). Newbury Park, CA: Sage.

Infante, D. A., & Gorden, W. I. (1987). Superior and subordinate communication profiles: Implications for independent-mindedness and upward effectiveness. *Central States Speech Journal, 38*, 73-80.

Infante, D. A., & Gorden, W. I. (1989). Argumentativeness and affirming communicator style as predictors of satisfaction/dissatisfaction with subordinates. *Communication Quarterly, 37*, 81-90.

Itard, J. M. G. (1962). *The wild boy of Aveyron* (G. Humphrey & M. Humphrey, Trans.). New York: Appleton-Century-Crofts. (Original work published 1807).

Kerlinger, F. N. (1986). *Foundations of behavioral research* (3rd ed.). New York: Holt, Rinehart & Winston.

Kimble, G. A. (1993). Evolution of the nature-nurture issue in the history of psychology. In R. Plomin & G. E. McClearn (Eds.), *Nature, nurture, & psychology* (pp. 3-25). Washington, DC: American Psychological Association.

Koch, H. L. (1966). *Twins and their relations*. Chicago: University of Chicago.

Lenneberg, E. (1967). *Biological foundations of language*. New York: Wiley.

Loehlin, J. C., & Nichols, R. C. (Eds.). (1976). *Heredity, environment, & personality: A study of 850 sets of twins*. Austin: University of Texas Press.

Lykken, D. T. (1982). Research with twins: The concept of emergenesis. *Psychophysiology, 19*, 361-373.

Magnusson, D., & Endler, N. S. (1977). Interactional psychology: Present status and future prospects. In D. Magnusson & N. S. Endler (Eds.), *Personality as the crossroads: Current issues in interactional psychology* (pp. 3-36). New York: Wiley.

Matthews, K. A., & Krantz, D. S. (1976). Resemblances of twins and their parents in pattern A behavior. *Psychosomatic Medicine, 38,* 140-144.

McCroskey, J. C., & Richmond, V. P. (1987). Willingness to communicate. In J. C. McCroskey & J. A. Daly (Eds.), *Personality and interpersonal communication* (pp. 129-156). Newbury Park, CA: Sage.

McGue, M., Bouchard, T. J., Iacono, W. G., & Lykken, D. T. (1993). Behavioral genetics of cognitive ability: A life-span perspective. In R. Plomin & G. E. McClearn (Eds.), *Nature, nurture, & psychology* (pp. 59-76). Washington, DC: American Psychological Association.

Mendel, G. J. (1866). Versuche uver Pflanzen-Hybriden [Research on hybrid plants]. *Verhandlungen des Naturforshunden in Breuen, 4,* 3-47.

Mischel, W. (1968). *Personality and assessment.* New York: Wiley.

Neubauer, P. B., & Neubauer, A. (1990). *Nature's thumbprint.* Reading, MA: Addison-Wesley.

Norton, R. W. (1977). Teacher effectiveness as a function of communicator style. *Communication Yearbook, 1,* 525-542.

Norton, R. W. (1978). Foundation of a communicator style construct. *Human Communication Research, 4,* 99-112.

Norton, R. (1983). *Communicator style: Theory, applications, and measures.* Beverly Hills: Sage.

Norton, R., & Nussbaum, J. (1980). Dramatic behaviors of the effective teacher. *Communication Yearbook, 4,* 565-579.

Norton, R. W., & Pettegrew, L. S. (1977). Communicator style as an effect determinant of attraction. *Communication Research, 4,* 257-282.

Plomin, R. (1990). *Nature and nurture: An introduction to behavioral genetics.* Belmont, CA: Brooks-Cole.

Plomin, R., Loehlin, J. C., & DeFries, J. C. (1985). Genetic and environmental components of "environmental" influences. *Developmental Psychology, 3,* 391-402.

Rotter, J. B. (1964). *Social learning and clinical psychology* (3rd ed.). Englewood Cliffs, NJ: Prentice-Hall.

Rowe, D. C. (1993). Genetic perspectives on personality. In R. Plomin & G. E. McClearn (Eds.), *Nature, nurture, & psychology* (pp. 179-195). Washington, DC: American Psychological Association.

Rubin, R. B., & Feezel, J. D. (1986). Elements of teacher communication competence. *Communication Education, 35*, 255-268.

Rutter, M., Korn, S., & Birch, H. G. (1963). Genetic and environmental factors in the development of primary and secondary reaction patterns. *British Journal of Social and Clinical Psychology, 2*, 161-173.

Schlesinger, K., & Groves, P. M. (1976). *Psychology: A dynamic science*. Dubuque, IA: William C. Brown.

Singh, J. A., & Zingg, R. M. (1942). *Wolfchildren and feral man*. New York: Harper & Row.

Stern, C. (1949). *Principles of human genetics*. San Francisco: Freeman.

Thoday, J. M., & Parkes, A. S. (1968). *Genetic and environmental influences on behavior*. New York: Plenum.

Torgersen, A. M., & Kringlen, E. (1979). Genetic aspects of temperamental differences in infants. In S. Chess & A. Thomas (Eds.), *Annual progress in child development* (pp. 251-262). New York: Brunner Mazel.

4

Personality and Self-Perceptions About Communication

James B. Weaver, III
Auburn University

This chapter examines several aspects of communication within the well-developed conceptual framework of H. Eysenck's (1947, 1990) psychobiological model of personality. First, several conceptual commonalties between contemporary communication and personality theories are highlighted. Next, the methodology employed in a series of studies is outlined. Then empirical evidence of linkages between three personality dimensions—psychoticism, extraversion, and neuroticism—and six inventories assessing self-perceptions about communication—empathetic responsiveness, communication apprehension, receiver apprehension, fear of intimacy, interaction involvement, listening style preferences, and communication style— is detailed. Taken together, the data at hand provide informative initial sketches of distinctive communication preference profiles of each personality dimension.

PERSONALITY AND COMMUNICATION: INTERTWINED
INDIVIDUAL DIFFERENCES

On cursory reflection, most people seem to agree that when it comes to the way we communicate, individuals are often distinctively different. Indeed, everyday parlance is filled with natural language terms people use to categorize themselves and others. Statements like "He's so quiet," "She's very assertive and to the point," and "They just love to talk" illustrate how social perceptions are often colloquially expressed through attention to communication behaviors (Bandura, 1986). Through social interactions, we drop clues about who we are and, in turn, learn about others. Communication, in other words, goes beyond simply being a mode for exchanging linguistic content; the manner in which information is transmitted and received—a person's communication preference profile—also provides a key point of reference toward assessing numerous aspects of the individual. Indeed, many argue that the essence of one's personality (i.e., self-conception) emerges from and is refined through communicative interactions with others in society (cf. Allport, 1937, Blumer, 1969; Marlowe & Gergen, 1969; Mead, 1934).

The idea that communication and personality characteristics are "inherently intertwined" (Daly, 1987) has intrigued scholars since the late 1930s. Allport (1937), for instance, recognizing the heuristic value of natural language terms, advanced a "dispositional model" on which most contemporary personality theories are grounded. Employing a lexical approach, Allport and his colleagues identified more than 18,000 words they believed described common personality characteristics. Approximately one fourth of the terms—including *friendliness, ambitiousness, cleanliness, enthusiasm, punctuality, shyness, talkativeness, dominance submissiveness*—were considered of particular importance because they had the potential "to distinguish the behavior of one human being from another" (Allport & Odbert, 1936, p. 24).

The fact that a large proportion of the personality descriptor terms highlighted by Allport involves some aspect of communication behavior has not been overlooked. Indeed, numerous investigations have provided evidence suggesting that consideration of individual differences emerging from relatively stable and enduring personality characteristics could substantially enlighten our understanding of how people communicate (cf. Marlowe & Gergen, 1969; McCroskey & Daly, 1987). Consolidation of these findings has been hampered, however, by the seemingly haphazard manner in which personality variables have been selected and operationalized. Daly (1987) framed the dilemma perceptively:

Communication research emphasizing personality has had no obvious structure or "master plan" associated with it. Each individual investigator selects his or her favorite trait and proceeds to explore the measurement, manifestations, or consequences of the disposition without much regard for how it fits within some larger domain. (p. 31)

Furthermore, Daly concluded that casting future research within an integrative model of personality was a theoretically critical challenge facing communication scholars. It was this notion that grasped my intellectual curiosity and fostered the work summarized here.

CONTEMPORARY PERSONALITY THEORY

Contemporary ideas about personality are rooted in antiquity. Ancient Greek and Roman philosophers, for instance, advanced a taxonomy of personality involving four temperaments—choleric, sanguine, phlegmatic, and melancholic—that provides the conceptual foundation for much modern inquiry (cf. H. Eysenck & Eysenck, 1985).

Most contemporary theories of personality have been constructed within hierarchical structural models that involve at least three levels (John, 1990; Liebert & Spiegler, 1994). At the lowest level of these models are "habitual cognitions or behaviors" (H. Eysenck, 1990, p. 244). These everyday "habits" are conceptualized as specific mental and/or behavioral responses to social stimuli that an individual experiences and exhibits across a variety of circumstances.

Personality traits are conceived as the next level in most models of personality. Such traits are viewed as emerging from sets of habits that are "generalized and personalized determining tendencies—consistent and stable modes of an individual's adjustment to his environment" (Allport & Odbert, 1936, p. 26). If a person is described as "talkative," for example, several consistent habits—such as always talking to people despite the situation and always having something to say—typically come to mind as underlying such a trait.

Finally, at the highest level, traits are clustered together to form predominant personality dimensions. Although a variety of labels have been assigned to these personality dimensions—for instance, *central dispositions* (Allport, 1937), *primary factors* (Cattell, 1946, 1990), *supertraits* (McCrae & Costa, 1985, 1987), and *types* (H.

Eysenck, 1947, 1990)—theorists agree that they emerge from intercorrelations of personality traits. H. Eysenck and Eysenck (1985), for example, referred to personality dimensions as second-order factors that reduce "the total complexity of sometimes thousands of intercorrelations to the relative simplicity of a few factors" (p. 19). The notion of personality dimensions, in other words, permits classification of individuals into distinct groups based on their similarities and differences across several personality trait characteristics.

Of the variety of personality models (cf. John, 1990), the one developed by H. Eysenck (1947, 1990) provides an excellent framework for examining potential interrelationships between personality characteristics and communication self-perceptions. Working since the late 1940s, using extensive, culturally diverse samples, H. Eysenck demonstrated that numerous personality traits cluster into three, essentially orthogonal, personality types—*extraversion, neuroticism,* and *psychoticism* (cf. H. Eysenck, 1990). Equally important, other research (e.g., Zuckerman, Kuhlman, & Camac, 1988) provided considerable validation of the Eysenck model and further illuminated the definition of each of the three personality types.

Two dimensions of H. Eysenck's model are consistent with those isolated in essentially all contemporary personality theories (cf. John, 1990). The extraversion personality type is conceptualized as tapping trait characteristics such as an individual's level of sociability and/or social adaptability, affiliation, participation, activity, and positive self-esteem. The neuroticism personality type, on the other hand, involves traits such as an individual's level of anxiety and emotionality and a negative self-image.

Differing from the other personality types and unique to H. Eysenck's conceptualization, psychoticism is conceptualized as accessing traits such as an individual's tendencies toward egocentricity, sensation-seeking, and autonomy (i.e., internal locus of control). More specifically, individuals evidencing the psychoticism personality type typically display a high level of social deviance, impulsivity, and "a lack of restraint, responsibility, need for cognitive structure, and willingness to live by society's rules and mores (socialization)" (Zuckerman, Kuhlman, & Camac, 1988, p. 104).

Within this framework, psychoticism, extraversion, and neuroticism are seen as influencing an individual's primary communication style via both cognitive/affective and physiological mechanisms (H. Eysenck, 1990; Zuckerman, 1991). Specifically, these personality characteristics are conceptualized as central components within the nexus of attitudes, beliefs, and values that guide our interactions with the social environment (cf. Daly, 1987; Daly &

Diesel, 1992). In other words, it seems reasonable to expect that consideration of the extent to which individuals exhibit psychoticism, extraversion, or neuroticism should greatly facilitate explanation and prediction of their self perceptions about communicating.

OVERVIEW OF METHOD

The series of studies summarized here were conducted from September 1992 through June 1996. Large samples of participants (*n*s between 500 and 2,500) were recruited for each study with specific sample size details included in the tables.

Unless otherwise noted, each inventory was administered and the various indices were computed in a manner consistent with that outlined by the developers. Because the procedures and operationalizations employed in these studies were relatively standardized, much of the technical information typical in empirical presentations has been omitted here. In the interest of brevity, for example, the sample statistics, reliability estimates, and intercorrelations for the various measures are discussed only if these scale characteristics deviated substantially from normative data. Readers interested in such details are encouraged to review the referenced citations or contact the author.

Participants. Participants were students enrolled in an introductory-level professional communication course at a large university in the southeastern United States. The course is a requirement for essentially all undergraduate majors at the university and draws students from a variety of interests and disciplines.

Questionnaire. A broad-ranging "communication preference" questionnaire was administered during the first week of each academic quarter. Respondents voluntarily completed the questionnaire during class hours.

Personality Measures. Respondents completed a short form version of the Eysenck Personality Questionnaire (EPQ-R; S. Eysenck, Eysenck, & Barrett, 1985) that was adapted for these studies. Specifically, the wording of some EPQ-R items was modified to enhance the meaning for American respondents and to permit responses on the scale *always* (4), *frequently* (3), *sometimes* (2), *infrequently* (1), and *never* (0).

As outlined by S. Eysenck et al. (1985), the items from the EPQ-R were organized and summed to form three personality measures—labeled *psychoticism, extraversion,* and *neuroticism*—that ranged from 0 to 48. Respondents were then categorized into three mutually exclusive groups based on their predominant personality type (see Weaver, Watson, & Barker, 1996). This task involved a three-step procedure. First, the responses for each personality type were standardized within each sex. Next, respondents scoring either below or above the mean on all three measures were excluded. This step, in other words, isolated the "nay sayers" and "yeah sayers" (Frey, Botan, Freedman, & Kreps, 1992) for whom no distinctive personality type was evident. Then, difference scores between the personality measures were computed and respondents were classified into discrete personality type groups based on these scores. The resulting categorical variable—with psychotic (P), extravert (E), and neurotic (N) as nominal levels—was the personality type measure used in subsequent analyses.

Empathic Response Style. A 20-item inventory composed by Richendoller and Weaver, (1994; Weaver & Kirtley, 1995) was used to assess three empathic response styles—empathetic responsiveness, perspective-taking, and sympathetic responsiveness. Specifically, seven items were used to operationalize empathetic responsiveness. These included, for example, "I don't get upset just because a friend is acting upset" and other statements that tapped (both positively and negatively) the respondent's tendency to experience an affective reaction congruent with another's emotion. Perspective-taking was operationalized by the five items—including "When I'm upset with someone I usually try to 'put myself in his or her shoes' for a while"—that assessed the tendency to imagine oneself in the place of another. And, sympathetic responsiveness, defined as the feeling of pity, sorrow or concern for another, was operationalized using the eight items. "I am the type of person who is concerned when others are unhappy" is an example. Respondents rated the applicability of each statement to themselves on a scale ranging from *strongly agree* (4), *agree* (3), *neutral* (2), *disagree* (1), and *strongly disagree* (0).

Communication Apprehension. The Personal Report of Communication Apprehension (PRCA-24; Richmond & McCroskey, 1992) was used to assess communication apprehension (CA). Respondents were asked to report how well each of the 24 statements of the PRCA characterized their feelings and/or behaviors on the *always* (4) to *never* (0) scale.

As detailed by Richmond and McCroskey (1992), responses were transformed and combined to create measures of communication apprehension—that ranged from *no apprehension* (6) to *extreme apprehension* (30)—in four settings: public, meeting, small group, and interpersonal interaction. Examples of the items presented to the respondents include: public CA, "I feel relaxed when giving a speech" (reversed); meeting CA, "Usually I am calm and relaxed while participating in meetings" (reversed), small group CA, "I am calm and relaxed while participating in group discussions" (reversed); and interpersonal CA, "Ordinarily I am calm and relaxed in conversations" (reversed).

Receiver Apprehension. The 20-item Receiver Apprehension Test (RAT; L. Wheeless, 1975) was presented in a random order. Respondents were asked to respond to statements such as "I am generally overexcited and rattled when others are speaking to me" and "I often feel uncomfortable when listening to others" on the *strongly agree* (4) to *strongly disagree* (0) scale. A single index was computed via item transformation and averaging.

Fear of Intimacy. The Fear of Intimacy Scale (FIS; Descutner & Thelen, 1991) is a 35-item inventory designed to measure individuals' anxiety about close relationships. Respondents were asked to report how well each statement characterized their feelings and/or behaviors toward their closest friend on the *strongly agree* (4) to *strongly disagree* (0) scale.

A principle components factor analysis followed by oblique rotation was used to reduce the FIS to three indices. The first factor, emotional intimacy fear, was defined by six items including "I would feel uneasy with my closest friend depending on me for emotional support." "I would feel uneasy talking with my closet friend about something that has hurt me deeply" is an example of the 10 items that defined the communicative intimacy fear factor. Relational intimacy fear, the third factor, was defined by 10 items such as "I have done things in previous relationships to keep me from developing closeness." The items defining each factor were averaged to form the three measures used in subsequent tests.

Listening Style Preferences. Listening style preferences (LS) were assessed using the 16-item Listening Styles Profile (LSP16; Watson, Barker, & Weaver, 1995). Responses were reported on the 5-point scale, *always* (4) to *never* (0).

Consistent with Watson et al. (1995), responses to the four items that defined each LS were averaged to produce the people,

action, content, and time LS preferences. Examples of the items
included in each index are as follows: people LS, "I focus my
attention on the other person's feelings when listening to them";
action LS, "I am frustrated when others don't present their ideas in
an orderly, efficient way"; content LS, "I like the challenge of
listening to complex information"; and time LS, "I interrupt others
when I feel time pressure."

  Interaction Involvement. The 18-item Interaction
Involvement Scale (IIS; Cegala, 1981) examines how individuals
perceive their own interpersonal communication competence.
Respondents were asked to indicate their individual perceptions on
the 5-point scale *always* (4) to *never* (0).
  As outlined by Cegala (1981), responses to the IIS were
transformed and combined to create three measures. The
responsiveness index was composed of items such as "Often in
conversations I'm not sure what my role is; that is, I'm not sure how
I'm expected to relate to others" (reversed). "I carefully observe how
others respond to me during my conversations" is an item typical of
the perceptiveness index. And, the attentiveness index included
items such as "My mind wanders during conversations and I often
miss parts of what is going on" (reversed).

  Communication Style. A version of the Communication Style
Profile Test (CSPT; McCallister, 1992) that was modified to enhance
the meaning for young adult respondents was employed.
Respondents were asked to indicate how well each of 48 items on the
CSPT described them on the *always* (4) to *never* (0) scale.
  According to McCallister (1992), the CSPT is designed to
assess three predominant communication styles that people may
employ when interacting with others in both interpersonal and group
settings. However, even a cursory review of the inventory items
highlighted the fact that a variety of communication concepts
underlay each communication style. Constructs such as
communication competence, willingness to communicate, and
communication apprehension were all intermingled; thus, thwarting
efforts to compose valid and reliable indices for each communication
style. Consequently, the individual items were retained for
subsequent analysis.

SUMMARY OF FINDINGS

Emphatic Response Style

Exploring individual differences in empathic response style was the focus of our initial examination of linkages between personality and communication self-perceptions (Richendoller & Weaver, 1994). Despite its apparent centrality and importance to communication "the notion of empathy is, and always has been, a broad, somewhat slippery concept—one that has provoked considerable speculation, excitement and confusion" (Eisenberg & Strayer, 1987, p. 3). However, building on the ideas of several contemporary theorists, Richendoller and Weaver (1994) isolated three constructs of empathy—empathetic responsiveness, perspective-taking, and sympathetic responsiveness—that converge on emotional and cognitive reactions manifest when communicating with others.

Briefly, empathetic responsiveness was conceptualized as a congruent affective response to overt or covert cues of another's affective state that can be experienced in both joyful and sad situations. Perspective-taking, both conceptually and semantically the most widely agreed upon empathy construct, was defined as a process that broadly involves imagining oneself in the place of another. On the other hand, the essence of sympathetic responsiveness, the newest and least clearly developed empathy construct, is this: when you feel sympathy for another with a problem, you do not actually experience emotions parallel to theirs; instead, you experience different emotions that are associated with concern or sorrow for another.

It was expected that an individual's empathic response style should correspond, at least to some degree, with their predominant personality characteristics. Consequently, the empathic response styles profile of psychotics should reflect their tendencies toward egocentricity and lack of concern for others. Extraverts might display a profile consistent with their desire to be viewed as sociable and affiliated with others. Analogously, the profile evidenced by neurotics should reflect their tendency toward anxiety, emotionality, and social isolation.

The results of a discriminant analysis, reported in Table 4.1, lend considerable support to these expectations. Specifically, using the 20 empathic response style items as predictor variables, the three-level personality type measure (P, E, N) was subjected to a stepwise discriminant analysis. Minimization of Wilks' lambda was used as the selection criterion in this procedure in order to maximize group separation.

Table 4.1. Discriminant Analysis: Empathic Response Styles as a Function of Personality Type.

	Function One	Function Two
Summary Statistics		
Canonical correlation	0.42	0.38
Eigenvalue	0.22	0.17
Wilks' Lambda	0.70	0.85
Chi-square	700.15	315.83
Degrees of freedom	22	10
Significance	<0.0001	<0.0001
Structure Coefficients		
"I become nervous if others around me seem nervous."	0.70	0.04
"I am able to remain calm even though those around me worry."	-0.68	-0.16
"The people around me have a great influence on my moods."	0.61	0.19
"When I see someone who badly needs help in an emergency, I go to pieces."	0.47	-0.19
"I don't get upset just because a friend is acting upset."	-0.38	-0.04
"I am the type of person who is concerned when others are unhappy."	0.03	0.75
"When someone else is upset, I almost always try to console them."	0.08	0.74
"Other people's misfortunes do not usually disturb me a great deal."	-0.15	-0.59
"I often have tender, concerned feelings for people less fortunate than me."	0.19	0.59
"I sometimes don't feel very sorry for people when they are having problems."	-0.01	-0.51
"When I'm upset at someone I usually try to 'put myself in his or her shoes' for a while.	-0.07	0.38

Classification Information

	n	Classified correctly	Group centroids	
			Function 1	Function 2
Psychoticism	577	46.3%	-0.26	-0.60
Extraversion	732	62.6%	-0.38	0.42
Neuroticism	663	59%	0.65	0.06

As can be seen, two significant discriminant functions emerged. The first function consisted of five items designed to assess empathetic responsiveness. Alternatively, Function 2 was composed of five items designed to tap sympathetic responsiveness and one measure reflecting perspective-taking (the last item defining Function 2). These functions permitted correct classification of about 57% of the respondents.

Inspection of the group centroids revealed that individuals evidencing P as their predominant personality type experience neither empathetic or sympathetic responsiveness, thus suggesting a certain callous nature within such individuals. Extraverts reported a tendency to be sympathetic but not empathetic toward others. Conversely, N were very empathetic but reported little sympathy for others. This latter finding, which at first glance appears paradoxical, suggests that neurotics, recognizing their own emotionality, may insulate themselves from feeling concern for others to avoid the anxiety such sorrow causes.

Communication Anxiety

Recent research suggests that what Americans fear most—more than disease or even death—is speaking before others (cf. Motley, 1988). Against this backdrop, McCroskey (1978, 1984) has focused considerable attention on the anxiety or fear an individual associates with "either real or anticipated communication with another person" (p. 13). Specifically, through the PRCA-24, Richmond and McCroskey (1992) have isolated four contexts or settings in which apprehensions can emerge: public speaking, speaking at a meeting, speaking in a small group, and speaking in a dyadic interaction.

Other inventories assessing CA have also emerged. L. Wheeless (1975), for example, developed the RAT to assess anxiety arising during the decoding, receiving, and responding function of communication. Alternatively, Descutner and Thelen (1991) articulated the FIS to appraise the "inhibited capacity of an individual, because of anxiety, to exchange thoughts and feelings of personal significance with another individual who is highly valued" (p. 219). As detailed earlier, three aspects of anxiety—emotional, communicative, and relational intimacy fear—were extracted from the FIS scale.

To what extent do our anxieties about communicating with others vary as a function of our personality type? Rather clear expectations for Es and Ns can be advanced. Because of their effluently sociable tendencies, Es are expected to report the least apprehension. Conversely, in light of the anxious and emotional dispositions, Ns are expected to evidence the most apprehension. Predictions for the egocentric and socially autonomous Ps are less conspicuous.

In order to test these expectations, the four measures derived from the PRCA, the single index computed from the RAT, and the three measures extracted from the FIS were subjected to analysis of variance with respondent sex (male, female) and personality type (P, E, N) as independent measure factors. Significant respondent sex main effects emerged for five of the measures. Examination of the means revealed that females reported greater apprehension than males on the RAT and three FIS indices, but the opposite pattern appears for the public CA measure. Furthermore, the respondent sex by personality type interactions all yielded only trivial ($F \leq 1$) variation.

Of interest to our task at hand, significant personality type main effects were evident for all eight measures. The means associated with these effects are presented in Table 4.2. As can be seen, distinct differences between the three personality types are apparent. Consistent with expectations, Es reported the least apprehension across all eight measures. Furthermore, for the PRCA and RAT measures, the findings for Ns are also concordant with expectations; Ns report significantly greater apprehension than either Es or Ps. Interestingly, the means for Ps fall between the E and N means on the PRCA and RAT measures. Notice that the pattern of differences that emerges for the three FIS indices is less unique (P = N > E).

Styles of Communicating

The notion of communication style has been with us for more than two millennia. In ancient Rome, for example, style was one of the "five canons of rhetoric" (Norton, 1978, 1983, p. 7). Even today, Aristotle's observations and recommendations for public speaking style remain an instructional staple in many contemporary college rhetoric courses (e.g., Griffin, 1997).

Among contemporary scholars, Norton's (1983) conceptualization of communication style as existing along a single continuum ranging from a "nondirective" to a "directive" manner of interpersonal interaction has received considerable attention (e.g., Dion & Notarantonio, 1992; V. Wheeless & Lashbrook, 1987). Within this framework, individuals who are accommodating, attentive, and supportive of others during interactions display a nondirective communication style. On the other end of the continuum, those who are dominant, talk frequently and animatedly, and generally take

Table 4.2. Communication Apprehension, Receiver Apprehension, and Fear of Intimacy as a Function of Personality Type.

Apprehension Inventory	Predominant Personality Type		
	Psychoticism	Extraversion	Neuroticism
Communication Apprehension			
Public CA	18.58[b]	16.74[a]	21.10[c]
Meeting CA	16.17[b]	13.63[a]	18.26[c]
Small-group CA	15.62[b]	12.45[a]	16.90[c]
Interpersonal CA	14.88[b]	12.30[a]	16.61[c]
n	218	279	247
Receiver Apprehension			
Total	1.49[b]	1.28[a]	1.64[c]
n	119	169	139
Fear of Intimacy			
Emotional fear	1.44[b]	1.11[a]	1.49[b]
Communicative fear	1.75[b]	1.45[a]	1.80[b]
Relational fear	2.10[b]	1.78[a]	2.18[b]
n	119	169	139

Note. Means with different superscripts differ at $p < 0.005$ by the Student-Newman-Keuls *t* test.

control of social situations exhibit the directive communication style. The notion of a communication style continuum has been supported by congruent findings emerging from diverse methodologies and operationalizations (e.g., Hansford & Hattie, 1987; Hart, Carlson, & Eadie, 1980; O'Keefe, 1988).

Three inventories were included here to examine individual differences in styles of communicating. The LSP16 (Watson et al., 1995) was examined first (Weaver et al., 1996). Conceptualizing listening preferences as attitudes, beliefs, and predispositions about the how, where, when, who, and what of information reception and encoding, Watson et al. (1995) identified four distinct LS: people-, action-, content-, and time- oriented. The people LS emerged as a preference where concern for others' feelings and emotions appear paramount. The action LS delineates a preference for listening to concise, error-free presentations. The content LS highlights a preference for listening to complex and challenging information in an evaluative manner. And the time LS accentuates a preference for brief or hurried interactions with others.

A second inventory that is conceptually consistent with the notion of communication style is the IIS (Cegala, 1981). Cegala, defining interaction involvement as "the extent to which an individual partakes in a social environment" (p. 112), articulated the IIS as a cognitive assessment of communication competence. As detailed earlier, three dimensions of interaction involvement—responsiveness, perceptiveness, and attentiveness—focusing on distinct communication competencies were isolated.

Evolving from the earlier work of Norton (1978, 1983), McCallister's (1992) CSPT incorporates questions exploring several communication constructs (e.g., apprehension, competence, and willingness to communicate) in an attempt to profile respondents on the nondirective-directive continuum. Although giving rise to questions of validity and reliability, the assemblage of diverse constructs within the CSPT inventory, in light of the exploratory nature of this endeavor, was deemed advantageous (Weaver, Richendoller, & Kirtley, 1995).

What differences in self-perceptions of communication style should we expect across the three personality types? Locating the outgoing and socially adaptive extraverts along Norton's continuum is more difficult because they often endorse positive characteristics typical of both the nondirective (e.g., attentive, supportive) and directive (animated, talkative) anchors. Commonly displaying confidence, patience, and skill when communicating with others, Es are expected to perceive themselves as people-oriented listeners who are very responsive, perceptive, and attentive during interactions.

Conversely, a communication style that sanctions minimal involvement with, if not avoidance of, others could be a prominent characteristic of neurotics. The anxious and emotional Ns, in other words, are expected to endorse characteristics antithetical to the anchors of Norton's continuum perceiving themselves as action- and time-oriented listeners who are unresponsive, imperceptive, and inattentive when involved in interpersonal interactions.

The clearest expectations emerge for Ps. Indeed, endorsing a communication style that reflects outspokenness and social callousness toward others, Ps may exemplify Norton's directive anchor. Specifically, the egocentric Ps are expected to reject the notions of people- and content-oriented listening and perceive themselves as unresponsive, imperceptive, and inattentive communicators.

These possibilities were tested in two ways. First, the four LSP and three IIS measures were subjected to analyses of variance with respondent sex (male, female) and personality type (P, E, N) as independent measure factors. A stepwise discriminant analysis using the 48 items of the CSPT as predictor variables and the personality type (P, E, N) as the grouping variable was the second procedure.

The ANOVAs on the LSP and IIS measures revealed significant personality type main effects for all seven measures. The means associated with these effects, displayed in Table 4.3, highlight distinct differences between Ps, Es, and Ns.

Consistent with expectations, Es perceived themselves as friendly, open, and supportive listeners. Compared with the other personality type groups, Es endorsed both the people and content LS most strongly while rejecting the action and content listening styles. Furthermore, Es perceived themselves as significantly more responsive, perceptive, and attentive than their counterparts.

The pattern of responses revealed for Ns is distinguished by an apparent indifference toward listening and interacting with others. The Ns, for example, emerged as intermediate to the two other personality types on the people LS and parallel with the Ps on the content listening style. The responses of the neuroticism group proved most distinctive on the action LS suggesting that a tendency to become frustrated and impatient punctuates their interactions with others. Furthermore, across the three interaction involvement measures, Ns perceived themselves as significantly less responsive than the Es and Ps and were equal with the Ps on the perceptiveness and attentiveness measures.

Table 4.3. Interaction Involvement and Listening Style Preferences As a Function of Personality Type.

	Predominant personality type		
Inventory	Psychoticism	Extraversion	Neuroticism
Listening Style Preferences			
People	2.96[a]	3.33[c]	3.13[b]
Action	2.06[ab]	1.98[a]	2.13[b]
Content	2.25[a]	2.37[b]	2.26[a]
Time	1.83[b]	1.76[a]	1.86[b]
n	374	478	458
Interaction Involvement			
Responsiveness	3.35[b]	3.67[c]	3.15[a]
Perceptiveness	2.58[a]	2.85[b]	2.66[a]
Attentiveness	3.19[a]	3.42[b]	3.15[a]
n	218	279	247

Note. Means with different superscripts differ at $p < 0.005$ by the Student-Newman-Keuls t test.

Consistent with expectations, Ps rejected the notion that, when listening to other people, concern for their feelings and emotions should be important. Specifically, Ps emerged as significantly lower on the people LS than did Es and Ns and intermediate to the other personality types on the action LS and responsiveness measure. On the other four indices, the pattern of responses of Ps were equivalent to Ns.

Significant sex differences were also apparent across the seven measures. Examination of the means revealed that females endorsed the people LS and responsiveness, perceptiveness, and attentiveness measures more strongly than males, but the opposite pattern appeared for the action, content, and time LS. A single-respondent sex by personality type interaction emerged. Inspection of the interaction means for the attentiveness measure showed that female Ps perceived themselves as significantly more attentive than their male counterparts.

The discriminant analysis, details of which are presented in Table 4.4, yielded two functions that permitted correct classification of about 61% of the respondents. The first discriminant function appears to reflect the antipode of Norton's directive communication style. Taken together, the seven items composing the first function suggest a demure, unsupportive, and inattentive communication style. The second discriminant function also seems less aligned with Norton's notion than might have been expected. The five items defining the second function converge on a supportive, nondirective communication style but also suggest that acquiescence and frustration are strong underlying components.

Examination of the group centroids revealed that strong rejection of the first discriminant function was a prominent characteristic of extraverted respondents. Consistent with the pattern observed for the LSP and IIS measures, Es emerge as outgoing, supportive, and attentive communicators.

The patterns for P and N respondents appear more complex. Rejection of the second discriminant function along with moderate endorsement of the first function was evident for Ps. This suggests that Ps perceive themselves as outspoken, dogmatic, and impersonal communicators who exhibit little regard for others. Neurotics, on the other hand, reported moderate endorsement of both discriminant functions. This pattern paints an image of individuals who perceive themselves to be polite, but demure, acquiescent, but unsupportive, and attentive, but frustrated, communicators.

Table 4.4. Discriminant Analysis: Communication Style Profile Test as a Function of Personality Type.

	Function One	Function Two
Summary Statistics		
Canonical correlation	0.52	0.43
Eigenvalue	0.37	0.23
Wilks' Lambda	0.59	0.82
Chi-square	443.93	173.36
Degrees of freedom	24	11
Significance	<0.0001	<0.0001
Structure Coefficients		
"I really like to sit and talk with other people."	-0.57	0.38
"I am soft-spoken."	0.46	0.20
"I do not tell others about my personal feelings."	0.46	-0.11
"Sometimes it appears that people tune me out when I am talking."	0.43	0.24
"I am direct, straightforward, frank, and spontaneous when I talk."	-0.41	-0.33
"I am willing to listen to another person, but I really don't like to give advice on what to do."	0.37	-0.19
"I am a very patient person."	-0.15	-0.13
"I tend to 'give in' more than other people, and sometimes this bothers me."	0.39	0.56
"I am polite, supportive, and warm when I talk."	-0.38	0.51
"I try to show the other person that I am listening by nodding my head and saying 'yes, I see, uh-huh,' and so on."	-0.20	0.49
"There is a right and a wrong way to do most things."	-0.05	0.31
"I make a lot of 'you should' statements."	0.15	0.20

Classification information

			Group centroids	
	n	Classified correctly	Function 1	Function 2
Psychoticism	285	57.2%	0.38	-0.69
Extraversion	329	73.3%	-0.77	0.07
Neuroticism	246	50%	0.56	0.51

CONCLUSIONS

The findings of this investigation, consistent with the arguments of others (cf. McCroskey & Daly, 1987), reveal a great deal about the mediating impact of personality on our perceptions of how we communicate with others. In particular, the data at hand illustrate that an amalgamation of different communication characteristics are linked with each personality type suggesting that the role played by communication in the "development and maintenance of dispositional tendencies" (Daly, 1987, p. 29) may be even more substantial than initially expected.

Looking across the various findings reported in this chapter, we can sketch out distinctive communication preferences profiles that emerge for each personality type. Displaying a strong tendency toward callousness and social deviance when interacting with others, respondents reporting psychoticism as their predominant personality type endorse a communication preferences profile that involves an unsupportive, rude, and unresponsive approach to interactions. Evidencing moderate communication apprehension, this type of individual appears to dislike interpersonal interaction, tends to be judgmental of others, and often fails to recognize social boundaries or conventions during communication.

In stark contrast, individuals reporting extraversion as their predominant personality type perceive themselves as confident, patient, and skilled communicators. Extraverts tend to be friendly, open, and supportive during interactions, freely express sympathy for others, and display little anxiety over communication in any circumstances.

The communication preferences profile revealed by individuals reporting neuroticism as their predominant personality type is distinguished by an apparent indifference toward and frustration during interaction with others. Perhaps because they suffer substantial emotionality and communication apprehension, Ns appear as acquiescent and demure communicators who prefer circumstances that permit minimal contact with, if not avoidance of, others. However, Ns also report considerable hostility and frustration emerging from their interactions—feelings arising from beliefs that they are often either dishonest with or ignored by others. Apprehensive, imperceptive, and frustrated, neurotics evidence both impatience and a lack of finesse when communicating.

The portrait etched by these findings extends our understanding of the neurotic communicator and points, perhaps, to one fountainhead from which their negative perceptions of the communication process may spring. Specifically, it appears that neurotic individuals perceive themselves as easily falling into a "spiral of miscommunication" (cf. Coupland, Wiemann, & Giles, 1991). Apprehension and frustration could merge for these individuals because they may be unable to realize an effective balance between the illocutionary acts (i.e., the promises, requests, warning, threats, etc. of a speaker) and perlocutionary effects (i.e., the receiver's reaction to what is said) that evolve during an interaction (cf. Austin, 1975; Searle, 1969). These considerations suggest that future research exploring the perceptions of communicative competence (Wiemann, 1977) and discourse strategies (Villaume & Cegala, 1988) associated with the neuroticism personality type should prove particularly insightful.

Although the findings of this investigation are informative, some caveats must be acknowledged. The cultural diversity of the sample was limited. Ninety-five percent of the respondents were Caucasian; diverse ethnic groups were under represented. Because both personality and communication characteristics result, at least to some extent, through socialization, the potential influence of ethnic diversity must be considered. The southern university sampling of the volunteers could also be a weakness. Typically, undergraduates from this region tend to have rather conservative values and attitudes that could be reflected in their communicative characteristics. Additionally, their higher education level may have enabled them to be more aware of personality differences and the importance of effective communication thus causing them to present image management biases in their responses. These factors, however, should only inflate the error variance, which ultimately leads to more conservative statistical tests.

The fact that the findings summarized here are limited to perceptions about communication is another important limitation. We must be sensitive to the fact that self-reports of "how we feel" about an activity like communication may not provide the most reliable estimates of actual behavior. With this in mind, future research should consider the potential of direct behavioral assessments to provide valuable insights into linkages between personality and communication.

In summary, the data at hand highlight significant individual differences in perceptions about communication. The results show that the psychoticism personality type is linked to a socially callous approach to communication. Conversely, the extraversion personality type is associated with an expressive, supportive communication style. The neuroticism personality type, on the other hand, evidences perceptions about interacting with others that are punctuated by both acquiescence and frustration. These distinctively different communication preference profiles highlight the necessity for incorporating individual personality differences into our understanding of the communication process.

ACKNOWLEDGEMENTS

A word of thanks is extended to my colleagues Don Richardson, Deborah Barker, and Dave Sutton and to Behavioral Research Laboratory research assistants Jeanne Gartenschlaeger, Lola McCord, Nadine Richendoller, Michelle Kirtley, Stephanie Sargent, and Christian Kiewitz. For the instrumental contribution of these individuals to this endeavor I am grateful.

REFERENCES

Allport, G. W. (1937). *Personality: A psychological interpretation.* New York: Holt.

Allport, G. W., & Odbert, H. S. (1936). Trait-names: A psycho-lexical study. *Psychological Monographs, 47*(1), 1-171.

Austin, J. L. (1975). *How to do things with words* (2nd ed.). Cambridge, MA: Harvard University Press.

Bandura, A. (1986). *Social foundations of thought and action.* Englewood Cliffs, NJ: Prentice-Hall.

Blumer, H. (1969). *Symbolic interactionism.* Englewood Cliffs, NJ: Prentice-Hall.

Cattell, R. B. (1946). *Description and measurement of personality.* Yonkers-on-Hudson, NY: World.

Cattell, R. B. (1990). Advances in Cattellian personality theory. In L. A. Pervin (Ed.), *Handbook of personality and research* (pp. 101-110). New York: Guilford.

Cegala, D. J. (1981). Interaction involvement: A cognitive dimension of communicative competence. *Communication Education, 30*, 109-121.

Coupland, N., Wiemann, J. M., & Giles, H. (1991). *"Miscommunication" and problematic talk.* Newbury Park, CA: Sage.

Daly, J. A. (1987). Personality and interpersonal communication: Issues and directions. In J. C. McCroskey & J. A. Daly (Eds.), *Personality and interpersonal communication* (pp. 13-41). Newbury Park, CA: Sage.

Daly, J. A., & Diesel, C. A. (1992). Measures of communication-related personality variables. *Communication Education, 41,* 405-414.

Descutner, C. J., & Thelen, M. H. (1991). Development and validation of a fear-of-intimacy scale. *Psychological Assessment: A Journal of Consulting and Clinical Psychology, 3,* 218-225.

Dion, P. A., & Notarantonio, E. M. (1992). Salesperson communication style: The neglected dimension in sales performance. *Journal of Business Communication, 29*(1), 63-77.

Eisenberg, N., & Strayer, J. (1987). Critical issues in the study of empathy. In N. Eisenberg & J. Strayer (Eds.), *Empathy and its development* (pp. 3-13). Cambridge: Cambridge University Press.

Eysenck, H. J. (1947). *Dimensions of personality.* New York: Praeger.

Eysenck, H. J. (1990). Biological dimensions of personality. In L. A. Pervin (Ed.), *Handbook of personality and research* (pp. 244-276). New York: Guilford.

Eysenck, H. J., & Eysenck, M. W. (1985). *Personality and individual differences: A natural science approach.* New York: Plenum.

Eysenck, S. G. B., Eysenck, H. J., & Barrett, P. (1985). A revised version of the psychoticism scale. *Personality and Individual Differences, 6,* 21-29.

Frey, L. R., Botan, C. H., Friedman, P. G., & Kreps, G. L. (1992). *Interpreting communication research.* Englewood Cliffs, NJ: Prentice-Hall.

Griffin, E. A. (1997). *A first look at communication theory.* New York: McGraw-Hill.

Hansford, B., & Hattie, J. (1987). Perceptions of communication style and self concept. *Communication Research, 14,* 189-203.

Hart, R. P., Carlson, R. E., & Eadie, W. F. (1980). Attitudes toward communication and the assessment of rhetorical sensitivity. *Communication Monographs, 47,* 1-22.

John, O. P. (1990). The "big five" factor taxonomy: Dimensions of personality in the natural language and in questionnaires. In L. A. Pervin (Ed.), *Handbook of personality and research* (pp. 66-100). New York: Guilford.

Liebert, R. M., & Spiegler, M. D. (1994). *Personality: Strategies and issues* (7th ed.). Pacific Grove, CA: Brooks/Cole.

Marlowe, D., & Gergen, K. J. (1969). Personality and social interaction. In G. Lindzey & E. Aronson (Eds.), *The handbook of social psychology* (2nd ed., pp. 590-665). Reading, MA: Addison-Wesley.

McCallister, L. (1992). *"I wish I'd said that!"* New York: Wiley.

McCrae, R. R., & Costa, P. T. (1985). Comparison of EPI and psychoticism scales with measures of the five factor model of personality. *Personality and Individual Differences, 6,* 587-597.

McCrae, R. R., & Costa, P. T. (1987). Validation of the five-factor model of personality. *Journal of Personality and Social Psychology, 52,* 81-90.

McCroskey, J. C. (1978). Validity of the PRCA as an index of oral communication apprehension. *Communication Monographs, 45,* 192-203.

McCroskey, J. C. (1984). The communication apprehension perspective. In J. A. Daly & J. C. McCroskey (Eds.), *Avoiding communication: shyness, reticence, and apprehension* (pp. 13-38). Beverly Hills, CA: Sage.

McCroskey, J. C., & Daly, J. A. (1987). *Personality and interpersonal communication.* Newbury Park, CA: Sage.

Mead, G. H. (1934). *Mind, self and society.* Chicago: University of Chicago Press.

Motley, M. T. (1988, January). Taking the terror out of talk. *Psychology Today,* pp. 46-49.

Norton, R. (1978). Foundation of a communicator style construct. *Human Communication Research, 4,* 99-112.

Norton, R. (1983). *Communicator style.* Beverly Hills: Sage.

O'Keefe, B. (1988). Three logics of message design: Individual differences in reasoning about communication. *Communication Monographs, 55,* 80-103.

Richendoller, N. R., & Weaver, J. B., III (1994). Exploring the links between personality and empathic response style. *Personality and Individual Differences, 17,* 303-311.

Richmond, V. P., & McCroskey, J. C. (1992). *Communication: Apprehension, avoidance, and effectiveness* (3rd ed.). Scottsdale, AZ: Gorsuch Scarisbrick.

Searle, J. R. (1969). *Speech acts.* Cambridge: Cambridge University Press.

Villaume, W. A., & Cegala, D. J. (1988). Interaction involvement and discourse strategies: The patterned use of cohesive devices in conversation. *Communication Monographs, 55,* 22-40.

Watson, K. W., Barker, L. L., & Weaver, J. B. (1995). The Listening Styles Profile (LSP-16): Development and validation of an instrument to assess four listening styles. *International Journal of Listening, 9,* 1-13.

Weaver, J. B., III, & Kirtley, M. D. (1995). Listening styles and empathy. *The Southern Communication Journal, 60*(2), 131-140.

Weaver, J. B., III, Richendoller, N. R., & Kirtley, M. D. (1995, November). *Individual differences in communication style.* Paper presented at the annual meeting of the Speech Communication Association, San Antonio, TX.

Weaver, J. B., III, Watson, K. W., & Barker L. L. (1996). Personality and listening preferences: Do you hear what I hear? *Personality and Individual Differences, 20*, 381-387.

Wheeless, L. R. (1975). An investigation of receiver apprehension and social context dimensions of communication apprehension. *The Speech Teacher, 24*, 261-268.

Wheeless, V. E., & Lashbrook, W. B. (1987). Style. In J. C. McCroskey & J. A. Daly (Eds.), *Personality and interpersonal communication* (pp. 243-272). Newbury Park, CA: Sage.

Wiemann, J. M. (1977). Explication and test of a model of communicative competence. *Human Communication Research, 3*, 195 - 213.

Zuckerman, M. (1991). *Psychobiology of personality*. Cambridge: Cambridge University Press.

Zuckerman, M., Kuhlman, D. M., & Camac, C. (1988). What lies beyond E and N? Factor analyses of scales believed to measure basic dimensions of personality. *Journal of Personality and Social Psychology, 54*, 96-107.

5

Willingness to Communicate

James C. McCroskey
Virginia P. Richmond
West Virginia University

Although talk is a vital component of communication, and a critical factor for the development of most human relationships, people differ dramatically in the degree to which they actually do talk, and probably even more dramatically in the extent to which they would prefer to talk. Some people tend to speak only when spoken to by others, and some not even then. Others tend to be extremely high verbalizers, even being driven compulsively to communicate to excess.

Every person's characteristic communication behavior falls somewhere along a continuum between the extremes of high and low verbalization. This behavior is a manifestation of the individual's preference for initiating communication in interaction with the everyday environments with which the individual comes in contact.

More than 2,000 years ago the Greeks wrote of people who were reluctant to speak. Similarly, in today's popular literature there are many references to people who are "quiet," as well as descriptions of some people as being those who "talk too much" (McCroskey &

Richmond, 1993, 1995). It is clear that such strong tendencies represent trait-driven behavior. Such trait-based behavior is genetically programmed in the individual at birth, much as size is genetically programmed at birth. Of course, appropriate diet and/or exercise may be able to modify an individual's size and/or proportions to some extent. Similarly, an individual's genetic tendencies with regard to talk may also be shaped as a function of the environment in which he or she is raised. For example, even though two children might have very similar genetic predispositions, the child raised in a typical Japanese home would be less likely to be highly verbal than the one raised in a typical North American home. One should not, however, make too much of the potential of environment to overpower genetic communication tendencies. Available evidence indicates a very powerful genetic impact and a comparatively very weak environmental influence (Bates & Wachs, 1994).

Whether a person is willing to communicate with another person in a given situation, of course, certainly is affected by the situational constraints of that encounter. Many situational variables can have an impact. How the person feels that day, what communication the person has had with others recently, who the other person is, what that person looks like, what might be gained or lost through communicating, and what other demands on the person's time are present can all have a major impact, as can a wide variety of other elements not specified here.

An individual's level of willingness to communicate, even though it is primarily genetically driven, is in part situationally dependent. Nevertheless, individuals exhibit regular willingness-to-communicate tendencies across situations. Consistent behavioral tendencies with regard to frequency and amount of talk have been noted in the research literature since the 1940s (Borgatta & Bales, 1953; Chapple & Arensberg, 1940; Goldman-Eisler, 1951). Such regularity in communication behaviors across communication contexts confirms the existence of the personality-type trait we have chosen to call *willingness to communicate* (WTC; McCroskey & Richmond, 1987). The WTC trait is an individual's predisposition to initiate communication with others. It is this trait orientation that explains why one person will initiate communication, whereas another will not even under identical or virtually identical situational constraints. It is believed by many that this trait is the one that is the most central trait to human communication. Certainly, the predisposition toward approaching or avoiding communication must be one of the most critical aspects of communication behavior (Gray, 1991).

FORMULATION OF THE WTC CONSTRUCT

Foundations of the WTC Construct

Although it had its earliest origins with the work of Phillips (1965, 1968) on reticence, the present WTC construct has evolved from the earlier work of Burgoon (1976) on unwillingness to communicate, Mortensen, Arntson, and Lustig (1977) on predispositions toward verbal behavior, and McCroskey and Richmond (1982) on shyness. All of these writings center on a presumed traitlike predisposition toward communication.

Unwillingness to Communicate. Burgoon (1976) originated the first construct that clearly falls within this area. She labeled her construct *unwillingness to communicate.* She described this predisposition as "a chronic tendency to avoid and/or devalue oral communication" (p. 60). To argue the existence of such a predisposition, Burgoon drew on work in the areas of anomie and alienation, introversion, self-esteem, and communication apprehension (CA). All of these areas of research (which are considered later) indicate variability in people's willingness to talk in various communication settings.

A self-report measure, the Unwillingness-to-Communicate scale (UCS), was developed as an operational definition of the construct. The measure was found to include two factors. One factor was labeled *approach-avoidance* and subsequently was found to be so highly correlated with a measure of communication apprehension as to be virtually interchangeable with such a measure. The other factor was labeled *reward.* This factor was not correlated with a measure of apprehension ($r = .01$).

Data reported by Burgoon (1976), while pointing to the potential usefulness of one dimension of the UCS to measure apprehension, also demonstrated it was not a valid operationalization of the construct that had been advanced. The scores on the approach-avoidance (apprehension) factor were found to be correlated with a measure of CA, total participation in a small group, and amounts of information giving and information-seeking in a small group. The reward factor was uncorrelated with any of these criterion measures. In contrast, scores on the reward factor were correlated with satisfaction with a group, attraction to group members, and perceived coordination in a group, whereas scores on the approach-avoidance factor were uncorrelated with these criterion measures.

These results were discouraging because the behavioral measures of communication, which could be taken as validating a willingness or unwillingness to communicate predisposition, were only correlated with the apprehension factor scores. Thus, the results did not provide support for a general predisposition of unwillingness to communicate. Rather, they only replicated other research that indicates that people who are fearful or anxious about communication are likely to engage in less communication than others—a finding observed many times before and since this investigation.

The results of the validation research for the UCS, then, suggest that the measure is not a valid operationalization of the construct of a global predisposition to be willing or unwilling to communicate. Subsequent research employing the UCS has reinforced this conclusion. Although the apprehension factor of the instrument may be used appropriately as a measure of CA neither factor has been demonstrated to measure the construct for which it was developed. However, the results of this research do not deny the possible existence of such a predisposition. In fact, they provide additional evidence that there is some regularity in the amount a person communicates.

Predispositions toward Verbal Behavior. Mortensen et al. (1977) argued that "the more global features of speech tend to be consistent from one class of social situations to another" (p. 146). Although they recognize the importance of variance in situational characteristics in determining how much a person will communicate, they note findings from more than 25 years of research that indicate consistency in the amount of an individual's communication exists across communication situations. They suggest there is a characteristic predisposition of an individual to talk a given amount and that predisposition operates within the constraints of individual situations. They label this phenomenon *predispositions toward verbal behavior.*

Unlike Burgoon (1976), these authors do not explore the possible causes of the global predisposition. Rather, they simply argue that it exists and provide a self-report scale that is designed to measure it. This measure is known as the Predispositions toward Verbal Behavior (PVB) scale. It is a 25-item, Likert-type scale employing a seven-step response option.

On the basis of the data reported by Mortensen et al. (1977), the PVB appears to be a unidimensional scale, although they indicate an interpretable multiple-factor solution can be forced. Only one of the five factors interpreted centered on a general disinclination to engage in communication. The remaining factors appeared to measure dominance in communication, initiating and maintaining interpersonal communication, frequency and duration of communication, and anxiety about communication.

Data on validity indicate the ability of the PVB to significantly predict both number of words spoken and duration of talk in interpersonal interactions. This is a positive indication of validity of the scale. However, since only 5 of the 25 items focus directly on a general willingness or unwillingness to communicate (the communication disinclination factor), the reason for the obtained predictive validity is in considerable doubt.

A reported high correlation of the PVB with a measure of communication apprehension ($r = .67$) increases that doubt. As noted previously, considerable research prior and subsequent to the development of the PVB has found apprehension to be predictive of the amount a person talks in various settings. CA measures are not presumed to be direct measures of a global predisposition to approach or avoid communication. Rather, they are presumed to be indicants of the amount of fear or anxiety an individual is likely to experience about communication. Such fear or anxiety, however, is likely to be one of the antecedents of general predispositions to be willing or unwilling to communicate, although certainly not the only one.

The PVB, therefore, does not appear to be a valid operationalization of a general predisposition to be willing or unwilling to communicate. As was the case with the UCS, however, the research results based on the PVB provide additional indications that some regularity exists in the amount an individual communicates.

Shyness. *Shyness* is a term that has been used by many researchers when investigating traitlike predispositions toward communication. Unfortunately, some researchers fail to provide any definition of the term, and those who do are far from universal agreement on its definition. Leary (1983), basing his efforts on earlier work on shyness, generated a construct he called *social anxiety.* He noted two components in his construct—an internally experienced discomfort and an externally observable behavior. Some writers in the area of shyness have focused on the internal experience. Their work has paralleled work in the area of CA. Others have focused on shyness as reduced communication behaviors. This approach appears to be consistent with a concern for a predisposition toward WTC.

Our work (McCroskey & Richmond, 1982) falls into the latter category. We defined *shyness* as "the tendency to be timid, reserved, and most specifically, talk less." We suggested that apprehension is one of possibly numerous elements that could impact that tendency, but stress that the two predispositions are conceptually distinct.

In earlier work, the attempt was made to develop a simplified version of a measure for use in a study with preliterate children (McCroskey, Andersen, Richmond, & Wheeless, 1981). As a serendipitous artifact of that work, a self-report scale was developed that was factorially distinct from, yet substantially correlated with, a measure of CA. The items on the scale centered on the amount of talking that people report they do. Initially, the new instrument was named the Verbal Activity scale (VAS), but we reversed the scoring of the scale and changed its name to the Shyness scale (SS) in later reports of its use. It has come to be known as the McCroskey Shyness Scale (MSS) to distinguish it from a number of other shyness measures developed by other people. Most of these other scales focus on anxiety about communication rather than shyness as a behavioral construct. Hence, we refer to this scale as the MSS here.

We believed the MSS was tapping a construct distinctly different from, although related to, the construct of CA. We attempted to validate both of the measures (shyness—MSS and CA—PRCA) by examining their independence through factor analysis and their relationships with reports of communication behaviors taken from untrained observers who were friends of the subjects completing the measures. Employing both normal college student and older adult samples, we found that the measures were factorially distinct, as had been found in the early work, and were both significant predictors of observer reports of communication behavior. The validity coefficient for the MSS with observer reports of behavior was .53, a level generally considered quite high for self-report data with observation of actual behavior (McCroskey & Richmond, 1982).

Although these results suggest the MSS is a valid measure of something, it is not evidence indicating that something is a predisposition to be willing or unwilling to communicate. The MSS is a self-report of the amount of talk in which one typically engages. The data from the McCroskey and Richmond (1982) study suggests the scores generated are valid predictors of the amount of talk in which observers see the individual engage. Even if we grant the validity of observer reports as quality indicants of actual behavior, this simply means the MSS is a valid report of behavioral tendencies in communication. It does not validate the existence of a personality-based predisposition to be willing or unwilling to communicate. That a person can with considerable accuracy, self-report whether he or she talks a lot or a little does not necessarily demonstrate that the behavior being reported is consistent with a predispositional desire, much less produced by such a predisposition.

As was the case with the research involving the UTC and PVB noted previously, the research involving the MSS lends additional support for the argument that some regularity exists in the amount an individual communicates. Unfortunately, it is not clear that the MSS is a measure of a personality-based predisposition to be willing or unwilling to communicate, even though it may be a valid measure of a behavioral tendency to communicate more or less.

The Current WTC Construct

With the development and validation of the WTC scale (McCroskey, 1992; McCroskey & Richmond, 1987), we now have an appropriate measure to employ in studies of willingness to communicate. This has permitted refinement of the earlier conceptualization of WTC, particularly in terms of the variables that were originally indicated as the antecedents of WTC.

In the original conceptualization of the antecedents of WTC, a number of probable antecedents were introduced. Three of these (anomie, alienation, and self-esteem) were found to have statistically significant, but very modest, correlations with WTC ($r < .25$). Thus, although it remains reasonable to presume that people who are anomic or alienated from the people around them, or who have low self-esteem, are less likely to be willing to communicate than others, any causal link of WTC with these antecedents would of necessity be quite small, given the observed correlations, and could be expected to account for very little variance in WTC.

In contrast, correlations of WTC with introversion, CA, and self-perceived communication competence have been found to be much more substantial and to be present in a variety of cultures (McCroskey & Richmond, 1990). The relationship between WTC and introversion has varied across cultures from -.19 to -.43. The relation with CA has been consistently higher, -.44 to -.52, and the relation with self-reported communication competence even higher, .44 to .80. The relation between WTC and introversion/extraversion suggests that WTC is most likely a very stable trait. As McCrae and Costa (1994) noted:

Stability appears to characterize all five of the major domains of personality—neuroticism, extraversion, openness to experience, agreeableness, and conscientiousness. This finding suggests that an adult's personality profile as a whole will change little over time, and studies of the stability of configural measures of personality support that view. (p. 173)

Because CA and self-perceived communication competence are correlated with introversion at levels similar to the relation of introversion and WTC, it appears that all of these constructs may fall within the general introversion/extraversion domain of personality. Because introversion/extra-version has been demonstrated to have a substantial genetic component, this is an indication that these communication predispositions probably are genetically produced and not primarily a function of environmental influence as some have thought. In any event, the two antecedents of WTC that have been demonstrated to have the highest correlation with the WTC scale are CA and self-perceived communication competence. We consider CA in a subsequent chapter. In the following section, we examine the theoretic linkage between self-perceived communication competence and WTC.

SELF-PERCEIVED COMMUNICATION COMPETENCE

Phillips' (1965, 1968) early writings on "reticence" made clear that he was interested in studying people who had a tendency to avoid communication. That view of reticence and our contemporary view of WTC are very similar. It should not be surprising, therefore, that Phillips' two views of the causes of reticence—anxiety about communication and lack of communication skills—have received support from the empirical research on WTC.

The support for Phillips' early anxiety explanation is direct. Correlations across cultures between CA and WTC range from -.44 to -.52. Clearly, people who are highly communication apprehensive are less willing to communicate than are others who are less apprehensive.

The support for the communication skills explanation is less direct, and we must modify Phillips' position somewhat to claim full support. Earlier work by reticence researchers (Kelly, 1982) failed to support the skills explanation. The communication skills of self-identified reticent speakers were not found to differ from those of nonreticent speakers. The reason for this lack of support may well be that it is not a person's actual communication competence or skill that determines one's WTC, but rather it may be the individual's self-perception of that competence or skill. Phillips implicitly confirmed that assumption by selecting people to be treated for reticence in large part on the basis of their self-reports of their competence and skills through a questionnaire followed by an interview rather than using observations of their behavior as the primary aspect of this diagnosis.

We have indicated elsewhere that self-reports are not necessarily a valid way to measure a person's actual communication competence or skill (McCroskey & McCroskey, 1988). Validity of such measures must be demonstrated by correlations with more direct behavioral or observational measures. However, it is questionable whether some people really are aware of their own competence or skill. Given the number of incompetent communicators we daily come in contact with who continue to force their communication on others, self-reports of communication competence do not have an overpowering level of face validity as true measures of competence.

Regardless of the validity of our self-perceptions, however, we do make decisions about whether or not to initiate communication (at both trait and situational levels) on the basis of how competent we think we are. Hence, on *a priori* grounds we predicted a substantial correlation between such self-perceptions of communication competence and scores on the WTC, and this prediction was confirmed across cultures with positive correlations between self-perceived communication competence, as measured by the Self-Perceived Communication Competence (SPCC) scale (McCroskey & McCroskey, 1988), and WTC, as measured by the WTC scale. The correlations ranged from a low of .44 in Sweden (McCroskey, Burroughs, Daun, & Richmond, 1990) to a high of .80 in Micronesia (Burroughs & Marie, 1990).

The extremely high correlation in Micronesia is particularly interesting. The subjects in that study were college students at the University of Guam. The students come to the university from the various islands of Micronesia with a very wide variety of first languages. English is a second language for the overwhelming majority of these students and all instruction, as well as most interpersonal contact, is conducted in that second language. Competence in English, therefore, is closely equated with competence in communication. Thus, communication skills developed over a lifetime in a first language may be seen as (or actually be) irrelevant when speaking in English. This group reported both the lowest WTC and the lowest SPCC scores of any cultural group yet studied, as well as the highest correlation between these scores.

It is clear from the research that has involved measurement of WTC, CA, and SPCC that these are very distinct constructs. However, these constructs are related in predictable ways. At this point, WTC appears to the best predictor of actual communication approach—avoidance behavior, whereas CA and SPCC appear to measure the factors which make the major contribution to prediction of a person's WTC.

Although we presume that the relations discussed here are causal ones, and the limited data available that permit causal inferences point in this direction (MacIntyre, 1994), more research is needed to clearly delineate the nature of causality in this area. At this time we certainly cannot rule out an overwhelming impact of genetics in the determination of individuals' levels of WTC, CA, and SPCC, as well as the interrelationships among these variables. In fact, we presently see the genetic explanation of these predispositions as clearly the most justified.

Effects of WTC

The presumed direct impact of a person's level of WTC is to push the individual to initiate communication more, or less, in accordance with that predisposition. Thus, if a person has a lower level of willingness, we would presume he or she would take steps to avoid or withdraw from contexts where others would initiate communication or where he or she would be expected to initiate communication. In contrast, if a person has a high level of willingness, we might expect that person to be present in contexts where communication is expected, or even demanded. High WTC people would be expected to gravitate into occupations that encourage or demand communication, whereas low WTC people would be expected to gravitate toward occupations that demand less communication.

Research has provided extremely strong support for these speculations, including research that was conducted prior to the conceptualization and operationalization of WTC. People who are more willing to communicate do indeed talk more, and they do so across virtually every context studied—and, of course, people who are less willing do talk less. The fact that these assumptions have been confirmed is important for the validation of the construct and its measure. But the next level of effect is of considerably greater importance.

Research in the United States has generally confirmed the hypothesis that more talk is seen as a positive attribute and less talk is seen as a negative attribute (e.g., Daly, McCroskey, & Richmond, 1977; Hayes & Metzger, 1972). Increased talkativeness is associated with perceptions of competence, leadership, friendliness, intelligence, attractiveness, and a whole array of other positive characteristics. Low levels of talkativeness, on the other hand, are associated with perceptions of coldness, incompetence, unfriendliness, and an array of other negative characteristics. Thus, in general positive perceptions of people have a linear relation with the amount of talk in which they engage.

Caution should be exercised when generalizing this research to cultures outside North America. Some research has indicated the impact of talk is similar to that in the United States in other Western societies. However, it is highly unlikely that these patterns will be found to exist in many African and Asian cultures. It may well be that reverse relation will be found in some of these cultures.

With the exception of possible cultural variations, then, it can be concluded that a higher willingness to communicate is a more positive trait for an individual to possess. High levels of this trait will typically lead to a wide variety of positive outcomes (Daly & Stafford, 1984; Richmond, 1984). An extremely large number of these outcomes have been confirmed through research in interpersonal, instructional, and organizational contexts.

Future research involving the WTC construct needs to examine the impact of this trait in a variety of contexts not yet examined, such as contexts where we would presume that one would be expected to be less talkative. There are contexts in interpersonal relationships (such as when conflict occurs) when reduced communication might be expected to be a wise strategy. Similarly, high talkativeness in some organizational contexts might be very detrimental.

It is also important to examine this construct in varied cultural environments. The general U.S. stereotype is that "talk is good." That stereotype is not shared by many Confucian cultures. What impact does this have when cultures with varying views of the value of talk come in contact? Can people be taught to moderate their WTC trait under such circumstances? These are important questions given that in the next century the isolation of divergent cultures from one another will be reduced to a level even lower than today.

REFERENCES

Bates, J. E., & Wachs, T. D. (Eds.). (1994). *Temperament: Individual differences at the interface of biology and behavior.* Washington, DC: American Psychological Association.

Borgatta, E. F., & Bales, R. F. (1953). Interaction of individuals in reconstituted groups. *Sociometry, 16,* 302-320.

Burgoon, J. K. (1976). The unwillingness-to-communicate scale: Development and validation. *Communication Monographs, 43,* 60-69.

Burroughs, N. F., & Marie, V. (1990). Communication orientations of Micronesian and American students. *Communication Research Reports, 7,* 139-146.

Chapple, E. D., & Arensberg, C. M. (1940). Measuring human relations: An introduction to the study of the interaction of individuals. *Genetic Psychology Monographs, 22*, 143-147.

Daly, J. A., McCroskey, J. C., & Richmond, V. P. (1977). The relationships between vocal activity and perceptions of communicators in small group interaction. *Western Speech Communication, 41*, 175-187.

Daly, J. C., & Stafford, L. (1984). Correlates and consequences of social-communicative anxiety. In J. A. Daly & J. C. McCroskey (Eds.), *Avoiding communication: Shyness, reticence, and communication apprehension* (pp. 125-143). Beverly Hills, CA: Sage.

Goldman-Eisler, F. (1951). The measurement of time sequences in conversational behavior. *British Journal of Psychology, 42*, 355-362.

Gray, J. A. (1991). The neuropsychology of temperament. In J. Stela & A. Angleitner (Eds.), *Explorations in temperament* (pp. 105-128). New York: Plenum.

Hayes, D., & Metzger, L. (1972). Interpersonal judgements based on talkativeness: Fact or artifact. *Sociometry, 35*, 538-561.

Kelly, L. (1982). *Observers' comparisons of the interpersonal communication skills of reticent and non-reticent students*. Paper presented at the annual Speech Communication Association Convention, Louisville, KY.

Leary, M. R. (1983). Social anxiousness: The construct and its measurement. *Journal of Personality Assessment, 47*, 65-75.

MacIntyre, P. D. (1994). Variables underlying willingness to communicate: A causal analysis. *Communication Research Reports, 11*, 135-142.

McCrae, R. R., & Costa, P. T., Jr. (1994). The stability of personality: Observations and evaluations. *Current Directions in Psychological Science, 3*, 173-175.

McCroskey, J. C. (1992). Reliability and validity of the willingness to communicate scale. *Communication Quarterly, 40*, 16-25.

McCroskey, J.C., Anderson, J.F., Richmond, V. P., & Wheeless, L.R. (1981). Communication apprehension of elementary and secondary students and teachers. *Communication Education, 30*, 122-132.

McCroskey, J. C., Burroughs, N. F., Daun, A., & Richmond, V.P. (1990). Correlates of quietness: Swedish and American perspectives. *Communication Quarterly, 38*, 127 - 137.

McCroskey, J. C., & McCroskey, L. L. (1988). Self-report as an approach to measuring communication competence. *Communication Research Reports, 5*, 108-113.

McCroskey, J. C., & Richmond, V. P. (1982). Communication apprehension and shyness: Conceptual and operational distinctions. *Central States Speech Journal, 33*, 458-468.

McCroskey, J. C., & Richmond, V. P. (1987). Willingness to communicate. In J. C. McCroskey & J. A. Daly (Eds.), *Personality and interpersonal communication* (pp. 129-156). Beverly Hills, CA: Sage.

McCroskey, J. C., & Richmond, V. P. (1990). Willingness to communicate: Differing cultural perspectives. *The Southern Communication Journal, 56*, 72-77

McCroskey, J. C., & Richmond, V. P. (1993). Identifying compulsive communicators: The talkaholic scale. *Communication Research Reports, 10*, 107-114.

McCroskey, J. C., & Richmond, V. P. (1995). Correlates of compulsive communication: Quantitative and qualitative characteristics. *Communication Quarterly, 43*, 39-52.

Mortensen, D. C., Arntson, P. H., & Lustig, M. (1977). The measurement of verbal predispositions: Scale development and application. *Human Communication Research, 3*, 146-158.

Phillips, G. M. (1965). The problem of reticence. *Pennsylvania Speech Annual, 22*, 22-38.

Phillips, G. M. (1968). Reticence: Pathology of the normal speaker. *Speech Monographs, 35*, 39-49.

Richmond, V. P. (1984). Implications of quietness: Some facts and speculations. In J. A. Daly & J. C. McCroskey (Eds.), *Avoiding communication: Shyness, reticence, and communication apprehension* (pp. 145-155). Beverly Hills, CA: Sage.

6

Sociocommunicative Style and Sociocommunicative Orientation

Virginia P. Richmond
Matthew M. Martin
West Virginia University

Individuals exhibit trait differences in their basic communication styles (Norton, 1983). In addition to the work of Norton, communication styles have been examined under such labels as *personal style* (Merrill & Reid, 1981), *social style* (Lashbrook, 1974), and *psychological androgyny* (Bem, 1974; Wheeless & Dierks-Stewart, 1981). Other than Norton's work, the various approaches to communication style have been rooted in Jungian psychology. This work has its best known manifestation in the Myers-Briggs personality inventory. All of these approaches are based on the assumption that trait differences in communication behavior are produced by an individual's temperament or personality.

The style-based approaches typically identify either two or three dimensions of an individual's style that are assumed to produce different communication behaviors. The two primary dimensions commonly are labeled *assertiveness* (called *masculinity* by Bem) and *responsiveness* (called *femininity* by Bem) and are presumed to represent the core elements in style. The third dimension usually is called *versatility* or *flexibility* and represents the degree to which the individual is capable of adapting her or his style to varying situational constraints.

The constructs of sociocommunicative style (SCS) and sociocommunicative orientation (SCO) are based on these earlier research programs (Thomas, Richmond, & McCroskey, 1994). Both constructs presume three dimensions. The two constructs are essentially the same. SCO represents the way one perceives oneself. It is that person's image of his or her own trait behavior pattern. SCS, on the other hand, is the perception others have of that individual—presumably based on his or her regular communication behavior patterns. The two need not be highly correlated, because the individual may not be particularly perceptive of his or her own behaviors, and/or that individual may behave quite differently with different observers. Because both sources and receivers make many decisions based on their perceptions of themselves and others with whom they communicate, both SCO and SCS are seen as very important for understanding communication behavior.

Because SCO and SCS are based in part on the work of Merrill and Reid (1981), it is useful to examine the way they interpret various combinations of scores on measures of assertiveness and responsiveness. Merrill and Reid indicated that social style is a collection of observable communication behaviors that impact one's effectiveness in interpersonal and organizational relationships. They argued that people are creatures of habit and by identifying their own and others' social style, people could have more beneficial and satisfying relationships. Depending on whether people are high or low in assertiveness and high or low in responsiveness, Merrill and Reid would classify them into one of four categories: amiable, analytical, driver, and expressive.

Amiables are high in responsiveness but low in assertiveness. Merrill and Reid (1981) stated that amiable individuals are those who focus on relationships, people who enjoy interacting with others, and who attempt to use mutual understanding versus compliance in attempting to influence others. Amiables often focus their attention on the people in the situation, not the task at hand. According to Merrill and Reid, amiables are slow or reluctant to change, especially when they perceive change as possibly hurting a personal relationship that they have. Commitment is a very important factor to these individuals.

Analyticals are low in responsiveness and low in assertiveness. Sometimes these people may appear cold, aloof, or unenthusiastic because they tend to focus on facts and reasoning. Merrill and Reid (1981) noted that analyticals have a "show me" attitude; these people often do not make decisions based on personal relationships, but instead make decisions on evidence and experience. Although analyticals might be slow in making a decision or in being persuaded, once a decision is made, analyticals tend to stand by it because the decision was arrived at rationally.

Drivers are low in responsiveness but high in assertiveness. Merrill and Reid (1981) stated that drivers know what they want and they do whatever it takes in order to accomplish their given goals. These individuals are action-oriented and are not very patient. Drivers initiate action, are power-driven, and are often very independent thinkers. In comparison to analytics, they are more likely to take risks in making decisions, allowing their instincts to overrule the apparent evidence. Drivers also have a high need for control.

Expressives are high in responsiveness and high in assertiveness. Merrill and Reid (1981) suggested that expressive individuals value relationships, but at the same time, are very goals-focused, and many times may use their relationships in order to attain personal goals. Like drivers, expressives are very action-oriented, but whereas drivers tend to consider evidence more, expressives trust their intuition. Expressives are creative, imaginative, future-oriented, adaptable, and status-oriented (Merrill & Reid, 1981). Expressives do not have a high need for regularity in their routines and are quite flexible in their behaviors.

Although people might identify one of these styles as more attractive to them than the others, Merrill and Reid (1981) argued that each style has value and that no one style is necessarily better than the others. They also pointed out the need for versatility: Individuals need to be able to change and adapt their behaviors according to the situation.

COMPONENTS OF SCO AND SCS

The three variables that influence a person's SCO and SCS are assertiveness, responsiveness, and versatility. The following sections review each of these three constructs.

Assertiveness

When people stand up for themselves and do not let others take advantage of them, without taking advantage of others themselves, they are acting assertively. It is also acting assertively to speak up for one's self, whether that is making a request or expressing a feeling. Assertive communicators are also able to initiate, maintain, and terminate conversations, according to their interpersonal goals (McCroskey & Richmond, 1996). Assertive communicators talk faster and louder, use more gestures, make more eye contact, and lean forward more in interactions (Merrill & Reid, 1981). Assertiveness focuses on the task dimension of relationships (Wheeless & Lashbrook, 1987). Many of these assertive behaviors are considered to be masculine behaviors (Bem, 1974), but this does mean that these behaviors are limited only to men. Both men and women can display assertive behaviors. Stereotypically, however, males are more assertive than women are in the general U.S. culture.

It is often difficult to distinguish between assertiveness and aggressiveness. Although it is true that assertive behavior often is aggressive (i.e., defending one's self against attacks instead of quietly accepting another person's condemnation), there is an important distinction to be made between the two constructs. McCroskey and Richmond (1996) argued that aggressiveness could be considered as "assertiveness plus." In other words, the aggressive person acts similarly to the assertive person in that both will speak up to demand what is rightfully theirs, but the aggressive person will attempt to be successful, many times forcing others to yield their own rights. The assertive person does not hinder others' chances of being successful, whereas the aggressive person has a "win-at-all-costs" mentality. Another distinction is that the assertive person makes requests while the aggressive person makes demands (McCroskey & Richmond, 1996). Although either assertive or aggressive behavior can lead to goal achievement, assertive behavior is more likely to lead to long-term effectiveness while maintaining good relationships with others. The aggressive person might win in the short term, but probably burns a few bridges along the way.

One variable that impacts greatly a person's assertiveness is communication apprehension (CA) (Richmond & McCroskey, 1995). A person who is likely to be reluctant to communicate is less likely to defend him or herself or voice his or her opinion. The unassertive individual will often be taken advantage of and often would be unable to reach personal goals due to lack of assertiveness.

Responsiveness

Responsiveness involves being other-oriented. In other words, the responsive person is sensitive to others. The responsive individual considers other's feelings, listens to what others have to say, and recognizes the needs of others (McCroskey & Richmond, 1996). Words that are commonly used to describe the responsive communicator include *friendly, compassionate, warm, sincere*, and *helpful* (Talley & Richmond, 1980). The responsive communicator is able to be empathic and immediate when interacting with others. Responsive communicators speak with greater inflection, use open body gestures, and show animated facial expressions (Merrill & Reid, 1981). Responsiveness focuses on the relational dimension of relationships. Many of these responsive behaviors are considered to be feminine (Bem, 1974). This does not imply that only women can be responsive. Just like there are men and women who are assertive, there are men and women who are responsive. Stereotypically, however, females are more responsive than males are in the general U.S. culture.

Being responsive does not mean that a person always complies with the wishes and demands of others. There is an important difference between being submissive and being responsive. Submissives yield their rights to others, even when yielding their rights goes against their own goals or needs. Submissive communicators sacrifice their own goals in order to benefit others. On the other hand, although the responsive communicator is considerate of other's needs, the responsive communicator also pays attention to his or her own goals. The responsive person recognizes and considers the other person's needs and rights, but does this without sacrificing his or her own legitimate rights. McCroskey and Richmond (1996) noted that being submissive or responsive will probably produce short-term liking from another person, but they added that responsive communicators are able to maintain liking in a relationship and still reach their own interpersonal goals.

Similar to the relation between assertiveness and CA, CA also has an impact on responsiveness. Shy people or those reluctant to communicate in general are also likely to be apprehensive about communicating responsively. In order to avoid future interactions, to decrease CA or due to lack of interpersonal capabilities, people may act cold and indifferent, instead of communicating responsively. Responsive behaviors often send nonverbal messages inviting ongoing or future interactions. The CA person would not want interaction to continue, and thus would be less inclined to communicate responsively.

Versatility

Because all communication takes place in a given context, it is difficult, if not impossible, to identify communication behaviors that are appropriate and effective in all situations. Thus, the third dimension of SCO is versatility (McCroskey & Richmond, 1996). Other terms that are used for versatility include *accommodating, adaptability, flexibility, rhetorical sensitivity,* and *style-flexing* (Duran, 1992; Hart, Carlson, & Eadie, 1980; Martin & Rubin, 1994, 1995; Richmond & McCroskey, 1992; Spitzberg & Cupach, 1984). Words that demonstrate a lack of versatility include *rigid, dogmatic, uncompromising,* and *unyielding* (McCroskey & Richmond, 1996). The importance of versatility is that in addition to being assertive and responsive, individuals must be versatile; they need to know when to be assertive and when to be responsive. Similarly, they need to also know when not to be assertive and when not to be responsive. The idea behind versatility is that people need to be able to adapt their behavior within a situation and from situation to situation (Wiemann, 1977).

Another way of looking at versatility (i.e., flexibility) is a person's ability to relate in new ways when necessary (Bochner & Kelly, 1974). Flexible people recognize that in any given situation there are various alternatives from which to choose. People need to choose from their assertive and responsive behaviors which messages would be appropriate and effective in given situations. In identifying the flexible person, Bochner and Kelly noted that the person high in flexibility would likely have a high number of interactions with others, would make a high number of owning statements, and would offer constructive, versus damaging, feedback to others. Seemingly, the communicator who has a wide repertoire of assertive and responsive behaviors, who also has flexibility, would be able to adapt messages according to the contextual elements of the situation. "Communicating effectively with different people on different topics and at different times requires flexible communication behaviors" (Richmond & McCroskey, 1992, p. 86).

MEASUREMENT OF SCO AND SCS

In 1990, Richmond and McCroskey formally introduced their assertiveness-responsiveness measure. Their intention was to recognize a measure that was currently being used in instructional settings, as well as in research projects, as reliable and independent measures of assertiveness and responsiveness.

Based on the earlier work (Bem, 1974; Merrill & Reid, 1981; Wheeless & Dierks-Stewart, 1981), Richmond and McCroskey identified 10 items for assertiveness and 10 items for responsiveness.

The 10 assertiveness items are as follows: defends own beliefs, independent, forceful, has strong personality, assertive, dominant, willing to take a stand, acts as a leader, aggressive, and competitive. The 10 responsiveness items are as follows: helpful, responsive to others, sympathetic, compassionate, sensitive to the needs of others, sincere, gentle, warm, tender, and friendly. When used as a measure of SCO, individuals are asked to indicate how accurately each of the characteristics applies to them when they normally communicate with others. Individuals respond on a five-step continuum from 5 (*strongly agree*) to 1 (*strongly disagree*). When used as a measure of SCS, of course, individuals are asked to indicate how accurately each of the characteristics applies to another person.

Richmond and McCroskey (1990) reported that a factor analysis of the 20 items indicated that all of the items loaded on the two intended dimensions. Additionally, the two factors, assertiveness and responsiveness, were both internally reliable and not significantly correlated with each other. Thus, the measure appeared to be measuring two specific constructs that are not necessarily related to one another (i.e., just because a person is high in assertiveness does not necessarily mean that the individual is high or low in responsiveness). Both measures have consistently been found to be internally reliable in college and noncollege populations (Martin & Anderson, 1996c; Martin, Anderson, & Sirimangkala, 1996).

According to McCroskey and Richmond (1996), in order to interpret the SCO or SCS of individuals, assertiveness and responsiveness scores must be classified as either high (above 30) or low (below 30). The SCO/SCS of people who are high in assertiveness and responsiveness is described as *competent*. The SCO/SCS of people who are high in assertiveness but low in responsiveness is called *aggressive*. On the other hand, the SCO/SCS of people who are low in assertiveness but high in responsiveness is labeled *submissive*. When people are low in assertiveness and responsiveness, their SCO/SCS is classified as *noncompetent*. When people are rating their own communication behavior, the measure is called the SCO scale. When people are rating others communication behavior, the measure is called the SCS scale.

There are various measures of adaptability/flexibility/ versatility, but these measures have not been used consistently with the sociocommunicative measures to recognize individuals who are assertive, responsive, and versatile. Using the Social Style Profile (Buchholz, Lashbrook, & Wenberg, 1976), Bacon and Severson (1986) found that procedural leaders of groups were more assertive, responsive, and to some extent, versatile than the nonleaders in the groups. Martin and Anderson (1996b) looked at the relation between cognitive flexibility and assertiveness and responsiveness, using the SCO measure. Cognitive flexibility was moderately correlated with both assertiveness and responsiveness, while consistent with previous findings, assertiveness and responsiveness were not meaningfully correlated with one another. At this time however, it is difficult to recommend with confidence a communication measure for versatility that can be used along with the SCO measure to tap into the third aspect of sociocommunicative style.

RESEARCH ON SCO AND SCS

This section focuses on research that used the SCO and SCS measures. Although other research has focused on assertiveness and responsiveness specifically, and interpersonal communication competence in general, the focus here is on how assertiveness and responsiveness interact together in influencing a person's communicative behavior.

SCO and Other Communication Variables

Investigating the relation between various communication variables provides additional validity for the constructs (or identifies weaknesses in the constructs) and allows for studying how communication variables often interact with one another to achieve various relational outcomes. Several studies have used the SCO measure to study how communicator style is related to other communication variables. Some of these studies are briefly reported here.

In looking at students' perceptions of their teachers, Thomas, et al. (1994) found that teacher immediacy was positively related to assertiveness and responsiveness. Although immediacy and the two other variables were moderately correlated, the correlation between assertiveness and responsiveness was not significant. This is meaningful, according to Thomas et al., because others had proposed that immediacy was just another name for being responsive. Their results demonstrated, however, that producing perceptions of immediacy involved both assertive and responsive behaviors. Thomas et al. alluded to the fact that teachers would also need to be versatile in order to adapt their assertive and responsive behaviors in order to be effective in the classroom. Also looking at students' perceptions of their teachers, Wooten and McCroskey (1996) found that when students perceived their instructors as high in assertiveness and responsiveness, they had higher interpersonal trust with those instructors. This relationship was strongest with assertive students. When assertive students perceived their teachers as assertive and responsive, there was a higher level of trust between student and instructor. In this case, communicating assertively and responsively leads to a stronger relationship between the two parties.

Martin and Anderson (1996a) reported on the relation between SCS with the communication traits of argumentativeness and verbal aggressiveness. In defining these two aggressive communication traits, Infante (1987) stated that argumentativeness could be considered a subset of assertiveness and that verbal aggressiveness involves a lack of responsiveness toward others. Based on how each of these constructs are defined, Martin and Anderson expected that assertive communicators would be more argumentative whereas responsive communicators would be lower in verbal aggressiveness. These hypotheses were supported; people with the competent and aggressive communicator styles were more argumentative whereas those people with the competent and submissive communicator styles were less verbally aggressive.

Several studies have considered the relation between SCO and nonverbal communication behaviors. Myers and Avtgis (1996) reported that people differ in their nonverbal immediacy behaviors depending on their communicator style. Competent communicators were more nonverbally immediate; competent communicators were less tense, smiled more, and moved more than submissive and aggressive communicators. Communicator style was also found to make a difference on individuals' tendency to be touch avoidant. Martin and Anderson (1993) reported that aggressive communicators were more same-gender touch avoidant than the other types of communicators, whereas noncompetent communicators were more opposite-gender touch avoidant than the three other types of communicators. The results from both of these studies provide further support for the importance of possessing assertive and responsive behaviors.

Another study that shows real-life application for being assertive and responsive is Neupauer's (1996) investigation of the role that communication traits play in determining individuals' earnings in media occupations. In comparing higher paid television and radio workers with lower paid television and radio workers, the higher paid workers were significantly more assertive and less responsive than those who were lower paid. Thus, in this sample of members of the media, the aggressive communicator style appears to be the style to possess for financial success. Chances are, people do not receive more money just because they are high or low on a particular communication trait, but they are more likely to be rewarded or punished based on their communication messages (which are influenced by their communication traits). The following section looks at how the different SCS have differed in how they communicate.

SCO as Antecedent of Communication

Given that SCO is a communication trait, people's SCO should influence how they communicate. People high in assertiveness and responsiveness would be expected to communicate differently than people who are low in assertiveness and responsiveness. Because high responders are more focused on the feelings of others, it would be expected that they would be more other-oriented in the encoding of their messages. Several studies have looked at how the different communicator styles affect the communication choices that individuals make.

In looking at the mending of a relationship after an altercation, Patterson and Beckett (1995) asked what affinity-seeking strategies individuals used in order to increase affinity in their relationships. High assertives, compared to low assertives, were more likely to assume control and were less likely to show sensitivity. High responsives, in comparison to low responsives, were more likely to encourage self-disclosure. Patterson and Beckett concluded that their study provides evidence for the argument that SCO does influence the communication strategies individuals make.

Also looking at communication strategies, Martin, et al. (1996) studied the conflict strategies that subordinates use with their superiors in the workplace. Martin et al. found that assertive communicators (i.e., competents and aggressives), in comparison to nonassertives (i.e., noncompetents and submissives) tended not to use nonconfrontation conflict strategies and were more likely to use collaboration and control conflict strategies. In other words, people that reported being more assertive also said that they use more aggressive and less avoidant conflict strategies when in conflict with their superiors. Martin et al. also investigated how subordinates with different communicator styles differed in their use of argumentativeness and verbal aggressiveness with their superiors. Supporting the findings of Martin and Anderson (1996a), aggressive and competent subordinates claimed that they were more argumentative than submissive and noncompetent subordinates. Differing from the earlier findings, they also reported that the four different styles did not differ in their use of verbal aggressiveness with their superiors. Martin et al. proposed that all subordinates might realize that being verbally aggressive with their superiors is not only inappropriate, but also could be very detrimental to one's organizational health.

To know more about how people with different communicator styles differ in general, Anderson and Martin (1995) studied how SCO influences the reasons why people talk to one another. They found that, depending on their communicator style, people differed in their interpersonal motives for communicating with others. Competent communicators reported talking to others more to satisfy affection and pleasure needs, whereas noncompetents reported communicating more for control and escape needs. Competent communicators, in fact, communicated more for affection than submissives and aggressives as well. Although competent communicators reported talking to others more for inclusion than aggressives, aggressives said that they talked more for control. Their results support the position that in order for communicators to achieve their goals for affection, inclusion, and pleasure, they need to demonstrate versatility in their communicator styles (McCroskey & Richmond, 1996). Based on their findings, Anderson and Martin concluded that communicators high in responsive and assertive skills flexibly engage in expressive-type communication behaviors that serve both functional and relational needs.

INTERCULTURAL STUDIES

Because SCO is considered to be a communication trait, questions are then raised concerning the role of assertiveness and responsiveness in other cultures and whether the SCO measure can be adapted to be used in different cultures. Like many communication and personality traits, most of the introductory research for SCO was based on samples of individuals that live in the United States. Whether the constructs of assertiveness and responsiveness exist in a similar fashion in other cultures remains to be tested. Various researchers, however, have done preliminary work in studying assertiveness and responsiveness in other cultures.

In a cross-cultural study involving Americans, Finns, Japanese, and Koreans, Thompson and Klopf (1991) reported that U.S. males and females and Korean males were more assertive than the Finnish and Japanese males and females. Additionally, U.S. females were more responsive than males and females from the other cultures. In comparing the Americans to the Japanese specifically (Thompson, Klopf, & Ishii, 1991), U.S. females were higher in responsiveness than

Japanese females (there was no difference between the males from the two cultures). For assertiveness, U.S. males and females were more assertive than Japanese males and females. Thompson and Klopf also noted that cross-culturally, females were more responsive than males, whereas males were more assertive.

Investigating a different Asian population, Anderson, Martin, and Zhong (1996) tested a Chinese version of the SCO scale for internal reliability, separation of factors, and gender differences. People affiliated with a university in Beijing completed the Chinese version. Both the assertiveness and responsiveness measures proved to be internally reliable. A factor analysis showed that all but one of the items loaded on the appropriate factors of assertiveness and responsiveness (i.e., compassion loaded on the assertiveness factor instead of the responsiveness factor). Anderson et al. reported that Chinese males are more assertive than Chinese females, but the two groups did not differ on responsiveness.

The SCO scale has also been used in a study of Russian communication traits. Christophel (1996) reported that compared to Americans, Russians are lower in assertiveness, but slightly higher in their responsiveness. In comparing Russian males to Russian females, Russian males were more assertive whereas Russian females were more responsive. This finding is consistent with U.S. and other cultural samples (Martin & Anderson, 1996c; Thompson & Klopf, 1991).

When using any measure in a different culture, it must be realized that cultural differences may change the meaning of the items, and possibly a totally different construct could be being measured. This would be especially true for translating measures into other languages (no matter how good the translation is perceived to be). Thus, results must be considered with a great deal of caution. McCroskey (personal communication, October 1996) suggested that a possible better way of studying SCO would be to discover if the constructs of assertiveness and responsiveness are relevant in a culture, and to create culturally specific measures. Although this does not allow for direct comparison of measures, it may allow for a better understanding of communicator style and other communication variables in a given culture.

THE FUTURE OF SCO AND SCS RESEARCH

It is our view that SCO is a manifestation of the individual's basic personality or temperament. Consistent with the view advanced by

Beatty and McCroskey (chapter 2), we believe temperament, and hence, SCO is genetically based. It is important, therefore, to determine in future research the impact of varying SCOs on actual communication behavior as well as on the perceptions of others with whom the individual interacts. Equally important is research that examines other meaningful outcomes of communication of communicators with divergent SCOs. Research to date suggests that varying SCS can have a major impact on communication outcomes and the consequences of communication behavior. We would be very surprised if future research did not confirm and extend what has been found to date. If this is the case, a critical concern becomes how much a genetically influenced trait can be shaped or altered by instruction in communication. Although some work has indicated that people can be taught assertiveness skills, there is less information about instruction in responsiveness skills.

Presuming both can be taught, the crucial concern becomes whether it will make any difference. In other words, can versatility be taught? To possess assertiveness and/or responsiveness skills is of little value if one is not oriented toward using those skills and/or is unable to determine when and where those skills are appropriate and able to use them in those circumstances. We know that debating skills, for example, can be taught. But it sometimes appears that people who have developed those skills choose to use them at inappropriate as well as appropriate times. If this is the case, wouldn't it be the case with other skills as well? Future research needs to examine these concerns.

If our assumptions about the foundation of SCO are correct, it is important that we map the associations between the dimensions of SCO and the major dimensions of temperament. Are some people really born to be more effective communicators, or is effective communication a learned ability, as most in our field claim? At this point, the question remains an empirical one.

REFERENCES

Anderson, C. M., & Martin, M. M. (1995). Communication motives of assertive and responsive communicators. *Communication Research Reports, 12,* 186-191.

Anderson, C. M., Martin, M. M., & Zhong, M. (1996). *Reliability, separation of factors, and sex differences on the Assertiveness-Responsiveness measure: A Chinese sample.* Manuscript submitted for publication.

Bacon, C. C., & Severson, M. L. (1986). Assertiveness, responsiveness, and versatility as predictors of leadership emergence. *Communication Research Reports, 3,* 53-59.

Bem, S. L. (1974). The measurement of psychological androgyny. *Journal of Consulting and Clinical Psychology, 42,* 155-162.

Bochner, A. P., & Kelly, C. W. (1974). Interpersonal communication instruction—theory and practice, a symposium. I. Interpersonal competence: Rationale, philosophy, and implementation of a conceptual framework. *Speech Teacher, 23,* 279-301.

Buchholz, S., Lashbrook, W. B., & Wenberg, J. R. (1976). *Toward the measurement and processing of social style.* Paper presented at the annual meeting of the International Communication Association, Portland, OR.

Christophel, D. M. (1996). Russian communication orientations: A cross-cultural examination. *Communication Research Reports, 13,* 43-51.

Duran, R. L. (1992). Communication adaptability: A review of conceptualization and measurement. *Communication Quarterly, 40,* 253-268.

Hart, R. P., Carlson, R. E., & Eadie, W. F. (1980). Attitudes toward communication and the assessment of rhetorical sensitivity, *Communication Monographs, 47,* 1-22.

Infante, D. A. (1987). Aggressiveness. In J. C. McCroskey & J. A. Daly (Eds.), *Personality and interpersonal communication* (pp. 157-194). Newbury Park, CA: Sage.

Lashbrook, W. B. (1974). *Toward the measurement and processing of the social style profile.* Eden Prairie, MN: Wilson Learning Corporation.

Martin, M. M., & Anderson, C. M. (1993). Biological and psychological differences in touch avoidance. *Communication Research Reports, 11,* 33-44.

Martin, M. M., & Anderson, C. M. (1996a). Argumentativeness and verbal aggressiveness. *Journal of Social Behavior and Personality, 11,* 547-554.

Martin, M. M., & Anderson, C. M. (1996b). *The Cognitive Flexibility scale: Validity studies and classroom applications.* Manuscript submitted for publication.

Martin, M. M., & Anderson, C. M. (1996c). Communication traits: A cross-generational investigation. *Communication Research Reports, 13,* 58-67.

Martin, M. M., Anderson, C. M., & Sirimangkala, P. (1996). *The relationship between use of organizational conflict strategies with socio-communicative style and aggressive communication traits.* Manuscript submitted for publication.

Martin, M.M., & Rubin, R.B. (1994). Development of a communication flexibility scale. *Southern Communication Journal, 59,* 171-178.

Martin, M. M., & Rubin, R. B. (1995). A new measure of cognitive flexibility. *Psychological Reports, 76,* 623-626.

McCroskey, J. C., & Richmond, V. P. (1996). *Fundamentals of human communication: An interpersonal perspective.* Prospect Heights, IL: Waveland Press.

McCroskey, J. C., Richmond, V. P., & Stewart, R. A. (1986). *One on one: The foundations of interpersonal communication.* Englewood Cliffs, NJ: Prentice-Hall.

Merrill, D. W., & Reid, R. H. (1981). *Personal styles & effective performance.* Radnor, PA: Chilton.

Myers, S. A., & Avtgis, T. (1996). *The impact of socio-communicative style and relational context on perceptions of nonverbal immediacy.* Unpublished manuscript, Kent State University, OH.

Neupauer, N. C. (1996). Individual differences in on-air television and radio personalities. *Communication Research Reports, 13,* 77-85.

Norton, R. (1983). *Communicator style: Theory, applications, and measures.* Beverly Hills, CA: Sage.

Patterson, B. R., & Beckett, C. S. (1995). A reexamination of relational repair and reconciliation: Impact of socio-communicative style on strategy selection. *Communication Research Reports, 12,* 235-240.

Richmond, V.P., & McCroskey, J.C. (1990). Reliability and separation of factors on the assertiveness-responsiveness measure. *Psychological Reports, 67,* 449-450.

Richmond, V.P., & McCroskey, J.C. (1992). *Organizational communication for survival.* Englewood Cliffs, NJ: Prentice-Hall.

Richmond, V. P., & McCroskey, J. C. (1995). *Communication: Apprehension, avoidance and effectiveness* (3rd ed.). Scottsdale, AZ: Gorsuch-Scarisbrick.

Spitzberg, B. H., & Cupach, W. R. (1984). *Interpersonal communication competence.* Beverly Hills, CA: Sage.

Talley, M. A., & Richmond, V. P. (1980). The relationship between psychological gender orientation and communication style. *Human Communication Research, 6,* 326-344.

Thomas, C. E., Richmond, V. P., & McCroskey, J. C. (1994). The association between immediacy and socio-communicative style. *Communication Research Reports, 11,* 107-115.

Thompson, C. A., Ishii, S., & Klopf, D. W. (1990). Japanese and Americans compared on assertiveness/responsiveness. *Psychological Reports, 66,* 829-830.

Thompson, C. A., & Klopf, D. W. (1991). An analysis of social style among disparate cultures. *Communication Research Reports, 8,* 65-72.

Thompson, C. A., Klopf, D. W., & Ishii, S. (1991). A comparison of social style between Japanese and Americans. *Communication Research Reports, 8,* 165-172.

Wheeless, V. E., & Dierks-Stewart, K. (1981). The psychometric properties of the Bem sex-role inventory: Questions concerning reliability and validity. *Communication Quarterly, 29,* 173-186.

Wheeless, V. E., & Lashbrook, W. B. (1987). Style. In J. C. McCroskey & J. A. Daly (Eds.), *Personality and interpersonal communication* (pp. 243-274). Newbury Park, CA: Sage.

Wiemann, J. M. (1977). Explication and test of a model of communication competence. *Human Communication Research, 3,* 195-213.

Wooten, A. G., & McCroskey, J. C. (1996). Student trust of teacher as a function of socio-communicative style of teacher and socio-communicative orientation of student. *Communication Research Reports, 13,* 94-100.

7

Argumentativeness

Andrew S. Rancer
The University of Akron

Communication traits and predispositions have occupied a central place in the communication discipline since the 1960s. Communication journals show that a large percentage of the research and theory building activity in the discipline has been directed at understanding how communication traits and predispositions emerge, and how they influence not only actual communication *behavior,* but communication-based *perceptions* as well. Understanding the communication behavior of others can be enhanced by knowledge of the traits that individuals possess, as well as by understanding factors associated with the situations in which individuals communicate. Here and in chapter 9 (by Wigley), the "aggressive communication predispositions" of *argumentativeness* and *verbal aggressiveness* are discussed. These two communication predispositions were conceptualized by Infante (1987a). Infante, Wigley, and I worked on the explication of the traits, on the scales used to measure both dispositions, and on studies designed to see how these dispositions influence individual's perceptions and behavior in communication situations.

If you review your interactions with others you will no doubt recall instances in which your communication was marked by supportive communication and a great deal of agreement. In many interactions, you and others seemed to see the world in the same way, the positions you held on issues seemed to be almost identical. At other times, your interpersonal communication with others may have been fraught with disagreement or conflict, that is, you and your friends did not agree on issues you were discussing. The conflict may have been about something "major" such as where to take a vacation (e.g., you want to visit Cape Cod , your partner wants to go to Malibu Beach), or about something "minor" such as what flavor toothpaste to buy (e.g., you want mint-flavor, your partner wants fruit-flavored). The manner in which you and your partner manage these disagreements can help determine whether the relationship will thrive or whither. The discussion of conflict as it is exhibited via aggressive communication is the basis of the material for two chapters in this book.

Almost 20 years ago, Infante and I were attempting to develop a measure of interpersonal communication competence. We examined the literature and observed discussions of several important interpersonal communication behaviors such as empathy, openness, self-disclosure, listening, feedback, supportive communication, and paraphrasing. In examining this list of interpersonal competence behaviors we observed a lack of discussion of several other behaviors that also constitute interpersonal communication, behaviors that deal with communication during interpersonal conflict, communication behaviors that are considered aggressive in nature. We sought to study aggressive communication. We began by defining *aggressive communication*, then developed a conceptualization and measure of one form of aggressive communication, *argumentativeness*.

AGGRESSIVE COMMUNICATION

A communication behavior is aggressive "if it applies force . . . symbolically in order, minimally to dominate and perhaps damage, or maximally, to defeat and perhaps destroy the locus of the attack" (Infante, 1987a, p. 58). Aggressive communication behaviors have certain elements that distinguish them from other types of interpersonal communication behaviors. In aggressive communication, at least one person applies force to another person. The individuals involved in aggressive communication probably have elevated levels of arousal. They may, and usually do, experience some anger. "Attack" and "defend" orientations are activated. Aggressive communication behaviors are usually more active than passive, and are usually more attention-getting rather than mundane.

Infante (1987a) developed a model that suggests that aggressive communication is controlled by a cluster of four communication traits that interact with situational factors to influence a person's message producing behavior. Two traits (*assertiveness* and *argumentativeness*) are considered constructive, and two traits (*hostility* and *verbal aggressiveness*) are considered destructive. Argumentativeness is a subset of assertiveness because all argumentative behavior is considered assertive, but not all assertive behavior is considered argumentative (e.g., a request).

In your life you probably can recall instances in which an argument you had with someone was stimulating, exciting, exhilarating, and even "constructive." You may recall examples of conversations such as when you and your friends argued about who was the best pitcher in the major leagues, or which musical group was the best (I can recall arguments I had with friends about who was the better group, the Beatles or the Rolling Stones). I can still recall the excitement many of us felt when presenting our arguments on a variety of such subjects, and how satisfied I felt when I was able to convince someone that my position was the best, leading them to agree with me. Arguing with friends and colleagues was considered "fun," and was seen as almost a type of recreational activity. Because of these feelings of excitement, interest, and enjoyment you may have come to believe that arguing is a very positive activity, and is one of the best and most satisfying ways of communicating with people.

Conversely, you can probably recall several examples of arguments that were anything but constructive. That is, the argument you were in led to feelings of anger, hurt, confusion, embarrassment, and may have even led to the damaging or termination of the interpersonal relationship. Perhaps you can recall an example of an argument that became so destructive that it quickly turned to name-calling, and may have even ended up with individuals exhibiting physical aggression (e.g., shoving, pushing, hitting) and other forms of violence directed at each other! These situations may have led you to believe that arguing is a destructive form of communication, something to be avoided at all costs, even if it means having to suppress your true feelings and yield to another person's wishes.

Infante and I were perplexed by the apparent unfavorable attitudes toward arguing that existed among many individuals. Among a large number of people, the term *arguing* was equated with *fighting,* that is, people tended to use these two terms almost interchangeably. To many people with whom we spoke, having an argument with someone was seen as fighting with them. The confusion between the two terms held by many people (including several students of communication) was especially confusing to us because the communication discipline has taught since antiquity that arguing is a constructive communication activity. For example, the early sophists taught Greek citizens how to argue effectively, and the principles of argumentation have been passed down through the centuries as a rather cohesive framework of principles that today is called *argumentation theory.* The central purpose of argumentation theory, we believe, is to enable people to argue effectively and constructively. Learning how to argue effectively remains at the core of the curriculum in most U.S. schools of communication.

CONCEPTUALIZING ARGUMENTATIVE COMMUNICATION

Infante and I reasoned that at least part of the problem for the confusion with the term *arguing* existed because what people call *arguing* may not be. To clarify this point, we first set out to distinguish between *argumentativeness* and *verbal aggressiveness* (Infante & Rancer, 1982; Infante & Wigley, 1986). We defined *argumentativeness* "a generally stable trait which predisposes individuals in communication situations to advocate positions on controversial issues and to attack verbally the *positions* which other people hold on these issues" (Infante & Rancer, 1982, p. 72). Argumentativeness is contrasted with another aggressive communication trait, verbal aggressiveness, in which individuals attack the self-concept of another instead of, or in addition to another's positions on controversial issues (Infante & Wigley, 1986). Chapter 9 more fully presents the conceptualization of verbal aggressiveness. To reiterate, when individuals engage in argumentativeness, they attack the positions that others take or hold on controversial issues. When individuals engage in verbal aggressiveness they attack the self-concept of the other.

The trait of argumentativeness includes individuals advocating and defending positions on controversial issues simultaneously with the ability to refute the positions that others hold on those issues (Infante & Rancer, 1982, 1996). The dispositional approach to understanding argumentative communication has focused on the general trait to be argumentative (ARGgt), which is composed of two competing motivational tendencies: the tendency to approach arguments (ARGap), and the tendency to avoid arguments (ARGav). The more the motivation to approach arguments exceeds the motivation to avoid arguments, the more argumentative the individual is. Thus, a high argumentative is a person who is high on ARGap and low on ARGav. A low argumentative is low on ARGap, and high on ARGav. There are at least two types of individuals who are considered moderate on argumentativeness. Conflicting feelings moderates are high on both ARGap and ARGav; they argue mainly when they feel sure that they can succeed or "win" during an argument. Apathetic moderates are low on both ARGap and ARGav; they neither like nor dislike arguing and engage in argument only when they feel they must do so.

BELIEFS ABOUT ARGUING

Several studies have explored the beliefs about arguing of individuals who vary in argumentativeness in order to better understand why people differ in this trait. A framework was used that suggests that behavior is linked to attitudes and beliefs. Predispositions (such as argumentativeness) are controlled by the set of beliefs an individual learns to associate with the object of the predisposition (Fishbein & Ajzen, 1975). It was reasoned that one way to understand why people differ in argumentativeness is to examine their beliefs about arguing.

Rancer, Baukus, and Infante (1985) identified several beliefs individuals hold about arguing. They labeled these beliefs *hostility, activity/process, control/dominance, conflict/dissonance, self-image, learning*, and *skill*. It was found that these beliefs distinguish between individuals who differ in argumentativeness. For example, high argumentatives hold more positive beliefs about activity/process, control/dominance, conflict/dissonance, self-image, learning, and skill than do low argumentative individuals. That is, argumentative individuals view arguing as a productive communication activity which tends to enhance their self-esteem, they see arguing as an activity in that both participants learn something new, and one that demonstrates their argumentative and rhetorical skills. They also believe arguing is a means to reduce conflict. Low argumentatives' beliefs were found to be in the opposite direction.

Rancer, Kosberg, and Baukus (1992) recommend that a major component of argumentation, interpersonal, and communication conflict courses should focus on the presentation of these positive beliefs associated with arguing. The relation among argumentative skill and self-concept, practical outcomes associated with arguing constructively, and motivation to argue should do much to enhance individuals' level of argumentativeness.

THE INTERACTIONIST APPROACH TO UNDERSTANDING ARGUMENTATIVE BEHAVIOR

In addition to the trait component, the model of argumentativeness (Infante & Rancer, 1982) also includes situational factors in order to more accurately predict motivation to argue in a given situation. A part of this theory suggests that a person's motivation to argue in a particular situation is determined by the interaction of a person's trait (ARGgt), and that person's perceptions of the probability and importance of success and failure in the situation. Including both the trait and situational factors in the model is consistent with the interactionist approach to studying personality (e.g., Andersen, 1987; Epstein, 1979; Magnusson & Endler, 1977). Including the situational probability and importance perceptions along with trait argumentativeness improves predictions about exactly how argumentative a person is expected to be in any given situation (Infante, 1987b; Infante & Rancer, 1982).

Several studies have identified situational factors that allow us to more accurately predict an individual's argumentative behavior in a given situation. For example, Onyekwere, Rubin, and Infante (1991) found that a person's ego involvement in the topic of an argument affected the behavior of high and low argumentativeness. Issues that were more involving to the individual stimulated more motivation to argue, and enhanced actual argumentative behavior. Religious orientation (extrinsic vs. intrinsic) is another factor that has been found to influence argumentative behavior. Stewart and Roach (1993) studied how the topic of argument and religious orientation influenced willingness to argue. Although trait argumentativeness was found to influence willingness to argue greatly, extrinsically religious persons were more will to argue than intrinsically religious persons. High argumentatives have also been found to argue more on certain topics (e.g., social, political, moral-ethical issues) than low or moderate argumentatives (Infante & Rancer, 1993).

MEASURING ARGUMENTATIVENESS

Infante and I developed a way to measure trait argumentativeness. We did this in order to classify individuals according to their levels of the trait in order to better understanding of how people behave during conflict communication. We developed the Argumentativeness Scale (Infante & Rancer, 1982), a personality measure that contains 20 items. Ten items measure motivation to approach situations (ARGap), and 10 items measure motivation to avoid situations (ARGav). The scale asks individuals to respond to 20 items about "arguing controversial issues."

A shorter, 10 item form of the scale has been used to study argumentative behavior in particular contexts, such as the organization (Infante, Anderson, Martin, Herington, & Kim, 1993; Infante & Gorden, 1987, 1989, 1991). A version of the Argumentativeness scale has also been developed to measure argumentativeness in adolescents (Roberto & Finucane, 1997). The results suggest that the concepts and measurement of argumentativeness can be generalized to adolescent populations.

The Argumentativeness scale has been translated into several languages. To study differences between high-context (e.g., Asian) and low-context (e.g., American) cultures, Suzuki and Rancer (1994) translated the scale into Japanese and tested it for conceptual and measurement equivalence across the two cultures. This research found that the ARGap and ARGav factors developed in the United States is generalizable to Japanese culture. In addition, the construct validity of the scale was established for the cross-cultural sample.

Another possible method of measuring argumentativeness was used in a recent study (Infante & Rancer, 1993). Participants were asked the number of times during the past week they had advocated a position or attempted to refute another person's position on 11 different types of controversial issues (e.g., social issues such as welfare reform; family issues such as family chores and responsibilities; entertainment issues such as whether a movie was good; work issues such as whether a boss is fair with employees; personal behavior issues such as what one should or should not do; religious issues such as the value of religion; and political issues such as who should be elected to a particular national, state, or local office.) The sum of their advocacy and refutation behaviors can be used as a measure of their "argumentativeness."

SOME IMPORTANT FINDINGS REGARDING
ARGUMENTATIVENESS

The research on argumentativeness has tended to focus on how the trait functions within several communication contexts. The results of that research allows several conclusions to be drawn about the way argumentativeness functions in communication situations. Perhaps the most important overall finding based on this body of research is that all of the outcomes or consequences of being argumentative are positive. That is, being motivated and skilled in argumentative communication is clearly considered positive across contexts and situations. Furthermore almost all of the outcomes of being verbally aggressive are negative. In chapter 9 Wigley describes the consequences of being verbally aggressive. The strong and unequivocal support for the assertion that argumentativeness is a constructive and positive trait is surely comforting for the communication discipline, because teaching students to argue effectively and constructively (Infante, 1988) has been a major preoccupation of the discipline for more than 2,000 years.

Benefits of Argumentativeness

Research has uncovered several benefits of being high in motivation to argue. Arguing stimulates curiosity and increases learning because we seek out more information on the issues we argue about. Arguing reduces egocentric thinking and forces us to explore issues from multiple perspectives (Johnson & Johnson, 1979). Moreover, arguing enhances social perspective-taking, which is related to persuasiveness (Delia, O'Keefe, & O'Keefe, 1982).

Some research has examined how argumentativeness is related to persuasion. It was reasoned that ability to argue should be related to persuasive ability, thus, differences between individuals in motivation to argue should be evident in their own persuasive efforts and in resisting the persuasive efforts of others. For example, high argumentatives have been found to use a greater diversity of strategies to influence others, and are sometimes more persistent in their influence attempts (Boster & Levine, 1988; Boster, Levine, & Kazoleas, 1993). They are also less willing to use compliance-gaining strategies that create negative feelings in others (Infante et al., 1993). Argumentatives are more reluctant to use their power, even legitimate power, to force compliance (Roach, 1992, 1995); and tend to encourage other people to express their views on controversial issues (Gorden, Infante, & Graham, 1988).

Several studies have explored situations when argumentatives are the recipients of persuasive attempts of others. In these situations, argumentatives are more inflexible in their position when others try to persuade them (Infante, 1981); they generate more counterarguments hence, are persuaded less (Kazoleas, 1993); they generate more ideas favorable to a persuader when they initially agree with the persuader's position (Levine & Badger, 1993); and display more attitude-behavioral intention consistency in response to persuasive messages (Mongeau, 1989).

Argumentativeness are seen as higher in credibility than those low in argumentativeness. Argumentativeness and credibility have been examined because of the assumption that higher levels of the trait may indicate more skill in arguing. Research has indicated that more skillful advocacy, refutation, and rebuttal behavior in argumentative situations indicate that the argumentative individual is a more competent communicator (Infante, 1981, 1985; Onyekwere et al., 1991; Richmond, McCroskey, & McCroskey, 1989). High argumentatives score higher on the competence dimension of credibility, and argumentatives are also seen as being higher in dynamism and trustworthiness (Infante, 1981, 1985; Onyekwere et al., 1991). Argumentatives may be perceived as more trustworthy because others may feel that the information obtained from them is dependable, that argumentative individuals are more sincere, and they can be relied on. That argumentatives are seen as higher in dynamism may stem from the fact that high argumentatives enjoy arguing, and this enjoyment may be reflected in their actual communication behavior that tends to be quite active and animated during argument.

Individuals high in argumentativeness are also seen as more interested in communication (Infante, 1981). High argumentatives are less likely to be provoked into verbal aggression, which is considered negative and destructive to interpersonal relationships. Argumentatives are more likely than low argumentatives to be seen as leaders in group problem-solving discussions (Schultz, 1982). Higher levels of self-esteem, especially perceptions of personal power and competence have been associated with trait argumentativeness (Rancer, Kosberg, & Silvestri, 1992).

The conclusion that argumentativeness is a constructive communication predisposition is not limited to a particular communication context. Argumentativeness has been investigated in interpersonal, organizational, family, intercultural, and educational contexts, among others. A discussion of the function of this trait in several of these contexts is presented here.

Positive Consequences of Argumentativeness in Family Communication

Researchers in family communication have applied the aggressive communication traits in several ways, a major focus being on marriages troubled by violence. A great deal of the work supports what has been called the *argumentative skill deficiency* explanation for intrafamily violence (Infante, Chandler, & Rudd, 1989). This model has also been used to help predict and explain unwanted sexual aggression in dating encounters.

The argumentative skill deficiency explanation suggests that individuals low in motivation and skill in argumentative communication quickly "run out of things to say" (i.e., arguments) when they are engaged in an argument with someone. This explanation suggests that these low argumentative individuals do not have much ability to generate arguments as they are needed or called for. Remember that one characteristic of aggressive communication is that we are in an attack-and-defend mode of behavior (Infante, 1988). Our attention is focused on attacking the position our adversary holds on the controversial issue, and on defending our own position on the issue. People with little ability to generate arguments have great difficulty in generating arguments to support their position, and quickly "use up" their meager store of arguments. If the conflict continues, the "attack-and-defend" mode is still operational, that is, individuals continue to feel the need to say something to defend themselves and attack their opponent. If they cannot attack their adversary's position on the controversial issue with arguments (i.e., engage in argumentativeness), they redirect their attack to the person's self-concept (i.e., engage in verbal aggressiveness).

Infante et al. (1989) developed and tested the argumentative skill deficiency model of intrafamily violence. The basic idea is that verbal aggression in a marriage is a catalyst to violence especially under certain conditions, such as when one or both spouses have a hostile disposition because of undissipated anger, and when the spouses are low in argumentative motivation, and unskilled in argumentative communication. That is, argumentative skill deficiencies can lead to verbal attacks being directed to the other person's self-concept instead of his or her position on a controversial issue. This in turn can lead to increased anger that may ultimately lead to physical aggression. Being skilled argumentatively can reduce the likelihood that this cycle will ensue because skilled and motivated arguers are able to direct the attack to the other person's position and not the other's self-concept. The researchers tested this model in a study that found that abused wives and abusive husbands were lower in argumentativeness and higher in verbal aggressiveness than a control group of nonviolent husbands and wives.

The argumentative skill deficiency model of intrafamily violence has also been used to test the relation between the aggressive communication predispositions and antecedents of date rape. Andonian and Droge (1992) found that acceptance of date rape myths is positively related to verbal aggressiveness and negatively related to argumentativeness. That is, males who accepted myths about date rape (e.g., "women say 'no' when they mean 'yes' to avoid being seen as promiscuous") were lower in argumentativeness and higher in verbal aggressiveness than men high in argumentativeness and low in verbal aggressiveness. This trend held for females as well.

Studies have explored whether married couples similar or dissimilar in aggressive communication exhibited differences in marital satisfaction. Payne and Sabourin (1990) found that husbands were more satisfied with their marriages when their wives were high argumentatives, whereas Rancer, Baukus, and Amato (1986) found that couples who were dissimilar on argumentativeness reported more overall marital satisfaction than couples classified as similar. Because most of the couples in the dissimilar group had husbands higher than wives in argumentativeness, Rancer et al. (1986) speculated that for "traditional couples" (see Fitzpatrick, 1988) a more argumentative husband may be acceptable according to conventional gender role norms.

Research has explored how communication between parents and children is influenced by argumentativeness and verbal aggressiveness. Bayer and Cegala (1992) investigated the styles of parents of 5- to 12-year-old children. They found parents with an "authoritative" style (e.g., used reasoning with children, encouraged a give-and-take) were higher in argumentativeness and lower in verbal aggressiveness. On the other hand, parents with an "authoritarian" style (e.g., used authority-based control messages, discouraged responses from children, did not show much emotion) were lower in argumentativeness and higher in verbal aggressiveness. This may be especially important because as Bayer and Cegala (1992) pointed out, the development of positive self-concepts in children has been negatively associated with an authoritarian style of parenting. Thus, the studies reviewed in this section indicate that argumentativeness and verbal aggressiveness are relevant to a range of concerns in family communication.

Positive Consequences of Argumentativeness in Organizational Communication

A good deal of research has explored how the aggressive communication traits (argumentativeness and verbal aggressiveness) function in the organizational context. The application of these aggressive communication dispositions has led to the development of the of independent-mindedness theory of organizational communication (Gorden & Infante, 1987; Infante & Gorden, 1987). The research has also focused on the development of "profiles" of superior and subordinate communication styles that seem to produce the most favorable organizational outcomes.

Independent-mindedness involves the tendency of employees to have their own thoughts and opinions rather than to passively accept the opinions of supervisors in the organization. The theory of independent-mindedness suggests that when superiors encourage freedom of speech among their employees and promote individualism and independent-mindedness, more favorable organizational outcomes will result. The most favorable conditions for organizational communication is when superiors and subordinates are high in argumentativeness, low in verbal aggressiveness, and communicate with an "affirming communicator style." This is a style in which the individual communicates in a highly relaxed, highly friendly, and highly attentive manner. That is, individuals communicate with a great deal of attention and eye contact, have relaxed and composed gestures, and use positive facial expressions that include smiling, head nods, and so on. Several studies (Infante & Gorden, 1987, 1989, 1991) found support for the contention that argumentativeness is a constructive communication trait when coupled with an affirming communicator style in the organizational context.

Argumentativeness and Intercultural Communication

Since the 1980s, interest in intercultural communication has increased. Popular interest in communication between cultures has been stimulated by increased attention to cultural diversity, increased international business, greater cooperation between countries, growth in international travel, growth in electronic communication that has made the "global village" more of a reality, and increased numbers of multinational organizations. Expansion in research activity has accompanied this increased interest in intercultural and cross-cultural communication. The traits of argumentativeness and verbal aggressiveness have been examined within the context of intercultural communication. Differences in conflict styles across and between cultures have been identified and clarified.

Several cultures have been compared regarding trait argumentativeness. Several studies have explored how Asian cultures compare with Western/U.S. cultures on argumentativeness. For example, Prunty, Klopf, and Ishii (1990a, 1990b) found that Americans are higher than the Japanese on argumentativeness. Americans were also found to be higher than Koreans in argumentativeness, but no significant differences were observed between Korean and American males (Jenkins, Klopf, & Park, 1991). The difference between Americans and Koreans apparently is that U.S. women are more argumentative than Korean women.

Cross-cultural differences in aggressive communication between low-context cultures have also been observed. For example, both Finnish and Norwegian cultures have been found to be higher than U.S. culture in argumentativeness (Klopf, Thompson, & Sallinen-Kuparinen, 1991; Rahoi, Svenkerud, & Love, 1994). Regional differences in aggressive communication, and regional identification have also been studied. One study (Geddes, 1992) classified Americans by geographical location, and found northerners higher on argumentativeness than southerners, although this difference ($p = .057$) was not quite statistically significant employing the traditional $p < .05$ criterion.

Enhancing Argumentativeness and Skill in Arguing

The constructive nature of argumentativeness and the destructive nature of verbal aggressiveness is supported by a large body of research (see, Infante & Rancer, 1996). In this chapter, we have presented a synthesis of the numerous positive consequences of being high in trait argumentativeness and skilled in arguing. Several studies cited in this chapter, and numerous studies cited in chapter 9 reveal a number of negative outcomes associated with being high in verbal aggressiveness.

The communication discipline has long advanced the notion that individuals can be trained to enhance their argumentative skill. Recently, several programs have been offered that attempt to increase motivation to argue and enhance actual argumentative behavior. For example, Anderson, Schultz, and Courtney Staley (1987) demonstrated that "cognitive training" in argument and conflict management can positively influence individuals to increase their motivation to argue. This finding is especially powerful for females who are low in argumentativeness.

Using the assumptions of the argumentativeness model, Schultz and Anderson (1984) suggested that "if one is to resolve a conflict situation, one will have to be argumentative; that is, be willing to argue in one's own behalf, providing information and reasoning, asserting conclusions, and refuting positions that others are asserting" (p. 336). They concluded that the use of cognitive material can affect changes in motivation to argue. Several assumptions are inherent in this cognitive training model: Conflict management requires a willingness to be argumentative; substantial cognitive data must be presented in order to change unfavorable perceptions of conflict and argumentativeness; and, after negative perceptions are altered, skill in conflict management can be taught using a model drawing on theories of argumentation and persuasion (Anderson et al., 1987).

These assumptions were the basis of the content of a training program designed to test the effect of training on motivation to argue. Anderson et al. (1987) reported a study in which one group received this cognitive training in argumentativeness and conflict management, whereas a control group did not. The training occurred over a 3 week period. The results supported the contention that cognitive training enhances argumentativeness, "Exposing subjects to information that expands and alters their perceptions about argumentativeness and conflict in positive directions will influence them to change their attitudes in positive directions" (Anderson et al., 1987, p. 64).

Other methods of enhancing argumentativeness and skill in arguing have produced equally positive results. Nelson (1970); Infante (1971); Nelson, Petelle, and Monroe (1974); and Kosberg and Rancer (in press) demonstrated that topical systems (systematic methods that use a specific rhetorical devise, topoi, to help individuals develop arguments) can enhance the ability to generate arguments. In addition, Infante (1985) used a cued-argument procedure in which some individuals were provided with a number of arguments relevant to the topics and were told to use those arguments in a forthcoming discussion. Results indicated that cued subjects were perceived more favorably than those individuals not cued on credibility, quality of arguments, and willingness to argue. Colbert (1993) found that students with experience in competitive debate were significantly lower in verbal aggressiveness and higher in argumentativeness than those students without debate training or experience. Sanders, Wiseman, and Gass (1994) found that training in argumentativeness helped students' enhance their critical thinking skills, especially their ability to judge weak arguments, improved their self-reported effectiveness in arguing, and decreased verbal aggressiveness.

Infante (1988) offered a two-part Inventional System designed to enhance individuals' motivation and skill in arguing. He advocated the use of informative, persuasive, and argumentative components to enhancing motivation and skill in argument. The informative component of the model involves helping the individual to state the nature of the conflict or controversy in propositional form. This is done in order to let the adversary know where the individual stands on the issue. When the controversy is stated in propositional form (e.g., Resolved: "That this family should buy a new car"), the parties can "agree on what to disagree" (Infante, 1988, p. 42).

The persuasive component of the model involves the individual explaining his or her position on the controversial issue, and inventing arguments to support that position. The Inventional System, which includes the components of Problem-blame-solution-consequences, is sometimes referred to as the *problem-solution* format. This inventional system requires the individual to ask questions such as: "What are the signs of a problem?" "What is to blame?" or "What is the cause of the problem?" "What are the possible solutions to the problem?" and "What favorable outcomes/consequences will result from adopting this solution?" (Infante, 1988, p. 47).

The argumentative component of the model includes techniques for presenting and defending arguments, as well as techniques for attacking the adversary's position on issues. Procedures are outlined to present and defend arguments as well as to attack the arguments of others. Other components of the model include;: analyzing an opponent's message structure-tactics such as the placement of disliked evidence sources, managing credibility, enhancing verbal and nonverbal presentational ability, and the use of language tactics designed to enhance the chance of "winning" an argument (Infante, 1988).

Kosberg and Rancer (in press) tested the impact of three methods of training in argument (Infante's inventional system, Wilson and Arnold's topical system, and the Anderson, Schultz, and Staley's cognitive training in argument and interpersonal conflict) in order to determine if one method was "superior" to another in enhancing argumentative behavior. Results of the study indicated that all three methods were productive in providing individuals with the tools necessary to generate arguments. Participants were able to generate an average of eight arguments for a given proposition, across the three methods, after the training was completed.

Recently, Rancer, Whitecap, Kosberg, and Avtgis (1997) used a modified version of Infante's inventional system to teach seventh-grade students how to argue constructively. Objectives of the training included enhancing the students' argumentative behavior by using Infante's (1988) system to formulate arguments, and to have students correctly identify messages as either argumentative or verbally aggressive. The inventional system was modified to accommodate the learning styles of the age group. The results of the training support the contention that adolescents can improve their ability to generate arguments, hence improve their argumentative behavior by using the inventional system. After the training, students were also able to distinguish between messages that attack a person's position (argumentativeness) from messages that attack a person's self-concept (verbal aggressiveness), and were able to generate more arguments.

LOOKING AHEAD

One consequence of the distillation of past research on aggressive communication traits (Infante & Rancer, 1996) was to illuminate directions for future research. Many questions remain unanswered about the influence of argumentativeness and verbal aggressiveness.

In the context of family communication, several studies suggest marital satisfaction is related to argumentativeness and verbal aggressiveness in husband-wife interactions. Whether the relation is causal is an issue that needs to be resolved. Methods for training spouses to argue constructively need to be developed and tested with both spouses in distressed marriages to see if argumentation (with low verbal aggressiveness) produces satisfaction. Perhaps the application of the inventional system can be used to train married couples to argue constructively. In the area of parent-child communication, Bayer and Cegala (1992) suggested parental education programs might benefit from the inclusion of a unit for developing argumentative competencies. Programs such as they suggest, could be valuable not only for parents, but also with children, especially those with a hostile disposition who would benefit by having aggressive but constructive (i.e., argumentative) alternatives available in conflict situations.

Additionally, some basic knowledge of argument is needed to answer such research questions as: What positive affective states are related to greater argumentativeness in families? Which topics tend to be associated with the most/least constructive family arguments? What are the main determinants of a family argument becoming verbally aggressive, hence, destructive? What kinds of messages can change a family argument from being destructive to being constructive?

Although the organizational communication research has produced results that support the idea that argumentativeness is constructive, the data has been based primarily on superiors' and subordinates' perceptions. Although this is a major interest in research from a psychological perspective, additional "bottomline" criteria such as employee productivity rates, or generally quantifiable successes and failures of both supervisors and their subordinates need to be applied to test the model. This would establish more precisely what it means for an organization to have superiors and subordinates communicate according to certain styles (i.e., high in argumentativeness, low in verbal aggressiveness, highly relaxed, friendly, and attentive). Such data would provide an even stronger rationale for training employees to communicate in this way.

Research on argumentativeness in the organizational context would also benefit from more specificity. That is, of the many forms of argumentative behavior (e.g., developing cases, refuting evidence, recognizing faulty reasoning) which are most valuable to organizations? Which organizational roles are most in need of competent argumentative behavior—upper level management, sales personnel, line supervisors, and so forth? What are essential guidelines for argumentation between superiors and subordinates to be constructive? What typically leads to destructive arguments?

Additional research on the role of argumentativeness in the intercultural context appears warranted. For example, what values in a culture promote the argumentativeness trait? Because the Finnish culture has been found to be especially argumentative, it may warrant further study. What overt and subtle behaviors do cultures and ethnic groups employ to promote high motivation to argue? What sanctions are imposed in other cultures to dampen an individual's motivation to argue? If there are differences in argumentativeness between one culture and another, how may members of one culture argue with members of the other and still have the outcomes be constructive? What factors lead to destructive arguments when the disputants are from different cultures? What underlying beliefs about arguing are evident in high-context versus low-context cultures? What types of cross-cultural training in argument would increase the likelihood of successful conflict management between members of different cultures, races, and ethnic groups? Finally, is argumentativeness considered a constructive and valuable trait for individuals to possess across cultures?

The interpersonal context in general offers a rich source of application issues for the continued study of argumentativeness. In particular, what other factors in an interpersonal situation are related to motivation to argue? Factors such as power, dominance, and status differences between communicators should help explain additional variance in motivation to argue. Are there additional environmental factors that impact on argumentativeness? Does argumentative skill relate to an individual's ability to form and maintain friendships? What influence does the enhancement of argumentativeness and skill in arguing have on self-esteem?

Because argumentative communication is such an integral part of the communication discipline, studying argumentativeness, we believe, is a way of understanding essential features of the field. If future research and application follows at least some of these suggestions offered here, we should be further enlightened.

REFERENCES

Andersen, P.A. (1987). The trait debate: A critical examination of the individual differences paradigm in interpersonal communication. In B. Dervin & M. J. Voigt (Eds.), *Progress in communication sciences* (Vol. 7, pp. 47-52). Norwood, NJ: Ablex.

Anderson, J., Schultz, B., & Courtney Staley, C. (1987). Training in argumentativeness: New hope for nonassertive women. *Women's Studies in Communication, 10,* 58-66.

Andonian, K. K., & Droge, D. (1992, October). *Verbal aggressiveness and sexual violence in dating relationships: An exploratory study of antecedents of date rape.* Paper presented at the annual meeting of the Speech Communication Association, Chicago, IL.

Bayer, C.L., & Cegala, D.J. (1992). Trait verbal aggressiveness and argumentativeness: Relations with parenting style. *Western Journal of Communication, 56,* 301-310.

Boster, F. J., & Levine, T. (1988). Individual differences and compliance-gaining message selection: The effects of verbal aggressiveness, argumentativeness, dogmatism, and negativism. *Communication Research Reports, 5,* 114-119.

Boster, F. J., Levine, T., & Kazoleas, D. (1993). The impact of argumentativeness and verbal aggressiveness on strategic diversity and persistence in compliance-gaining behavior. *Communication Quarterly, 41,* 405-414.

Colbert, K. R. (1993). The effects of debate participation on argumentativeness and verbal aggression. *Communication Education, 42,* 206-214.

Delia, J. G., O'Keefe, B.J., & O'Keefe, D.J. (1982). The constructivist approach to communication. In F. E. X. Dance (Ed.), *Human communication theory* (pp. 147-191). New York: Harper & Row.

Epstein, S. (1979). The stability of behavior: 1. On predicting most of the people much of the time. *Journal of Personality and Social Psychology, 37,* 1097-1126.

Fishbein, M., & Ajzen, I. (1975). *Belief, attitude, intention, and behavior: An introduction to theory and research.* Reading, MA: Addison-Wesley.

Fitzpatrick, M. A. (1988). *Between husbands and wives.* Newbury Park, CA: Sage.

Geddes, D.S. (1992). Comparison of regional interpersonal communication predispositions. *Pennsylvania Speech Communication Annual, 48,* 67-93.

Gorden, W.I., & Infante, D.A. (1987), Employee rights: Context, argumentativeness, verbal aggressiveness, and career satisfaction. In C. A. B. Osigweh (Ed.), *Communicating employee responsibilities and rights* (pp. 149-163). Westport, CT: Quorum.

Gorden, W.I., Infante, D.A., & Graham, E.E. (1988). Corporate conditions conducive to employee voice: A subordinate perspective. *Employee Responsibilities and Rights Journal, 1,* 101-111.

Infante, D.A. (1971). The influence of a topical system on the discovery of arguments. *Speech Monographs, 38,* 125-128.

Infante, D.A. (1981). Trait argumentativeness as a predictor of communicative behavior in situations requiring argument. *Central States Speech Journal, 32,* 265-272.

Infante, D.A. (1985). Inducing women to be more argumentative: Source credibility effects. *Journal of Applied Communication Research, 13,* 33-44.

Infante, D.A. (1987a). Aggressiveness. In J. C. McCroskey & J. A. Daly (Eds.), *Personality and interpersonal communication* (pp. 157-192). Newbury Park, CA: Sage.

Infante, D.A. (1987b). Enhancing the prediction of response to a communication situation from communication traits. *Communication Quarterly, 35,* 308-316.

Infante, D.A. (1988). *Arguing constructively.* Prospect Heights, IL: Waveland Press.

Infante, D. A., Anderson, C. M., Martin, M. M., Herington, A. D., & Kim, J. (1993). Subordinates' satisfaction and perceptions of superiors' compliance-gaining tactics, argumentativeness, verbal aggressiveness and style. *Management Communication Quarterly, 6,* 307-326.

Infante, D.A., Chandler, T. A., & Rudd, J. E. (1989). Test of an argumentative skill deficiency model of interspousal violence. *Communication Monographs, 56,* 163-177.

Infante, D. A., & Gorden, W. I. (1987). Superior and subordinate communication profiles: Implications for independent-mindedness and upward effectiveness. *Central States Speech Journal, 38*, 73-80.

Infante, D.A., & Gorden, W.I. (1989). Argumentativeness and affirming communicator style as predictors of satisfaction/dissatisfaction with subordinates. *Communication Quarterly, 37*, 81-90.

Infante, D.A., & Gorden, W.I. (1991). How employees see the boss: Test of an argumentative and affirming model of superiors' communicative behavior. *Western Journal of Speech Communication, 55*, 294-304.

Infante, D.A., & Rancer, A.S. (1982). A conceptualization and measure of argumentativeness. *Journal of Personality Assessment, 46*, 72-80.

Infante, D.A., & Rancer, A.S. (1993). Relations between argumentative motivation, and advocacy and refutation on controversial issues. *Communication Quarterly, 41*, 415-426.

Infante, D.A., & Rancer, A.S. (1996). Argumentativeness and verbal aggressiveness: A review of recent theory and research. In B. Burleson (Ed.), *Communication yearbook 19* (pp. 319-351). Thousand Oaks, CA: Sage.

Infante, D.A., & Wigley, C.J. (1986). Verbal aggressiveness: An interpersonal model and measure. *Communication Monographs, 53*, 61-69.

Jenkins, G.D., Klopf, D. W., & Park, M.S. (1991, July). *Argumentativeness in Korean and American college students: A comparison.* Paper presented at the annual meeting of the World Communication Association, Jyvaskyla, Finland.

Johnson, D. W., & Johnson, R. T. (1979). Conflict in the classroom: Controversy and learning. *Review of Educational Research, 49*, 51-70.

Kazoleas, D. (1993). The impact of argumentativeness on resistance to persuasion. *Human Communication Research, 20*, 118-137.

Klopf, D. W., Thompson, C.A., & Sallinen-Kuparinen, S. (1991). Argumentativeness among selected Finnish and American college students. *Psychological Reports, 68*, 161-162.

Kosberg, R. L., & Rancer, A.S. (in press). Enhancing argumentativeness and argumentative behavior: The influence of gender and training. In L. Longmire & L. Merrill (Eds.), *Untying the tongue: Gender, power, and the word*. Westport, CT: Greenwood Press.

Levine T. R., & Badger, E.E. (1993). Argumentativeness and resistance to persuasion. *Communication Reports, 6*, 71-78.

Magnusson, D., & Endler, N.S. (1977). Interactional psychology: Present status and future prospects. In D. Magnusson & N.S. Endler (Eds.), *Personality at the crossroads: Current issues in interactional psychology* (pp. 3-35). Hillsdale, NJ: Lawrence Erlbaum Associates.

Mongeau, P. A. (1989). Individual differences as moderators of persuasive message processing and attitude-behavior relations. *Communication Research Reports, 6,* 1-6.

Nelson, W. F. (1970). Topoi: Functional in human recall. *Speech Monographs, 37,* 121-126.

Nelson, W. F., Petelle, J. L., & Monroe, C. (1974). A revised strategy for idea generation in small group decision making. *The Speech Teacher, 23,* 191- 196.

Onyekwere, E.O., Rubin, R. B., & Infante, D. A. (1991). Interpersonal perception and communication satisfaction as function of argumentativeness and ego-involvement. *Communication Quarterly, 39,* 35-47.

Payne, M. J., & Sabourin, T. C. (1990). Argumentative skill deficiency and its relationship to quality of marriage. *Communication Research Reports, 7,* 121- 124.

Prunty, A. M., Klopf, D. W., & Ishii, S. (1990a). Argumentativeness: Japanese and American tendencies to approach and avoid conflict. *Communication Research Reports, 7,* 75-79.

Prunty, A. M., Klopf, D. W., & Ishii, S. (1990b). Japanese and American tendencies to argue. *Psychological Reports, 66,* 802.

Rahoi, R., Svenkerud, P., & Love, D. (1994). *Searching for subtlety: Investigating argumentativeness across low-context cultural boundaries.* Unpublished manuscript, Ohio University, OH.

Rancer, A.S., Baukus, R.A., & Amato, P.P. (1986). Argumentativeness, verbal aggressiveness, and marital satisfaction. *Communication Research Reports, 3,* 28-32.

Rancer, A.S., Baukus, R.A., & Infante, D.A. (1985). Relations between argumentativeness and belief structures about arguing. *Communication Education, 34,* 37-47.

Rancer, A. S., Kosberg, R. L., & Baukus, R. A. (1992). Beliefs about arguing as predictors of trait argumentativeness: Implications for training in argument and conflict management. *Communication Education, 41,* 375-387.

Rancer, A. S., Kosberg, R. L., & Silvestri, V. N. (1992). The relationship between self-esteem and aggressive communication predispositions. *Communication Research Reports, 9,* 23-32.

Rancer, A. S., Whitecap, V. G., Kosberg, R. L., & Avtgis, T. A. (1997). Testing the efficacy of a communication training program to increase argumentativeness and argumentative behavior in adolescents. *Communication Education, 46,* 273-286.

Richmond, V. P., McCroskey, J. C., & McCroskey, L. L. (1989). An investigation of self-perceived communication competence and personality orientations. *Communication Research Reports, 6,* 28-36.

Roach, K. D. (1992). Teacher demographic characteristics and level of teacher argumentatives. *Communication Research Reports, 9,* 65-71.

Roach, K. D. (1995). Teaching assistant argumentativeness: Effects on affective learning and students perceptions of power use. *Communication Education, 44,* 15-29.

Roberto, A. J., & Finucane, M. E. (1997). The assessment of argumentativeness and verbal aggressiveness in adolescent populations. *Communication Quarterly, 45,* 21-36.

Sanders, J. A., Wiseman, R. L., & Gass, R. H. (1994). Does teaching argumentation facilitate critical thinking? *Communication Reports, 7,* 27-35.

Schultz, B. (1982). Argumentativeness: Its effect in group decision-making and its role in leadership perception. *Communication Quarterly, 30,* 368-375.

Schultz, B., & Anderson, J. (1984). Training in the management of conflict: A communication theory perspective. *Small Group Behavior, 15,* 333-348.

Stewart, R. A., & Roach, K. D. (1993). Argumentativeness, religious orientation, and reactions to argument situations involving religious versus nonreligious issues. *Communication Quarterly, 41,* 26-39.

Suzuki, S., & Rancer, A.S. (1994). Argumentativeness and verbal aggressiveness: Testing for conceptual and measure equivalence across cultures. *Communication Monographs, 61,* 256-279.

Wilson, J. F. & Arnold, C. C. (1983). *Public speaking as a liberal art* (5th ed.). Boston: Allyn & Bacon.

8

Emotionality and Affective Orientation

Melanie Booth-Butterfield
Steven Booth-Butterfield
West Virginia University

Lust. Suspicion. Loneliness. Embarrassment. In communication research we are more likely to examine how such emotions should be coped with or handled than how they are used to provide information and guidance. Statements such as "I know I'm lonely, but I try not to let it interfere with my work," or "I was suspicious, but I didn't let that affect how I acted," are typical of this orientation. Nevertheless, some people are predisposed to notice and pay attention to their emotional states. They readily implement that emotional information to direct their communicative behavior, rather than rejecting and ignoring it. The study of affective orientation examines how this personality trait is displayed.

One of the controversies facing social scientists is determining the extent to which communication and behavior are a function of circumstances and environment as opposed to learned traits and inherited predispositions. In the area of emotions, the question is whether we communicate emotionally because some situation triggered the feelings, or, whether we act emotionally because we are predispositionally emotional individuals. Recent studies have found unexpected adult social patterns such as divorce to be related to genetics, or at least to the personality patterns inherited from the family (Jockin, McGue, & Lykken, 1996). Even traits such as alcoholism and aggression appear to be heritable (Holden, 1987).

The most complete explanations of social behavior/ communication appear to integrate both trait influences (whether learned early or genetically based) and situational factors (e.g., the immediate circumstances surrounding the interaction). Models have been posed for other social problems such as child maltreatment (Belsky, 1993) and communication anxiety and avoidance (Booth-Butterfield & Booth-Butterfield, 1992; McCroskey, 1984). But to understand the situational outcomes, we must understand the personality factors that predispose us to respond in predictable ways to immediate influences.

The focus here is an examination of how awareness and use of one's affective state, specifically one's emotions, influence communication. The predisposition to actively scrutinize, consider, and subsequently use one's emotions as guiding information is termed *affective orientation* (AO). In this chapter, we describe existing AO research and findings, present a model of how AO is integrated in the communication process, describe the utility of a more direct measure of AO, and report preliminary results of our recent study involving affective orientation and health behaviors.

EXTANT RESEARCH ON AFFECTIVE ORIENTATION

Since its conceptualization (Booth-Butterfield & Booth-Butterfield, 1990), AO has gained the attention of both communication and psychology researchers. Basically, affectively oriented communicators are very sensitive to their own emotional states, noticing even subtle changes. Moreover, not only are high AOs aware of their emotions, but they consider them substantive information and weigh emotions positively when making behavioral decisions. In contrast, low AOs tend to be unaware of their emotions, unless at a high level of arousal, and tend to reject their emotions as useful, important information. Thus, even when they are aware of their affective state, low AOs disregard those cues in favor of more fact-based analysis.

Many researchers are interested in how high or low trait affective communication may be problematic in relationships. For example, Yelsma (1995) studied AO and spousal abuse. He found that individuals who were higher in AO were also more likely to say they would express negative emotions, although they did not necessarily do so in an abusive manner. Sidelinger and Booth-Butterfield (1997) found a significant positive relation between AO levels between parents and children, and that low AO families were also less likely to have satisfactory family interaction styles. Taylor (1994; Bagby & Taylor, in press) discussed the relation between AO and alexithymia. People who are alexithymic have difficulty in identifying and describing feelings, and this condition often contributes to a variety of psychological problems. Lower AOs were more likely to be alexithymic (see also Johnston, Stinski, & Meyers, 1993).

AO has also been linked with more positive social patterns. Booth-Butterfield and Andrighetti (1993) and Dolin and Booth-Butterfield (1993) found AO to be positively associated with nonverbal sensitivity and comforting behaviors respectively. More affectively oriented individuals were more sensitive to nonverbal cues around them and also had a more extensive repertoire of nonverbal comforting communication messages compared to low AOs. Wanzer, Booth-Butterfield, and Booth-Butterfield (1995) examined AO with humor production. They reported that people who were higher in AO also tended to be more likely to enact humorous messages to communicate in a variety of situations.

Cognitive processing and retrieval differences have also been noted. In Booth-Butterfield and Booth-Butterfield (1990) higher AOs were able to recall more emotion words in a general timed test than did low AOs. Similarly, when given oral examples of self-relevant incidents employing affect, low AOs exhibited longer latencies to start and more pausing in the recounting compared to high AOs. This suggests that high-trait AO enhances facility of communication production when dealing with the topic of emotion.

In a related area, Dillard, Plotnick, Godbold, Freimuth, and Edgar (1996) studied how AO influences individuals' responses to fear appeals in health related public service announcements. They found that high AOs respond with more emotion and attitude change to fear inducements compared to low AOs. Conversely, fear messages had less impact on low AOs. This result has implications for how we frame messages to achieve the maximum change in audiences. Now we know that AO is not associated with need for cognition (Booth-Butterfield & Booth-Butterfield, 1990, 1996), which means that AOs are not simply avoiding thinking, but the focus of their thinking and cognitively processing is emotion-based and what that emotion means for them.

Booth-Butterfield and Booth-Butterfield (1990) found AO to be positively related to the personality traits of conversational sensitivity and femininity, indicating that AOs are more responsive and sympathetic to others and tend to be cognizant of conversational undercurrents and agendas. A later study (Booth-Butterfield & Booth-Butterfield, 1994) indicated (not surprisingly perhaps) that affect intensity and private self-consciousness were positively correlated with AO. Hence, people who are more affectively oriented tend to feel their emotions more strongly and to be aware of even subtle changes in how they view themselves and the interactions around them. That same study also noted that high AOs tend to be more romantic and idealistic in their beliefs about interpersonal relationships.

Cross-cultural differences in sensitivity to and use of emotion have also been noted. Frymier, Ishii, and Klopf (1990) reported that Japanese individuals had lower levels of AO than Americans. Furthermore, there were minimal male-female differences in the trait among Japanese respondents. (Because this is the only cross-cultural comparison of which we are aware, additional research among different cultures seems to be a fruitful area to pursue.)

McCroskey and Richmond (1995) used AO to establish the divergent validity of talkaholism, reporting that AO was not related to compulsive talking. Students with different college majors have even been found to differ on AO (Booth-Butterfield & Crayton, 1994), with students in the fine arts and literature being more likely to have high AO and students with engineering and physics majors more likely to have low AO. Such findings have implications for instructional communication (see Table 8.1 for the correlations found in affective orientation studies).

What emerges is a pattern of responding where high AOs sense and respond to affective cues, whether their own or among people around them. They then consider those affect cues and allow them to guide their reactions and communicative behavior.

MODEL OF THE PROCESS

Examination of the composition, emergence, and influence of emotions on thinking and behavior is controversial and complex (Berscheid, 1987; Zajonc, 1980). Simply put, AO conceptually focuses on cognition about affect. This approach involves the individual's thought and rumination about his or her emotional state, typically under circumstances of low to moderate autonomic system arousal.

Table 8.1. Correlations of Affective Orientation.

	AO Correlation	N	Authors
Need for cognition	.07	94	Booth-Butterfield and Booth-Butterfield (1990)
Communication apprehension	-.03		
Masculinity	.13	94	
Femininity	.31	94	
Conversational sensitivity	.28	37	
Self-monitoring	.02	43	
Affect intensity	.37	172	Booth-Butterfield and Booth-Butterfield (1994)
Extroversion	.19	172	
Neuroticism	.14	172	
Public self-consciousness	.19	172	
Private self-consciousness	.36	172	
Blunting style	.09	172	
Monitoring style	.18	172	
Romantic beliefs	.22	172	
Humor Orientation	.26	161	Wanzer, Booth-Butterfield, and Booth-Butterfield (1995)
Comforting	.19	93	Dolin and Booth-Butterfield, (1993)
Nonverbal sensitivity	.45	122	Booth-Butterfield and Andrighetti (1993)
Assertiveness	.00	122	Booth-Butterfield and Andrighetti (1993)
Talkaholism	.00	660	McCroskey and Richmond (1995)
Expression of negative emotions	.30	78	Yelsma (1995)
Expression of positive emotions	.14	78	Yelsma (1995)
Parent-child	.45	133 pairs or 266	Booth-Butterfield and Sidelinger (in press)

The model we present here describes the sequence of cognitive events leading up to communication action. The model does not specify behavior, but explains how AO mediates the process, resulting in different antecedents of behavior. The model begins with some form of triggering event.

If an external triggering event is direct and extreme, one's level of AO will have negligible influence on the outcome. For instance, if a real danger such as a gunbearing mugger is presented, most people, whether high or low AO, will react with intense fear and will attempt to escape. Additionally, high intensity emotions tend to demand immediate action, whereas low intensity emotional situations typically allow more time for cognitive work. In cases demanding immediate, emergency actions there is little time for even high AOs to ruminate about feelings. But as we see here, if time is available, high AOs will use the cognitive time between trigger and decision differently, or come to different conclusions than low AOs.

Extremely dangerous events requiring instantaneous reaction are uncommon. For the most part, we contend with day-to-day situations and interactions. Potentially emotional communication events such as the threat imposed when someone invades our personal space in line, when we receive notification of insufficient bank funds, our partner demands more commitment, or we face loneliness and choices about what to do with our time are much more realistic occurrences. It is when confronting these types of circumstances that the trait of AO exhibits the most influence (see figure 8.1.).

The first step in describing the role of AO is to examine the impact of emotional intensity. If the emotion felt is very strong and immediate to the situation (e.g., annoyance when someone carelessly knocks our lunch out of our hands, extreme fear brought on by claustrophobia, or joy at receiving a prize) the emotion is readily recognized by most individuals.

However, if the intensity is low to moderate, we will observe differences due to AO. High AOs tend to recognize and interpret even subtle emotional responses within themselves. This leads to internal scrutiny or cognition about the relevance of the emotion for the situation. Low AOs, in contrast, are unlikely to recognize low-level emotional responses until they reach a much stronger level of intensity.

To illustrate, low AOs may overlook feelings of emotional discomfort in the presence of another person. They may simply be unaware of their reactions until the discomfort reaches a higher level, breaches a threshold of awareness, and demands cognitive attention. (This is the *interrupt* that Mandler 1984, referenced when he stipulated that we experience emotion when the normal cognitive flow is interrupted.

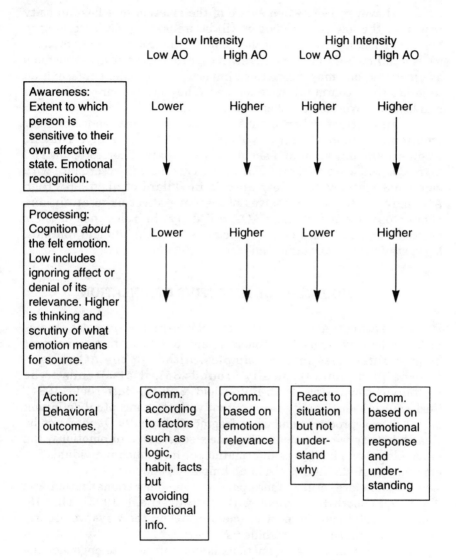

Figure 8.1. Emotional responses

However, even when aware of the emotion in a low-intensity response, the low AO responder will be unlikely to act according to his or her feelings because of the denial of the relevance of emotions as useful. Low AOs may eventually recognize their affective reactions as emotions, but may reject their importance as salient information to guide their communicative actions. They may ignore affect cues and look for diversion to other forms of data.

In contrast, when high AOs consider the relevance of their emotional responses, they typically view it positively. That is, emotions are important and should be listened to. Therefore, low and high AOs will act differently. The high AO will act in accordance with emotional response (e.g., fear appeals in Dillard et al., 1996). High AOs may act to rid themselves of negative affect or to attain and bolster positive affect. Low AOs will deny the relevance of their emotions and act based on other factors such as habits and routines, logic, statistical information, and so on.

MEASUREMENT OF AFFECTIVE ORIENTATION

Relation between AO and other variables exhibited in most studies have tended to be small to moderate, and to demonstrate consistent gender differences in U.S. samples. Although the AO scale is internally reliable (typically around .85), it also tends to be multidimensional (see Booth-Butterfield & Booth-Butterfield, 1994). Such multidimensionality is consistent with the conceptual definition of AO, it can produce somewhat fragmented results. It may not be clear whether we are measuring one's sensitivity to emotions, the value placed on emotion as information, or how much individuals use emotions to guide their decision making and behavior.

Therefore, a new, more parsimonious operationalization was developed (Booth-Butterfield & Booth-Butterfield, 1996). This 15-item scale refocuses the measurement of AO on the ways we use our emotions as information to guide us.

Mere sensitivity to emotions is not sufficient to engender the communication behaviors that follow. Mandler (1984) contended that an "emotion" occurs when an expected sequence is interrupted, causing autonomic nervous system arousal (see also Berscheid, 1987). Thus, when we become attentive to the interruption, we experience and label the emotion. But use of that emotion as information is subsequent to the sensitivity stage. That is, we could regularly be aware of our affective state without following its dictates.

Similarly, valuing our emotions is not the same as considering them seriously in interactions. Most people would agree that emotions are important to them, but what do they do with them? We are primarily interested in those individuals who not only sense and value their emotions, but actually scrutinize and give them credence to influence behavior. Their affect is a guiding force for them. We reason that if people report that they consider and use their emotions, then the awareness and valuation of their emotions must be presumed (see Buck, 1985). Hence, the focus for the new AO measurement is on the using and direction given by affect in one's life.

An important point to make about measuring AO and its effects revolves around triggering the affect in research. If participants' emotion is not "triggered", trait AO will not necessarily influence outcomes. This has been an issue in some correlational research. High AOs do not necessarily respond significantly differently than do low AOs if the trait is not made salient to the situation. For example, if people are in a "happy mood" but the mood has nothing to do with the current task or situation, it may exert negligible influence even among high AOs. This pattern is comparable to activating trait communication apprehension, verbal aggression, and the like. People who are high on the trait do not automatically communicate or behave any differently than others unless the trait is activated. For affectively oriented thinking and communication production to be activated people have to be in an emotional state, or have to have their emotions elicited for perusal. If research participants are sitting passively in classrooms while responding to scales, it is not surprising that effects for AO will tend to be small or unfocused. Therefore, efforts should be made to elicit emotion that is salient to the research situation at hand, in order to uncover the clearest affective orientation effects.

COMPARISON OF TWO MEASURES

At this point it is an appropriate to consider which version is preferable when a researcher is looking for a measure of AO. The answer depends somewhat on the focus of the study.

The original AO (Booth-Butterfield & Booth-Butterfield, 1990) is highly reliable (i.e., over .80) and taps in to several dimensions associated with emotions and communication. It contains items addressing sensitivity to or awareness of one's own emotions, the relative importance or value the communicator holds for felt emotions, and the extent to which sources consult or use their emotional responses to give direction to decisions they must make and to interactive behavior produced. Thus, if a researcher plans to study an array of emotion-related processing, the 20-item AO scale might be preferable. For example, in studying alexithymia, Taylor (1994) found the sensitivity factor of AO most strongly associated with lack of awareness of feelings.

However, for most AO research we believe the AO15 is the preferable measure for three reasons. It offers a more definitionally focused, concise operationalization of AO, it exhibits minimal gender differences in mean scores, and it is psychometrically more sound than the original AO scale.

First, it makes conceptual sense that AO measurement should focus on whether one considers and implements emotional information. Such an approach presumes awareness, as illustrated in Figure 8.1. If communicators react with knee-jerk emotional responses when highly aroused, this fails to illustrate the AO process. Similarly, mere sensitivity to emotion, without examining message formation, is largely internal. As communication researchers, it is also appropriate that we focus most directly on communicative outcomes of the process of being aware of, valuing, and subsequently allowing emotion to guide interactions.

Second, the original AO scale has demonstrated a consistent, approximate 5-point gap in the mean scores of males versus females. In our society, females tend to learn to be emotionally sensitive and vigilant about their own emotional state. There are well-documented patterns of male-female differences in both the encoding and decoding of emotional nonverbal expressions (Hall, 1984). Thus, it is more productive, in terms of understanding human interactions, to directly assess deliberation and use rather than sensitivity to emotions, the dimension that exhibits such consistent gender bias. Indeed, the AO15 scale shows much reduced differences between the sexes on actual utilization of emotions (Booth-Butterfield & Booth-Butterfield, 1996).

Finally, the AO15 appears to be a psychometrically superior instrument to the original version. Confirmatory factor analysis shows that the factors fit the conceptual structure more closely than the 20-item measure (Booth-Butterfield & Booth-Butterfield, 1996). Thus, this version of the scale is likely to discern effects at a lower level, and hence reveal stronger relationships with researchers' constructs of interest because is it psychometrically more focused.

Importantly, the introduction of the AO15 does not undermine any of the previous research conducted with the 20-item scale. Rather, if the research were to be redone with the newer scale, any effects found would be likely to be larger.

NEW DIRECTIONS IN RESEARCH ON AFFECTIVE ORIENTATION

We are currently investigating the effects of AO with a variety of health applications. This is a potentially useful and important area for applied communication research because of the critical role communication plays in the uptake, maintenance, and/or cessation of risky behaviors such as drug and tobacco use, unsafe sex, poor nutrition, and sedentary lifestyle. In this section, we detail preliminary results of our research looking at the role AO plays in tobacco use.

BACKGROUND ON TOBACCO USE

At present, the United States faces an unexpected and unwanted increase in youth tobacco use (Escobedo & Peddicord, 1996; Nelson, et al., 1995; Nelson, Tomar, & Siegel, 1996; Pierce & Gilpin, 1995, 1996). Since 1992 a variety of surveys have indicated that increasingly children under the age of 18 have tried and are using tobacco compared to a long decline during the 1970s and 1980s. AO seems to be an especially good candidate for understanding and explaining why youth take up tobacco in the first place and how tobacco use is maintained. Consider each of these two points in detail.

First, tobacco uptake is connected with emotion-based factors (Evans, Farkas, Gilpin, Berry, & Pierce, 1995; Pierce & Gilpin, 1995; Schooler, Feighery, & Flora, 1996). Marketing strategies make emotional appeals (belonging, being cool) and peer influence depends in part on the emotional relationship among the peers. Family modeling depends on emotions as the links within the family are maintained or strengthened. It seems reasonable to assume that tobacco uptake is positively associated with AO.

Second, research demonstrates that tobacco use has important affect-maintenance properties. People use tobacco to relieve stress and boredom, to catch a "buzz," and in general manipulate their emotions (Anderson, Booth-Butterfield, & Williams, 1996; Evans et al., 1995). And, of course, nicotine, in addition to being physiologically addictive, also has demonstrated effects on mood and affect (Henningfield, 1995). It seems reasonable again, that continuing tobacco use is positively associated with AO.

TOBACCO STUDY METHODS

We administered a three-page survey to people enrolled in basic communication courses at West Virginia University. The participants completed the 15-item AO scale, the Need for Cognition scale (Cacioppo & Petty, 1982), and a five-choice scale that assessed their stage of change (Prochaska, 1994; Prochaska & DiClemente, 1983), age at tobacco startup (if a tobacco user), and an estimate of the number of cigarettes smoked on a daily basis (again if a tobacco user). Because our focus in this chapter is on AO, we only report here on the results with the AO scale and not discuss results of other measures. Researchers interested in additional information should contact us for details.

The stages of change is a descriptive model usually composed of five sequential steps people experience as they move from an old behavior (a health-risk action like smoking or leading a sedentary lifestyle) to a new behavior (tobacco-free, regular exercise). Similar to previous research with tobacco and stages, we identified these five steps: Never Smoked (people who had never smoked in their lives); Quit Smoking (people who had smoked, but had quit at least 6 months ago); Tried to Quit (current smokers who had made an attempt to quit smoking within the last 6 months); Thinking about Quitting (current smokers who were actively thinking about and preparing to quit smoking); and last, Current Smokers (people who were smokers and had not tried to quit or make plans to quit.

We hypothesized that AO should be related to the stages of change in two ways. First, given our rationale that links tobacco uptake to affective factors, Never Smokers should show lower AO scores compared to the other four stages (including quitters) because people in these four stages had used tobacco. Second, given the description of the Thinking about Quitting stage, these people should show a stronger cognitive orientation and therefore report lower AO compared to the remaining three smoking categories (Quitters, Triers, Current Smokers).

TOBACCO STUDY RESULTS

There were 234 respondents who completed the surveys. The average age of the sample was 21.7 years with a range of 17 to 51 years (SD = 4.7 years). Males composed 51% of the sample. Of the 72 respondents (31%) reported using tobacco at some time (current or former smokers), a proportion that is consistent with other surveys of people this age. The mean age at smoking startup was 16.4 years (SD = 2.2 years). Thus, the majority of tobacco users in this sample started as adolescents, a finding consistent with recent research (Nelson et al., 1995; Nelson et al., 1996).

The stages of change analysis divided respondents into one of five mutually exclusive categories (category N and percentage): Never Smoked (162, 69%), Quit in the last 6 months (13, 6%), Smoke, but Tried to Quit in last 6 months (20, 9%), Smoke, but Thinking about Quitting (28, 12%), and Currently Smoking (11, 5%).

Our main focus was to understand the relation between AO and tobacco use. Recall our first hypothesis that posits an AO difference between Never Smokers and the other four smoking categories. Table 8.2 displays AO means by the five stages. We ran a comparison of the Never Smokers versus those who were Current or Former Smokers. An F test showed a statistically reliable effect (F[1, 229) = 4.14, p < .043, d = .22, a "small" effect size) showing that respondents who never smoked had lower AO than current or former users. This evidence supports the first hypothesis.

Our second hypothesis claimed a difference between those Thinking about Quitting versus all other smoking categories. We therefore, ran another comparison between those Thinking about Quitting versus Smokers, Quitters, and Tried to Quit. This F test also showed a statistically reliable effect (F[1, 229] = 4.79, p < .03, d = .25, a "small" effect size) showing that Thinkers also had lower AO than other user categories. This evidence supports the second hypothesis.

We also explored whether AO interacted with the age or gender of the respondent, but found no statistically significant effects at the .05 alpha level. We also investigated the main effects of these variables on smoking and found no significant effects.

TOBACCO STUDY CONCLUSIONS

This survey discloses a potential link between an important health behavior, smoking, and AO. These results suggest that smoking uptake and maintenance are related to AO in theoretically predictable ways. Specifically, the data indicate that tobacco users are more likely to use their emotions as a guide to action in tobacco uptake and/or maintenance. This link partly explains why tobacco advertising may be more successful with some younger people compared to other youngsters. Children who are more affectively oriented will respond more favorably to emotion-oriented marketing appeals by using their positive feelings as a motivation or guide to tobacco uptake. Conversely, lower AO children, those who are guided

Table 8.2. Mean AO Scores by Stage of Change.

Smokers	Quitters	Tried	Think	Never
53.5	57.4	54.6	50.5	51.1

by factual information, appear to be less influenced by emotional marketing. This evidence also helps explain the modeling effects in tobacco uptake whereby children imitate family members and peers. Doubtless, the positive affect these relationships hold motivates higher AO children to try tobacco.

Assuming that these results are not sample-specific, there are interesting implications for prevention campaigns. Our read of this data is to suggest that prevention messages should make strong emotional appeals that accomplish two goals. First, the campaign should stimulate negative affect (fear, anger, disgust) in the receiver. Second, the campaign should link that negative affect with tobacco. We would predict that such a campaign would be a successful method for creating and strengthening negative attitudes toward tobacco uptake. Given that people with higher AO appear to be at slightly higher risk of uptake, emotion-focused messages might show greater impact.

The evidence from the second hypothesis demonstrates a subtle effect of AO. Although the data indicate that people who use tobacco have higher AO compared to those who never used tobacco, there is yet another distinction among the users. Those who are thinking about quitting report lower AO compared to their peers. We see this as a comparison that is demanded by the definition of this particular stage. The "planning" stage is described as a high cognition phase where people actively consider and make plans for changing their behavior. Given that we followed current practice described in this stage, we would expect that AO scores for this category should be lower. We would predict that if the wording of the stage was changed to reflect a more emotional orientation ("I have felt like trying to quit") the results might be quite different.

CONCLUSIONS ABOUT AO AND HEALTH

Our results here are certainly preliminary and we need to explore the link between AO and tobacco use with other populations before we can be confident of it. However, the results are encouraging enough to support continued investigation with tobacco. Furthermore, we think that the results here demonstrate that AO might be a profitable variable to study in a variety of health-risk areas. (See also Bleiker, van der Ploeg, Hendricks, & Adler, 1996.)

We are also exploring the indirect role the AO plays in health through an investigation of its effect on message processing. As part of a multiphase campaign to encourage people to drink low fat milk (Reger, Wootan, Booth-Butterfield, & Smith, 1996), we are looking at how campaign messages are processed by level of AO. We suspect that emotion-based advertising messages should play a stronger role in influencing high AO viewers to switch. This is consistent with Dillard et al.'s (1996) work that demonstrated differential effects for recipients of mediated messages.

Health communication is certainly not the only application of AO. The health and message processing applications just discussed might be usefully extended to mass media research in general. Preliminary evidence (Booth-Butterfield & Crayton, 1994) suggests that AO may be salient in classroom contexts—both for teachers and students. Because interpersonal relationships are so often centered around emotions and the expression of affect, the area of relational communication is a primary area for further research on AO.

From a less trait approach, it would be productive to examine communication situations that bring affect to the foreground. It seems reasonable to conjecture that some circumstances, tasks, or communicative goals (e.g., high-level government decisions) are more firmly based on logic and factual data. Other tasks accentuate affective-oriented thinking in most communicators (e.g., a decision concerning what type of art to purchase).

However, even in the latter situation, an argument could be made that depending on the AO trait, people would rely on different forms of data to make their art decision. The low AO buys art because it has high resale value, or it blends with the existing decor. In comparison, high AOs select art because of they ways in which it gives them pleasure, soothes them, or in some way plays on their emotions.

Research on how emotions are used by individuals to guide communication production is in its early stages. We know that some individuals disregard their own affective reactions until the level of arousal becomes so high that it cannot be ignored. They then may act according to their emotional response, but they might not know why. It is mere reaction, not considered communication production. We know that others actively engage their affective state, readily recognize and consult their feelings in making decisions. Thus, some people orient to their communicative world through their emotions— hence the construct's label, *affective orientation*.

AFFECTIVE ORIENTATION

Directions: The following statements refer to the feelings and emotions people have and how people use their feelings and emotions to guide their behaviors. There are no right or wrong answers. Also realize that emotions and feelings can be positive or negative. One person can feel anger; another can feel love and tenderness. Both cases, however, are emotion. Use the following 5-point scale to indicate your answer.

Strongly Agree	Agree	Uncertain	Disagree	Strongly Disagree
5	4	3	2	1

_____ 1. I use my feelings to determine what I should do in situations.

_____ 2. I listen to what my "gut" or "heart" says in many situations.

_____ 3. My emotions tell me what to do in many cases.

_____ 4. I try not to let feelings guide my actions.

_____ 5. I am aware of and use my feelings as a guide more than others do.

_____ 6. I won't let my emotions influence how I act most of the time.

_____ 7. I follow what my feelings say I should do in most situations.

_____ 8. Most of the time I avoid letting my emotions guide what I do.

_____ 9. I usually let my internal feelings direct my behavior.

_____ 10. Usually my emotions are good predictors of how I will act.

_____ 11. My actions are often influenced by my awareness of my emotions.

_____ 12. My emotions provide me solid direction in my life.

_____ 13. How I act often depends on what my feelings tell me to do.

_____ 14. Even subtle emotions often guide my actions.

_____ 15. When I am aware of my emotional response, I listen to it to determine what to do.

Figure 8.2. Affective Orientation 15 (AO15)

REFERENCES

Anderson, R., Booth-Butterfield, M., & Williams, K. (1996). *Adolescent tobacco use: What's in it for them?* Paper presented at the annual conference of the American Public Health Association, New York.

Bagby, M., & Taylor, G. (in press). Measurement and validation of the alexithymia construct. In G. Taylor, M. Bagby, & J. Parker (Eds.), *Disorders of affect regulation: Alexithymia in medical and psychiatric illness* (pp. 56-76). Cambridge, UK: Cambridge University Press.

Belsky, J. (1993). Etiology of child maltreatment: A developmental-ecological analysis. *Psychological Bulletin, 114*, 413-434.

Berscheid, E. (1987). Emotion and interpersonal communication. In M. Roloff & G. R. Miller (Eds.), *Interpersonal processes: New directions in communication research* (pp. 77-88) Newbury Park, CA: Sage.

Bleiker, E., van der Ploeg, H., Hendricks, J., & Adler, H. (1996). Personality factors and breast cancer development: A prospective longitudinal study. *Journal of the National Cancer Institute, 88*, 1478-1482.

Booth-Butterfield, M., & Andrighetti, A. (1993). *The role of affective orientation and nonverbal sensitivity in the interpretation of communication in acquaintance rape.* Paper presented at the annual convention of the Eastern Communication Association, New Haven, CT.

Booth-Butterfield, M., & Booth-Butterfield, S. (1990). Conceptualizing affect as information in communication production. *Human Communication Research, 16*, 451-476.

Booth-Butterfield, M., & Booth-Butterfield, S. (1992). *Communication apprehension and avoidance in the classroom.* Edina, MN: Burgess International Group.

Booth-Butterfield, M., & Booth-Butterfield, S. (1994). The affective orientation to communication: Conceptual and empirical distinctions. *Communication Quarterly, 42*, 331-344.

Booth-Butterfield, M., & Booth-Butterfield, S. (1996). Using your emotions: Improving the measurement of affective orientation. *Communication Research Reports, 13*, 157-163.

Booth-Butterfield, M., & Crayton, M. (1994). *A known-groups comparison of affective orientation.* Unpublished manuscript.

Booth-Butterfield, M., & Sidelinger, R. (in press). The relationship between parental traits and open family communication: Affective orientation and verbal aggression. *Communication Research Reports, 13*.

Buck, R. (1985). Prime Theory: An integrated view of motivation and emotion. *Psychological Review, 92*, 389-413.

Cacioppo, J., & Petty, R. (1982). The need for cognition. *Journal of Personality and Social Psychology, 42*, 116-131.

Dillard, J., Plotnick, C., Godbold, L., Freimuth, V., & Edgar, T. (1996). The multiple affective outcomes of AIDS PSAs: Fear appeals do more than scare people. *Communication Research, 23*, 44-72.

Dolin, D., & Booth-Butterfield, M. (1993). Reach out and touch someone: Analysis of nonverbal comforting responses. *Communication Quarterly, 41*, 383-393.

Escobedo, L., & Peddicord, J. (1996). Smoking prevalence in US birth cohorts: The influence of gender and education. *American Journal of Public Health, 86,* 231-236.

Evans, N., Farkas, A., Gilpin, E., Berry, C., & Pierce, J. (1995). Influence of tobacco marketing and exposure to smokers on adolescent susceptibility to smoking. *Journal of the National Cancer Institute, 87,* 1538-1545.

Frymier, A., Klopf, D., & Ishii, S. (1990). Affect orientation: Japanese compares to Americans. *Communication Research Reports, 7,* 63-66.

Hall, J. (1984). *Nonverbal sex differences.* Baltimore, MD: Johns Hopkins University Press.

Henningfield, J. (1995). Nicotine medications for smoking cessation. *The New England Journal of Medicine, 333,* 1196-1203.

Holden, C. (1987). Genetics of personality. *Science, 237,* 598-601.

Jockin, V., McGue, M., & Lykken, D. (1996). Personality and divorce: A genetic analysis. *Journal of Personality and Social Psychology, 71,* 288-299.

Johnston, D., Stinski, M., & Meyers, D. (1993). Development of an alexithymia instrument to measure the diminished communication of affect. *Communication Research Reports, 10,* 149-160.

Mandler, G. (1984). *Mind and body: Psychology of emotion and stress.* New York: Norton.

McCroskey, J. (1984). The communication apprehension perspective. In J. Daly & J. McCroskey (Eds.), *Avoiding communication: Shyness, reticence, and communication apprehension* (pp. 13-33). Beverly Hills, CA: Sage.

McCroskey, J., & Richmond, V. (1995). Correlates of compulsive communication: Quantitative and qualitative characteristics. *Communication Quarterly, 43,* 39-52.

Nelson, D., Giovino, G., Shopland, D., Mowery, P., Mills, S., & Eriksen, M. (1995). Trends in cigarette smoking among US adolescents, 1974 through 1991. *American Journal of Public Health, 85,* 34-40.

Nelson, D., Tomar, S., & Siegel, P. (1996). Trends in smokeless tobacco use among men in four states, 1998 through 1993. *American Journal of Public Health, 86,* 1300-1302.

Pierce, J., & Gilpin, E. (1995). A historical analysis of tobacco marketing and the uptake of smoking by youth in the United States: 1890-1977. *Health Psychology, 14,* 500-508.

Pierce, J., & Gilpin, E. (1996). How long will today's new adolescent smoker be addicted to cigarettes? *American Journal of Public Health, 86,* 253-257.

Prochaska, J. (1994). Strong and weak principles for progressing from precontemplation to action on the basis of twelve problem behaviors. *Health Psychology, 13*, 47-51.

Prochaska, J., & DiClemente, C. (1983). Stages and processes of self-change of smoking: Toward an integrative model of change. *Journal of Consulting and Clinical Psychology, 51*, 390-395.

Reger, W., Wootan, M., Booth-Butterfield, S., & Smith, H. (1996). *1% or less: A community-based nutrition campaign.* Manuscript submitted for publication.

Schooler, C., Feighery, E., & Flora, J. (1996). Seventh graders' self-reported exposure to cigarette marketing and its relationship to their smoking behavior. *American Journal of Public Health, 86*, 1216-1221.

Sidelinger, R., & Booth-Butterfield, M. (1997). *The influence of family communication on the college-age child: Openness, attitudes about sex and alcohol use, and Affective Orientation.* Paper presented at the annual convention of the International Communication Association, Montreal.

Taylor, G. (1994). The alexithymia construct: Conceptualization, validation, and relationship with basic dimensions of personality. *New Trends in Experimental and Clinical Psychiatry, 10*, 61-74.

Wanzer, M., Booth-Butterfield, M., & Booth-Butterfield, S. (1995). The funny people: A source-orientation to the communication of humor. *Communication Quarterly, 43*, 142-154.

Yelsma, P. (1995). Couples' affective orientations and their verbal abusiveness. *Communication Quarterly, 43*, 100-114.

Zajonc, R. (1980). Feeling and thinking: Preferences need no inferences. *American Psychologist, 35*, 151-175.

9

Verbal Aggressiveness

Charles J. Wigley III
Canisius College

Sometimes, when we have really good ideas, we express these ideas as if they belong to us. We say, "Here's my idea" and "I think you'll like my idea." We take pride in offering our ideas to others, and, in many ways, treat the idea as an extension of ourselves. Similarly, when we attack ideas, we often associate them with a particular person. We say things like, "I disagree with your idea because . . . " and "Your idea isn't so good, because. . . ." We treat the idea as if it is owned by the other person, and as if it is an extension of that person. People become personally involved with the ideas they discuss, and, sometimes, people view an attack on an idea as an attack on themselves. It becomes risky to argue ideas with others because losing an argument might lead us to feel that we have suffered a personal loss.

In some cases (which happen often), when two people are arguing, one of them will start to sense that he or she is losing the argument. Because the person feels attached to his or her own argument, a sense of personal loss, and a feeling of defensiveness may surface. Perhaps sensing that the best defense is a good offense,

191

the person tries even harder to defeat the opponent's position. However, as the argument continues, and the person runs out of good evidence and reasons why his or her opponent's ideas are wrong, it is easy to see how the person might personally attack his or her opponent with verbal assaults. After all, if the idea cannot be defeated directly, maybe the source of the idea can be defeated!

When people are unable to generate enough arguments to defeat the opponent's position, they suffer from a deficiency in arguing skills. Incapable of generating enough evidence or reasons to meet the heavy burden of destroying the opponent's position, the person resorts to attacking the opponent's self concept. Whereas argumentation involves the use of evidence and reason to reach conclusions, verbal aggression involves the use of attacks on the other person's self-concept, such as character attacks, in order to "win" during an argument. Such a win is likely to result in a sense of personal loss by the opponent, but a sense of victory by the aggressor. Because people feel good about winning, they begin to associate verbal aggression with the rewards of winning, and they start to rely on verbal aggression when dealing with others. When reliance on verbal aggression becomes so frequent that it can be predicted that the individual will use verbal aggression in future encounters, the individual is said to be verbally aggressive. Verbal aggressiveness refers to the tendency to attack the self-concept of another person in face-to-face encounters, instead of, or in addition to, attacks on another's arguments (Infante & Rancer, 1982). The attack is directed against the other person, rather than against the person's ideas.

Whereas some people resort to particular forms of aggression, such as attacking an opponent's character or background, other people resort to a variety of aggressive messages. In order to gain a better understanding of how verbal aggression is actually used by people, Infante (1987) researched the primary kinds of verbally aggressive messages. He found that verbally aggressive people resort to using one or more of the following kinds of messages: character attacks, competence attacks, background attacks, physical appearance attacks, maledictions, teasing, swearing, ridicule, threats, and nonverbal emblems. Infante (1995) said that other forms of aggression are sometimes used, such as blame, personality attacks, commands, global rejection, disconfirmation, negative comparison, sexual harassment, and attacking target's significant others. There seems to be no shortage of ways to cause other people to feel badly about themselves. However, when we think of these specific types of aggressive messages, we start to see how easily a person can become aggressive toward other people.

Although some people are generally more verbally aggressive than others it also seems likely that some situations are more likely to lead to aggressive exchanges. When the topic is of great importance and the consequences of the discussion are meaningful to those involved, the motivation for winning is greater. These high motivation situations arise in dating relationships, family settings, work environments, and a host of other situations. When positive conflict becomes negative controversy, constructive arguers become destructive aggressors. Although the aggressive individual might protest that the situation justified the aggression, our research suggests that, more often than not, aggression leads to aggression, misunderstanding, bad feelings, and negative long-term consequences. The value of studying verbal aggression lies not only in identifying highly aggressive individuals so that they can get better control of their aggressions, but in identifying how verbal aggression operates in particular settings, so that people can try to avoid and minimize the negative consequences of aggression.

In Infante and Wigley (1986), we set out to develop a way to identify aggressive individuals so that we could better understand them as people, and so that we could gain a better understanding of how they behave in particular settings. We developed the Verbal Aggressiveness scale. This is a 20-item personality test that asks people about their aggressions toward others. We assume that people know whether they are aggressive toward others, and that they would honestly report their level of aggression to us. Because some people, no doubt, recognize that verbal aggression is, often, damaging to relationships, we tried to make the questions seem as if we (the researchers) think aggression is sometimes justifiable. People might find their aggressions easier to admit when they report on the behavior to others who seem to share the view that, sometimes, aggression is called for in the situations. A shorter, 10-item version of the questionnaire has been used to study verbally aggressive behavior between spouses (Infante, Chandler, & Rudd, 1989; Infante, Chandler, Sabourin, Rudd, & Shannon, 1990; Rudd, Burant, & Beatty, 1994; Sabourin, Infante, & Rudd, 1993). A copy of the 10-item questionnaire can be found in Rudd et al. (1994).

Another way to discover people's levels of aggressiveness involves describing a variety of social situations and asking people which of six different kinds of messages they would use in each particular situation (Infante & Wigley, 1986). For each of the social situations, people are told that they want to convince someone else to do something. Four of the messages are not at all verbally aggressive, whereas two of the possible messages imply that the person would resort to verbal aggression. More aggressive people are more likely to select the aggressive messages. A similar method, using 18 messages for each scenario, 4 of which were verbally aggressive, has also been used (Infante, Trebing, Shepherd, & Seeds, 1984).

We know that verbal aggressiveness differs from person to person, but what causes it? What are the consequences of verbal aggressiveness? What steps can we take to reduce aggressiveness? These are important questions, because human relationships are precious commodities that take a long time to develop and a short time to destroy. The questions are discussed here.

CAUSES OF VERBAL AGGRESSIVENESS AS A CROSS-SITUATIONALLY CONSISTENT PREDISPOSITION

Why does verbal aggressiveness occur? One of the earliest articles (Infante, Trebing, et al. 1984) specifically addressing the primary causes of verbal aggression identified four main causes, including psychopathology (an individual expresses previously repressed hostility), disdain for the target of aggression, social learning of aggression, and an argumentative skill deficiency (ASD; an individual fails to attack the opponent's ideas successfully, and, instead, attacks the advocate of the disfavored idea).

A psychopathological basis for aggression seems likely in some of the extreme cases, and its investigation is more appropriately reserved for trained psychologists. The focus of this chapter is on those causes of verbal aggression that might meaningfully be addressed through skills enhancement achieved through personal efforts. "Disdain for the target of aggression" helps us understand why some people are consistently verbally aggressive toward some individuals, but not toward others. Long-standing interpersonal difficulties and misunderstandings might prevent an individual from effectively dealing with particular others. However, it seems that the aggression problem is not usually restricted to a select group of opponents. Rather, most verbally aggressive individuals seem to express aggression toward any number of other people. Although further research is needed to explore this issue, current research seems to provide substantial evidence that the two main causes of verbal aggressiveness are social learning and ASD.

The social learning explanation is strongly supported by a number of studies. As a socially learned way of dealing with others, verbal aggression might become strongly ingrained in one's personality. In fact, verbal aggression might become one of a person's more noticeable characteristics. Building on earlier research by

Norman (1963), McCrae and Costa (1987), said that personality characteristics can be broken into five main groups that they label *neuroticism, extraversion, openness, agreeableness,* and *conscientiousness.* Infante (1987) explained that verbal aggressiveness is, generally, a way of expressing hostility and, therefore, is an aspect of neuroticism. In contrast, it is easy to see how *argumentativeness,* defined by Infante and Rancer (1982) as the tendency to advance and refute controversial issues, has been considered a form of extraversion (Infante, 1987). Because Neuroticism appears to categorize a large number of negative characteristics, verbal aggressiveness might incubate and grow with this aspect of one's personality. Consistent with this theoretical conceptualization, research evidence suggests that argumentativeness and verbal aggressiveness are not generally related (Infante & Wigley, 1986) and that high, moderate, and low argumentatives are equally likely to use any of the 10 primary forms of verbal aggression (Infante & Rancer, 1993).

If a person sees others succeed through the use of aggression, he or she might experiment by also using verbal aggression. If the individual views the experiment as successful, his or her sense of reward for using aggression will generate and reinforce its use in the future. It is easy to see how modeling the behaviors of successful aggressors can result in development of the characteristic. Certainly, a number of movie heroes are models for aggression (e.g., Clint Eastwood's "Do ya' feel lucky punk, well, do ya' . . ."), as well as television personalities such as Roseanne and Don Rickles.

There is strong support for the conclusion that some verbal aggression results from an ASD. The study by Infante, Trebing et al. (1984) was particularly significant in its finding that high, moderate, and low argumentatives were equally likely to use verbally aggressive messages with adaptable opponents (people willing to change). Additionally, although moderate and low argumentatives were more likely to favor verbally aggressive messages with obstinate than adaptable opponents, high argumentatives did not alter their preferences based on whether the opponent was adaptable or obstinate. This set of research findings is particularly valuable because it shows that training in argumentation might reduce the likelihood that a person will rely on verbal aggression. Finally, the study found that situational variables might have a major role in determining any apparent differences in verbal aggressiveness between males and females. Although gender did not predict preference for verbally aggressive messages, men were more likely than women to use verbally aggressive messages when the opponent was perceived as adaptable.

Verbal Aggressiveness as Genetically Determined

Beatty and McCroskey (1997) argued that verbal aggressiveness is largely the result of genetics. They demonstrated that a neurobiological explanation of verbal aggressiveness is much more complete than theoretical models based on social learning. In their explanation of a temperament-based model of verbal aggressiveness, Beatty and McCroskey strongly underscored the need for understanding neurobiological bases of verbal aggressiveness. These authors cited some of the empirical evidence available to support the neurobiologically based perspective. For example, Horvath (1995) contrasted monozygotic (identical) and dyzygotic (fraternal) twins to determine the extent to which communicator style characteristics are genetically influenced. Using conservative measurement criteria, she found four characteristics that are likely to be influenced by genetic composition. The four characteristics, and the percentage of variance for each characteristic accounted for by genetic makeup, included openness (78%), communicator image (66%), relaxedness (62%), and dominance (50%). Horvath suggested that confidence in communication may be largely an inherited characteristic. Her findings have important ramifications for understanding people's levels of verbal aggressiveness. If genetics is an extremely strong influence on communicator style, why would it not be an extremely strong influence on verbal aggressiveness? Beatty and McCroskey (1997) advocated a paradigm shift that would allow for a more complete understanding of the causes of verbal aggressiveness. However, for now, I return to more traditional explanations of verbal aggressiveness.

Some Situational Determinants of Verbal Aggression

In a consideration of situational variables, Infante (1989) asked people to read a scenario describing a situation in which another individual is asked to engage in a particular behavior. The other individual was described as being highly argumentative and nonresponsive to the request. For the first communicative exchange, people were asked which of four particular messages they would use to try to persuade the other person to alter his or her position. A response by the other person was then indicated. These responses were either verbally aggressive or argumentative. In the second exchange, people were given an opportunity to indicate which of four particular messages they would use in response to the other person. A third exchange, similar to the second exchange, was then employed. Results indicate that when the other person gave an argumentative response to the advocate, gender failed to predict whether the advocate would select an argumentative or verbally aggressive response. However, when the other person gave a verbally aggressive response, males were more likely than females to respond in kind, and females were more likely than males to respond argumentatively. Gender of the other person failed to predict the advocate's preference for an argumentative or a verbally aggressive strategy. This study evidences the reciprocity effect of verbal aggressiveness for males (in other words; for males, aggressiveness begets aggressiveness), and suggests females may be particularly adept as mediators attempting moderation of verbally aggressive interaction (Infante, 1989). It builds on previous research that found that males were more likely than females to be verbally aggressive when arguing with a same-gender opponent (Infante, Wall, Leap, & Danielson, 1984).

When a listener (the target) responds negatively to a compliance-gaining effort, the compliance seeker (the persuader) is likely to engage in follow-up influence attempts. Lim (1990) found that persuaders were more verbally aggressive when targets were unfriendly rather than friendly, and, after a brief delay, persuaders resorted to higher levels of verbal aggression more quickly when targets showed more rather than less intense resistance. In situations in which targets showed intense resistance, persuaders delayed using higher levels of aggression. Initial levels of verbal aggression were slightly lower than in the weak resistance condition. According to Lim, this may be the result of efforts by the persuader at de-escalation (when they first encounter the strong resistance). However, soon afterward, when it becomes apparent that the effort at persuasion is about to fail, the persuader rapidly resorts to higher levels of aggression.

Lim's (1990) study is particularly valuable in demonstrating that situational factors (such as the friendliness and intensity of resistance of the target) play an important role in determining whether a persuader will manifest verbal aggressiveness. Hence, one's general level of verbal aggressiveness is, alone, not fully explanatory of the degree of verbal aggression evident in any given situation.

Overall, more research needs to investigate the causes of verbal aggressiveness. At this time, however, the evidence seems to point most clearly toward the social learning and ASD explanations of the trait. Additionally, situational factors include consideration of the behaviors of the receiver, such as whether the receiver responds in a friendly way, in an intense-negative manner, or with reciprocity (to an aggressive message). The second question concerns the consequences of verbal aggression.

CONSEQUENCES OF VERBAL AGGRESSIVENESS-INFLUENCES
ON THE INDIVIDUAL

Early studies describing the effects of verbal aggression frequently made reference to the damage to people's self-concepts, and some articles referenced the works of social psychologists (for an especially detailed review of the social psychology research on verbal aggressiveness, see Infante, 1987). More recently, the focus has shifted from an analysis at the more general level to the study of aggressiveness in particular contexts. This seems only natural because some relationships are more intense and more intimate than others. The value of success in dealing with others takes on greater importance in some situations more than it does in others.

Verbal aggression may occur more frequently when individuals become less sensitive to the variety of destructive consequences stemming from it. Infante, Riddle, Horvath, and Tumlin (1992) contrasted high and low verbal aggressives to determine whether they differed on the basis of type of aggressive messages sent, type of aggressive message received, perceived hurtfulness by type of verbally aggressive message, and reasons for endorsing verbal aggression. Subjects were asked to consider the previous 4-week period and indicate the frequency with which they sent the 10 types of messages (as described in Infante, 1987). They were also asked to indicate how frequently they received the 10 types of messages, and the degree of self-perceived psychological pain in receiving these messages. They were then asked to estimate the extent to which they used each of 12 reasons to endorse their use of verbally aggressive messages. The reasons were as follows: reciprocity, disdain for the target, feeling angry, unable to think of an effective argument, a rational discussion degenerating into a verbal fight, being taught to use verbal aggression, the situation reminding one of past hurt, being in a bad mood, trying to be humorous but not hurtful, having observed a television or movie character using verbal aggression effectively, trying to appear "tough," and wanting to be mean to the other person.

High verbal aggressives can be characterized and distinguished from low verbal aggressives by their use of competence attacks, teasing, and nonverbal emblems. Although background attacks, ridicule, and physical appearance attacks distinguish high and low aggressives, these three message types were not selected as frequently and, therefore, should probably not be considered as characteristic choices of verbal aggressives. The percentage of cases correctly classified was 48% for highs, and 84% for lows. The researchers could not find any significant differences in the types of verbally aggressive messages received by high versus low aggressives. Perceived threats, competence attacks, and physical appearance attacks were viewed as less hurtful by high verbal aggressives than low verbal aggressives. When high verbal aggressives are contrasted with low verbal aggressives, highs perceived threats, competence attacks, character attacks, maledictions, nonverbal emblems, and ridicule as less hurtful. The reasons for endorsing verbal aggression differentiated the groups, with high verbal aggressives endorsing the following reasons more frequently than low verbal aggressives: trying to appear "tough," being in rational discussions that degenerate into verbal fights, wanting to be mean to the target of verbal aggression, and wanting to express disdain for the message receiver. The percentage of cases correctly classified was 61% for highs, and 82% for lows. The lows, typically, were consistent across the types of aggression, whereas the highs were less consistent.

As the researchers suggested, these findings are valuable because they provide insight about individuals who are verbally aggressive. The ability correctly to classify such a greater percentage of low as opposed to high verbal aggressives on the basis of messages sent and reasons for using aggression suggests that low verbal aggressiveness might act more as a personality characteristic (generally stable) than high aggressiveness (more erratically demonstrated); (Infante, Riddle, et al.,1992). Situational influences may play a more significant role in understanding high verbal aggressiveness than low verbal aggressiveness (Infante, Riddle, et al., 1992). Perhaps the most important finding is that high verbal aggressives seemed less sensitive to the hurtfulness of verbally aggressive messages than did low verbal aggressives. The investigators explained that heightened awareness of the dire consequences of verbal aggressiveness among high verbal aggressives might inhibit its use.

Martin and Anderson (1996) provided some empirical support for the claim that heightened awareness of verbal aggressiveness might inhibit its use. They reported that more responsive individuals tend to be less verbally aggressive than low responsive individuals. Martin and Anderson highlighted consistent research findings suggesting that verbal aggressiveness leads to negative relational consequences. As they explained, because responsive individuals tend to be empathic and "other-oriented," they are less likely to be verbally aggressive. Confirmation of this relationship evidences that awareness by an individual of the costly consequences of verbal aggressiveness might play a pivotal role in reducing the individual's verbal aggressiveness. For example, Martin, Anderson, and Horvath (1996) found a positive relation between verbal aggressiveness and the perception that it is justified. If the negative consequences of verbal aggression are more fully understood by the verbally aggressive individual, the act of verbal aggression may seem less justifiable.

Source credibility has been a favored line of investigation by communication investigators for years. Infante, Hartley, Martin, Higgins, Bruning, and Hur (1992) hypothesized that message sources who initiate a high degree of verbal aggression in a discussion, as contrasted with sources initiating lower verbal aggression, will be perceived as less credible (measured as perceived character and competence) and as having produced fewer valid arguments. Also, targets of verbal aggression failing to reciprocate verbal aggression will be more credible and credited with having presented more valid arguments than reciprocating targets. People were separated into five groups and each group listened to one of five different audiotaped messages. The five taped messages varied as follows:(a) high verbal aggression and matching reciprocity (HR), (b) high verbal aggression and no reciprocity (HN), (c) low verbal aggression and matching reciprocity (LR), (d) low verbal aggression and no reciprocity (LN), and (e) no verbal aggression (NN: the control condition). The first hypothesis was partially confirmed in that sources initiating a high degree of verbal aggression were less credible, both in terms of perceived character and competence. Furthermore, they were credited with fewer valid arguments than were their targets. However, the number of valid arguments credited to the source did not meaningfully distinguish these sources (high in verbal aggression) from sources initiating lower verbal aggression. For the second hypothesis, the target of verbal aggression was perceived as more credible and as having more valid arguments than the initiator of verbal aggression. However, an interesting finding, and one contrary to the investigators' initial reasoning, was that individuals reciprocating verbal aggression were credited with having more valid arguments than nonreciprocating targets. Interestingly, the target's character was less favorably perceived when using a higher degree of verbal aggression (when compared to the control condition, i.e., when comparing HR with NN). The authors raised new questions in the discussion of their findings. Is restraint or reciprocity expected from the target of verbal aggression? What are the normative expectations? If further research demonstrates that reciprocity is a rewarded norm, then additional research will have to identify the circumstances where the norm operates.

Negative Consequences in Organizational Settings

Organizational communication research has benefited from studies of verbal aggressiveness. Infante and Gorden (1985) found that the more subordinates perceived superiors to be high in argumentativeness and low in verbal aggressiveness, the more subordinates were satisfied with their superior, believed their employee rights were protected, and had career satisfaction. Understanding levels of perceived partner verbal aggressiveness in the superior-subordinate relationship may provide considerable insight as to why some managers fail.

In a follow-up investigation, Infante and Gorden (1991) found that when superiors were perceived as verbally aggressive, subordinates had particularly low levels of organizational commitment, and they tended to be far less satisfied with their work and with their superiors. Conversely, superiors who were perceived as relaxed, attentive, friendly, and low in aggressiveness were more likely to have more committed and satisfied employees. One interesting implication is that a superior's perceived affirming style might be more instrumental in achieving employee satisfaction and commitment than the superior's perceived willingness to engage employees in constructive arguments. Subordinates may prefer superiors perceived as more argumentative over most other superiors. However, subordinates especially prefer superiors perceived as nonaggressive.

Infante, Anderson, Martin, Herington, and Kim (1993) found that subordinates' levels of satisfaction with their superiors steadily increased as superiors became more argumentative, more affirming in style (i. e., more relaxed, attentive, and friendly), and less verbally aggressive. Their research suggests that superiors have a threshold for stimulating negative affect in subordinates, and that superiors with more positive communication traits were less likely to cross that threshold for negative affect. As in the earlier study by Infante and Gorden (1991), subordinates were particularly dissatisfied with superiors perceived as verbally aggressive.

Infante, Myers, and Buerkel (1994) suggested that factors in the workplace may inhibit verbal aggression, such as fear of economic reprisal and reluctance to engage in negative personal displays in public. Individuals were significantly less likely to resort to verbally aggressive messages in the public organizational setting than in the private familial setting. Heightened awareness of the negative consequences of verbal aggression might diminish its use in the workplace.

Verbal Aggression as an Influence in Jury Selection and Deliberation

Other research has examined the role of verbal aggressiveness in trial courts. Excused jurors may be more aggressive than empaneled jurors in municipal criminal court cases (Wigley, 1986). Although the results of the study are somewhat inconclusive, a comparison of selected and excused jurors suggests that verbally aggressive jurors might be significantly more likely to be excused than less verbally aggressive jurors. A follow-up investigation is currently re-examining this issue. In addition, the study investigates whether proportional frequency and duration of juror contributions is influenced by such factors as jurors' levels of communication apprehension, willingness to communicate, and overall level of argumentativeness. Communication characteristics may have a very powerful impact on the level of thoroughness of debate among jurors in the deliberation process.

Verbal Aggression in Family Communication

Research in the marital domain has grown rapidly since the 1980s. One of the first sets of studies in this area focused on gender by trait differences between violent and nonviolent couples (Infante, et al., 1989). Individuals reported their own levels of argumentativeness and verbal aggressiveness, and perceived levels of the traits with respect to their spouses (no married couples were in the sample). In general, verbal aggressiveness scores were higher in violent than in nonviolent marriages, and argumentativeness scores were higher in nonviolent than in violent marriages. Infante et al. found that in violent marriages there was a significant negative correlation between the individual's self reported level of argumentativeness and the perceived argumentativeness of the spouse. However, in nonviolent marriages the correlation between the variables was significant and positive. In violent marriages, individuals rated their own argumentativeness as lower than that of their spouse, but they rated the spouse's verbal aggressiveness as higher than their own. The authors explained that the combination of traits might interact to produce negative results. If so, then verbal aggressiveness might be considered a catalyst for interspousal violence, and the ASD of one spouse might be a primary cause of the verbal aggressiveness (Infante et al., 1989). Maybe greater use of argumentation would result in less verbal aggression.

In a study by Infante et al. (1990), abused wives wrote accounts of their most recent spousal disagreement resulting in physical violence, whereas nonabused wives recounted their most recent spousal disagreement. Participants then answered a questionnaire, called the Recall of Verbal Aggression Instrument, by indicating the frequency with which they and their husbands used 10 types of verbally aggressive messages (listed in Infante, 1987; Infante & Wigley, 1986) during the recounted disagreements. The four main findings of this study are as follows: (a) there is a perception of higher levels of verbal aggression in violent as opposed to nonviolent disagreements, (b) a substantial relation exists between the number of verbally aggressive messages that wives reported for themselves and the number reported by the wives for their husbands, (c) character attacks, swearing, and competence attacks were the three types of verbally aggressive messages explaining the vast majority of variance between the abusive and nonabusive wives; and (d) character attacks, curses, and threats were the three message strategies explaining nearly all of the variance between the abusive and nonabusive husbands. For the last two findings, the authors reported that the role of verbal aggression in spousal interaction does not fully account for the abusiveness in the most recent accounts. Of the abused wives, 45% reported their own levels of verbal aggression and nearly 28% reported their husbands' verbally abusive behaviors in a manner not distinguishable from the nonabused wives. An additional finding, peripheral to the main study, should be noted. This is the first study to provide strong support for the notion that the 10 types of verbally aggressive messages noted in earlier research may be fairly inclusive of the construct. Subjects recalling the types of messages used did not frequently respond to an 11th option labeled *other*.

Sabourin et al. (1993) contrasted three types of married couples, that is, violent, distressed-nonviolent (couples in marital therapy), and nondistressed-nonviolent. This study involved both partners, as opposed to studies where only one of the marital partners participates. The research investigators measured four type of reciprocity, including (a) objective reciprocity (OR: both spouses self-report the same level of the traits of argumentativeness or verbal aggressiveness), (b) husband-claimed reciprocity (HC: husband claims both spouses demonstrate the same levels of the traits), (c) wife-claimed reciprocity (WC: wife claims both spouses manifest similar trait levels), and (d) inferred reciprocity (IR: frequency of similarity with which each spouse claimed the other spouse used argumentative or verbally aggressive messages). In addition, the frequency of use of the 10 types of verbally aggressive messages

(Infante, 1987) for each type of reciprocity, across the three types of marriages, was examined.[1]

Major findings of the study included the following:

1. While the two distressed groups could not be distinguished on the basis of marital satisfaction, nondistressed-nonviolent marriages reported higher levels of marital satisfaction than either of the other groups.
2. While the number of verbally aggressive messages did not distinguish the two nonviolent groups, violent marriages reported a significantly greater number of such messages than the other groups.
3. Reported reciprocity of verbal aggression did not distinguish the two nonviolent groups, but the violent group reported higher levels of verbal aggression reciprocity than the other groups.
4. Spouses agreed that in violent marriages, husbands used more verbal aggression than wives.
5. Nondistressed-nonviolent marital partners rated their spouses as higher in argumentativeness than verbal aggressiveness, but violent-distressed marriages could not be distinguished by measuring the difference between perceived argumentativeness and verbal aggressiveness of spouse.
6. Violent couples reported higher levels of all four types of reciprocity than the nondistressed-nonviolent group, but violent couples were distinguishable from the distressed-nonviolent group only on the basis of HC and IC.

---

[1]Readers interested in examining the original study by Sabourin, et al. (1993) might find the design of the study interesting: type of marriage (violent, distressed-nonviolent, nonviolent-nondistressed) was the between-groups variable, and type of reciprocity (OR, HC, WC, IR) was a within-groups variable, for a 4 X 3 design. Furthermore, type of reciprocity (OR, HC, WC, IR) was treated as a between-groups variable, and type of verbally aggressive message (character attack, competence attack, background attack, physical appearance attack, malediction, teasing, ridicule, threat, swearing, nonverbal emblem) constituted the within-groups variable, for a 10 X 4 design. Finally, the investigators examined marital satisfaction for husbands and wives (a within-groups variable) across the types of marriage, that is violent, distressed-nonviolent, nonviolent-nondistressed (the between-groups variable), by a 2 X 3 ANOVA.

7. Character attacks and threats most strongly differentiated between violent marriages and both other groups for HC reciprocity.

8. Swearing, ridicule and character attacks most strongly differentiated between violent marriages and nondistressed-nonviolent couples for WC reciprocity.

9. Character attacks and threats discriminated most powerfully between violent couples and both nonviolent groups.

10. Nonviolent groups (i.e., distressed-nonviolent and nondistressed-nonviolent) were not distinguishable on the basis of type of reciprocity.

11. Subjects' argumentativeness, verbal aggressiveness, and dispute message all correlated with the subjects' marital partners' perceptions across all three marital types, except that the wife's perception of her verbal aggression did not relate to husband's perception in distressed-violent marriages, and husband's perception did not correlate with wife's dispute messages in violent marriages.

Of particular note is the finding that the correlation between wife's dispute messages and husband's perception was statistically stronger in the nondistressed marriages ($r = .82$) than in the violent marriages ($r = .40$). The authors suggested that husbands in nondistressed-nonviolent marriages may more accurately perceive their wives' intentions to send verbally aggressive messages than husbands in violent or distressed but nonviolent marriages.

These findings are valuable because, as the authors explained, the results evidence that an ASD may cause verbal aggression, that there is a reciprocity effect in verbally aggressive exchanges, that a more satisfactory marriage is likely to involve partners who are mutually more argumentative than verbally aggressive, and that IR, and, to a lesser extent, OR, may be particularly powerful variables for discriminating among marital types on the basis of style of verbally aggressive messages.

When we try to get another person to comply with our wishes, we often select a strategy that we perceive will be most effective. One such method is to select an effective message strategy. Rudd et al. (1994) investigated the role of compliance-gaining message strategies as a function of the communication traits of argumentativeness and verbal aggressiveness. Participants were abused women residing in protective housing. Participants reported the frequency with which they employed 16 different compliance-gaining strategies (ingratiation, promise, debt, esteem, allurement, aversive stimulation, threat, guilt, warning, altruism, direct request, explanation, hint, deceit, empathetic, bargaining), and they were asked to respond to the category "other." Subjects completed the 10-item verbal aggressiveness questionnaire and the 10 item argumentativeness questionnaire that have been used in some previous investigations of interspousal violence. Mean scores suggested the following ordering of compliance-gaining strategies (most frequently used to least frequently used); ingratiation, aversive stimulation, explanation, promise, deceit, empathetic, hint, debt, guilt, bargaining, threat, esteem, direct request, allurement, altruism, and warning. People higher on verbal aggressiveness and lower on argumentativeness are more likely to use guilt, bargaining, debt, threat, aversive stimulation, and warning than the other strategies. In comparison to the other strategies, the strategy least likely to be used is ingratiation. People who are higher on argumentativeness and lower on verbal aggressiveness are more likely to utilize allurement, hinting, direct request, and aversive stimulation than the other strategies. It is less likely, compared to other strategies, that either threat or deceit will be used. The authors noted that abused women are lacking in direct power bases, and this would explain their preference for indirect strategies (e.g., ingratiation, aversive stimulation) and their disfavoring of direct strategies (e.g., warning). These findings are important because, as the authors indicated, the traits of argumentativeness and verbal aggressiveness appear to influence compliance-gaining message selection ("very distinct strategies" are selected) and understanding message selection may be critical to understanding (and preventing!) further abuse.

    Segrin and Fitzpatrick (1992) explored the role of verbal aggressiveness and depression in spousal relationships. In addition, the authors examined the two variables across three marital types (i.e., traditional, independents, and separates). Each marital type is distinguished on three dimensions, namely, marital and family ideology (conventional vs. nonconventional), degree of interdependence (high vs. low), and level of willingness to engage in conflict (high vs. low). Traditionals are of conventional ideology, high interdependence, and low conflict. Independents are of nonconventional ideology, low interdependence, and high conflict. Separates are of conventional ideology, low interdependence, and low conflict. Finally, the authors considered mixed marriages (i.e., marriages where one spouse falls into one of the three marital types and the other spouse falls into another of the three marital types).

The authors confirmed their hypothesis that personal levels of depression and verbal aggressiveness would covary for both spouses. However, although husbands' depression covaried with wives' verbal aggressiveness, in general, no relation was found between wives' depression and husbands' verbal aggressiveness. One notable and significant exception was found. For marriages classified as traditional, wives' depression was negatively related to husbands' verbal aggression. The authors reasoned that in these marriages, husbands perceiving their wives' depression might reduce their own levels of aggressive communication. A similar pattern may exist in the separates marital type. However, the small sample size for the separates classification reduced the likelihood of obtaining meaningful results.

Research Involving Parent-Child Communication

Research in the family setting sheds some light on the expectations of parents and children. Bayer and Cegala (1992) examined the relation between parenting style and the two variables of argumentativeness and verbal aggressiveness. In this study, parenting style was examined as a two-dimensional construct, namely, autonomy-control and love-hostility. Specifically, the authoritative parenting style involved individuals who were higher on love (expressing positive affect) and autonomy (allowing child greater degrees of independence); authoritarian parenting style involved higher levels of hostility (expressing negative affect) and control (restricting freedom of the child); and the permissive parenting style involved higher levels of control and love. As hypothesized, verbally aggressive individuals who were lower in argumentativeness tended to be authoritarian in parenting style. Authoritative parenting style reflected lower levels of aggressiveness and higher levels of argumentativeness. It is worth noting, however, that the verbal aggressiveness variable was considerably stronger than argumentativeness in distinguishing the parenting styles. Bayer and Cegala (1992) underscored the significance of viewing verbal aggression as a form of child abuse, and that the authoritative parenting style is a more competent style than the authoritarian style.

An interesting question is whether adult children's perceptions of their parents' levels of verbal aggressiveness are accurate. Beatty, Zelley, Dobos, and Rudd (1994) examined the degree of correspondence between fathers' self-reports of verbal aggressiveness and sons' reporting of the levels of verbal aggressiveness of their fathers. The authors found that fathers' verbal aggressiveness contributed 44% of the variance in sons' perception of fathers' aggressiveness. These findings suggest that sons' accounts of fathers' verbal aggressiveness are meaningfully accurate. Fathers' verbal aggressiveness significantly correlated with sons' perceptions of father's sarcasm, father's criticism, and father's general verbal aggressiveness. These results have important ramifications for correctly identifying aggressive fathers. Specifically, not only might the reports of adult sons provide a meaningful basis for assessing fathers' verbal aggressiveness, but, as the authors suggested, a better understanding of sons' process of socialization might result.

REDUCING VERBAL AGGRESSIVENESS

How can we reduce verbal aggressiveness? If the four primary causes of verbal aggressiveness are, in fact, disdain, psychopathology, social learning, and ASD, then addressing each of the causal factors might reduce a substantial portion of the consequences of verbal aggression. However, this is not entirely clear because we do not know whether this list of causes is exhaustive of the primary causes of aggression, and because we do not know whether these four causes operate synergistically (Infante, 1989). ASD might be addressed by training in argumentation (Infante, Trebing, et al., 1984). Infante often noted that the communication discipline probably knows more about improving arguing skills than any other single area of skill development. Such training is more consonant with the activities within the academic discipline than within any other discipline (Infante, 1995).

The findings with respect to compliance-gaining strategies (Rudd, et al., 1994) have enormous ramifications, especially if it can be demonstrated that some compliance-gaining strategies are more effective and less likely to result in further abuse. The reasoning here is that if the interactional pattern is as follows: verbal aggressiveness leads to selection of compliance-gaining strategy leads to manifestation of higher levels of aggressiveness, then it might be possible to break the connection in the logical chain at the beginning by removing an ASD, in the middle by improving on message selection strategies, or at the end by selecting further strategies to reduce aggression. Such communication-specific remedies rely on the verbal plan's conceptualization.

Another important issue is whether sensitization to the harmful effects of verbal aggression might moderate its use (Infante,

Riddle et al., 1992). Although extreme cases might require the assistance of a psychologist or other mental health professional, it seems reasonable to conclude that high-but-nonextreme verbally aggressive individuals would benefit from skills training in arguing and studying argumentation. However, as Infante warned, learning about the consequences of verbal aggression by role-playing or other simulations might actually increase the tendency toward verbal aggressiveness because the individual will have practiced and developed aggression skills, and may feel rewarded for demonstrating verbally aggressive behaviors (Infante, 1995)

One complex issue is whether the primary cause of verbal aggressiveness is an ASD with psychopathology, disdain, and social learning having a less salient role in causing aggressiveness. It might be that the ASD model only operates in argumentative situations (Infante, Trebing, et al., 1984). If other catalysts operate as trigger mechanisms for aggression, then programs designed to remediate aggressive tendencies through the teaching of argumentation might be ineffective and, therefore, needlessly costly.

One study examining the relation between sensitivity to conversational cues and verbal aggressiveness failed to demonstrate a significant difference in reported verbal aggressiveness scores between high and low conversationally sensitive individuals (Wigley, Pohl, & Watt, 1989). One explanation, offered by the authors for this finding, is that individuals low in sensitivity might use aggression to avoid conversation, whereas high conversational sensitives might use it to influence others (e.g., people who are perceived to be more likely to be influenced by hostile messages). Given the growing body of literature that reveals the negative consequences of verbal aggression, it might be desirable to investigate the types of message strategies that conversationally sensitive individuals would accept as adequate substitutes for aggressive messages. It may be easier to train these individuals than individuals who report lower levels of conversational awareness. If so, then this would help mitigate the expense involved in training in argumentation.

LOOKING AHEAD

The undesirable consequences of verbal aggressiveness manifest themselves in meaningful and measurable ways, including damage to self-concept, desensitization leading to increased aggression, loss of credibility, deficient workplace skills, decreased workplace satisfaction, possible interference with one's ability to function on a par with others in society (e.g., on jury duty), inhibiting one's ability to select effective message strategies, decreased marital satisfaction, reciprocity of aggression, and as catalyst for more (and worse) aggression.

Although psychopathology, disdain for target, social learning of aggression, and ASD are probably (according to traditional approaches to the study of communication) the main causes of verbal aggressiveness, other causes may exist. In any event, there is strong evidence that ASD plays a substantial role in causing a significant amount of verbal aggression. Infante's research findings suggest that ASD is a prime target for remediation efforts. Alternatively, a neurobiological approach to verbal aggressiveness would probably find that genetics is the primary cause of verbal aggressiveness, and that situational and environmental influences are quite small (Beatty & McCroskey, 1997). If so, then efforts targeting ASD for remediation may be doomed to failure. Finding the most fruitful approach to understanding the causes of verbal aggressiveness is essential in designing the most effective remediation efforts. However, the dire consequences of verbal aggressiveness suggest that we should continue efforts toward remediation concurrent with our efforts to more fully understand its causes.

Can we have meaningful solutions to the verbal aggressiveness problem? Sometimes, there is a considerable delay between identifying a problem, the study of its causes, and implementation of workable, practical, and desirable solutions. However, Infante took especially meaningful steps toward enhancing arguing skills, not only through his popular textbook *Arguing Constructively* (1988), but by revealing specific instructional plans that teachers can use to help students reduce their levels of verbal aggression (Infante, 1995). As more people become aware of the differences between argumentation and verbal aggression, the constructive nature of one and the destructive nature of the other, it seems likely that verbal aggression will decrease and its consequences diminished.

People often plan what they will say in conversation (Infante, 1979, 1980). Perhaps one method for reducing verbal aggression would involve training people to formulate more appropriate and effective verbal plans. If individuals are more capable of generating issues, exploring topics, and understanding the expectations of others, then their verbal plans may be executed more favorably. Message selection, message construction, and message delivery skills are teachable, and the verbal plans conceptualization (Infante, 1980) provides a useful model for understanding why people communicate in a given situation. Research by Beatty, Burant, Dobos, and Rudd (1996) suggests, for example, that fathers high in verbal aggressiveness tend to construct less appropriate and less effective verbal plans for interaction with their adult sons.

Most of the studies on verbal aggression were recently reviewed by Infante and Rancer (1996). A seemingly endless list of untested hypotheses remain. Some hypotheses are as follows:

> Hypothesis 1: The threat of greater sanctions by valued others for using verbal aggression will result in decreased verbal aggression.
>
> Hypothesis 2: The threat of sanctions by more valued others for using verbal aggression will result in less verbal aggression than the threat of sanctions by less valued others.
>
> Hypothesis 3: Verbal aggression negatively covaries with the number of valued others that expect compliance with standards of nonaggression.
>
> Hypothesis 4: As one becomes more aware of the undesirable consequences of verbal aggression, the probability of executing planned verbal aggression will decrease.
>
> Hypothesis 5: As one perceives that the likelihood of desirable consequences increases with verbal aggression, the probability of planned verbal aggression increases.
>
> Hypothesis 6: Executed verbal plans of a verbally aggressive nature are more likely to have been initially formulated as argumentative verbal plans than verbally aggressive verbal plans.

Some unanswered research questions are as follows:

> RQ1: What situational determinants most strongly covary negatively with one's plan to comply with the expectations of valued others that the use of verbal aggression should be avoided?
>
> RQ2: Are verbally aggressive individuals aware of their targets' perceptions of the hurtfulness of verbal aggression?
>
> RQ3: Under what conditions is verbally aggressive behavior the *sine qua non* of the verbal plan (aggression merely for the sake of aggression)?
>
> RQ4: In cases of reciprocal spousal verbal aggression, do individuals perceive the verbal aggression of spouse as a statement of an expectation that verbal aggression is more acceptable than nonaggression?

RQ5: In cases of nonreciprocal interspousal verbal aggression, is the nonreciprocating spouse more aware than the aggressor spouse of the undesirable consequences of verbal aggression?

RQ6: Do verbal plans of an argumentative nature spend more time in the planning stage than verbal plans of a verbally aggressive nature?

As we continue testing hypotheses and attempt to answer these research questions, we improve our understanding of each other. As we understand the nature of verbal aggressiveness, its causes, its consequences, and ways of reducing it, people's lives will be filled with more kindness and less verbal and physical aggression. These are worthy objectives, and illustrate the substantial role that the study of human communication can take in helping society in general, and individual relationships, in particular, to grow and be healthy.

REFERENCES

Bayer, C. L., & Cegala, D. J. (1992). Trait verbal aggressiveness and argumentativeness: relations with parenting style. *Western Journal of Communication, 56*, 301-310.

Beatty, M. J., Burant, P. A., Dobos, J. A., & Rudd, J. E. (1996). Trait verbal aggressiveness and the appropriateness and effectiveness of fathers' interaction plans. *Communication Quarterly, 44*, 1-15.

Beatty, M. J., & McCroskey, J. C. (1997, May). *It's in our nature: verbal aggressiveness as temperamental expression.* Paper presented at the annual convention of the International Communication Association, Montreal, Canada.

Beatty, M. J., Zelley, J. R., Dobos, J. A., & Rudd, J. E. (1994). Fathers' trait verbal aggressiveness and argumentativeness as predictors of adult sons' perceptions of fathers' sarcasm, criticism, and verbal aggressiveness. *Communication Quarterly, 42*, 407-415.

Horvath, C. W. (1995). Biological origins of communicator style. *Communication Quarterly, 43*, 394-407.

Infante, D. A. (1979). Predicting response to semantic differential scales from verbal behavior. *Southern Speech Communication Journal, 44*, 355-363.

Infante, D. A. (1980). Verbal plans: A conceptualization and investigation. *Communication Quarterly, 28*, 3-10.

Infante, D. A. (1987). Aggressiveness. In J. C. McCroskey & J. A. Daly (Eds.), *Personality and interpersonal communication* (pp. 157-192). Beverly Hills, CA: Sage.

Infante, D. A. (1988). *Arguing constructively.* Prospect Heights, IL: Waveland Press.

Infante, D. A. (1989). Response to high argumentatives: Message and sex differences. *Southern Communication Journal, 54,* 159-170.

Infante, D. A. (1995). Teaching students to understand and control verbal aggression. *Communication Education, 44,* 51-63.

Infante, D. A., Anderson, C. M., Martin, M. M., Herington, A. D., & Kim, J. (1993). Subordinates' satisfaction and perceptions of superiors' compliance-gaining tactics, argumentativeness, verbal aggressiveness, and style. *Management Communication Quarterly, 6,* 307-326.

Infante, D. A., Chandler, T. A., & Rudd, J. E. (1989). Test of an argumentative skill deficiency model of interspousal violence. *Communication Monographs, 56,* 163-177.

Infante, D. A., Chandler T. A., Rudd, J. E., & Shannon, E. A. (1990). Verbal aggression in violent and nonviolent marital disputes. *Communication Quarterly, 38,* 361-371.

Infante, D. A., & Gorden, W. I. (1985). Superiors' argumentativeness and verbal aggressiveness as predictors of subordinates' satisfaction. *Human Communication Research, 12,* 117-125.

Infante, D. A., & Gorden, W. I. (1991). How employees see the boss: test of an argumentative and affirming model of supervisors' communicative behavior. *Western Journal of Speech Communication, 55,* 294-304.

Infante, D. A., Hartley, K. C., Martin, M. M., Higgins, M. A., Bruning, S. D., & Hur, G. (1992). Initiating and reciprocating verbal aggression: Effects on credibility and credited valid arguments. *Communication Studies, 43,* 182-190.

Infante, D. A., Myers, S. A., & Buerkel, R. A. (1994) Argument and verbal aggression in constructive and destructive family and organizational disagreements. *Western Journal of Communication, 58,* 73-84.

Infante, D. A., & Rancer, A. S. (1982). A conceptualization and measure of argumentativeness. *Journal of Personality Assessment, 46,* 72-80.

Infante, D.A., & Rancer, A. S. (1993). Relations between argumentative motivation, and advocacy and refutation on controversial issues. *Communication Quarterly, 41,* 415-426.

Infante, D. A., & Rancer, A. S. (1996). Argumentativeness and verbal aggressiveness: A review of recent theory and research. In B. R. Burleson (Ed.), *Communication yearbook 19* (pp. 319-351). Beverly Hills, CA: Sage.

Infante, D. A., Riddle, B. L., Horvath, C. L., & Tumlin, S. A. (1992). Verbal aggressiveness: Messages and reasons. *Communication Quarterly, 40,* 116-126.

Infante, D. A., Trebing, D. J., Shepherd, P. E., & Seeds, D. E. (1984). The relationship of argumentativeness to verbal aggression. *Southern Speech Communication Journal, 50*, 67-77.

Infante, D. A., Wall, C. H., Leap, C. J., & Danielson, K. (1984). Verbal aggression as a function of the receiver's argumentativeness. *Communication Research Reports, 1*, 33-37.

Infante, D. A., & Wigley, C. J. (1986). Verbal aggressiveness: An interpersonal model and measure. *Communication Monographs, 53*, 61-69.

Lim, T. (1990). The influences of receivers' resistance on persuaders' verbal aggressiveness. *Communication Quarterly, 38*, 170-188.

Martin, M. M., & Anderson, C. M. (1996). Argumentativeness and verbal aggressiveness. *Journal of Social Behavior and Personality, 11*, 547-554.

Martin, M. M., Anderson, C. A., & Horvath, C. L. (1996). Feelings about verbal aggression: Justifications for sending and hurt from receiving verbally aggressive messages. *Communication Research Reports, 13*, 19-26.

McCrae, R. R., & Costa, P. T., Jr. (1987). Validation of the five-factor model of personality across instruments and observers. *Journal of Personality and Social Psychology, 52*, 81-90.

Norman, W. T. (1963). Toward an adequate taxonomy of personality attributes: Replicated factor structure in peer nomination personality ratings. *Journal of Abnormal and Social Psychology, 66*, 574-583.

Rudd, J. E., Burant, P. A., & Beatty, M. J. (1994). Battered women's compliance-gaining strategies as a function of argumentativeness and verbal aggression. *Communication Research Reports, 11*, 13-22.

Sabourin, T. C., Infante, D. A., & Rudd, J. E. (1993). Verbal aggression in marriages: A comparison of violent, distressed but nonviolent, and nondistressed couples. *Human Communication Research, 20*, 245-267.

Segrin, C., & Fitzpatrick, M. A. (1992). Depression and verbal aggressiveness in different marital couple types. *Communication Studies, 43*, 79-91.

Wigley, C. J. (1986). *Communication variables as predictors of decisions in the voir dire process.* Unpublished doctoral dissertation, Kent State University, Kent, OH.

Wigley, C. J., Pohl, G. H., & Watt, M. G. S. (1989). Conversational sensitivity as a correlate of trait verbal aggressiveness and the predisposition to verbally praise others. *Communication Reports, 2*, 92-95.

10

Communication Apprehension

James C. McCroskey
West Virginia University
Michael J. Beatty
Cleveland State University

The original conceptualization of *communication apprehension* (CA); McCroskey, 1970) viewed it as "a broadly based anxiety related to oral communication" (p. 269). Subsequent writings made minor modifications to this definition. For the past two decades, CA has been defined as "an individual's level of fear or anxiety associated with either real or anticipated communication with another person or persons" (McCroskey, 1977, 1978).

Although the conceptualization of CA has remained reasonably stable, two important conceptual modifications have occurred. The first concerned the oral communication focus of CA and the other concerned whether CA was restricted to a trait conceptualization.

THE ORAL FOCUS OF CA

In the original article that advanced the construct of CA, the focus clearly was on oral communication (McCroskey, 1970). Although in this article *communication* frequently was used without the "oral" qualifier, the earlier work in the areas of stage fright and reticence were acknowledged as the foundations on which the CA construct was developed. Both of these areas focused exclusively on oral communication at that time.

In some subsequent writings, the oral context of CA received less emphasis. Of particular importance were two research programs that were conducted under the general rubric of CA but that did not focus on speaking. The first was the research concerned with apprehension about writing (Daly & Miller, 1975). This stream of research, initially led by Daly and his associates, continues and has received considerable attention in the field of English. The measure developed by Daly and Miller (1975), the Writing Apprehension Test (WAT), has been employed widely and has been found to have only a moderate correlation with oral CA measures. The second research area was that concerned with apprehension about singing. Although receiving far less attention than the articles and measures concerned with speaking and writing, research involving the Test of Singing Apprehension (TOSA) also discovered low correlations between the TOSA and CA measures (Andersen, Andersen, & Garrison, 1978).

In summary, the CA construct has been broadened substantially. Although it was originally restricted to talking, it now encompasses all modes of communication. Consequently, it should be recognized that current instruments labeled as CA measures (notably the Personal Report of Communication Apprehension, PRCA; McCroskey, 1970, 1978, 1982) are restricted to oral CA, specifically apprehension about talking to or with others. The focus in the remainder of this chapter is on this form of CA and when the term *CA* is employed this is the referent. Most of what follows applies equally well to other forms of CA. However, our interest here is exclusively with oral (talking) communication. Such legitimate concerns as apprehension about writing, singing, touching, or listening are not addressed directly in this chapter. Of course, much of what is discussed here may also hold true with regard to these other forms of CA.

THE TRAIT CONCEPTUALIZATION OF CA

The original article that advanced the construct of CA included no explicit mention of whether it was seen as a trait of an individual or as a response to the situational elements of a specific communication transaction. However, the implication was clear that the construct was viewed from a trait orientation. Not only was the discussion directed toward a response generalized across situations and time, but also the measures advanced clearly focused on a traitlike pattern.

The overwhelming majority of the early research studies employing the CA construct took a trait approach (McCroskey, 1977). Many referred to CA with phrases such as "a traitlike, personality-type variable." The CA construct, however, has been expanded explicitly to encompass both trait and situational views (McCroskey, 1977). Considerable research has been reported that has investigated CA either as a state or in both the trait and state form (see, e.g., Beatty, Balfantz, & Kuwabara, 1989; Beatty & Friedland, 1990; Prisbell & Dallinger, 1981; Richmond, 1978).

In summary, the CA construct has been broadened substantially. Although it originally was restricted to a trait orientation, it is now viewed as representing both trait and state approaches. Although the original definition of CA restricts the construct to a trait perspective, the revised definition noted previously is consistent with the broader view. It should be recognized, however, that the most popular measures of CA are restricted to a trait conceptualization. Research based on more situational perspectives must employ other instruments. Because our concern in this chapter is centered on the relation between personality and human communication, we center most of our attention here on the trait approach to CA. Readers interested in our earlier views related to situational or state CA should turn to McCroskey (1984) and Beatty et al. (1989). Currently, we are inclined to view state CA as simply a manifestation of trait CA and other traits of the individual.

A CONTEMPORARY CONCEPTUALIZATION OF CA

In the following sections a conceptualization of the CA trait is enunciated in four major areas: etiology of CA, pathological CA, effects of CA, and treatment of CA.

Etiology OF CA

Throughout the social sciences only two major explanations of the differential trait behaviors of individuals hold sway: heredity and environment. Simply put, we can be born with it or we can learn it. It is our view that the most powerful and justified explanation focuses on genetic factors involved in temperament.

Most early writers, particularly those influenced by the political-social-scientific orthodoxy of the 1960s and 1970s, adhered to the politically correct views of their era and discounted out-of-hand the notion of heredity as a cause of traitlike CA. However, some writers since 1980 have acknowledged that there indeed must be a hereditary contribution. The work of social biologists, particularly their research with twins, has provided compelling evidence that something other than environmentally based, social-learning is having an impact on human behavior tendencies. McCroskey and Richmond (1980) summarized the thrust of the early research in this area:

> Researchers in the area of social biology have established that significant social traits can be measured in infants shortly after birth, and that infants differ sharply from each other on these traits. One of these traits is referred to as "sociability"—the degree to which we reach out to other people and respond positively to contact with other people. Research with identical twins and fraternal twins of the same sex reinforces this theoretical role of heredity. Identical twins are biologically identical, whereas fraternal twins are not. Thus, if differences between twins raised in the same environment are found to exist, biology (heredity) can be discounted as a cause in one case but not in the other. Actual research has indicated that biologically identical twins are much more similar in sociability than are fraternal twins. This research would be interesting if it were conducted only on twin infants, but it is even more so because it was conducted on a large sample of adult twins who had the opportunity to have many different and varied social experiences. (p.6)

Since the late 1980s, numerous studies of twins have extended the conclusions about sociability to other personality traits that are subcomponents of CA. For example, Beatty and McCroskey (1997) showed that the multiple correlation between introversion and neuroticism (both largely genetic personality traits) is approximately .90. Temperament theorists now argue that we are born with neurobiological systems with individual differences in thresholds or "set points" for stimulating reactions. Recently, we have begun to investigate the connections between CA and low thresholds for stimulating the neurobiological systems responsible for avoidance behavior and anxiety reactions (Beatty & McCroskey, 1997). These and other neurobiological systems are described elsewhere (chapter 2, this volume).

Children, it seems, are born with certain personality predispositions or tendencies. Inborn predispositions and tendencies, of course, do not provide perfect predictability of an individual's communication behavior. Thus, although genetic factors have a heavy influence on communication behavior, what happens in the child's environment will have some impact on the predispositions and tendencies the child carries over into later life. However, because children are born with different predispositions and tendencies, they will react differently to the same environmental conditions.

Psychobiologists estimate that the contribution of genetics to environment in the etiology of introversion and neuroticism follows an 80 to 20 ratio. Although we are rapidly moving toward a genetic theory, we are not yet in position to rule out all environmental effects. However, Beatty and McCroskey (1997) did point out that measures of personality factors, including CA, are imperfect. Hence, improving the validity of such measures is likely to tip the balance farther toward genetics. In the late 1990's, the interaction of heredity and environment are seen as factors leading to adult temperamental predispositions and tendencies such as CA. This theory does not leave room for a purely situational explanation of CA.

Causes of Situational CA. Much has been made of the factors in communication situations that presumably impact the CA people experience in those situations. The causes of situational CA appear to be clear, at least to authors of basic public speaking books. As we have indicated in previous writings, the causal elements outlined by Buss (1980) appeared particularly insightful. Buss suggested that the major elements in the situation that can result in increased CA are novelty, formality, subordinate status, conspicuousness, unfamiliarity, dissimilarity, and degree of attention from others. In most instances, the opposite of these factors would be presumed to lead to decreased CA in the situation. In other work, Daly and Hailey (1980) noted two elements that go beyond those advanced by Buss as causes of situational CA. These are degree of evaluation and prior history.

Although these causes are intuitive and have been suggested as probable causes by authors in many books (including those written by McCroskey), research reported by Beatty and his colleagues has raised very serious questions as to whether these factors are, in fact, meaningfully causally related to an individual's fear or anxiety responses. This work provides convincing evidence that these presumably situationally produced perceptions are, in reality, the product of traitlike predispositions to perceive situations differently and that trait CA, or an overiding temperamental factor, is the factor driving these perceptual predispositions. Beatty has found, for example, that regardless of situational manipulation, high apprehensives see themselves as being more conspicuous, for example, than do low apprehensives (Beatty et al., 1989; Beatty & Friedland, 1990). In fact, when researchers control for the effects of trait CA, these "situational" factors contribute no significant variation in state CA (e.g., Beatty, 1988). What is reported as situational variability is merely a projection of individuals' predispositions to experience a given situation differently.

Simply put, situational variation does not produce any significant impact on trait CA behavior. Rather, individuals have traitlike responses to interpreting situations so that they are consistent with their trait CA responses. There are no situational causes of CA, only misunderstood trait responses to situational variations in the communication environment. Traits drive individuals' communication behavior and responses to the communication behavior of others.

Pathological CA

In its earliest research form, stage fright or public speaking anxiety, CA was viewed as a serious problem. The contemporary perspective takes a similar view. CA is seen as a problem—for the person who experiences it and, often, for others who have contact with that person. At very high levels, CA can become an extremely negative, dominating force that controls virtually all of an individual's life. This feature of CA is represented in the high correlation between CA and neuroticism (Beatty, McCroskey, & Heisel, in press).

To place the problematic nature of CA in perspective, it is important to recognize that every individual experiences CA to either a greater or lesser degree. It is a truly rare individual, if one actually exists, who never experiences CA under any circumstance. Such an individual would be seen as evidencing pathological behavior, because fear is a natural human response to a truly threatening situation. Similarly, it is comparatively rare individual who experiences CA in all communication situations, although such people do exist. With the exception of these rare individuals, even people with very high traitlike CA find some circumstances in which they can communicate comfortably. The most common of these situations involve communication with close friends. It is not so much that close friends produce less apprehension as it is that people who produce less apprehension are allowed to become close friends, whereas more threatening individuals are avoided.

Because in the previous literature much has been made of the pathological nature of high CA, high reticence, and high shyness, we need to consider what we should view as pathological, or abnormal, levels of CA. This distinction can be made both conceptually and empirically, although the distinctions are not fully isomorphic.

At the conceptual level, we view abnormal behavior to be that which is nonadaptive, nonresponsive, or nonfunctional in the environment in which it is engaged. Normal individuals are sensitive to their environment, respond to its demands, and adapt their behaviors so that they are a functional part of that environment. Experiencing no fear or anxiety in a nonthreatening environment and continuing to function in that environment is normal. The reverse responses are abnormal. If such responses become characteristic of the individual, he or she may be regarded as pathological and in need of professional help. The question, of course, is one of degree. Abnormal responses in one or few circumstances certainly should not generate a judgment of "pathological." Only when such behavior represents a consistent pattern of the individual would such a judgment seem warranted. Most importantly, such judgments should not be restricted to only one end of the CA continuum. Extremely low CA can be just as abnormal as extremely high CA.

Empirically, the distinction between normal and abnormal is a bit more easily determined. The empirical distinction made most frequently in the previous research is based on the normal curve, an approximation of which is generated by scores on most of the common CA measures. People with scores beyond one standard deviation above or below the mean score of the population are identified as high or low in CA. In normally distributed scores, approximately 68% of the population falls within one standard deviation of the mean, with 16% scoring over one standard deviation higher and 16% scoring over one standard lower. The latter two groups are, in fact, statistically significantly different at alpha = .05.

For research purposes, this is a particularly good distinction. The researcher can be reasonably assured that the people classified as "high" are truly different from those classified as "low." These two groups are the ones that theoretically should manifest differential behaviors related to the measure. Those in the middle, the "normals," actually may have no consistent pattern of behavior, particularly if the measure is a personality-type measure. The middle scores most likely indicate that this is a facet of personality not highly associated with the behavior of these individuals. Other personality elements may completely dominate their behavior to the exclusion of this particular personality variable.[1]

This system of classification was introduced into the literature as a function of observing groups of students brought into rooms for treatment of high trait CA. It was observed that groups of students composed entirely of individuals with scores beyond one standard deviation from the mean simply did not talk. The behavior of individuals in groups composed of people with scores between one-half and one standard deviation above the mean did not have such a consistent pattern. Some were totally noncommunicative, but others were willing to interact.[2] Thus this classification scheme is not purely arbitrary. It does seem to have a behavioral justification.

Two cautions should be stressed, however. First, some samples may not be representative of the overall population. Therefore, the classification-by-standard-deviation procedure should be sensitive to the mean and standard deviation of the population norms rather than the particular sample studied. A sample of successful salespersons or trial lawyers, for example, probably would include few people with high CA. Second, although this procedure is excellent for research involving comparatively large samples and based on aggregate data analyses, such a procedure is far too subject to measurement error to be applied to single individuals. Judgments about individuals should never be based on a single score or any scale. Rather, such a score should be only one of many factors to be considered. This is particularly important for people to recognize when developing or implementing intervention programs designed to alter high or low CA.

---

[1]It has been demonstrated repeatedly in the personality literature that any given personality variable may be relevant to behavioral prediction for some people but not for all people. People scoring in the midrange of the measure are least predictable. For such people, the variable may be irrelevant and their behavior may be controlled by the situation and/or other personality characteristics. For a discussion of these problems see Bem and Allen (1974) and Bem and Funder (1978).

[2]These observations were made during data collection for the study reported by Ertle (1969).

Effects of CA

The effects of CA have been the target of extensive research, particularly concerning trait CA, and have been summarized elsewhere. Our focus here is not on such specific variable research, but rather on theoretically more global effect patterns. The previous research, although extremely valuable for generating an understanding of how CA is manifested in ongoing communicative relationships of individuals, has been subject to considerable overinterpretation, if not misinterpretation. Effects observed in aggregate data analyses often are seen as regular behavioral outcome patterns for individual people with high or low CA. Such interpretations fail to recognize the high potential for the individual to deviate from the aggregate norm and the possibility of choosing from numerous behaviors, all of which would be theoretically consistent with the individual's CA level. Our concern here, therefore, is directed toward the internal impact of CA, possible external manifestations of CA, and the role CA plays as a mediator between communicative competence/skill and ultimate communicative behavior.

Internal Impact of CA. Although CA indeed has some behavioral implications, as we note later, it is primarily experienced by the individual internally. The only effect of CA that is predicted to be universal across both individuals and types of CA is an internally experienced feeling of discomfort. The lower the CA, the less the internal discomfort. Because people's cognitions are imperfectly related to their levels of physiological arousal, no physiological variable is predicted to be universally highly associated with CA across all people or across all types of CA.

The implications of this conceptualization of CA for both research and treatment cannot be overemphasized. Because CA is experienced internally, the only potentially valid indicant of CA is the individual's report of that experience. Thus, self-reports of individuals, whether obtained by paper-and-pencil measures or careful interviews, obtained under circumstances where the individual has nothing to gain or avoid losing by lying, provide the only potentially valid measures of CA. Measures of physiological activation and observations of behavior can provide, at best, only indirect evidence of CA and thus are inherently inferior approaches to measuring CA. Thus, physiological and behavioral instruments intended to measure CA must be validated with self-report measures, not the other way around. To the extent that such measures are not related to self-report measures, they must be judged invalid.

Currently available data indicate that such physiological measures and behavioral observation procedures have low to moderately low validity.[3]

External Impact of CA. As previously noted, there is no behavior that is predicted to be a universal product of varying levels of CA. Nevertheless, there are some externally observable behaviors that are more likely to occur or less likely to occur as a function of varying levels of CA. However, CA will be manifested in behavior in a given situation only as it interacts with the constraints of that situation. A person with low CA, for example, may behave in a manner no different from anyone else if called to a meeting to be reprimanded by a superior. The behavioral manifestations of high CA discussed here, therefore, presuppose that CA actually is present to a sufficient degree to consistently trigger the behavior. The behavioral prediction is only likely to be confirmed when considering aggregate behavioral indicants of the individual across time and across contexts.[4] Predicting individual behaviors of a given person at a single time is tenuous at best, no matter how extreme the person's CA. There are always behavioral options for the highly apprehensive person, and more than one of the options will be completely consistent with the experience of high CA.

Three patterns of behavioral response to high CA may be predicted to be generally applicable and one pattern can be described as sometimes present, but an atypical response pattern. The three typical patterns are communication avoidance, communication withdrawal, and communication disruption. The atypical pattern is excessive communication. Let us consider each.

When people are confronted with a circumstance that they anticipate will make them uncomfortable, and they have a choice of whether or not to confront it, they may decide either to confront it

---

[3]For earlier research, see Clevenger (1959). More recently, it has been found that although self-reported trait-like CA, as measured by the PRCA, is not highly correlated with physiological arousal, as measured by heart rate, the two combined are able to predict more than 80% of the variance in self-reported state apprehension, as measured by a modification of the Spielberger state anxiety measure. The beta weights for the two predictors are nearly equal with little colinearity. See Behnke and Beatty (1981). This indicates physiological measurement has some validity for estimating state CA, but is not associated meaningfully with trait CA.

[4]For suggestions for testing this type of prediction, see Jaccard and Daly (1980). Recent research reports validity coefficients in the neighborhood of .50 for the PRCA and a measure of shyness when tested in this way. See McCroskey and Richmond (1982).

and make the best of it or avoid it and thus avoid the discomfort. Some refer to this as the choice between fight and flight. Research in the area of CA indicates that the latter choice should be expected in most instances. In order to avoid having to experience high CA, people may select occupations that involve low communication responsibilities, may pick housing units that reduce incidental contact with other people, may choose seats in classrooms or in meetings that are less conspicuous, and may avoid social settings. At the lowest level, if a person makes us uncomfortable, we may simply avoid being around that person. Avoidance, then, is a common behavioral response to high CA.

Avoidance of communication is not always possible. In addition, a person can find her- or himself in a situation that generates a high level of CA with no advance warning. Under such circumstances, withdrawal from communication is the behavioral pattern to be expected. This withdrawal may be complete (i.e., absolute silence) or partial (i.e., talking only as much as absolutely required). In a public speaking setting, this response may be represented by the very short speech. In a meeting, class, or small group discussion, it may be represented by talking only when called on. In a dyadic interaction, it may be represented by answering questions only when directly questioned by the other dyad member or supplying agreeing responses with no initiation of discussion.

Both of these patterns reflect a distinct reduction in willingness to communicate and represent avoidance responses. If the person cannot avoid communication, however, the third pattern is likely.

Communication disruption is the third typical behavioral pattern associated with high CA. The person may have disfluencies in verbal presentation or unnatural nonverbal behaviors. Equally as likely are poor choices of communicative strategies, sometimes reflected in the after-the-fact "I wish I had (had not) said . . ." phenomenon. It is important to note, however, that such behaviors may be produced by inadequate communication skills as well as by high CA. Thus inferring CA from observations of such behavior often is not appropriate.

Overcommunication is a response to high CA that is not common but is the pattern exhibited by a small minority. This behavior represents overcompensation. It may reflect the fight rather than the flight reaction, the attempt to succeed despite discomfort. The person who elects to take a public speaking course despite her or his extreme stage fright is a classic example. Less easily recognizable is the individual with high CA who attempts to dominate social situations. Most of the time, people who employ this behavioral option are seen as poor communicators but are not recognized as having high CA; in fact, they may be seen as people with very low CA. In research on compulsive communication, it was found that people who recognized themselves as "talkaholics" were equally as likely to be high as they were to be low CAs (McCroskey & Richmond, 1993, 1995).

To this point, we have looked at the typical behaviors of people with high CA levels. We might assume that the behaviors of people with low CA would be the exact reverse. That assumption might not always be correct. Although people with low CA should be expected to seek opportunities to communicate rather than avoid them, and to participate in dyads and groups of which they are members rather than withdraw from them, people with low CA may also have disrupted communication and/or over-communicate. The disruptions may stem from pushing too hard rather than tension, but the behaviors may not always be distinctly different to the observer. Similarly, persons who over-communicate engage in very similar behavior whether the behavior stems from high or low CA. Although future research may permit us to train observers who can distinguish disrupted communication resulting from high CA from that resulting from low CA and possibly distinguish between over-communication behaviors stemming from the two causes, these behaviors are, and probably will remain, indistinguishable by the average person in the communication situation.

CA and Communication Behavior. Although recognizing the central role of genetic predispositions in the development and manifestation of CA, we view communication behavior (and most other human behavior) as in part a learned response to one's environment. Because we wish to explore the role of CA as it relates to human communication behavior more generally, it is important to enunciate our assumptions about human learning. Following the lead of contemporary writers in educational psychology, we view human learning as composed of three domains: the cognitive (understanding or knowing),[5] the affective (feeling of liking or disliking), and the psychomotor (the physical capability of doing).

Because of inconsistent and confused use of terms within the communication literature, when we apply these domains to communication learning it is important that we make a distinction

---

[5]Our use of cognitive previously referred to the distinction made in psychology between cognitivists and behaviorists. This is a broader use of the term than the one relating to the domains of leaning. The reader should avoid confusing the two usages.

between communication competence and communication *skill*. We see communication competence as falling within the cognitive domain and communication skill as falling within the psychomotor domain. More specifically, communication competence is "the ability of an individual to demonstrate knowledge of the appropriate communicative behavior in a given situation" (Larson, Backlund, Redmond, & Barbour, 1978, p. 16). Communication competence, then, can be demonstrated by observing a communication situation and identifying behaviors that would be appropriate or inappropriate in that situation. Communication skill, on the other hand, involves actual psychomotor behavior. Communication skill is the ability of an individual to perform appropriate communicative behavior in a given situation. To be judged skilled, then, a person must be able to engage physically in appropriate behaviors.

The three components of desired communication learning, then, are communication competence (knowing and understanding appropriate communication behaviors), communication skill (being able to produce appropriate communication behaviors physically), and positive communication affect (valuing and wanting to produce appropriate communication behaviors). Any desired impact on long-term behavior of the individual requires that production of all of these types of learning be achieved, whether by the "natural" environment, by a formal instructional system, or by some combination of the two.

CA can have a major impact in all three areas of communication learning, and consequently, on the long-term behavior of individuals. High CA is seen as a potential inhibitor of the development of both communication competence and communication skill and as a direct precursor of negative communication affect. Low CA, on the other hand, is seen as a facilitator of the development of communication competence and communication skill and as a precursor of positive communication affect.

With regard to communication competence, high CA is projected as a barrier to accurate observation of the natural environment and sufficient experience within it and as a barrier to the formal study of communication. Not only do people try to avoid studying things that cause them discomfort, but such discomfort may inhibit their learning when they do study it. The projected pattern for learning communication skills is seen in the same way. A major facet of psychomotor learning is practice. High CA will lead to less practice and possible misinterpretations of the outcomes of what practice is attempted. The impact of CA in terms of communication affect is even more direct. If we are fearful or anxious about something, we are not given to liking it. On the other hand, things that are not threatening are more likely to generate positive affect.

A major conclusion we can draw from this conceptualization of CA and communication learning is that high CA is highly associated with ineffective communication. As such, CA must be considered a central concern of any instructional program concerned with more effective communication as a targeted outcome, whether the program is labeled a program in communication competence or a program in communication skill. Basic competencies and basic skills cannot be separated from the problem of high CA.

Treatment of CA

Because CA is something that an individual is born with, it should not come as a surprise to learn that changing one's CA level typically is very difficult, and for some, impossible. Many people think that if they just take a good public speaking class, they will get their CA (or at least the manifestation commonly known as stage fright) to go away. Although such classes may be very beneficial for people with low CA in helping them become more skilled speakers, and may help people with only moderate CA to understand what CA they have and control it better as well as increasing their speaking skills, the person with high CA will receive little benefit from such instruction—and may even see their problems become worse.

Although formal instruction under a highly qualified teacher of public speaking may be of little help, "help" from others may do significant harm. Many teachers think they are speech or communication teachers—from elementary teachers who direct students to participate in "show and tell" and "read out loud" to the entire class, to language arts teachers who demand students present "oral book reports," to social studies teachers who insist their students make "current events" presentations, to science teachers who require their students to make oral presentations based on their "science projects." Not to mention ministers who want children to perform for others by bible reading or praying and parents who want their children to perform in plays and all sorts of other public exhibitions. Such efforts, when mandatory or coerced rather than truly voluntary, are very likely to reinforce and strengthen the CA response. As in many other instances in life, often the people trying the hardest to help do the most harm!

It has been determined that CA, when treated as a phobic response, is quite responsive to two behavioral therapies—systematic desensitization and cognitive restructuring (Fremouw, 1984; McCroskey, 1972; McCroskey, Ralph, & Barrick, 1970; Meichenbaum,

1976; Paul, 1966). Both of these methods involve a relatively brief time span for treatment (4-7 hours over a period of 1-7 weeks) and, hence, are relatively inexpensive procedures and can be performed by any psychologist who has studied behavior therapy (and many individuals with less training under appropriate supervision). Both of these approaches provide the person receiving the treatment with cognitive skills for coping with CA in a constructive way. These methods do not remove genetically transmitted behavior tendencies, but rather teach the individual to manage those tendencies in order to be able to communicate effectively without extreme apprehension. Simply put, these therapies do not change the individual's basic temperament, but they allow the individual to control some of the negative aspects of that temperament.

REFERENCES

Andersen, P. A., Andersen, J. F., & Garrison, J. P. (1978). Singing apprehension and talking apprehension: The development of two constructs. *Sign Language Studies, 19*, 155-186.

Beatty, M. J. (1988). Situational and predispositional correlates of public speaking anxiety. *Communication Education, 37*, 28-39.

Beatty, M. J., Balfantz, G. L., & Kuwabara, A. Y. (1989) Trait-like qualities of selected variables assumed to be transient causes of performance state anxiety. *Communication Education, 38*, 277-289.

Beatty, M. J., & Friedland, M. H. (1990). Public speaking state anxiety as a function of selected situational and predispositional variables. *Communication Education, 39,* 142-147.

Beatty, M. J., McCroskey, J. C., & Heisel, A. (in press). Communication apprehension as temperamental expression: A communibiological paradigm. *Communication Monographs*.

Beatty, M. J., & McCroskey, J. C. (1997, February). *Communication apprehension as temperamental expression: Toward the development of a communibiological theory of communicative inhibition.* Paper presented at the annual meeting of the Western States Communication Association, Monterey, CA.

Behnke, R. R., & Beatty, M. J. (1981). A cognitive-physiological model of speech anxiety. *Communication Monographs, 48*, 158-163.

Bem, D. J., & Allen, A. (1974). On predicting some of the people some of the time: The search for cross-situational consistencies in behavior. *Psychological Review, 81*, 506-520.

Bem, D. J., & Funder, D. C. (1978). Predicting more of the people more of the time: Assessing the personality of situations. *Psychological Review, 85,* 485-501.

Buss, A. H. (1980). *Self-consciousness and social anxiety.* San Francisco: Freeman.

Clevenger, T., Jr. (1959). A synthesis of experimental research in stage fright. *Quarterly Journal of Speech, 45,* 134-145.

Daly, J. A., & Hailey, J. L. (1980). *Putting the situation into writing research: Situational parameters of writing apprehension as disposition and state.* Paper presented at the National Council of Teachers of English Convention, Cincinnati.

Daly, J. A., & Miller, M. D. (1975). The empirical development of an instrument to measure writing apprehension. *Research in the Teaching of English, 9,* 242-249.

Ertle, C. D. (1969). *A study of the effect of homogeneous grouping on systematic desensitization for the reduction of interpersonal communication apprehension.* Unpublished doctoral dissertation, Michigan State University, East Lansing.

Fremouw, W. J. (1984). Cognitive-behavioral therapies for modification of communication apprehension. In J. C. McCroskey & J. A. Daly (Eds.), *Avoiding communication: Shyness, reticence, and communication apprehension* (pp. 209-215). Beverly Hills, CA: Sage.

Jaccard, J., & Daly, J. A. (1980). Personality traits and multiple-act criteria. *Human Communication Research, 6,* 367-377.

Larson, C. E., Backlund, P. M., Redmond, M. K., & Barbour, A. (1978). *Assessing communicative competence.* Falls Church, VA: Speech Communication Association and ERIC.

McCroskey, J. C. (1970). Measures of communication-bound anxiety. *Speech Monographs, 37,* 269-277.

McCroskey, J. C. (1972). The implementation of a large-scale program of systematic desensitization for communication apprehension. *Speech Teacher, 21,* 255-264.

McCroskey, J. C. (1977). Classroom consequences of communication apprehension. *Communication Education, 26,* 27-33.

McCroskey, J. C. (1978). Validity of the PRCA as an index of oral communication apprehension. *Communication Monographs, 45,* 192-203.

McCroskey, J. C. (1982). *An introduction to rhetorical communication* (4th ed.). Englewood Cliffs, NJ: Prentice-Hall.

McCroskey, J. C. (1984). The communication apprehension perspective. In J. A. Daly & J. C. McCroskey (Eds.). *Avoiding communication: Shyness, reticence, and communication apprehension* (pp. 13-18). Beverly Hills, CA: Sage.

McCroskey, J. C., Ralph, D. C., & Barrick, J. E. (1970). The effect of systematic desensitization on speech anxiety. *Speech Teacher, 19*, 32-36.

McCroskey, J. C., & Richmond, V. P. (1980). *The quiet ones: Shyness and communication apprehension.* Scottsdale, AZ: Gorsuch Scarisbrick.

McCroskey, J. C., & Richmond, V. P. (1982). Communication apprehension and shyness: Conceptual and operational distinctions. *Central States Speech Journal, 33*, 458-468.

McCroskey, J. C., & Richmond, V. P. (1993). Identifying compulsive communicators: The talkaholic scale. *Communication Research Reports, 10*, 107-114.

McCroskey, J. C., & Richmond, V. P. (1995). Correlates of compulsive communication: Quantitative and qualitative characteristics. *Communication Quarterly, 43*, 39-52.

Meichenbaum, D. (1976). Toward a cognitive theory of self-control. In G. Schwartz & D. Shapiro (Eds.), *Consciousness and self-regulation: Advances in research* (pp. 113-132). New York: Plenum.

Paul, G. L. (1966). *Insight vs. desensitization in psychotherapy: An experiment in anxiety reduction.* Stanford, CA: Stanford University Press.

Prisbell, M., & Dallinger, J. (1981, February). *Trait and state communication apprehension and level of uncertainty over time.* Paper presented at the Western Speech Communication Association Convention, San Jose, February.

Richmond, V. P. (1978). The relationship between trait and state communication apprehension and interpersonal perception during acquaintance stages. *Human Communication Research, 4*, 338-349.

11

Cognitive Complexity

Brant R. Burleson
Scott E. Caplan
Purdue University

Cognitive complexity is an individual-difference variable associated with a broad range of communication skills and related abilities. In general, the term indexes the degree of differentiation, articulation, and integration within a cognitive system. That is, a cognitive system composed of a comparatively large number of finely articulated, abstract, and well-integrated elements is regarded as relatively complex. Strictly speaking, the term *cognitive complexity* is content free and can be applied to any cognitive domain. In practice, however, cognitive complexity has been treated as an aspect of social cognition, with research focusing on individual differences in the complexity of cognitive structures applicable to the self and, especially, other persons. Considerable research (reviewed later in this chapter) has found that individual differences in cognitive complexity underlie a diverse array of communication-related abilities, including skill in social perception, message production, message reception, and social interaction.

This chapter provides a detailed examination of the connections between cognitive complexity and communication processes. The initial section of the chapter considers several theoretical and methodological issues associated with the conceptualization and assessment of cognitive complexity. The second section, which constitutes the core of the chapter, reviews theory and research linking cognitive complexity with several major communication processes. Previous reviews of the literature on cognitive complexity and communication have focused heavily on the contributions of complexity to the production of sophisticated, finely adapted message strategies (see Applegate, 1990; Burleson, 1987; Delia, 1987; B. O'Keefe & Delia, 1988). This chapter is more comprehensive, providing reviews of research on the contributions of cognitive complexity to social perception, message reception, and conversational interaction as well as to message production. The final portion of the chapter details some current concerns and controversies in cognitive complexity research and sketches directions for future study and theoretical development.

THE THEORY AND MEASUREMENT OF COGNITIVE COMPLEXITY

Scope of the Review

Although most discussions about cognitive complexity make some reference to the notions of cognitive differentiation, abstractness, articulation, and integration, several quite distinct conceptualizations and operationalizations of the cognitive complexity construct have appeared since the 1950s (see Bieri, et al., 1966; Burleson & Waltman, 1988; Coopman, in press; Crockett, 1982; Goldstein & Blackman, 1978; Miller & Wilson, 1979; D. O'Keefe & Sypher, 1981; Scott, Osgood, & Peterson, 1979; Streufert & Streufert, 1978). Moreover, different measures of cognitive complexity have often been found either uncorrelated or only weakly correlated with each other—findings indicating that the varied measures of cognitive complexity cannot all be measuring the same thing (see D. O'Keefe & Sypher, 1981; Vannoy, 1965). Furthermore, many studies making use of the cognitive complexity construct focus on issues chiefly relevant in clinical, educational, industrial, and personality psychology (see Adams-Webber, 1979; R. Neimeyer, Baker, & Neimeyer, 1990); much of this work has only tangential relevance to research on human communication processes. For all these reasons, it is necessary to narrow the scope of this review to only a small portion of the total literature on cognitive complexity.

This chapter focuses on only one approach to the study of cognitive complexity, that introduced in the field of psychology by Crockett (1965) and developed in the field of communication by Delia and his associates (e.g., Delia, 1972; Delia, Clark, & Switzer, 1974). There are several reasons for adopting this specific focus. First, considerable evidence indicates that the procedure developed by Crockett for assessing cognitive complexity is superior to alternative assessment methods. For example, D. O'Keefe and Sypher (1981) carried out a comprehensive review of several commonly used measures of cognitive complexity and concluded that only Crockett's measure satisfied "all the criteria for an adequate complexity measure" (p. 85). This conclusion has been buttressed by several recent comparative studies that have found Crockett's procedure for assessing complexity superior to alternative measurement procedures (e.g., Applegate, Kline, & Delia, 1991; Kagan, 1988; Kline, Pelias, & Delia, 1991; H. Sypher, Witt, & Sypher, 1986).

Second, most of the studies on cognitive complexity appearing in the communication literature have made use of Crockett's operationalization of this variable (for exceptions, see Beatty & Payne, 1981, 1984a). This research has stemmed largely from the theoretical perspective of constructivism (see Delia, O'Keefe, & O'Keefe, 1982)—a framework that has subsumed Crockett's analysis of cognitive complexity within more general analyses of social cognition and sophisticated interpersonal functioning. Although research examining the contributions of cognitive complexity to communication processes is a central component of the constructivist approach, constructivism is clearly broader than cognitive complexity research. The constructivism of Delia and his associates offers analyses of relationship development processes (e.g., Burleson, 1995; Delia, 1980), cultural influences on communication (e.g., Applegate & Sypher, 1988), language acquisition and communicative development (e.g., Clark, 1980; Clark & Delia, 1979), socialization processes (e.g., Burleson, Delia, & Applegate, 1995; Burleson & Kunkel, 1996), and communication pedagogy (Clark, Willihnganz, & O'Dell, 1985; Rowan, 1984), as well as examinations of communication processes in business (e.g., B. Sypher, 1991), educational institutions (Applegate, 1980a), health care contexts (e.g., Kline & Ceropski, 1984), and political settings (e.g., Swanson, 1981). Reviews of the general constructivist program are widely available (e.g., Burleson, 1989; Delia et al., 1982; Gastil, 1995; Griffin, 1997; Nicotera, 1995).

Thus we do not attempt to provide a comprehensive review of literature on either cognitive complexity or the constructivist approach to communication. Rather, our review is defined by the intersection of the cognitive complexity and constructivist literatures. Although this is a narrow focus, a search of the literature conducted in 1996 indicated that the specified intersection contained more than 200 published empirical studies as well as several dozen theoretical articles and reviews.

A Constructivist Conceptualization of Cognitive Complexity

Personal Constructs and Their Development. Crockett's (1965) original analysis of cognitive complexity was based on a fusion of the personal construct psychology of Kelly (1955) and the structural developmental theory of Werner (1957). From Kelly, Crockett drew the basic unit of cognitive structure: the personal construct. Like modern day proponents of schema theory (see Fiske & Taylor, 1991), Kelly assumed that features of the world are never apprehended directly, but rather are grasped through the mediation of cognitive structures. For Kelly, the personal construct was the basic unit of the cognitive system; Kelly (1955) described *personal constructs* as "transparent templates" or bipolar dimensions that a person "creates and then attempts to fit over the realities of which the world is composed" (p. 9). Personal constructs thus constitute the basic cognitive structures through which persons interpret, anticipate, evaluate, and understand aspects of the world.

Kelly (1955) argued that each construct had a specific focus and range of convenience. That is, for each construct, some events fall within the specific focus of the construct, other events fall outside this focus but are still capable of being understood through the mediation of the construct, and still other events fall outside the range of the construct and thus are irrelevant to it. Kelly further maintained that constructs having a similar range of convenience (i.e., applying to roughly the same domain of phenomena) are organized with specific subsystems. Constructs are organized hierarchically, such that some elements in the subsystem subsume or imply other elements. Thus, for example, constructs whose range and focus of convenience include the thoughts, behaviors, characteristics, and qualities of other people form a subsystem of interpersonal constructs.

Werner's structural-developmental theory provided Crockett a way of dealing with systematic differences in the structure of individuals' personal constructs. According to Werner (1957), all things said to "develop" do so in accord with the Orthogenetic Principle: "Wherever development occurs, it proceeds from a state of relative globality and lack of differentiation to states of increasing differentiation, articulation, and hierarchic integration" (p. 126). Applied to personal constructs, the Orthogenetic Principle suggests that more developed systems of constructs will be more differentiated (contain greater numbers of constructs), articulated (consist of more refined and abstract elements), and integrated (organized and interconnected). These more developed systems of constructs can be characterized as relatively complex. That is, persons with relatively differentiated, abstract, and organized systems of constructs in a particular domain are considered cognitively complex in that domain. Thus, for example, someone with a relatively differentiated, abstract, and organized system of interpersonal constructs can be regarded as having a relatively high level of interpersonal cognitive complexity.

For both Kelly and Werner, development occurs in specific domains of activity and involvement. The degree of elaboration in any subsystem of constructs is partly a function of general maturational processes, but even more a function of socialization experiences and degree of activity with the domain of events for which the particular subsystem of constructs is developed. Thus, it is quite possible for an individual to possess a highly developed subsystem of interpersonal constructs while simultaneously possessing relatively undeveloped subsystems of constructs for other phenomenal domains (e.g., furniture, automobiles). This view of development is consistent with contemporary work in the psychology of expertise (see Bereiter & Scardamalia, 1993; Fiske & Taylor, 1991). From the viewpoint of schema theory, expertise is always domain specific; it is nonsensical (as well as oxymoronic) to speak of a "general expert."

Because development is viewed as proceeding in specific domains of activity and involvement, the constructivist perspective provides a way of addressing both age-related changes and systematic individual differences in the structure of the interpersonal construct system. Wernerian developmental theory suggests that over the course of childhood and adolescence, persons will elaborate more sophisticated and refined systems of interpersonal constructs. Consistent with this expectation, numerous studies have found that the individual's construct system becomes increasingly differentiated, abstract, and organized over the course of childhood and adolescence (e.g., Barenboim, 1977, 1981; Barratt, 1977; Bigner, 1974; Bliss, 1986; Livesley & Bromley, 1971; Peevers & Secord, 1973; Scarlett, Press, & Crockett, 1971).

Beyond these age-related changes in the construct system, any particular group of individuals (either adults or children of the same age) is likely to contain both persons with relatively differentiated, abstract, and organized systems of interpersonal constructs and persons with relatively sparse, concrete, and unorganized systems of interpersonal constructs. Stable individual differences in interpersonal cognitive complexity appear to originate in childhood (e.g., Jennings, 1975; Little, 1972) and persist across the life cycle (e.g., Crockett, 1965; D. O'Keefe, Shepherd, & Streeter, 1982). The socialization practices of parents have substantial impact on children's levels of interpersonal cognitive complexity. Particularly influential are parental modes of discipline and nurturance (e.g., Applegate, Burleson, & Delia, 1992; see also Burleson et al., 1995) and the frequency and manner in which parents talk about feelings and other internal states (e.g., Dunn, Brown, & Beardsall, 1991; Dunn, Brown, Slomowski, Tesla, & Youngblade, 1991). An additional factor influencing the emergence of individual differences in cognitive complexity appears to be frequency of social interaction, especially with peers (e.g., Crockett, 1965; Strayer & Mashal, 1983).

Conceptualizing Cognitive Complexity: Personality Trait or Social Information Processing Capacity? Is it appropriate to view cognitive complexity as a personality trait? Probably not. Classically, personality traits are conceptualized as motivating or predisposing individuals to act (or to avoid acting) in particular ways (see Daly, 1987; Hewes & Planalp, 1987; Steinfatt, 1987). Some traits are viewed as having a very broad influence on behavior whereas others are seen as exerting more limited, situationally specific effects. Regardless, personality traits are typically seen as affecting behavior by motivating (or inhibiting) the performance of certain acts. The distinctiveness of particular personality traits resides in the specific character of the motivational orientations with which they are associated.

Cognitive complexity should not be viewed as a personality trait because it is not best conceptualized as predisposing or motivating individuals to act in particular ways. Rather, cognitive complexity is better understood as an information processing variable. Individuals with developed (differentiated, articulated, and integrated) systems of personal constructs have greater information processing capacity in a particular domain, and thus possess greater expertise in that domain. Hence, studies comparing cognitively complex with less complex individuals are analogous to studies of expert-novice differences.

Research in the psychology of expert-novice differences (see Daly, Bell, Glenn, & Lawrence, 1985; Ericsson & Smith, 1991; Hoffman, 1992) indicates that compared to novices, experts have cognitive schemata that are more abstract (e.g., Hintzman, 1986), compact (e.g., Fiske & Dyer, 1985), and differentiated (e.g., Linville, 1982). Furthermore, "the well-developed schemas of experts contain more links among the elements and more complex organization" (Fiske & Taylor, 1991, p. 148; see also Chi & Koeske, 1983; McKiethen, Reitman, Rueter, & Hirtle, 1981). Obviously, this representation of the cognitive structures of experts is very similar to the conceptualization of cognitively complex individuals as possessing more differentiated, articulated, and integrated systems of personal constructs.

Research comparing experts and novices on a variety of information processing tasks has found that experts are better able to (a) develop detailed, discriminating representations of phenomena (e.g., Lurigio & Carroll, 1985); (b) recall information from memory quickly (e.g., Smith, Adams, & Schorr, 1978); (c) organize schema-consistent information quickly (e.g., Pryor & Merluzzi, 1985); (d) notice, recall, and use schema-inconsistent information (e.g., Bargh & Thein, 1985; Borgida & DeBono, 1989); and (e) resolve apparent discrepancies between schema-consistent and schema-inconsistent information (e.g., Fiske, Kinder, & Larter, 1983). These expert-novice differences correspond closely to contrasts distinguishing those who are more and less cognitively complex. For example, compared to those having less complex systems, persons with complex systems of interpersonal constructs (a) form more detailed and organized impressions of others (e.g., Delia et al., 1974), (b) are better able to remember impressions of others (e.g., B. O'Keefe, Delia, & O'Keefe, 1977), (c) are better able to resolve inconsistencies in information about others (e.g., Press, Crockett, & Delia, 1975), (d) learn complex social information quickly (e.g., Delia & Crockett, 1973), and (e) use multiple dimensions of judgment in making social evaluations (e.g., Shepherd & Trank, 1992). These results suggest that interpersonal cognitive complexity is properly viewed as indexing individual differences in social information-processing capacity.

It is appropriate to reiterate here that individual differences in cognitive complexity, like various forms of expertise, are domain specific. Thus, an individual with a high level of interpersonal cognitive complexity may be expected to display greater information-processing capacity and expertise in the domain of interpersonal relations, but not necessarily in other aspects of life (e.g., houseplants, architecture). Degree of expertise is a function of experience and involvement with the objects in a particular phenomenal domain. All people interact with others and all must develop, manage, and maintain a variety of interpersonal relationships. Hence, all people have minimally developed systems of interpersonal constructs and some level of expertise in managing interpersonal situations. Clearly, however, people differ in their levels of interpersonal experience and, consequently, in their degrees of interpersonal cognitive complexity and social expertise.

In summary, interpersonal cognitive complexity is best viewed as reflecting individual differences in social information-processing capacity, and not as a motivational orientation or predisposition. Persons with highly developed systems of interpersonal constructs are better able than those with less developed systems to acquire, store, retrieve, organize, and generate information about other persons and social situations. Whether and how people choose to use their social information-processing capacities is not something that can be determined directly from their levels of cognitive complexity.[1] As with other forms of expertise, people may use their social information-processing capacity for varied ends, and may even choose to not use it at all. Characteristically, however, we should expect that cognitively complex persons will spontaneously and routinely use the enhanced processing capacities at their disposal. Research on expert-novice differences (e.g., Bereiter & Scardamalia, 1993) indicates that use of enhanced capacities is not particularly burdensome for experts—at least up to certain limits. This suggests that individual differences in cognitive complexity may be reflected in a broad array of perceptual and interactive processes. The considerable evidence consistent with this notion is reviewed following a brief discussion of measurement issues.

---

[1]Although cognitive complexity is not best viewed as a personality trait, certain personality traits may influence (a) whether an individual initially develops a high level of complexity (e.g., attachment style), (b) the extent to which a given level of complexity is sustained or enhanced (e.g., emotional empathy), or (c) the ends to which individuals direct their social information-processing capacities (e.g., altruism or prosocial motivation). For example, cognitive complexity predicts how well an individual can take the perspective of another (see Hale & Delia, 1976), but is not necessarily predictive of whether the ability to take another's perspective will be used on a given occasion, and if used, for what purpose. Whether certain traits coincide with (or causally determine) interpersonal cognitive complexity is an empirical question—one on which there is considerable, and often conflicting, evidence. For example, compare Delia and O'Keefe (1976) with H. Sypher, Nightingale, Vielhaber, and Sypher (1981) on the influence of Machiavellianism, and Neuliep and Hazelton (1985) with Shepherd and Condra (1988) on the influence of communication apprehension.

Assessing Cognitive Complexity: The Role Category Questionnaire Measure

Structure and Use of the RCQ Measure. Many different measures of cognitive complexity have been developed since the 1950s, most of which have been based on grids associated with some version of Kelly's Role Construct Repertory Test (e.g., Bieri, 1955; Bieri et al., 1966; Easterby-Smith, 1981). However, most studies of cognitive complexity in relation to communication processes have employed a measurement approach that Crockett (1965) termed the Role Category Questionnaire (RCQ). Research participants responding to the RCQ typically provide free-response descriptions of several persons known to them. These descriptions are then coded for the number of interpersonal constructs they contain (or more precisely, reflect). The resulting number of constructs is viewed as an index of interpersonal cognitive complexity.

To obtain estimates of complexity levels, Crockett (1965) initially had subjects write descriptions of eight different peers. They were asked to do so in 3 minutes for each peer. Subsequent research has shown that valid and reliable estimates of complexity levels can be obtained by having participants describe only two peers for 5 minutes each (see Burleson & Waltman, 1988). Currently, the most commonly used version of the RCQ instructs participants to provide written descriptions of two well-known peers, one liked and one disliked. When writing their impressions, subjects are specifically instructed to describe each peer in as much detail as possible, focusing on the peer's habits, beliefs, mannerisms, ways of treating others, traits, and personality characteristics. The RCQ is a flexible instrument that readily permits variations in structure (e.g., number and type of targets described) and administration (e.g., oral vs. written descriptions) to enhance its utility with populations such as children and the elderly (for a discussion of variations and circumstances that may motivate their use, see Burleson & Waltman, 1988).

Procedures for scoring the impressions generated by the RCQ were detailed by Crockett, Press, Delia, and Kenny (1974); these procedures have been reproduced in several more accessible sources (e.g., Applegate, 1990; Burleson & Waltman, 1988). Most frequently, the impressions generated by the RCQ are scored for the number of different interpersonal constructs they contain. When only the number of constructs contained in the elicited impressions is coded, the resulting score is most properly regarded as a measure of interpersonal construct differentiation. The coding procedures for differentiation scorings have been found easy to follow and consistently result in high levels of intercoder reliability (see Burleson & Waltman, 1988). Procedures are also available for coding the abstractness of interpersonal constructs (see Applegate, 1980a, 1990; Burleson, 1984a; Delia et al., 1974) and estimating the degree of organization among constructs in the interpersonal system (Crockett, 1965, 1982; Crockett et al., 1974). Differentiation scores frequently have been found moderately to highly associated with abstractness and organization scores derived from the RCQ (see the review by D. O'Keefe & Sypher, 1981). Consequently, the differentiation score obtained from the RCQ can be regarded as a good, overall index of interpersonal cognitive complexity. Of course, construct abstractness or organization may prove to be a theoretically more appropriate index of construct system development in some circumstances (e.g., Delia, Kline, & Burleson, 1979; B. O'Keefe & Delia, 1979). Thus, the index of construct system development employed by researchers should be sensitive to the particular issues addressed by specific studies.

The RCQ is assumed to sample, rather than exhaustively tap, the interpersonal construct system (see Burleson, Applegate, & Delia, 1991; Crockett, 1965). That is, the constructs elicited by the RCQ are assumed to constitute a representative sample of the number of interpersonal constructs the individual has available. Individuals with larger numbers of interpersonal constructs available to them (i.e., those who have more differentiated construct systems) should express a greater number of constructs when responding to the RCQ (i.e., they should produce more differentiated impressions). Thus, it is assumed that the degree of differentiation observed in elicited impressions corresponds to the degree of differentiation that actually exists in the interpersonal cognitive system.

Reliability and Validity of Measures Derived from the RCQ. The reliability and validity of RCQ-based measures of construct system development, especially the frequently used measure of differentiation (or complexity), have been examined in numerous studies. The results of these investigations are summarized in several detailed reviews (see Burleson, 1987; Burleson et al., 1991; Burleson & Waltman, 1988; Delia et al., 1982; D. O'Keefe & Sypher, 1981; H. Sypher & Sypher, 1988), and thus are only glossed here. In general, the available evidence indicates that the measures generated by the RCQ are both reliable and valid, and frequently exhibit stronger validity coefficients than alternative measures of cognitive complexity. The RCQ measure of differentiation exhibits good test-retest reliability, as any measure of a stable individual difference should. The RCQ measure of complexity has also amassed considerable construct validity, evidenced in correlations with numerous indices of advanced socio-cognitive and communicative functioning (much of this evidence is summarized in the next section of this chapter).

Just as important, the RCQ measure of cognitive complexity exhibits good discriminant validity. Because the RCQ is a free-response task in which persons must verbally express their impressions of others, concern has quite naturally been expressed (e.g., Miller & Wilson, 1979) about the extent to which assessments derived from the RCQ might be confounded by factors such as verbal ability, intelligence, and writing skills. These concerns have been addressed in several studies, with results indicating that RCQ assessments of cognitive complexity are typically unrelated to independent assessments of variables such as verbal intelligence, verbal fluency, general intelligence, and academic achievement (see Burleson & Waltman, 1988, p. 18; also see Allen, Mabry, Banski, & Preiss, 1991). In addition, assessments of cognitive complexity obtained with written responses to the RCQ have been found uncontaminated by factors such as writing speed (e.g., Burleson, Applegate, & Neuwirth, 1981) and narrative writing skill (e.g., Burleson & Rowan, 1985).

Some researchers (e.g., Beatty & Payne, 1984b; Powers, Jordan, & Street, 1979) have argued that RCQ assessments of cognitive complexity may be confounded by loquacity, the propensity to wordiness in verbalizations. Because people must use words when expressing their constructs, it is not surprising to find that cognitive complexity scores derived from RCQ impressions are correlated with the number of words used in producing these impressions. However, several studies (e.g., Burleson et al., 1981; Burleson, Waltman, & Samter, 1987) have found little relation between RCQ assessments of cognitive complexity and independent measures of loquacity (e.g., the average number of words used to express a construct, the number of words used in an informal conversation, the number of conversational turns taken in a conversation, the average length of a conversational turn; see Burleson & Waltman, 1988). Other challenges to RCQ-based measures of construct system development have shown that scores generated by the RCQ can be altered by making substantial changes in how the task is administered (e.g., Allen, Mabry, Banski, Stoneman, & Carter, 1990; Beatty & Payne, 1985) and scored (Allen, Burrell, & Kellermann, 1993). These latter challenges to the RCQ's validity do not seem particularly problematic because the values generated by any instrument are likely to change as a result of major modifications in task instructions or scoring procedures (see Burleson et al., 1991).

In addition to being unconfounded by many verbal abilities, traits, and proclivities, RCQ-based assessments of cognitive complexity largely appear to be free from the influence of many personality traits (see Burleson & Waltman, 1988; B. O'Keefe & Delia, 1982). Furthermore, several studies (e.g., Samter & Burleson, 1984) found that controlling for the influence of diverse personality traits does not attenuate associations between RCQ measures of cognitive complexity and theoretically relevant criterion variables. Thus, RCQ measures of cognitive complexity appear to be uncontaminated by variables that might result in spurious associations.

In summary, although the reliability and validity of measures derived from the RCQ have been questioned by several researchers, the balance of the evidence weighs strongly in favor of RCQ-based measures. The RCQ appears to generate a reliable assessment of cognitive complexity that is not appreciably contaminated by general verbal orientations or skills, general intelligence, or a variety of personality traits. Moreover, measures of cognitive complexity based on the RCQ have been found substantially associated with indices of sophisticated socio-cognitive and communicative functioning. We now turn to a detailed examination of research exploring linkages between cognitive complexity and communication skills.

COGNITIVE COMPLEXITY AND COMMUNICATION SKILL

At a minimum, the communication process involves (a) perceiving others and defining social situations, (b) producing messages, (c) interpreting and responding to the messages of others, and (d) coordinating interaction with others (see Burleson, 1992; Delia et al., 1982; Motley, 1990). All of these components of the communication process draw on the individual's social information-processing capacity. Hence, individual differences in social information processing, indexed by level of interpersonal cognitive complexity, should be associated with corresponding differences in communication skills.

Cognitive Complexity and Social Perception Skills

Social perception processes are the "input-oriented" cognitive activities through which persons define social situations and perceive and interpret the qualities, thoughts, states, and behaviors of others.

Typical social perception processes include such cognitive activities as identifying types of persons and activities, determining intentions and affective states, inferring dispositional qualities from behavior, making causal attributions, forming impressions of others, retrieving information about situations and persons from memory, integrating new information with old, making inferences about the perspectives of others ("role-taking"), and evaluating aspects of others' conduct and traits. All these activities must take place through the application of cognitive structures. That is, through the application of cognitive structures, various social perception and social inference processes are carried out.

Contemporary social cognition researchers have proposed an array of cognitive structures through which the individual may generate and process social information; these structures include scripts, prototypes, exemplars, and several different types of social schemas (see Fiske & Taylor, 1991). Delia (1977; also see Delia et al., 1982) suggested that interpersonal constructs can be viewed as the basic socio-cognitive structure underlying the operation of all social perception processes. As a unit of cognitive structure, the interpersonal construct shares much in common with structures like the schema (see H. Sypher & Applegate, 1984); however, constructs are conceptualized primarily as representational structures rather than the loci in which the contents of memory reside.[2]

The notion that all social perception processes occur through the application of interpersonal constructs has important theoretical and empirical implications. In particular, it has been proposed that individuals with more developmentally advanced (i.e., differentiated, abstract, and integrated) systems of interpersonal constructs should exhibit more sophisticated social perception skills. Because interpersonal constructs are the basic schemes through which aspects of persons and social situations are represented, persons having more developed systems of constructs should generate more discriminating, abstract, and refined social perceptions. Furthermore, more developed systems of constructs should facilitate the retrieval and cognitive manipulation of social information (see Crockett, 1982, 1985; J.R. Meyer, 1996; H. Sypher & Applegate,

---

[2]For a discussion of social memory and the relation between memory and representation processes, see Fiske and Taylor (1991, especially chapter 8). Thus far, constructivist researchers have not developed detailed models of declarative memory for social phenomena, nor have they sought to integrate their work on social representation with existing models of social memory. Clearly, this constitutes a major hole in the constructivist program on social perception—one that is in urgent need of attention.

1984). This general prediction has been examined in numerous studies focusing on identifying others' states and inferring their dispositions, forming interpersonal impressions, integrating social information, making social evaluations, and taking the other's perspective.

Identifying Others' States and Inferring their Dispositions. When compared to their less complex counterparts, cognitively complex perceivers are more accurate at identifying others' emotional states, are more inclined to make sophisticated inferences about others' dispositional qualities, and are more likely to make use of information present in the situation when making inferences about dispositions. For example, both Burleson (1982a, 1994) and Applegate et al. (1992) found that children having high levels of cognitive complexity performed better than less complex children on an affect recognition task. Cognitive complexity has been found associated with the tendency to infer multiple causes for and consequences of the actions of others (e.g., Clark et al., 1985; B. O'Keefe, Murphy, Meyers, & Babrow, 1989). Moreover, Wilson and his colleagues (Wilson, Cruz, & Kang, 1992; Wilson & Kang, 1991) found that the dispositional attributions made by complex perceivers were comparatively sensitive and responsive to information available in social situations; this led to making dispositional attributions that were flexible and situationally sensitive. In contrast, less complex perceivers made less use of information available in the social situation and were more rigid in their attributions. Finally, Woods (1996) found cognitive complexity positively associated with performance on a test of nonverbal decoding ability (the capacity to correctly discern the intentions, states, and characteristics of others based on nonverbal cues). Thus, it appears that complex perceivers "read" people and social situations more deeply than do less complex perceivers and make more accurate judgments about affective and intentional states.

Impression Organization. The nature of others is not immediately given in their behavior; consequently, in forming impressions of others, perceivers must make inferences about the characteristics and qualities of others from observed behavior, infer other qualities from behavior-based inferences, and organize these inferences into a relatively complete and satisfying "picture" of the other. Highly organized impressions of others provide perceivers with a more comprehensive, flexible, and stable understanding of others. In contrast, poorly organized impressions provide a less complete account of the other's characteristics, are more labile, and are less stable.

Several studies have found that interpersonal construct differentiation, as assessed by the RCQ, is positively associated with the degree of organization exhibited in naturally formed impressions (e.g., Delia et al., 1974; B. O'Keefe, 1984), as well as impressions formed under various experimental conditions (e.g., Crockett, Gonyea, & Delia, 1970; Delia, 1972; Kenny, Press, & Crockett, 1972). Moreover, some research (e.g., Delia et al., 1974) indicates that RCQ-assessed construct differentiation is associated with the formation of more dispositionally and motivationally oriented impressions—qualities that presumably aid the perceiver in anticipating and understanding the other's behavior across an array of situations. Thus, measures of cognitive complexity based on the RCQ are good predictors of the level of organization attained in naturally formed impressions.

Information Integration. Considerable research also indicates that cognitive complexity, as assessed by the RCQ, is a good predictor of the ability to recognize, reconcile, and integrate potentially inconsistent information about others. Regardless of the mode in which inconsistent information has been presented to subjects, persons with highly differentiated systems of interpersonal constructs have been found better able than their less differentiated counterparts to reconcile and integrate information about others (e.g., Delia, Gonyea, & Crockett, 1971; Mayo & Crockett, 1964; McMahan, 1976; Meltzer, Crockett, & Rosenkrantz, 1966; Nidorf & Crockett, 1965; B. O'Keefe et al., 1977; Rosenbach, Crockett, & Wapner, 1973; Rosenkrantz & Crockett, 1965). Several factors have been found to attenuate the ability of cognitively complex individuals to integrate inconsistent information (e.g., emotional involvement, instructional sets, perceived similarity to the target); in particular, the induction of an evaluative set on the part of perceivers has been found to attenuate the effects of cognitive complexity with respect to information integration (e.g., see Crockett, Mahood, & Press, 1975; Press et al., 1975).

Social Evaluation and Reliance on Evaluative Consistency Principles. As just noted, the experimental induction of an evaluative set has been found to reduce the extent to which high complexity perceivers integrate inconsistent information about others. This finding suggests that, under most normal conditions, cognitively complex perceivers are less reliant on evaluative consistency principles in processing information and less dominated by global evaluations in making judgments and reaching decisions. More specifically, D. O'Keefe (1980) suggested that global evaluation (e.g., like-dislike, good-bad) constitutes one dimension of judgment all perceivers have available for cognizing features of the world or constructing plans of action. Because cognitively complex perceivers have many more dimensions of judgment available to them than less complex perceivers, they should be less reliant on and dominated by the dimension of global evaluation. Shepherd and Trank (1989, 1992) reported support for this notion, finding that cognitively complex students expressed more varied evaluations of teachers than did less complex students. Several other studies (Delia & Crockett, 1973; Delia, Crockett, & Gonyea, 1970; Press, Crockett, & Rosenkrantz, 1969) found that cognitively complex persons (as determined by the RCQ) exhibit less reliance on evaluatively based schemes (i.e., balance schemes) in learning patterns of social relationships than do noncomplex persons. In a related vein, D. O'Keefe and Brady (1980) found that cognitively complex perceivers were less likely than noncomplex perceivers to exhibit attitude polarization after brief periods of thought. Still other research (e.g., Nidorf & Argabrite, 1970) indicates cognitively complex perceivers are less likely than noncomplex perceivers to make extreme judgments. Overall then, cognitively complex social perceivers appear less reliant on evaluation as an organizing scheme than less complex individuals.

RCQ assessments of interpersonal cognitive complexity have also been found related to the strength of the attitude-behavior relation. D. O'Keefe and Delia (1981) reasoned that because cognitively complex persons should be less dominated by global evaluation in making decisions, high complexity individuals would exhibit less attitude-behavior consistency than low complexity persons. As expected, these researchers found that individuals with highly differentiated systems of interpersonal constructs displayed less consistency in their attitudes and behavioral intentions than did persons with less differentiated construct systems; similar findings have been reported in several other investigations (e.g., DeLancey & Swanson, 1981; D. O'Keefe & Shepherd, 1982; Shepherd, 1987). However, Babrow and O'Keefe (1984) found that RCQ-assessed complexity in a noninterpersonal domain (college classes) had no effect on the strength of the attitude-behavior relation in that domain. Thus, it is possible that cognitive complexity may have a moderating effect on the attitude-behavior relation only in the interpersonal domain. In any event, existing research clearly indicates that assessments of interpersonal cognitive complexity obtained through the RCQ are appropriately related to less reliance on global evaluation and evaluative consistency principles.

Social Perspective-Taking Ability. Role-taking or social perspective-taking ability, the capacity to infer and represent the cognitions and feelings of another, has frequently been regarded as a major socio-cognitive ability underlying competent and effective communication (Mead, 1934; Piaget, 1926; see the review by Burleson, 1984b). Individual differences in interpersonal construct system development, as assessed by the RCQ, have been found associated with perspective-taking ability in samples of both adults and children. For example, several studies (e.g., Beatty & Payne, 1984b; Hale & Delia, 1976; Kline et al., 1991) found construct system differentiation scores derived from the RCQ positively associated with adults' performance on Hale and Delia's (1976) Social Perspectives Task (SPT). Construct differentiation, however, was found by H. Sypher and O'Keefe (1980) to be only marginally associated with adults' performance on a perspective-taking measure developed by Pelias (1984). Children's performances on the SPT and Rothenberg's (1970) affective role-taking measure have also been found positively associated with both construct system differentiation and abstractness even when controlling for the potentially confounding effect of age (e.g., Burleson, 1982a; Clark & Delia, 1977). Quite clearly, individual differences in construct system development, as assessed by the RCQ, are related to varied measures of perspective-taking ability.

Cognitive Complexity and Message Production

Production of Person-Centered Messages. A central area of inquiry for cognitive complexity researchers has focused on the association between interpersonal construct system development and sophisticated modes of communicative functioning. In particular, one large body of research has focused on the association between interpersonal cognitive complexity and the production of person-centered messages. Several detailed reviews of this extensive empirical literature have appeared previously (e.g., Applegate, 1990; Burleson, 1987, 1989; Coopman, in press; Delia, 1987; Kline & Delia, 1990; B. O'Keefe & Delia, 1982, 1988). Hence, the review here is brief and selective.

Person-centered messages reflect an awareness of and an adaptation to the subjective, affective, and relational aspects of communicative contexts (for detailed discussions of the person-centered construct, see Applegate, Burke, Burleson, Delia, & Kline, 1985; Applegate & Delia, 1980; Burleson, 1987). Person-centeredness is an important quality of functional communication; person-centered messages tend to be more responsive to the aims and utterances of an interactional partner, are tailored to the characteristics of the partner and situation, attend to the identity-relevant features of

communicative contexts, and may encourage reflection about persons
and social situations (see Applegate et al., 1985). Some evidence
supports the functional effectiveness of person-centered modes of
communicating in contexts such as comforting (e.g., Burleson &
Samter, 1985a, 1985b; Samter, Burleson, & Murphy, 1987),
persuading (e.g., Burleson & Fennelly, 1981; B. O'Keefe & Shepherd,
1989), and disciplining or regulating (e.g., Adams & Shepherd, 1996;
Burleson, Delia, & Applegate, 1992).

In most research, the capacity to produce highly person-
centered messages has been assessed by having participants
generate messages in response to standard situations and then
coding these messages within hierarchical schemes for the degree of
person-centeredness manifested. For example, messages seeking to
persuade others have been coded for the extent to which the goals
and desires of the target are taken into account (Clark & Delia, 1976;
Delia, Kline, & Burleson, 1979), messages seeking to comfort others
have been coded for the extent to which distressed feelings are
acknowledged, elaborated, and legitimized (Applegate, 1980a;
Burleson, 1982b), regulative or disciplinary messages have been
coded for the extent to which they encourage an offender to reflect on
and reason through the consequences of problematic conduct
(Applegate et al., 1985; Kline, 1991). Messages have also been coded
for the degree of person-centeredness manifested with respect to such
subsidiary goals as face support and relationship enhancement (e.g.,
Applegate & Woods, 1991; Leichty & Applegate, 1991). The
rationales generated to explain or justify message choices can also be
coded for degree of person-centeredness (e.g., Applegate, 1980a;
Burleson, 1980; B. O'Keefe & Delia, 1979). Considerable evidence
supports the validity of these procedures for collecting and coding
message behavior (see Burleson, 1987; Kline & Delia, 1990); in
particular, research indicates that messages generated in response to
hypothetical situations approximate those used in "real-world"
situations (e.g., Applegate, 1980b; Kochanska, 1990; Kochanska,
Kuczynski, & Radke-Yarrow, 1989).

Initially, research efforts focused on establishing a relation
between cognitive complexity and the ability to produce person-
centered message strategies. Presumably, complex systems of
interpersonal constructs better facilitate the representation of
communication-relevant features of persons and situations, and thus
assist the production of person-centered messages (e.g, see Applegate,
1990; Burleson, 1987; Delia, 1987). Research has been quite
successful in demonstrating a moderate, positive association between
cognitive complexity (and related measures of construct system
development such as abstractness) and both the ability to produce

and tendency to use person-centered message forms in a variety of functional contexts. For example, individual differences in cognitive complexity have been found associated with the use of person-centered communication when people seek to persuade others (e.g., Applegate, 1982; Clark & Delia, 1977; Delia, Kline, & Burleson, 1979; Leichty & Applegate, 1991; B. O'Keefe & Delia, 1979; B. O'Keefe et al., 1989; Piche & Roen, 1987; Shepherd & Condra, 1988; H. Sypher et al., 1986), resist complying with another's persuasive effort (e.g., Kline & Hennen-Floyd, 1990), discipline or regulate the actions of others (e.g., Applegate et al., 1985; Applegate, Coyle, Seibert, & Church, 1989; Hale, 1986; Kline, 1988, 1991; Woods, 1996), comfort and provide emotional support to others (e.g., Burleson, 1983, 1984a; Samter & Burleson, 1984), manage interpersonal conflicts (Carrocci, 1985; Saine, 1974), convey information clearly (e.g., Hale, 1980, 1982), and make abstract concepts understandable (e.g., Rowan, 1990). The association between cognitive complexity and person-centered communication has proven to be quite robust, having been found to hold across the following:

1. Diverse subject populations (children, adolescents, college students, mothers of young children, teachers, daycare-workers, nurses, medical students, residence hall counselors, management executives, and police officers).
2. Differences in the media or modality used to assess both construct system development and communicative behavior (oral modality, written modality).
3. Differences in the means used to obtain samples of message behaviors (hypothetical situations, experimental analogue situations, real world situations).
4. Different measures of construct system development (differentiation, abstractness).
5. Different aspects of communicative behavior (quality of messages, quality of message rationales, number of messages, variety of messages).
6. The statistical control of numerous potentially confounding factors (age, gender, social class, verbal and intellectual abilities, personality traits, motivational orientations).
7. Different instrumental goals pursued by speakers (persuading, comforting, regulating, informing, explaining, etc.).

8. Different subsidiary objectives implicitly addressed by speakers (self-presentation, face support, relationship enhancement).

Detailed reviews of this literature are available in several sources (Applegate, 1990; Burleson, 1987; Coopman, in press; Delia, 1987; Kline & Delia, 1990; B. O'Keefe & Delia, 1988).

Models of Message Production: Accounting for the Association Between Cognitive Complexity and Message Forms. Much of the constructivist research conducted in the 1970s and 1980s focused on demonstrating a relation between cognitive complexity and person-centered message use. As the character of this link became increasingly established, more research began to concentrate on developing and testing different theoretical accounts for this relation. Today, research on the nature of the message production process, and the role of cognitive complexity in that process, is one of the most important and active areas of constructivist research.

Early explanations of the message production process (e.g., Clark & Delia, 1977; Delia & Clark, 1977) stressed that cognitive complexity contributed to role-taking skill which, in turn, enhanced an individual's capacity to edit and adapt messages to meet the characteristics of a specific listener. Research linking cognitive complexity to role-taking skill (e.g., Burleson, 1982a; Hale & Delia, 1976), and role-taking skills to the use of person-centered messages (e.g., Burleson, 1984b; Clark & Delia, 1977) provided support for this conception of message production. However, in an important critique, B. O'Keefe and Delia (1982) pointed out that the role-taking or adapted communication account presented a limited view of advanced message forms and the role social cognition played in the production of these message forms. Highly person-centered messages are not merely more adapted utterances; rather, these are sophisticated message structures that, depending on the circumstances, focus on psychological and relational states, address multiple aspects of what may be complicated social situations, engage the listener in reasoning about the situation, seek to manage or protect valued social identities, and so on. Furthermore, social cognition may enter into the message production process in several ways, influencing the kinds of communicative intentions or goals speakers develop, the capacity to reconcile or integrate potentially inconsistent goals, the degree of focus on the motivational and affective aspects of social situation, as well as the amount of editing or adaptation of message contents.

Recent research has sought to develop and test more detailed models of the message production process, examining how individual differences in cognitive complexity influence various phases or aspects of this process. For example, B. O'Keefe and Delia (1982, 1985) proposed that, in addition to attending to the instrumental demands of communicative situations, cognitively complex individuals would be more inclined to orient to relationship- and identity-relevant features of these situations. Hence, cognitively complex perceivers should be inclined to generate more complex goal sets for many communicative situations—goal sets that seek to address identity and relationship concerns, as well as instrumental ends. Research by Wilson (1990, 1995) provides direct support for this goal complexity account of the association between cognitive complexity and person-centered communication. Wilson found that persons with more complex systems of interpersonal constructs developed more complex sets of goals for challenging communication situations; furthermore, those who developed more complex goal sets generated more sophisticated, person-centered messages for these situations (also see Wilson et al., 1992; Wilson & Kang, 1991). Additional results supportive of the goal complexity account have been reported by several other researchers (e.g., Kline, 1991; Kline & Ceropski, 1984; Leichty & Applegate, 1991; B. O'Keefe & Shepherd, 1987; Shepherd & Condra, 1988; Waldron & Applegate, 1994).

The goal complexity account represents an important step in developing more comprehensive accounts of the message production process and the role cognitive complexity may play in that process. However, the models of message production thus far presented by constructivist researchers remain underspecified, failing to present a detailed portrait of the structures and processes involved in the movement from perception of situations, through goal formation, to message articulation. The development of richer models of message production will provide enhanced opportunities to investigate how cognitive complexity may influence this process. Integrating aspects of the constructivist analysis with more general models of message production, such as those suggested by Greene (1995; Greene, Lindsey, & Hawn, 1990), Berger (1995), and Kellermann (1995), may prove fruitful in this endeavor.

Communication Effectiveness. Several studies examined whether cognitively complex people tend to be more effective or successful in social relationships than their less complex counterparts. Numerous studies found that highly person-centered forms of communication are, compared to less person-centered forms, more effective at accomplishing both instrumental and relationship goals (e.g., Adams & Shepherd, 1996; Burleson, et al., 1986; Burleson & Samter, 1985a; B. O'Keefe & McCornack, 1987; Samter et al.,

1987). Cognitively complex individuals are more likely to use person-centered messages and also possess more advanced social perception skills. Thus, it has been hypothesized that complex persons should be more effective and successful in a variety of social circumstances. There is growing evidence supportive of this hypothesis.

For example, children with more developmentally advanced systems of interpersonal constructs tend to be better liked by peers and enjoy a greater number of reciprocated friendships with classmates (Burleson et al., 1992). Burleson and Waltman (1987) found that children with complex systems of interpersonal constructs were perceived by both teachers and peers to be likely to provide emotional support to peers during times of trouble or distress. However, complex and less complex persons tend to differ in their conceptions of the friendship relationship (Leichty, 1989) and in the forms of communication they value among friends (Burleson & Samter, 1990). This suggests that highly complex persons may be most attracted to others with similarly high levels of complexity, whereas less complex individuals may be more attracted to those with lesser levels of complexity. Consistent with this reasoning, studies have found similarity in level of cognitive complexity to characterize child friends (e.g., Burleson, 1994), adult friends (e.g., Burleson & Samter, 1996), and married couples (e.g., Burleson & Denton, 1992). In addition, relationship partners who have similar levels of cognitive complexity have been found to be more attracted to one another (Burleson, Kunkel, & Szolwinski, 1997) and to be more satisfied with their friendships (e.g., Burleson & Samter, 1996) than partners with dissimilar levels of complexity.

There does not appear to be a simple, straightforward relation between cognitive complexity and marital satisfaction. That is, complex couples have not been found to be happier or more satisfied than less complex couples (see Burleson & Denton, 1992; G. Neimeyer, 1984). However, some research (Denton, Burleson, & Sprenkle, 1995) suggests that cognitive complexity is positively associated with interaction skills particularly relevant in the marital context. In addition, a recent study suggests there are some important, but complicated, connections between cognitive complexity and marital quality. Burleson and Denton (in press) found that the association between wives' cognitive complexity and husbands' liking for their wives was moderated by the distressed status of the marriage. In this study, spouses in "distressed" marriages had significantly more negative intentions toward one another than those in "nondistressed" marriages. Burleson and Denton (in press) found that wives' cognitive complexity was *positively* associated with their husbands' liking for them when the marriage was nondistressed; however, among couples in distressed marriages, wives' cognitive complexity was *negatively* associated, at a significant level, with their husbands' liking for them. One explanation for this result is that complex wives use their advanced perceptual and behavioral skills in a fashion consistent with their feelings for and intentions toward their husbands—to help when they are happy, and to hurt when they are unhappy. In either case, complex wives appear to be more effective at attaining their goals than less complex wives.

Cognitive complexity is also an important correlate of effectiveness in the organizational context (see B. Sypher, 1984; also see Coopman, in press; Streufert & Swezey, 1986; Walton, 1985). For example, in a longitudinal study of managerial employees in a large insurance firm, B. Sypher and Zorn (1986) found assessments of cognitive complexity positively associated with both job level and upward mobility among employees. These results were subsequently replicated by Zorn and Violanti (1996). Zorn (1991) examined the leadership styles of small business owners and found that those with higher levels of cognitive complexity were more likely to practice a functional, "transformational" style of leadership. Several other studies (e.g., Penley, Alexander, Jernigan, & Henwood, 1991; B. Sypher, Bostrom, & Seibert, 1989; Zimmermann, 1994) also suggest that cognitive complexity is an asset in the work environment.

Although the available evidence is rather sparse, it is consistent: Cognitively complex actors are more interpersonally effective in a variety of social contexts than their less complex counterparts. Unfortunately, the simple correlational designs used in existing research permit few inferences about why complex individuals are more effective. It seems reasonable to speculate that the complex actors in these studies generally used more sophisticated and effective forms of message behavior, but this conclusion cannot be asserted with any degree of certainty. Clearly, what is needed are more precise conceptual models of how cognitive complexity may influence varied forms of interpersonal effectiveness, along with more sophisticated research designs that will permit the evaluation of these models.

In addition, the link between cognitive complexity and interpersonal effectiveness has been examined largely in contexts where greater complexity would appear to be an asset—that is, in complicated and demanding social circumstances such as dealing with another's distressed feelings, changing another's opinions or ideas, and managing others in high-pressure organizational environments. Thankfully, not all social settings are as challenging as these. Will a high level of cognitive complexity prove advantageous in less demanding, more mundane social circumstances As some (e.g., Griffin, 1997) have speculated, high levels of complexity might prove to be inhibiting, or even debilitating, in simple, routine social situations. It is possible that as a kind of expertise, high cognitive complexity might constitute a type of "trained incapacity" in some simple social situations. However, it seems more likely that cognitive complexity represents a flexible capacity for social information processing and social action that may be tapped in variable degrees depending on situational demands. Currently, however, there are no data that permit resolving this question; clearly, this issue should be examined in future research.

Cognitive Complexity and Message Reception

Message reception—the perception and processing of others' intentional efforts to convey some internal state—may be viewed as a special case of social perception. Because individuals with high levels of cognitive complexity enjoy more advanced social perception skills than those with lower levels of complexity, it seems reasonable to hypothesize that cognitive complexity is associated with capacities involved in the receipt, storage, and interpretation of messages. There is growing evidence in support of this hypothesis, although the body of work examining cognitive complexity in relation to message reception is small compared to the extensive research on message production.

Individual Differences in Listening, Comprehension, and Conversational Memory as a Function of Cognitive Complexity. Some studies suggest that high-complexity individuals generally have more sophisticated listening and message interpretation skills. For example, B. Sypher et al. (1989) had employees from a variety of organizational levels complete the RCQ measure of cognitive complexity and the Kentucky Comprehensive Listening Test, an instrument providing assessments of five aspects of listening. Cognitive complexity was associated, at moderate levels, with three of the five listening assessments.[3] Cognitive complexity also appears to aid the interpretation of written messages. Hynds (1985) found that cognitively complex high school students had more accurate interpretations (but not greater comprehension) of a story they read than did less complex students.

---

[3]Beatty and Payne (1984a) also found a positive association between listening comprehension and cognitive complexity, although these researchers employed a non-RCQ-based measure of complexity.

Research by Neuliep and Hazelton (1986) suggests that cognitive complexity underlies the ability to recall details from conversational interactions. Participants in this study completed the RCQ and then subsequently watched a videotaped conversational interaction in which a pair of actors discussed both person-relevant and nonperson-relevant topics. Immediately following the conversation, half the participants completed tasks assessing two aspects of conversational memory, recall of the conversation (assessed by an open-ended free-recall task) and cued recognition of conversational elements (assessed by an 18-item multiple-choice test). The other half of the participants were exposed to a 5-minute interference task before completing the assessments of conversational memory. Cognitively complex participants performed better on both recall and recognition tasks than did less complex participants; furthermore, the effects of cognitive complexity were not qualified by the interference manipulation.

The results of these three studies suggest that cognitive complexity facilitates the cognitive encoding and recall of the messages and conversational behaviors. Compared to less complex individuals, cognitively complex persons listen more attentively to the messages of others, interpret these messages more comprehensively, and recall more of what was said. Clearly, these are important communication capacities.

Differential Responses of Low and High Complexity Judges to Person-Centered, Behaviorally Complex Messages. A second line of research has examined whether perceivers differing in cognitive complexity get different things out of sophisticated, person-centered forms of communication. As indicated previously, highly person-centered messages constitute complex behavioral forms in which pursuit of an instrumental objective (e.g., informing, persuading, regulating, comforting) is integrated with attention to subsidiary identity- and relationship-relevant concerns (e.g., self-presentation, face support). Several recent studies have examined whether the cognitive complexity levels of message recipients (or judges) moderate the perception and effects of messages exhibiting different degrees of person-centeredness. In particular, research has focused on whether high complexity perceivers are more sensitive to, and appreciative of, messages incorporating facework than are less complex perceivers. Although the findings are mixed, most studies suggest that cognitively complex perceivers get more information from and respond more favorably to highly person-centered, behaviorally complex messages than do less complex perceivers.

Several studies have examined the influence of cognitive complexity on the evaluation of comforting messages exhibiting different levels of person-centeredness. For example, Burleson and Samter (1985b) had participants rate for overall quality 36 different messages, each of which exhibited one of nine levels of person-centeredness. Persons with more abstract (but not more differentiated) systems of interpersonal constructs evaluated the comforting messages in accord with their degree of person-centeredness, rating high person-centered messages positively and low person-centered messages negatively. However, Samter et al. (1987) found that cognitive complexity did not moderate the effect of message person-centeredness on the evaluation of comforting messages; in this study, both complex and less complex perceivers evaluated high person-centered comforting messages more positively than low person-centered messages. Samter, Burleson, and Basden-Murphy (1989) examined whether the cognitive complexity levels of perceivers would interact with the person-centered quality of the comforting message used by a source in determining the impression formed of the message source. Consistent with expectations, these researchers found that high complexity perceivers formed more differentiated impressions of the message source when the source employed highly person-centered, behaviorally complex messages, whereas the impressions of the source formed by low complexity perceivers did not vary as a function of message characteristics. Samter et al. (1989) interpreted these results as indicating that high complexity perceivers better recognize and appreciate sophisticated, behaviorally complex forms of communication than do low complexity perceivers. Overall then, there is some tendency for cognitively complex perceivers to be more sensitive than less complex perceivers to the person-centered qualities of comforting messages.

Cognitive complexity has also been found to moderate the effects of message qualities in regulative communication contexts. B. O'Keefe and McCornack (1987) asked participants to read and evaluate regulative messages directed at getting a problem group member to complete his portion of a group project. These messages varied in terms of both their goal structure (the extent to which relational and identity goals were addressed in addition to the core regulative goal) and their design logic (fundamental premises about communication assumed to underlie message production; see B. O'Keefe, 1988, 1990, 1991). Messages exhibiting more sophisticated design logics and goal structures were evaluated more positively on several scales tapping different dimensions of communicative effectiveness. More important, however, participants' levels of cognitive complexity interacted with the message variables such that highly complex perceivers evaluated sophisticated messages more positively, and unsophisticated messages more negatively, than did low complexity perceivers. Results quite similar to these were obtained by Bingham and Burleson (1989) in a study examining the perceived effectiveness of regulative messages responding to sexual harassment in the workplace, and by Adams and Shepherd (1996) in a study examining hospital volunteers' evaluations of regulative messages issued by their supervisors.

Research has also examined the moderating effects of cognitive complexity on the reception of persuasive messages exhibiting different levels of person-centeredness or goal complexity. In an early study, Burleson and Fennelly (1981) found that children responded more generously to highly person-centered altruistic appeals than they did to less person-centered messages. However, the predicted interaction between children's cognitive complexity and the person-centered quality of the persuasive appeals was not statistically significant, even though the cell means were in the expected directions. The cell sizes in this study were quite small, so the failure to observe the predicted interaction may have been due to low statistical power. Shepherd and O'Keefe (1984) sought to examine the interactive influence of target cognitive complexity and message person-centeredness on the willingness of college students to participate in a research study. The expected interaction between cognitive complexity and message sophistication was not observed; however, neither was a main effect for message sophistication observed, raising a question about the adequacy of the message operationalizations used in this study. More recently, B. O'Keefe and Shepherd (1989) assessed the influence of perceiver cognitive complexity and message qualities on outcomes in face-to-face persuasive interactions. These researchers paired participants who had different opinions on a controversial issue and instructed them to try to change the other's stance on the issue. Following the interactions, participants completed questionnaires providing measures of attitude change and evaluations of the partner. The interactions were videotaped and were subsequently transcribed and coded for participants' use of messages that reflected a sophisticated reconciliation of competing goals. The sophistication of the goal reconciliation strategy used by the partner had a much stronger effect for complex perceivers than noncomplex perceivers on the positive character of task-relevant and relational beliefs formed about the target.

In summary, research on message reception shows that the effects of message quality (whether conceptualized in terms of person-centeredness, goal complexity, or design logic) tend to be strong and are not always qualified by the cognitive complexity level of judges.

However, when message quality and perceiver cognitive complexity do interact, the character of the interaction is consistent: Highly complex perceivers are more sensitive to and appreciative of those features of messages that make them more sophisticated forms of behavior—the integrated pursuit of multiple goals, the focus on facework and identity management, and the person-centered attention to the needs and characteristics of the other. Sensitivity to these message features may be one reason why cognitively complex individuals tend to choose as friends those who have more developed skills at person-centered communication (see Burleson, 1994; Burleson & Samter, 1996).

Although there are increasingly good grounds for viewing cognitive complexity as an important determinant of message reception, we currently have little understanding of the precise role played by this variable in the message reception process. That is, extant research has focused on establishing that cognitive complexity has some effect on message reception and outcomes, but has not tested specific hypotheses regarding how these effects come about. Hence, future research should consider more general models of message comprehension and processing (such as those reviewed by Badzinski & Gill, 1994) and seek to integrate analyses of the effects of cognitive complexity within these more general frameworks.

Cognitive Complexity and the Management of Social Interactions

Most studies examining the influence of cognitive complexity on message production and reception have explored these processes abstracted from their natural operation in conversational interactions (for exceptions, see Applegate, 1982; Denton et al., 1995; Kline & Ceropski, 1984; B. O'Keefe & Shepherd, 1987, 1989; Samter & Burleson, 1984). This may be an important limitation in the research because the character of message production and reception processes, as well as the cognitive demands on these processes, may be quite different when people respond to a controlled task in the laboratory versus when they engage in natural interactions (see Street, 1993). Moreover, communication is not reducible to isolated processes of message production and reception; communication also involves ongoing efforts to manage an emergent interactional situation. Hence, a growing number of efforts have sought to understand how cognitive complexity influences the individual's general orientation to conversational interaction, as well as skill in conducting conversation. In particular, recent research has assessed the influence of cognitive complexity on representations of conversational interactions, topic management during the course of conversation, and the conversational planning process.

Representations of Conversational Interaction. An increasing number of studies indicate that cognitively complex individuals have deeper, more sophisticated representations of the nature, structure, and functions of conversational interactions. For example, Ellis, Hamilton, and Aho (1983) found cognitive complexity associated with the ability to reconstruct the opening sequence of a scrambled conversation, suggesting that complex individuals have a better understanding of how conversations are typically sequenced and patterned. Daly et al. (1985) found cognitive complexity positively associated with a measure of "conversational complexity," a construct referencing the extensiveness of persons' representations of conversational interaction.

Consistent with the results reported by Ellis et al. (1983) and Daly et al. (1985), Stacks and Murphy (1993) found cognitive complexity significantly associated with a self-report measure of "conversational sensitivity" developed by Daly, Vangelisti, and Daughton (1987). The conversational sensitivity scale taps several aspects of conversational behavior, including sensitivity to conversational control, ability to detect nuances of meaning, enjoyment of conversations, and memory for conversations; cognitive complexity was associated with subscales for each of these components, as well as with the total scale score. Of particular interest, the association between cognitive complexity and self-reported memory for conversations provides an important extension of results reported by Neuliep and Hazelton (1986), who found cognitive complexity positively associated with several aspects of memory for actual conversations. In summary, it appears that cognitively complex individuals have a more abstract understanding of the structure of conversation, more detailed representations of conversational interactions, greater sensitivity to meanings and interpersonal moves (such as power plays) in interactions, as well as better memories for conversation.

Topic Management During Conversation. One of the most important aspects of conversation is topic management, and several studies suggest that cognitive complexity is associated with numerous aspects of skill in managing the introduction, flow, and development of conversational topics. For example, some early studies of the influence of cognitive complexity on topic selection by Delia and his associates (Delia, 1974; Delia, Clark, & Switzer, 1979; Delia & Murphy, 1983) suggested that cognitively complex individuals spend, when interactional constraints permit, more time talking about the personal qualities of themselves and others, their relationships with others, and their relationship with their conversational partner. Consistent with these results, Samter and Burleson (1984) found that cognitively complex persons were more likely to structure interactions through the use of questions and disclosures so as to accommodate the needs of a distressed other during a comforting episode.

Daly et al. (1985) found cognitive complexity significantly associated with the use of verbal back channels ("uh-huh," "I see," "Mhmm") during an initial get-acquainted conversation. Verbal back channels have often been conceptualized as devices for controlling the conversational floor (see Duncan & Fiske, 1977). Verbal back channels may also signal interest, and are used often when encouraging conversational partners to amplify, elaborate, and extend their conversational contributions. More recently, Chen (1996) found that topical selections of high complexity conversationalists were comparatively sensitive and adaptive to the cultural composition of a dyad (same culture vs. different culture) during an initial, get-acquainted conversation. In contrast, the nature of the topics focused on by low complexity interactants differed little as a function of the cultural composition of the dyad.

Although most studies examining the influence of cognitive complexity on topic management have focused on informal social interactions, some research has found interesting effects for complexity on topic management in purposeful, task-focused interactions. For example, Kline, Hennen-Floyd, and Farrell (1990) had student dyads engage in problem-solving discussions regarding a course policy; these conversations were transcribed and coded within the interaction analysis system developed by Stiles (1978). Participants' levels of cognitive complexity were positively correlated with the proportion of questions and edifications they employed during the conversation, and were negatively correlated with the proportion of interpretations and reflections they used. Interpretations and reflections both presume knowledge of the other's frame of reference, whereas questions and edifications presume that a frame of reference is not shared, and so seek to create it (Stiles, 1978). Thus, compared to their less complex counterparts, the conversational actions of highly complex interactants made fewer assumptions about what the other knew and sought to create shared understanding through expressing their own thoughts and asking questions about the thoughts of others.

Kline et al.'s (1990) results are consistent with those reported by Kline and Ceropski (1984), who found that the construct system development of medical students was positively correlated with their efforts to provide information to (and solicit it from) patients during the course of a medical interview. Similarly, Samter and Burleson

(1984) found that cognitive complexity was positively associated with participants' information-seeking efforts as they sought to comfort a confederate who feigned emotional distress. In summary, the conversational actions of cognitively complex persons implicitly recognize the distinctiveness of individuals and the uniqueness of their perspectives, and seek to create shared understanding by explicitly elaborating their viewpoints and encouraging their talk partners to do the same.

Planning Processes During Conversation. Waldron and Applegate (1994) explored the influence of cognitive complexity on the conversational plans developed for conflict situations, as well as on the tactics actually used during the course of conflict interactions. Participants in this study discussed a controversial topic with a peer who held a divergent opinion; they subsequently completed a cued-recall task to elicit planning efforts during the interaction. The use of functional, integrative conflict management tactics during the interaction was significantly correlated with the sophistication and editing of conversational plans, but was uncorrelated with cognitive complexity. However, cognitive complexity was significantly associated with measures reflecting the sophistication and editing of conversational plans.

These findings are important, because they suggest that cognitive complexity may principally influence the interactional goals and plans individuals develop, with these goals and plans then shaping subsequent behavior. Several theorists (e.g., B. O'Keefe & Delia, 1982; Wilson, 1990) have proposed that cognitive complexity primarily affects how people perceive social situations and what goals they develop for these situations, with conversational goals and plans then having a major influence on behavior. Waldron and Applegate's results provide some confirmation of this notion and suggest the potential of further integrating constructivist work on communication processes with cognitive research on conversational planning (e.g., Berger, 1995; Kellermann, 1995).

CONCLUSION

The research reviewed in this chapter makes it quite clear that cognitive complexity contributes in important ways to several major communication processes. In particular, cognitive complexity is associated with critical aspects of social perception, message production, message reception, and interaction management. Scores of empirical studies support the broad conclusion that cognitively complex individuals are more socially skilled and interpersonally competent than less complex individuals. Specifically, cognitive complexity has been found associated with the ability to acquire, organize, and integrate social information; the ability to produce sophisticated, behaviorally complex message forms that are both interpersonally sensitive and pragmatically effective; the ability to interpret and comprehend the messages of others, especially those containing sophisticated facework; and the ability to manage conversational interactions in a coherent and effective fashion.

Although researchers have been quite successful in demonstrating associations between cognitive complexity and varied aspects of communication skill, many important conceptual and methodological problems remain to be addressed. Some of these problems pertain to the nature of the cognitive complexity construct itself, whereas others concern the ways in which cognitive complexity contributes to advanced interpersonal functioning.

Questions Regarding Constructs, Construct Systems, and Cognitive Complexity

One important set of issues facing researchers concerns the theoretical relation among constructs, schemas, prototypes, exemplars, and other cognitive elements (see H. Sypher & Applegate, 1984). Are these terms synonyms or do they refer to different entities? And, if these terms index somewhat different structures (as appears to be the case; see Fiske & Taylor, 1991), how are these entities related to one another both structurally and functionally? Generating answers to these questions should help researchers develop more detailed models of critical socio-cognitive processes, including person representation, social inference, information integration, and social evaluation. These models will need to specify the particular structures through which social information is acquired and represented, the character of the processes acting on the information (e.g., serial or parallel; additive or transformational), and the nature of the resulting information structure (see Greene, 1995). Then, theorists will need to explicate how having more constructs, more abstract constructs, and/or better integrated constructs facilitates the execution, operation, and outcome of various social perception processes. Furthermore, as Gastil (1995) suggested, constructivist scholars need to detail a model of social memory consistent with their view of person perception and social inference. Although some progress in these areas has been made recently (see Bargh & Thein, 1985; Crockett, 1985; J.R. Meyer, 1996), a great deal of work remains to be done.

A second issue concerns the nature of the interpersonal construct system. Is there just one system of interpersonal constructs or are there several interrelated systems? B. O'Keefe (1984) speculated that there are several relatively distinct systems of interpersonal constructs, each having a particular domain of relevance. According to this view, all persons have a system of "core constructs" that are "primarily functional for making decisions about relationships and, in particular, whether to pursue or avoid a close relationship with a target" (B. O'Keefe, 1984, p. 283). Additionally, however, persons develop other systems of interpersonal constructs based on their degree of experience with particular facets of the world (e.g., constructs for co-workers, constructs for relationships). These relatively distinct systems of constructs may be differentially accessed depending on the task at hand (see Kline, 1990).

Recent studies provide support for the notion that there are multiple systems of interpersonal constructs (a detailed review of this research is presented by Coopman, in press). For example, Daly et al. (1985) developed a measure of tapping the complexity of constructs for conversational interactions; this measure of conversational complexity was only moderately related to interpersonal cognitive complexity, as assessed by the RCQ. Martin (1991, 1992) showed that his measure tapping the complexity of constructs for personal relationships functioned independently of RCQ-based interpersonal cognitive complexity. More recently, several studies (J. C. Meyer & Sypher, 1993; Zimmermann, 1994; Zimmermann, Hart, Allen, & Haas, in press; Zorn, McKinney, & Moran, 1993) have shown that people tend to develop distinct systems of interpersonal constructs for co-workers. The evidence suggesting that people may develop several differentially elaborated systems of interpersonal constructs makes it imperative for theorists to detail the ways in which each of these systems operate independently, as well as in concert with other systems.

A third issue concerns the specific character of "complex" construct systems and the meaning of the scores generated by the RCQ. Crockett's (1965) original account maintained that persons producing more differentiated impressions in response to the RCQ had a larger number of constructs available to them than persons generating less differentiated impressions. This analysis is consistent with a view of the RCQ as tapping the level of differentiation within the interpersonal construct system as a whole. More recently, theorists (e.g., B. O'Keefe & Delia, 1982; H. Sypher & Applegate, 1984) have proposed that persons scoring highly on the RCQ might not have a larger number of constructs available to them, but instead can more easily access their constructs (see Burleson & Waltman, 1988). As

Gastil (1995) noted, if the RCQ is viewed as tapping construct accessibility, this has several important implications for the social perception process that need to be explored empirically. For example, if cognitively complex perceivers have more accessible constructs, this should be evident in speed of construct activation, information retrieval, and inference. Moreover, some researchers (Allen et al., 1990; Beatty & Payne, 1985) discount both the construct availability and accessibility explanations of cognitive complexity, suggesting instead that cognitively complex persons may be more motivated to use their constructs. All of these proposals merit further investigation.

A related concern expressed by some researchers (Allen et al., 1991; Beatty & Payne, 1985; Gastil, 1995) pertains to whether the index of construct differentiation generated by the RCQ provides a theoretically adequate operationalization of cognitive complexity. After all, complex systems were defined, following Werner (1957), as more differentiated, articulated (abstract), and integrated systems, so can a measure of just one of these attributes adequately capture the character of a complex cognitive system? We believe the answer to this question is yes. No operationalization exhausts the conceptual meaning of a theoretical term. Hence, the relevant issue is whether a given operationalization validly taps the construct it is intended to measure. The common index of construct differentiation generated by the RCQ has been shown repeatedly to be a sound, valid assessment of the complexity concept, correlating with measures of construct abstractness and organization, among other theoretically relevant variables (see Applegate, 1990; Burleson et al., 1991; Burleson & Waltman, 1988; D. O'Keefe & Sypher, 1981).

Questions Regarding Cognitive Complexity and Communication Processes

As the research reviewed in this chapter makes clear, cognitive complexity is moderately associated with message production, message reception, and interaction management processes. But precisely how does cognitive complexity contribute to these processes? Currently, we remain unable to specify exactly how cognitive complexity contributes to communicative functioning. In large measure, this is because we lack adequately detailed models of core communication processes.

Both Berger (1995) and Hewes and Planalp (1987) criticized constructivist research on message production for simply demonstrating that cognitive complexity is associated with the ability to generate highly person-centered messages. As these critics suggest, such correlational research does not explain how person-centered messages get produced or the role of cognitive complexity in the message production process. Recent research indicates that cognitive complexity contributes to message goals (e.g., Wilson, 1990) and planning (e.g., Waldron & Applegate, 1994); this represents a significant advance in the analysis of message production. Important as these findings are, they leave many key issues to be addressed. For example, do low and high complexity communicators primarily differ in the contents of their message producing systems (i.e., the contents of procedural memory), the processes used to generate messages (i.e., the structure or sequence of the processes used to produce messages or the rules used to combine information), or the activating conditions that initiate the message production process (i.e., the goals or intentions that presumably guide message design)? To answer these questions, researchers must develop—or appropriate—more detailed models of the message production process. Integrations such as those suggested by Wilson (1990), Waldron and Applegate (1994), and B. O'Keefe and Lambert (1995) hold promise for generating a comprehensive account of individual differences in message production.

Although constructivist models of message production have been fleshed out somewhat in recent years, models of message reception and interaction management remain on the thin side. General models of message reception and comprehension are available, and these certainly have the potential to inform analyses of individual differences in message reception (see the review by Badzinski & Gill, 1994). Furthermore, some aspects of message reception might be modeled on the social perception process. For example, it may be fruitful to regard high complexity message recipients as possessing a finer, more discriminating "ear" that allows them to sense and respond to nuances in messages such as person-centeredness, face support, and goal integration. Or, to borrow from research on the processing of persuasive messages, perhaps high complexity recipients are more disposed to process relationally relevant messages systematically while less complex recipients are more inclined to process these messages heuristically (for a discussion of systematic versus heuristic processing, see Chaiken, Liberman, & Eagly, 1989; also see Jorgensen, in press). In a somewhat different vein, Delia (1987) has proposed that cognitive complexity may facilitate interaction management by contributing to the individual's control over discourse-organizing schemes. This intriguing notion needs to be explored within the context of richer theories of language, conversation, and discourse.

Finally, research indicating that persons with high levels of interpersonal cognitive complexity tend to be more effective than less complex persons at achieving their social and communicative goals raises the important question as to whether training programs can be developed to enhance complexity levels (see Gastil, 1995; Griffin, 1997). To our knowledge, no such efforts have been undertaken. However, researchers have had some success with training efforts directed at enhancing both perspective-taking skills (e.g., Pelias, 1984) and the use of person-centered message strategies (e.g., Clark et al., 1985; Rowan, 1984). These efforts suggest it may be possible to develop programs affecting change in overall levels of cognitive complexity. Furthermore, by seeking to alter levels of interpersonal cognitive complexity, it is likely that we will learn more about the nature of this variable, as well as more about the character of the perceptual and communication processes it affects. Although such training efforts represent an exciting possibility, they should proceed cautiously because it remains unclear whether high levels of cognitive complexity consistently result in greater interpersonal effectiveness, greater personal happiness, and greater social good.

The theoretical tasks sketched here—formulating and testing more detailed models of cognitive structure, social perception, message production, message reception, and social interaction—are not, of course, the exclusive obligation of cognitive complexity researchers. Nor will constructivists be the only ones to gain from the development and articulation of these more refined models. In a very real sense, the major theoretical tasks facing constructivist researchers represent a core agenda for communication scholars, especially those focusing on the fundamental structures and processes underlying everyday communication activities. By addressing these tasks, we will advance our understanding of communication, as well as some of the individual differences that lead people to be more and less successful communicators.

REFERENCES

Adams, C., & Shepherd, G. (1996). Managing volunteer performance: Face support and situational features as predictors of volunteers' evaluations of regulative messages. *Management Communication Quarterly, 9,* 363-388.

Adams-Webber, J. R. (1979). *Personal construct theory: Concepts and applications.* New York: Wiley.

Allen, M., Burrell, N., & Kellermann, K. (1993). A comparison of observer and actor coding of the Role Category Questionnaire. *Communication Reports, 6,* 1-7.

Allen, M., Mabry, E. A., Banski, M., & Preiss, R. (1991). Valid and constructive thoughts: Continuing the dialog about the RCQ. *Communication Reports, 4,* 120-125.

Allen, M., Mabry, E. A., Banski, M., Stoneman, M., & Carter, P. (1990). A thoughtful appraisal of measuring cognition using the Role Category Questionnaire. *Communication Reports, 3,* 49-57.

Applegate, J. L. (1980a). Adaptive communication in educational contexts: A study of teachers' communicative strategies. *Communication Education, 29,* 158-170.

Applegate, J. L. (1980b). Person- and position-centered communication in a day-care center. In N. K. Denzin (Ed.), *Studies in symbolic interaction* (Vol. 3, pp. 59-96). Greenwich, CT: JAI Press.

Applegate, J. L. (1982). The impact of construct system development on communication and impression formation within persuasive contexts. *Communication Monographs, 46,* 231-240.

Applegate, J. L. (1990). Constructs and communication: A pragmatic integration. In G. Neimeyer (Ed.), *Advances in personal construct psychology* (Vol. 1, pp. 203-230). Greenwich, CT: JAI Press.

Applegate, J. L., Burke, J. A., Burleson, B. R., Delia, J. G., & Kline, S. L. (1985). Reflection-enhancing parental communication. In I. E. Sigel (Ed.), *Parental belief systems: The psychological consequences for children* (pp. 107-142). Hillsdale, NJ: Lawrence Earlbaum Associates.

Applegate, J. L., Burleson, B. R., & Delia, J. G. (1992). Reflection-enhancing parenting as antecedent to children's social-cognitive and communicative development. In I. E. Sigel, A. V. McGillicuddy-Delisi, & J. J. Goodnow (Eds.), *Parental belief systems: The psychological consequences for children* (2nd ed., pp. 3-39). Hillsdale, NJ: Erlbaum.

Applegate, J. L., Coyle, K., Seibert, J. H., & Church, S. (1989). Interpersonal constructs and communicative ability in a police environment: A preliminary investigation. *International Journal of Personal Construct Psychology, 2,* 385-399.

Applegate, J. L., & Delia, J. G. (1980). Person-centered speech, psychological development, and the contexts of language usage. In R. St. Clair & H. Giles (Eds.), *The social and psychological contexts of language* (pp. 245-282). Hillsdale, NJ: Lawrence Erlbaum Associates.

Applegate, J. L., Kline, S. L., & Delia, J. G. (1991). Alternative measures of cognitive complexity as predictors of communicative performance. *International Journal of Personal Construct Psychology, 4,* 193-213.

Applegate, J. L., & Sypher, H.E. (1988). Constructivist theory and intercultural communication research. In Y. Kim & W. Gudykunst (Eds.), *Theoretical perspectives in intercultural communication* (pp. 41-65). Beverly Hills, CA: Sage.

Applegate, J. L., & Woods, E. (1991). Construct system development and attention to face wants in persuasive contexts. *Southern Communication Journal, 56*, 194-204.

Babrow, A. S., & O'Keefe, D. J. (1984). Construct differentiation as a moderator of attitude-behavior consistency: A failure to confirm. *Central States Speech Journal, 35*, 160-165.

Badzinski, D. M., & Gill, M. M. (1994). Discourse features and message comprehension. In S. A. Deetz (Ed.), *Communication yearbook 17* (pp. 301-332). Thousand Oaks, CA: Sage.

Barenboim, C. (1977). Developmental changes in the interpersonal cognitive system from middle childhood to adolescence. *Child Development, 48*, 1467-1471.

Barenboim, C. (1981). The development of person perception in childhood and adolescence: From behavioral comparisons to psychological constructs to psychological comparisons. *Child Development, 52*, 129-144.

Bargh, J. A., & Thein, R. D. (1985). Individual construct accessibility, person memory, and the recall-judgment link: The case of information overload. *Journal of Personality and Social Psychology, 54*, 925-939.

Barratt, B. B. (1977). The development of peer perception systems in childhood and early adolescence. *Social Behavior and Personality, 5*, 351-360.

Beatty, M. J., & Payne, S. K. (1981). Receiver apprehension and cognitive complexity. *Western Journal of Speech Communication, 45*, 363-369.

Beatty, M. J., & Payne, S. K. (1984a). Listening comprehension as a function of cognitive complexity: A research note. *Communication Monographs, 51*, 85-89.

Beatty, M. J., & Payne, S. K. (1984b). Loquacity and quantity of constructs as predictors of social perspective-taking. *Communication Quarterly, 32*, 207-210.

Beatty, M. J., & Payne, S. K. (1985). Is construct differentiation loquacity? A motivational perspective. *Human Communication Research, 11*, 605-612.

Bereiter, C., & Scardamalia, M. (1993). *Surpassing ourselves: An inquiry into the nature and implications of expertise.* Chicago: Open Court.

Berger, C. R. (1995). A plan-based approach to strategic communication. In D. E. Hewes (Ed.), *The cognitive bases of interpersonal communication* (pp. 141-180). Hillsdale, NJ: Lawrence Erlbaum Associates.

Bieri, J. (1955). Cognitive complexity-simplicity and predictive behavior. *Journal of Abnormal and Social Psychology, 51*, 263.

Bieri, J., Atkins, A. L., Briar, S., Leaman, R. L., Miller, H., & Tripodi, T. (1966). *Clinical and social judgment.* New York: Wiley.

Bigner, J. J. (1974). A Wernerian developmental analysis of children's descriptions of siblings. *Child Development, 45,* 317-323.

Bingham, S. G., & Burleson, B. R. (1989). Multiple effects of messages with multiple goals: Some perceived outcomes of responses to sexual harassment. *Human Communication Research, 16,* 184-216.

Bliss, L. S. (1986). The development of the interpersonal construct system in educable mentally retarded children. *Journal of Mental Deficiency Research, 30,* 261-269.

Borgida, E., & DeBono, K. G. (1989). Social hypothesis-testing and the role of expertise. *Personality and Social Psychology Bulletin, 15,* 212-221.

Burleson, B. R. (1980). The development of interpersonal reasoning: An analysis of message strategy justifications. *Journal of the American Forensic Association, 17,* 102-110.

Burleson, B. R. (1982a). The affective perspective-taking process: A test of Turiel's role-taking model. In M. Burgoon (Ed.), *Communication yearbook 6* (pp. 473-488). Beverly Hills, CA: Sage.

Burleson, B. R. (1982b). The development of comforting communication skills in childhood and adolescence. *Child Development, 53,* 1578-1588.

Burleson, B. R. (1983). Social cognition, empathic motivation, and adults' comforting strategies. *Human Communication Research, 10,* 295-304.

Burleson, B. R. (1984a). Age, social-cognitive development, and the use of comforting strategies. *Communication Monographs, 51,* 140-153.

Burleson, B. R. (1984b). Role-taking and communication skills in childhood: Why they aren't related and what can be done about it. *Western Journal of Speech Communication, 48,* 155-170.

Burleson, B. R. (1987). Cognitive complexity. In J. C. McCroskey & J. A. Daly (Eds.), *Personality and interpersonal communication* (pp. 305-349). Newbury Park, CA: Sage.

Burleson, B. R. (1989). The constructivist approach to person-centered communication: Analysis of a research exemplar. In B.

A. Dervin, L. Grossberg, B. J. O'Keefe, & E. Wartella (Eds.), *Rethinking communication, Vol. 2: Paradigm exemplars* (pp. 29-46). Newbury Park, CA: Sage.

Burleson, B. R. (1992). Taking communication seriously. *Communication Monographs, 59,* 79-86.

Burleson, B. R. (1994). Friendship and similarities in social-cognitive and communication abilities: Social skill bases of interpersonal attraction in childhood. *Personal Relationships, 1,* 371-389.

Burleson, B. R. (1995). Personal relationships as a skilled accomplishment. *Journal of Social and Personal Relationships, 12,* 575-581.

Burleson, B. R., Applegate, J. L., Burke, J. A., Clark, R. A., Delia, J. G., & Kline, S. L. (1986). Communicative correlates of peer acceptance in childhood. *Communication Education, 35,* 349-361.

Burleson, B. R., Applegate, J. L., & Delia, J. G. (1991). On validly assessing the validity of the Role Category Questionnaire: A reply to Allen et al. *Communication Reports, 4,* 113-119.

Burleson, B. R., Applegate, J. L., & Neuwirth, C. M. (1981). Is cognitive complexity loquacity? A reply to Powers, Jordan, and Street. *Human Communication Research, 7,* 212-225.

Burleson, B. R., Delia, J. G., & Applegate, J. L. (1992). Effects of maternal communication and children's social-cognitive and communication skills on children's acceptance by the peer group. *Family Relations, 41,* 264-272.

Burleson, B. R., Delia, J. G., & Applegate, J. L. (1995). The socialization of person-centered communication skills: Parental contributions to the social-cognitive and communication skills of their children. In M. A. Fitzpatrick & A. L. Vangelisti (Eds.), *Explaining family interactions* (pp. 34-76). Thousand Oaks, CA: Sage.

Burleson, B. R., & Denton, W. H. (1992). A new look at similarity and attraction in marriage: Similarities in social-cognitive and communication skills as predictors of attraction and satisfaction. *Communication Monographs, 59,* 268-287.

Burleson, B. R., & Denton, W. H. (In press). The relationship between communication skills and marital satisfaction: Some moderating effects. *Journal of Marriage and the Family.*

Burleson, B. R., & Fennelly, D. A. (1981). Effects of cognitive complexity and persuasive appeal form on children's sharing behavior. *Child Study Journal, 11,* 75-90.

Burleson, B. R., & Kunkel, A. W. (1996). The socialization of emotional support skills in childhood. In G. R. Pierce, B. R. Sarason, & I. G. Sarason (Eds.), *Handbook of social support and the family* (pp. 105-140). New York: Plenum.

Burleson, B. R., Kunkel, A. W., & Szolwinski, J. B. (1997). Similarities in cognitive complexity and attraction to friends and lovers: Experimental and correlational studies. *Journal of Constructivist Psychology, 10,* 221-248.

Burleson, B. R., & Rowan, K. E. (1985). Are social-cognitive ability and narrative writing skill related? *Written Communication, 2,* 25-43.

Burleson, B. R., & Samter, W. (1985a). Consistencies in theoretical and naive evaluations of comforting messages: Two empirical studies. *Communication Monographs, 52,* 103-123.

Burleson, B. R., & Samter, W. (1985b). Individual differences in the perception of comforting messages: An exploratory investigation. *Central States Speech Journal, 36,* 39-50.

Burleson, B. R., & Samter, W. (1990). Effects of cognitive complexity on the perceived importance of communication skills in friends. *Communication Research, 17,* 165-182.

Burleson, B. R., & Samter, W. (1996). Similarity in the communication skills of young adults: Foundations of attraction, friendship, and relationship satisfaction. *Communication Reports, 9,* 125-139.

Burleson, B. R., & Waltman, M. S. (1988). Cognitive complexity: Using the Role Category Questionnaire measure. In C. H. Tardy (Ed.), *A handbook for the study of human communication: Methods and instruments for observing, measuring, and assessing communication processes* (pp. 1-35). Norwood, NJ: Ablex.

Burleson, B. R., Waltman, M. S., & Samter, W. (1987). More evidence that cognitive complexity is not loquacity: A reply to Beatty and Payne. *Communication Quarterly, 35,* 317-328.

Burleson, B. R., & Waltman, P. A. (1987). Popular, rejected, and supportive preadolescents: Social-cognitive and communicative characteristics. In M. L. McLaughlin (Ed.), *Communication yearbook 10* (pp. 533-552). Newbury Park, CA: Sage.

Carrocci, N. M. (1985). Perceiving and responding to interpersonal conflict. *Central States Speech Journal, 36,* 215-228.

Chaiken, S., Liberman, A., & Eagly, A. H. (1989). Heuristic and systematic information processing within and beyond the persuasion context. In J. S. Uleman & J. A. Bargh (Eds.), *Unintended thought* (pp. 212-252). New York: Guilford Press.

Chen, L. (1996). Cognitive complexity, situational influences, and topic selection in intracultural and intercultural dyadic interactions. *Communication Reports, 9,* 1-12.

Chi, M. T. H., & Koeske, R. (1983). Network representations of a child's dinosaur knowledge. *Developmental Psychology, 19,* 29-39.

Clark, R. A. (1980). Single word usage: Two stages. *Central States Speech Journal, 31,* 75-84.

Clark, R. A., & Delia, J. G. (1976). The development of functional persuasive skills in childhood and early adolescence. *Child Development, 47,* 1008-1014.

Clark, R. A., & Delia, J. G. (1977). Cognitive complexity, social perspective-taking, and functional persuasive skills in second- to ninth-grade children. *Human Communication Research, 3,* 128-134.

Clark, R. A., & Delia, J. G. (1979). *Topoi* and rhetorical competence. *Quarterly Journal of Speech, 65,* 187-206.

Clark, R. A., Willihnganz, S., & O'Dell, L. L. (1985). Training fourth graders in compromising and persuasive strategies. *Communication Education, 34,* 331-342.

Coopman, S. Z. (in press). Personal constructs and communication in interpersonal and organizational contexts. In G. Neimeyer & R. Neimeyer (Eds.), *Advances in personal construct psychology* (Vol. 4). Greenwich, CT: JAI Press.

Crockett, W. H. (1965). Cognitive complexity and impression formation. In B. A. Maher (Ed.), *Progress in experimental personality research* (Vol. 2, pp. 47-90). New York: Academic Press.

Crockett, W. H. (1982). The organization of construct systems. In J. C. Mancuso & J. R. Adams-Webber (Eds.), *The construing person* (pp. 62-95). New York: Praeger.

Crockett, W. H. (1985). Constructs, impressions, actions, responses, and construct change: A model of processes in impression formation. In F. Epting & A. W. Landfield (Eds.), *Anticipating personal construct psychology* (pp. 73-86). Lincoln: University of Nebraska Press.

Crockett, W. H., Gonyea, A. H., & Delia, J. G. (1970). Cognitive complexity and the formation of impressions from abstract qualities or from concrete behaviors. *Proceedings of the 78th Annual Convention of the American Psychological Association, 5,* 375-376.

Crockett, W. H., Mahood, S. M., Press, A. N. (1975). Impressions of a speaker as a function of set to understand or to evaluate, of cognitive complexity, and of prior attitudes. *Journal of Personality, 43,* 168-178.

Crockett, W. H., Press, A. N., Delia, J. G., & Kenny, C. T. (1974). *Structural analysis of the organization of written impressions.* (Mimeo). Department of Psychology, University of Kansas, Lawrence.

Daly, J. A. (1987). Personality and interpersonal communication: Issues and directions. In J. C. McCroskey & J. A. Daly (Eds.), *Personality and interpersonal communication* (pp. 13-41). Newbury Park, CA: Sage.

Daly, J. A., Bell, R. A., Glenn, P. J., & Lawrence, S. (1985). Conceptualizing conversational complexity. *Human Communication Research, 12,* 30-53.

Daly, J. A., Vangelisti, A. L., & Daughton, S. M. (1987). The nature and correlates of conversational sensitivity. *Human Communication Research, 14,* 167-202.

DeLancey, C. A., & Swanson, D. L. (1981, May). *Construct differentiation and the relationship of attitudes and behavioral intentions in the political domain.* Paper presented at the International Communication Association Convention, Minneapolis.

Delia, J. G. (1972). Dialects and the effects of stereotypes on interpersonal attraction and cognitive processes in impression formation. *Quarterly Journal of Speech, 58,* 285-297.

Delia, J. G. (1974). Attitude toward the disclosure of self-attributions and the complexity of interpersonal constructs. *Speech Monographs, 41,* 119-126.

Delia, J. G. (1977). Constructivism and the study of human communication. *Quarterly Journal of Speech, 63,* 66-83.

Delia, J. G. (1980). Some tentative thoughts concerning the study of interpersonal relationships and their development. *Western Journal of Speech Communication, 44,* 97-103.

Delia, J. G. (1987). Interpersonal cognition, message goals, and organization of communication: Recent constructivist research. In D. L. Kincaid (Ed.), *Communication theory: Eastern and western perspectives* (pp. 255-273). San Diego: Academic Press.

Delia, J. G., & Clark, R. A. (1977). Cognitive complexity, social perception, and the development of listener-adapted communication in six-, eight-, ten-, and twelve-year-old boys. *Communication Monographs, 44,* 326-345.

Delia, J. G., Clark, R. A., & Switzer, D. E. (1974). Cognitive complexity and impression formation in informal social interaction. *Speech Monographs, 41,* 299-308.

Delia, J. G., Clark, R. A., & Switzer, D. E. (1979). The content of informal conversations as a function of interactants' interpersonal cognitive complexity. *Communication Monographs, 46,* 274-281.

Delia, J. G., & Crockett, W. H. (1973). Social schemas, cognitive complexity, and the learning of social structures. *Journal of Personality, 41,* 413-429.

Delia, J. G., Crockett, W. H., & Gonyea, A. H. (1970). Cognitive complexity and the effects of schemas on the learning of social structures. *Proceedings of the 78th Annual Convention of the American Psychological Association, 5,* 373-374.

Delia, J. G., Gonyea, A. H., & Crockett, W. H. (1971). The effects of subject-generated and normative constructs upon the formation of impressions. *British Journal of Social and Clinical Psychology, 10*, 301-305.

Delia, J. G., Kline, S. L., & Burleson, B. R. (1979). The development of persuasive communication strategies in kindergartners through twelfth-graders. *Communication Monographs, 46*, 241-256.

Delia, J. G., & Murphy, M. A. (1983, November). *Roommates' construct differentiation, impressions, and person-centered communication: An analysis of perceiver and target effects.* Paper presented at the annual convention of the Speech Communication Association, Washington, DC.

Delia, J. G., & O'Keefe, B. J. (1976). The interpersonal constructs of Machiavellians. *British Journal of Social and Clinical Psychology, 15*, 435-436.

Delia, J. G., O'Keefe, B. J., & O'Keefe, D. J. (1982). The constructivist approach to communication. In F. E. X. Dance (Ed.), *Human communication theory: Comparative essays* (pp. 147-191). New York: Harper & Row.

Denton, W. H., Burleson, B. R., & Sprenkle, D. H. (1995). Association of interpersonal cognitive complexity with communication skill in marriage: Moderating effects of marital distress. *Family Process, 34*, 101-111.

Duncan, S., & Fiske, D. W. (1977). *Organization of behavior in face-to-face interaction.* Chicago: Aldine.

Dunn, J., Brown, J., & Beardsall, L. (1991). Family talk about feeling states and children's later understanding of others' emotions. *Developmental Psychology, 27*, 448-455.

Dunn, J., Brown, J., Slomkowski, C., Tesla, C., & Youngblade, L. (1991). Young children's understanding of other people's feelings and beliefs: Individual differences and their antecedents. *Child Development, 62*, 1352-1366.

Easterby-Smith, M. (1981). The design, analysis, and interpretation of repertory grids. In M. L. G. Shaw (Ed.), *Recent advances in personal construct technology* (pp. 9-30). London: Academic Press.

Ellis, D. G., Hamilton, M., & Aho, L. (1983). Some issues in conversation coherence. *Human Communication Research, 9*, 267-282.

Ericsson, K. A., & Smith, J. (Eds.). (1991). *Toward a general theory of expertise: Prospects and limits.* New York: Cambridge University Press.

Fiske, S. T., & Dyer, L. M. (1985). Structure and development of social schemata: Evidence from positive and negative transfer effects. *Journal of Personality and Social Psychology, 48*, 839-852.

Fiske, S. T., Kinder, D. R., & Larter, W. M. (1983). The novice and the expert: Knowledge-based strategies in political cognition. *Journal of Experimental Social Psychology, 19*, 381-400.

Fiske, S. T., & Taylor, S. E. (1991). *Social cognition* (2nd ed.). New York: McGraw-Hill.

Gastil, J. (1995). An appraisal and revision of the constructivist research program. In B. R. Burleson (Ed.), *Communication yearbook 18* (pp. 83-104). Thousand Oaks, CA: Sage.

Goldstein, K. M., & Blackman, S. (1978). *Cognitive style: Five approaches and relevant research.* New York: Wiley.

Greene, J. O. (1995). Production of messages in pursuit of multiple social goals: Action assembly theory contributions to the study of cognitive encoding processes. In B. R. Burleson (Ed.), *Communication yearbook 18* (pp. 26-53). Thousand Oaks, CA: Sage.

Greene, J. O., Lindsey, A. E., & Hawn, J. L. (1990). Social goals and speech production: Effects of multiple goals on pausal phenomena. *Journal of Language and Social Psychology, 9*, 119-134.

Griffin, E. (1997). Constructivism of Jesse Delia. In *A first look at communication theory* (3rd ed., pp. 128-139). New York: McGraw-Hill.

Hale, C. L. (1980). Cognitive complexity-simplicity as a determinant of communication effectiveness. *Communication Monographs, 47*, 304-311.

Hale, C. L. (1982). An investigation of the relationship between cognitive complexity and listener-adapted communication. *Central States Speech Journal, 33*, 339-344.

Hale, C. L. (1986). Impact of cognitive complexity on message structure in a face-threatening context. *Journal of Language and Social Psychology, 5*, 135-143.

Hale, C. L., & Delia, J. G. (1976). Cognitive complexity and social perspective taking. *Communication Monographs, 43*, 195-203.

Hewes, D. E., & Planalp, S. (1987). The individual's place in communication science. In C. R. Berger & S. H. Chaffee (Eds.), *Handbook of communication science* (pp. 146-183). Newbury Park, CA: Sage.

Hintzman, D. L. (1986). "Schema abstraction" in a multiple-trace memory model. *Psychological Review, 93*, 411-428.

Hoffman, R. R. (Ed.). (1992). *The psychology of expertise: Cognitive research and empirical findings.* New York: Springer-Verlag.

Hynds, S. D. (1985). Interpersonal cognitive complexity and the literary response processes of adolescent readers. *Research in the Teaching of English, 19*, 386-402.

Jennings, K. D. (1975). People versus object orientation, social behavior, and intellectual abilities in preschool children. *Developmental Psychology, 11,* 511-519.

Jorgensen, P. E. (in press). Affect, persuasion, and communication processes. In P. A. Andersen & L. K. Guerrero (Eds.), *Handbook of communication and emotion.* San Diego: Academic Press.

Kagan, D. M. (1988). Measurements of divergent and complex thinking. *Educational and Psychological Measurement, 48,* 873-884.

Kellermann, K. (1995). The conversation MOP: A model of patterned and pliable behavior. In D. E. Hewes (Ed.), *The cognitive bases of interpersonal communication* (pp. 181-221). Hillsdale, NJ: Lawrence Erlbaum Associates.

Kelly, G. A. (1955). *The psychology of personal constructs* (2 vols.). New York: W. W. Norton.

Kenny, C. T., Press, A. N., & Crockett, W. H. (1972). Individual differences in impression formation as a function of cognitive differentiation, social role, and amount of information. *Catalog of Selected Documents in Psychology, 2,* 63-64.

Kline, S. L. (1988). Social cognitive determinants of argument design features in regulative discourse. *Argumentation and Advocacy, 25,* 1-12.

Kline, S. L. (1990). Situational variability in personal construing and social cognitive development. *International Journal of Personal Construct Psychology, 3,* 327-337.

Kline, S. L. (1991). Construct differentiation and person-centered regulative messages. *Journal of Language and Social Psychology, 10,* 1-27.

Kline, S. L., & Ceropski, J. M. (1984). Person-centered communication in medical practice. In J. T. Wood & G. M. Phillips (Eds.), *Human decision-making* (pp. 120-141). Carbondale: Southern Illinois University Press.

Kline, S. L., & Delia, J. G. (1990). Reasoning about communication and communicative skill. In B. F. Jones & L. Idol (Eds.), *Dimensions of thinking and cognitive instruction: Implications for educational reform* (pp. 177-207). Hillsdale, NJ: Lawrence Erlbaum Associates.

Kline, S. L., & Hennen-Floyd, C. (1990). On the art of saying no: The influence of social cognitive development on messages of refusal. *Western Journal of Speech Communication, 54,* 454-472.

Kline, S. L., Hennen-Floyd, C. L., & Farrell, K. M. (1990). Cognitive complexity and verbal response mode use in discussion. *Communication Quarterly, 38,* 350-360.

Kline, S. L., Pelias, R., & Delia, J. G. (1991). The predictive validity of cognitive complexity measures on communication-relevant abilities. *International Journal of Personal Construct Psychology, 4,* 347-357.

Kochanska, G. (1990). Maternal beliefs as long-term predictors of mother-child interaction and report. *Child Development, 61,* 1934-1943.

Kochanska, G., Kuczynski, L., & Radke-Yarrow, M. (1989). Correspondence between mothers' self-reported and observed child rearing practices. *Child Development, 60,* 56-63.

Leichty, G. (1989). Interpersonal constructs and friendship form and structure. *International Journal of Personal Construct Psychology, 2,* 401-415.

Leichty, G., & Applegate, J. L. (1991). Social cognitive and situational influences on the use of face-saving persuasive strategies. *Human Communication Research, 17,* 451-484.

Linville, P. W. (1982). The complexity-extremity effect and age-based stereotyping. *Journal of Personality and Social Psychology, 42,* 193-211.

Little, B. R. (1972). Psychological man as scientist, humanist, and specialist. *Journal of Experimental Research in Personality, 6,* 95-118.

Livesley, W. F., & Bromley, D. B. (1971). *Person perception in childhood and adolescence.* New York: Wiley.

Lurigio, A. J., & Carroll, J. S. (1985). Probation officers' schemata of offenders: Content, development, and impact on treatment decisions. *Journal of Personality and Social Psychology, 48,* 1112-1126.

Martin, R. (1991). Examining relationship thinking: The relational cognition complexity instrument. *Journal of Social and Personal Relationships, 8,* 467-480.

Martin, R. (1992). Relational cognitive complexity and relational communication in personal relationships. *Communication Monographs, 59,* 150-163.

Mayo, C. W., & Crockett, W. H. (1964). Cognitive complexity and primacy-recency effects in impression formation. *Journal of Abnormal and Social Psychology, 68,* 335-338.

McKiethen, K. B., Reitman, J. S., Rueter, H. H., & Hirtle, S. C. (1981). Knowledge organization and skill differences in computer programmers. *Cognitive Psychology, 13,* 307-325.

McMahan, E. M. (1976). Nonverbal communication as a function of attribution in impression formation. *Communication Monographs, 43,* 287-294.

Mead, G. H. (1934). *Mind, self, and society: From the standpoint of a social behaviorist.* Chicago: University of Chicago Press.

Meltzer, B., Crockett, W. H., & Rosenkrantz, P. S. (1966). Cognitive complexity, value congruity, and the integration of potentially incompatible information in impressions of others. *Journal of Personality and Social Psychology, 4,* 338-343.

Meyer, J. C., & Sypher, B. D. (1993). Personal constructs as indicators of cultural values. *Southern Communication Journal, 58,* 227-238.

Meyer, J. R. (1996). What cognitive differences are measured by the Role Category Questionnaire. *Western Journal of Communication, 60,* 233-253.

Motley, M. T. (1990). On whether one can(not) not communicate: An examination via traditional communication postulates. *Western Journal of Speech Communication, 54,* 1-20.

Miller, A., & Wilson, P. (1979). Cognitive differentiation and integration: A conceptual analysis. *Genetic Psychology Monographs, 99,* 3-40.

Neimeyer, G. J. (1984). Cognitive complexity and marital satisfaction. *Journal of Social and Clinical Psychology, 2,* 258-263.

Neimeyer, R. A., Baker, K. D., & Neimeyer, G. J. (1990). The current status of personal construct theory. In G. Neimeyer & R. Neimeyer (Eds.), *Advances in personal construct theory* (Vol. 1, pp. 3-22). Greenwich, CT: JAI Press.

Neuliep, J. W., & Hazleton, V., Jr. (1985). Cognitive complexity and apprehension about communication: A preliminary report. *Psychological Reports, 57,* 1224-1226.

Neuliep, J. W., & Hazelton, V., Jr. (1986). Enhanced conversational recall and reduced conversational interference as a function of cognitive complexity. *Human Communication Research, 13,* 211-224.

Nicotera, A. M. (1995). The constructivist theory of Delia, Clark, and associates. In D. P. Cushman & B. Kovacic (Eds.), *Watershed research traditions in human communication theory* (pp. 45-66). Albany: State University of New York Press.

Nidorf, L. J., & Argabrite, A. H. (1970). Cognitive complexity and the tendency to make extreme judgments. *Perceptual and Motor Skills, 31,* 478.

Nidorf, L. J., & Crockett, W. H. (1965). Cognitive complexity and the organization of impressions of others. *Journal of Social Psychology, 79,* 165-169.

O'Keefe, B. J. (1984). The evolution of impressions in small working groups: Effects of construct differentiation. In H. E. Sypher & J. L. Applegate (Eds.), *Communication by children and adults:*

Social cognitive and strategic processes (pp. 262-291). Beverly Hills, CA: Sage.

O'Keefe, B. J. (1988). The logic of message design: Individual differences in reasoning about communication. *Communication Monographs, 55*, 80-103.

O'Keefe, B. J. (1990). The logic of regulative communication: Understanding the rationality of message designs. In J. P. Dillard (Ed.), *Seeking compliance: The production of interpersonal influence messages* (pp. 87-104). Scottsdale, AZ: Gorsuch Scarisbrick.

O'Keefe, B. J. (1991). Message design logic and the management of multiple goals. In K. Tracy (Ed.), *Understanding face-to-face communication: Issues linking goals and discourse* (pp. 131-150). Hillsdale, NJ: Lawrence Erlbaum Associates.

O'Keefe, B. J., & Delia, J. G. (1979). Construct comprehensiveness and cognitive complexity as predictors of the number and strategic adaptation of arguments and appeals in a persuasive message. *Communication Monographs, 46*, 231-240.

O'Keefe, B. J., & Delia, J. G. (1982). Impression formation and message production. In M. E. Roloff & C. R. Berger (Eds.), *Social cognition and communication* (pp. 33-72). Beverly Hills, CA: Sage.

O'Keefe, B. J., & Delia, J. G. (1985). Psychological and interactional dimensions of communicative development. In H. Giles & R. St. Clair (Eds.), *Recent advances in language, communication, and social psychology* (pp. 41-85). London: Lawrence Erlbaum Associates.

O'Keefe, B. J., & Delia, J. G. (1988). Communicative tasks and communicative practices: The development of audience-centered message production. In B. Rafoth, & D. L. Rubin (Eds.), *The social construction of written communication* (pp. 70-98). Norwood, NJ: Ablex.

O'Keefe, B. J., Delia, J. G., & O'Keefe, D. J. (1977). Construct individuality, cognitive complexity, and the formation and remembering of interpersonal impressions. *Social Behavior and Personality, 5*, 229-240.

O'Keefe, B. J., & Lambert, B. L. (1995). Managing the flow of ideas: A local management approach to message design. In B. R. Burleson (Ed.), *Communication yearbook 18* (pp. 54-82). Thousand Oaks, CA: Sage.

O'Keefe, B. J., & McCornack, S.A. (1987). Message design logic and message goal structure: Effects on perceptions of message quality in regulative communication situations. *Human Communication Research, 14*, 68-92.

O'Keefe, B. J., Murphy, M. B., Meyers, R. A., & Babrow, A. S. (1989). The development of persuasive communication skills: The influence of developments in interpersonal constructs on the ability to generate communication-relevant beliefs and on level of persuasive strategy. *Communication Studies, 40,* 29-40.

O'Keefe, B. J., & Shepherd, G. J. (1987). The pursuit of multiple objectives in face-to-face persuasive interaction: Effects of construct differentiation. *Communication Monographs, 54,* 396-419.

O'Keefe, B. J., & Shepherd, G. J. (1989). The communication of identity during face-to-face persuasive interactions: Effects of perceiver's construct differentiation and target's message strategies. *Communication Research, 16,* 375-404.

O'Keefe, D. J. (1980). The relationship of attitudes and behavior: A constructivist analysis. In D. P. Cushman & R. D. McPhee (Eds.), *The message-attitude-behavior relationship: Theory, methodology, and application* (pp. 117-148). New York: Academic Press.

O'Keefe, D. J., & Brady, R. M. (1980). Cognitive complexity and the effects of thought on attitude change. *Social Behavior and Personality, 8,* 849-856.

O'Keefe, D. J., & Delia, J. G. (1981). Construct differentiation and the relationship of attitudes and behavioral intentions. *Communication Monographs, 48,* 146-157.

O'Keefe, D. J., & Shepherd, G. J. (1982). Interpersonal construct differentiation, attitudinal confidence, and the attitude-behavior relationship. *Central States Speech Journal, 33,* 416-423.

O'Keefe, D. J., Shepherd, G. J., & Streeter, T. (1982). Role category questionnaire measures of cognitive complexity: Reliability and comparability of alternative forms. *Central States Speech Journal, 33,* 333-338.

O'Keefe, D. J., & Sypher, H. E. (1981). Cognitive complexity measures and the relationship of cognitive complexity to communication. *Human Communication Research, 8,* 72-92.

Peevers, B. H., & Secord, P. F. (1973). Developmental changes in the attribution of descriptive concepts to persons. *Journal of Personality and Social Psychology, 27,* 120-128.

Pelias, R. J. (1984). Oral interpretation as a training method for increasing perspective-taking abilities. *Communication Education, 33,* 143-151.

Penley, L. E., Alexander, E. R., Jernigan, T. E., & Henwood, C. I. (1991). Communication abilities of managers: The relationship to performance. *Journal of Management, 17,* 57-76.

Piaget, J. (1926). *The language and thought of the child.* London: Routledge & Kegan Paul.

Piche, G. L., & Roen, D. (1987). Social cognition and writing: Interpersonal cognitive complexity and the quality of students' persuasive writing. *Written Communication, 4,* 68-69.

Powers, W. G., Jordan, W. J., & Street, R. L. (1979). Language indices in the measurement of cognitive complexity: Is complexity loquacity? *Human Communication Research, 6,* 69-73.

Press, A. N., Crockett, W. H., & Delia, J. G. (1975). Effects of cognitive complexity and perceiver's set upon the organization of impressions of others. *Journal of Personality and Social Psychology, 32,* 865-895.

Press, A. N., Crockett, W. H., & Rosenkrantz, P. S. (1969). Cognitive complexity and the learning of balanced and unbalanced social structures. *Journal of Personality, 37,* 541-553.

Pryor, J. B., & Merluzzi, T. V. (1985). The role of expertise in processing social interaction scripts. *Journal of Experimental Social Psychology, 21,* 362-379.

Rosenbach, D., Crockett, W. H., & Wapner, S. (1973). Developmental level, emotional involvement, and the resolution of inconsistency in impression formation. *Developmental Psychology, 8,* 120-130.

Rosenkrantz, P. S., & Crockett, W. H. (1965). Some factors influencing the assimilation of disparate information in impression formation. *Journal of Personality and Social Psychology, 2,* 397-402.

Rothenberg, B. B. (1970). Children's social sensitivity and the relationship to interpersonal competence, intrapersonal comfort, and intellectual level. *Developmental Psychology, 2,* 335-350.

Rowan, K. E. (1984). The implicit social scientist and the implicit rhetorician: An integrative framework for the introductory interpersonal course. *Communication Education, 33,* 351-360.

Rowan, K. E. (1990). Cognitive correlates of explanatory writing skill: An analysis of individual differences. *Written Communication, 7,* 316-341.

Saine, T. J. (1974). Perceiving communication conflict. *Speech Monographs, 41,* 49-56.

Samter, W., & Burleson, B. R. (1984). Cognitive and motivational influences on spontaneous comforting behavior. *Human Communication Research, 11,* 231-260.

Samter, W., Burleson, B. R., & Basden-Murphy, L. (1989). Behavioral complexity is in the eye of the beholder: Effects of cognitive complexity and message complexity on impressions of the source of comforting messages. *Human Communication Research, 15,* 612-629.

Samter, W., Burleson, B. R., & Murphy, L. B. (1987). Comforting conversations: Effects of strategy type on evaluations of messages and message producers. *Southern Speech Communication Journal, 52*, 263-284.

Scarlett, H. H., Press, A. N., & Crockett, W. H. (1971). Children's descriptions of peers: A Wernerian developmental analysis. *Child Development, 42*, 439-453.

Scott, W. A., Osgood, D. W., & Peterson, C. (1979). *Cognitive structure: Theory and measurement of individual differences.* Washington, DC: Winston.

Shepherd, G. J. (1987). Individual differences in the relationship between attitudinal and normative determinants of behavioral intent. *Communication Monographs, 54*, 221-231.

Shepherd, G. J., & Condra, M. B. (1988). Anxiety, construct differentiation, and message production. *Central States Speech Journal, 39*, 177-189.

Shepherd, G. J., & O'Keefe, B. J. (1984). The relationship between the developmental level of persuasive strategies and their effectiveness. *Central States Speech Journal, 35,* 137-152.

Shepherd, G. J., & Trank, D. M. (1989). Individual differences in consistency of evaluation: Student perceptions of teacher effectiveness. *Journal of Research and Development in Education, 22,* 45-52.

Shepherd, G. J., & Trank, D. M. (1992). Construct system development and dimensions of judgment. *Southern Communication Journal, 57,* 296-307.

Smith, E. E., Adams, N., & Schorr, D. (1978). Fact retrieval and the paradox of interference. *Cognitive Psychology, 10,* 438-464.

Stacks, D. W., & Murphy, M. A. (1993). Conversational sensitivity: Further validation and extension. *Communication Reports, 6,* 18-24.

Steinfatt, T. M. (1987). Personality and communication: Classical approaches. In. J. C. McCroskey & J. A. Daly (Eds.), *Personality and interpersonal communication* (pp. 42-126). Newbury Park, CA: Sage.

Stiles, W. B. (1978). Verbal response modes and dimensions of interpersonal roles: A method of discourse analysis. *Journal of Personality and Social Psychology, 36,* 693-703.

Strayer, J., & Mashal, M. (1983). The role of peer experience in communication and role-taking skills. *Journal of Genetic Psychology, 143,* 113-122.

Street, R. L. (1993). Analyzing messages and their outcomes: Questionable assumptions, possible solutions. *Southern Communication Journal, 58,* 85-90.

Streufert, S., & Streufert, S. (1978). *Behavior in the complex environment.* Washington, DC: Winston.

Streufert, S., & Swezey, R. W. (1986). *Complexity, managers, and organizations.* Orlando, FL: Academic Press.

Swanson, D. L. (1981). A constructivist approach to political communication. In D. Nimmo & K. R. Sanders (Eds.), *Handbook of political communication.* Beverly Hills, CA: Sage.

Sypher, B. D. (1984). The importance of social-cognitive abilities in organizations. In R. N. Bostrom (Ed.), *Competence in communication* (pp. 103-127). Beverly Hills, CA: Sage.

Sypher, B. D. (1991). A message-centered approach to leadership. In J. A. Anderson (Ed.), *Communication yearbook 14* (pp. 547-557). Newbury Park, CA: Sage.

Sypher, B. D., Bostrom, R. N., & Seibert, J. H. (1989). Listening, communication abilities, and success at work. *Journal of Business Communication, 26,* 293-303.

Sypher, B. D., & Zorn, T. E. (1986). Communication-related abilities and upward mobility: A longitudinal investigation. *Human Communication Research, 12,* 420-431.

Sypher, H. E., & Applegate, J. L. (1984). Organizing communication behavior: The role of schemas and constructs. In R. N. Bostrom (Ed.), *Communication yearbook 8* (pp. 310-329). Beverly Hills, CA: Sage.

Sypher, H. E., Nightingale, J., Vielhaber, M., & Sypher, B. D. (1981). The interpersonal constructs of Machiavellians: A reconsideration. *British Journal of Social Psychology, 20,* 155-156.

Sypher, H. E., & O'Keefe, D. J. (1980, May). *The comparative validity of several cognitive complexity measures as predictors of communication-relevant abilities.* Paper presented at the International Communication Association convention, Acapulco, Mexico.

Sypher, H. E., & Sypher, B. D. (1988). Cognitive differentiation and communication behavior: The Role Category Questionnaire. *Management Communication Quarterly, 2,* 283-294.

Sypher, H. E., Witt, D. E., & Sypher, B. D. (1986). Interpersonal cognitive differentiation measures as predictors of written communication ability. *Communication Monographs, 53,* 376-382.

Vannoy, J. S. (1965). Generality of cognitive complexity-simplicity as a personality construct. *Journal of Personality and Social Psychology, 3,* 385-396.

Waldron, V. R., & Applegate, J. L. (1994). Interpersonal construct differentiation and conversational planning: An examination of two cognitive accounts for the production of competent verbal disagreement tactics. *Human Communication Research, 21,* 3-35.

Walton, E. (1985). The relevance of personal construct theory to management. In F. Epting & A.W. Landfield (Eds.), *Anticipating personal construct psychology* (pp. 95-108). Lincoln: University of Nebraska Press.

Werner, H. (1957). The concept of development from a comparative and organismic point of view. In D. B. Harris (Ed.), *The concept of development* (pp. 125-146). Minneapolis: University of Minnesota Press.

Wilson, S. R. (1990). Development and test of a cognitive rules model of interaction goals. *Communication Monographs, 81,* 81-103.

Wilson, S. R. (1995). Elaborating the cognitive rules model of interaction goals: The problem of accounting for individual differences in goal formation. In B. R. Burleson (Ed.), *Communication yearbook 18* (pp. 3-25). Thousand Oaks, CA: Sage.

Wilson, S. R., Cruz, M. G., & Kang, K. H. (1992). Is it always a matter of perspective? Construct differentiation and variability in attributions about compliance gaining. *Communication Monographs, 59,* 350-367.

Wilson, S. R., & Kang, K. H. (1991). Communication and unfulfilled obligations: Individual differences in causal judgments. *Communication Research, 18,* 799-824.

Woods, E. (1996). Associations of nonverbal decoding ability with indices of person-centered communicative ability. *Communication Reports, 9,* 13-22.

Zimmermann, S. (1994). Social cognition and evaluations of health care team communication effectiveness. *Western Journal of Communication, 58,* 116-141.

Zimmermann, S., Hart, J., Allen, M., & Haas, J. (in press). Detecting cultural knowledge in organization members' personal construct systems. *Journal of Constructivist Psychology.*

Zorn, T. E. (1991). Construct system development, transformational leadership, and leadership messages. *Southern Communication Journal, 56,* 178-193.

Zorn, T. E., McKinney, M. M., & Moran, M. M. (1993). The structure of interpersonal construct systems: One system or many? *International Journal of Personal Construct Psychology, 6,* 139-166.

Zorn, T.E., & Violanti, M.T. (1996). Communication abilities and individual achievement in organizations. *Management Communication Quarterly, 10,* 139-167.

12

Interpersonal Communication Motives

Rebecca B. Rubin
Kent State University
Matthew M. Martin
West Virginia University

Why do people communicate? Are communication motives stable personality factors or are they influenced by the situation? This chapter explores interpersonal needs and motives from a trait perspective. We propose that people have both traitlike primary need hierarchies that must be fulfilled in a specific order (from physiological to psychological) and secondary need hierarchies that are influenced by the situation. Primary need hierarchies have cross-situational consistency; communication motives across contexts are amazingly consistent. Secondary needs lead to secondary motives, behavioral goals, and plans that are not consistent across situations; goals and plans to accomplish these goals are inspired and created by the context or environment. Both primary and secondary needs, which are interrelated, motivate behavior.

Our position is that needs have such strong cross-situational consistency that they can be studied as personality variables. Needs may be either inherent (Cattell, 1957) or acquired (McClelland, 1960); however obtained, they drive behavior. Needs refer to things "lacked" (food and water), "human distentions" (sex hormones, milk production) or "stimuli" (pain, warmth, cold) that influence a person to act in a particular way. Needs are manifested in motives, which have an energizing and directing function. People can articulate their motives (i.e., we can ask people why they initiate communication and they can tell us), but often only the most introspective can articulate their needs.

Basic human needs produce motives to achieve particular goals; people then develop plans and enact behaviors ultimately to gratify those needs. "Communication motives are difficult to separate from needs since needs are manifested in motives. Motives are the expectations generated for communication behavior. A need to belong, for example, may produce a motive to use communication channels to seek companionship" (A. Rubin & Windahl, 1986, p. 185).

Because the terms *need* and *motive* are often used interchangeably, they are often confused. Adding to this confusion, a motive is the same as a drive (e.g., sex drive) in stimulus-response learning theory. Therefore, we refer to needs as *things lacked*, motives as *reasons for action*, goals as *aims or intended purpose*, and plans as *organized strategies for action*.

NEEDS

Although Murray (1938) projected at least 20 psychological needs, Maslow (1954) was the first scholar to identify a hierarchy of primary human needs. In his schema, basic needs (physiological—food, water) are fulfilled before others (safety—protection from harm), which then must be fulfilled before higher-order needs can be. Social (belonging, friendship, acceptance), ego (self-esteem, confidence, achievement, recognition, approval) and self-actualization (realizing one's own potential, creativity) are less basic in the hierarchy. All these needs motivate behavior.

Needs are central to the communication process. Although physiological and safety needs are most often met by the individual, Shaver and Hazan (1987) determined that people seek security by affiliating with others. Social needs—to belong, have friends, and feel accepted—are most closely related to interpersonal communication motives, yet ego needs, such as confidence, recognition, and approval, require others' participation and interaction. Mead (1934) argued that self-actualization can only come about through interaction with others. Thus, a person's need hierarchy is related to communication at several levels.

People have different levels of primary needs; the level is affected by the person's values, background, and experiences (Pasmore, 1979). Those who interact frequently with others and receive approval and recognition will more likely concentrate on self-actualization need fulfillment. Those with few friends will seek additional social interaction to feel accepted. Thus, people have a hierarchy of needs. Primary needs allow people to protect themselves and survive.

Having studied communication motives over the last few years, we now believe that some motives are related to these primary needs and some are not. As shown in Figure 12.1, motives such as inclusion/companionship and affection (to meet social needs) and control (to fulfill power or achievement needs) are primary motives related to primary needs. But we have discovered additional communication motives that move beyond this primary hierarchy. We refer to these as secondary needs (and motives). Secondary needs are not life-threatening and are often more affected by the situation or communication context.

Elements within the situation can create needs that lead to motives to fulfill these needs. For example, an extremely stressful day can motivate communication with others to relax. An upcoming storm can motivate viewing a TV weather station for information (note that safety needs might be involved if one were traveling in this storm). Boredom might motivate people to communicate with others for pleasure or to watch television for exciting entertainment. These secondary needs, then, are more situationally based and variable, whereas primary needs are more traitlike and stable across situations.

Secondary needs are both instrumental (e.g., a need for information or control) and ritualistic (e.g., need for regularity in life or arousal; A. Rubin, 1984). Secondary motives (just like secondary needs) are not basic but present, nevertheless. Relaxation and escape motives, for example, must be linked to a need for an uncomplicated, simple world.

MOTIVES

A *motive* is defined as "a relatively general disposition which will influence actions that are expected to lead to a particular kind of

NEEDS	MOTIVES	GOALS	PLANS	BEHAVIOR
PRIMARY	PRIMARY	PRIMARY		
Self-Actualization				
Ego-achievement	Control	Power	Target	
Social-affiliation	Inclusion	Belonging	Channel	
Safety/Security	Affection	Love	Actions	
Physiological				
SECONDARY	SECONDARY	SECONDARY		
Reduced Stress	Relaxation Escape	Rest Distraction	Target	
Information-certainty	Information	Knowledge	Channel	
Arousal	Pleasure Excitement	Amusement Entertainment	Actions	
Alleviate boredom	Pass time, Habit	Diversion Routine		

Figure 12.1. A needs-based model of communication

consequence or goal. When an individual confronts a series of tasks that differ in difficulty, the motive to achieve is general in the sense of having a multiplicative influence on the tendency to undertake each activity that is expected to lead to success" (Atkinson, 1965, p. 14).

Motives are potentials for behavior. The situation or environment can arouse motives. Different types of motivation satisfy different needs. Purposive behavior can be understood by identifying the actions that lead to achieving a particular goal.

Madsen (1965) identified and discussed two main types of motivation theories: personality dynamics and learning dynamics. According to Madsen, Maslow (1954), Cattell (1957), Lewin (1951), McClelland (1960), and Murray (1938) developed personality theories where *needs* represent "driving forces behind behavior" (p. 51) and can be studied as personality-type variables. Cattell hypothesized 16 different needs and Murray proposed more than 32. Cattell thought that needs were inherent ("constitutional") in the individual, whereas McClelland thought they were acquired. Murray's theory assumed both primary (viscerogenic) and secondary (psychogenic) needs.

Madsen (1965) identified Hull, Spence, Logan, Bown, Hebb, Olds, and Skinner as learning-dynamic researchers. In learning theory, motivation is comprised of both needs (peripherical processes outside the central nervous system (CNS)) and drives. Needs are lacks (food and water), distentions (sex hormones, milk production), or stimuli (pain, warmth, cold). Organic motives include hunger, thirst, sex, maternal, pain-avoidance, and rest. These involve non-CNS processes. Acquired motives (e.g., tobacco, alcohol) are secondary.

According to Madsen (1965), social motives include social contact (a most central, primary motive), power (competition for leadership, dominance, or influence), achievement (determined by external stimuli from competition situations, it is motivated by fear of failure, need for achievement, and need for contact), and acquisition (a secondary motive to collect objects stimulated by fear, power, and achievement motives). Thus, some motives are primary (social), but most are secondary (relaxation, escape).

Atkinson (1965) proposed a theory of motivation that accounts for "selectivity, preference, or direction in behavior that is governed in some way by the relation of particular actions to an objectively definable consequence, end, or goal, and for the tendency of action, once initiated, to persist until the end, or goal, is attained" (p. 3). He noted that Lewin (1951) provided the best guide to motivation through an equation stating that behavior occurs due to "the interaction of characteristics of personality and characteristics of the immediate environment at the time" (Atkinson, 1965, p. 4).

Important socio-psychological motives include fear, achievement, affiliation, and power. Need for achievement, affiliation, and power are three basic needs that have characteristic motives and behaviors associated with them. A need for power results in an interpersonal motive to communicate for control, a need for affiliation results in motives to seek affection and inclusion, and a need for achievement would motivate hard work, for instance.

Communication Motives

The study of communication motives is rooted in uses and gratifications (U&G) theory. U & G theory asserts that communicators are active agents who seek communication content to gratify a need. Whether they identify gratifications sought and obtained (Palmgreen & Rayburn, 1982) or television-viewing motives (Katz, Blumler, & Gurevitch, 1974; A. Rubin, 1981), the theory soundly focuses on the reasons why people watch television (or use mediated channels), how these reasons are affected by antecedent social-psychological traits, and how these motives lead to behaviors and resultant need gratification.

U&G researchers have explored many different media motives (A. Rubin, 1983; A. Rubin & Bantz, 1987; A. Rubin & Rubin, 1989; R. Rubin & Rubin, 1992). A. Rubin classified television-viewing motives into ritualized and instrumental motives. Instrumental television viewing motives are ones such as information seeking and control, whereas ritualistic motives are habit, pass time, and entertainment motives. Finn and Gore (1988) also identified two main motive dimensions: mood management (relaxation, entertainment, arousal, information) and social compensation (companionship, habit, escape, pass time).

These communication motives might be necessitated by primary or secondary needs. For example, an information-seeking television-viewing motive to find out a tornado's predicted path would fulfill a primary need for safety as well as a secondary need for information (if the tornado is not in the viewer's geographic area, but that of a friend or relative). Communication motives, then, may fulfill primary or secondary needs, depending on how basic they are to the person's survival and growth. This example also demonstrates how some more basic primary needs and secondary needs might be aroused by the situation (e.g., a drought, storm, or moving out of state) or environment, whereas higher order primary needs are more internal and psychological.

Interpersonal Communication Motives

Interpersonal communication is goal-directed. People use communication as a tool to mold their self-concepts (e.g., ego needs) and to fulfill other basic needs. People initiate conversations with others to satisfy needs.

Interpersonal communication motives research addresses the issues of why we talk, who we talk to, what we talk about, how we talk, and the outcomes of talking to others. Earlier research focused on the development of the measure for interpersonal communication motives and antecedents to interpersonal communication motives. Later research examined the relation between motives with other communication variables and the study of interpersonal communication motives contextually.

Schutz (1966) first identified three primary interpersonal needs: inclusion, affection, and control. Inclusion is the need to be part of a group, to be affiliated with others, or to have companions. According to Schutz, it can also be the need to embrace others in one's own group. Affection is the need to express love or be loved by others. Control is the need to exert power over others or give others power. These three primary needs are closely tied to Maslow's (1954) and Madsen's (1965) social needs.

Also, each of these three needs is discussed as a behavior and a feeling, so needs are fulfilled on both behavioral and cognitive levels (Schutz, 1966). Behaviorally, *inclusion* is the need to establish and maintain satisfactory associations with others; emotionally, it is the need to establish and maintain an interest in others. Behaviorally, *control* refers to a need to initiate or preserve power and influence over others; emotionally, it is the need to achieve/maintain mutual respect for another's competence. Behaviorally, *affection* is the need to initiate or maintain relationships based on love, adoration, and devotion (which always refers to a dyadic relationship and demonstrates close personal feelings); emotionally, it is the need to achieve or maintain mutual support of and connection with others.

Interpersonal needs are fulfilled through satisfactory relations with others (Schutz, 1966). How well these needs are fulfilled depends how much of the action is observed by others, the direction of the need fulfillment (who is the originator and who is the target), which need is being fulfilled, and the need state (desired, ideal, or pathological). Schutz's Fundamental Interpersonal Relations Orientations instrument identifies and measures interpersonal needs of inclusion, control, and affection.

Operating within a U&G framework, R. Rubin, Perse, and Barbato (1988) examined several interpersonal communication motives (based on diary reports and previously uncovered television-viewing motives) and discovered that inclusion, affection, and control motives were, indeed, central or primary motives. They also found three additional motives: pleasure, relaxation, and escape. The pleasure motive reflects a need to be entertained and aroused; people initiate communication with others to have fun and for excitement. The relaxation motive reflects a need to unwind, rest, or feel less tense; people communicate with others to calm down. Escape motives reflect a need to avoid other activities and worries by communicating with someone; people avoid potentially stressful situations by starting up conversations. Inclusion, affection, control, pleasure, relaxation, and escape, then, are basic interpersonal communication motives that have traditionally been examined in motives research. Recently, Graham (1994) reviewed the Interpersonal Communication Motives Scale and concluded that the scale is consistently reliable and valid.

The communication literature reveals consistent antecedents to interpersonal communication motives, which indicates that traitlike qualities exist for these motives. Barbato (1995) too has consistent relation between interpersonal motives and other traitlike communication variables in the research literature. This literature, then, supports the notion that people have some consistent motives for interpersonal communication.

Antecedents. Researchers have examined antecedents of interpersonal communication motives. Two antecedents that influence why people communicate interpersonally are locus of control (Brenders, 1987; Canary, Cunningham, & Cody, 1988; DeCharms, 1968; A. Rubin, 1993; R. Rubin & Rubin, 1992, Steinfatt, 1987) and communication apprehension (Kondo, 1994; A. Rubin, 1993; R. Rubin et al., 1988).

R. Rubin et al. (1988) reported that there was no relation between communicating for control and communication satisfaction. Although satisfaction was positively related to communicating for pleasure, affection, inclusion, and relaxation, there was no such relation for control. In comparing people with an internal locus of control versus those with an external locus of control, R. Rubin and Rubin (1989) found that Internals seek control in conversations, but so did externals who felt controlled by powerful others. They also found that mobility was related to control (people who were less mobile sought less interpersonal control).

When considering the effect of locus of control on communication motives in the interpersonal and mass media contexts, A. Rubin (1993) reported that externals scored higher on interpersonal and television inclusion, escape, and pass time, and interpersonal social ritual. Additionally, externals were motivated to communicate more ritualistically than internals. Externals also were more anxious when communicating with others and found interaction less rewarding and less satisfying than internals.

Another antecedent factor that has an influence on why and whether people talk to one another is communication apprehension (CA). Kondo (1994) found that high CAs communicate more so for escape whereas low apprehensives communicated for pleasure and relaxation. Previously, R. Rubin et al. (1988) found that high CAs were less likely to communicate for pleasure, control, inclusion, and affection than were low CAs. In the classroom setting, Myers (1996) found that students high in apprehension communicated more for inclusion and to escape than students low in communication apprehension. Certain motives, then, may be related to a general avoidance tendency.

Two other variables that can be considered to be antecedent factors are biological gender and age. When R. Rubin et al. (1988)

were establishing initial validity of the Interpersonal Communication Motives measure, they examined gender in relation to interpersonal communication motives. They found that women were less likely to communicate for control, but more likely to communicate for pleasure, to express affection, seek inclusion, and relax. In considering age differences, younger people communicated for pleasure, inclusion, and escape and older persons to give affection (R. Rubin et al., 1988). These results are based on trait differences; gender and age groups differ in their overall reasons for communicating with others.

R. Rubin and Rubin (1992) argued that attention should also be paid to contextual age in considering the relation between locus of control and interpersonal communication motives. In contrast to chronological age, contextual age considers how healthy, happy, economically stable, mobile, and socially interactive people are. R. Rubin and Rubin found that people who were less healthy and had an external locus of control reported communicating for escape, inclusion, and control. On the other hand, people who were more socially interactive, healthy, and happy communicated more for affection, pleasure, and inclusion.

Barbato and Perse (1992) also considered contextual age in elders' motives for communicating. Elders who viewed life negatively communicated more for control and comfort, whereas elders who viewed life positively communicated more for pleasure and affection. In their study of older adults, Downs and Javidi (1990) found that lonely elders communicated for escape, whereas less lonely elders communicated for pleasure, relaxation, and control. These last three studies demonstrate that there are mediating variables when studying the relation between age and motives.

Related Variables. Next we report on studies that have looked at the relation between interpersonal communication motives and other communication traits. Although an argument could be made that some of the communication variables could be antecedent factors that influence why people communicate with others, due to the nature of the studies (i.e., causation was not tested), they are here.

People with different interaction motives differ in their choice of typical interaction strategy. Javidi, Jordan, and Carlone (1994) investigated the relation between compliance-gaining strategies and interpersonal communication motives. They found that people who consistently use cooperative compliance-gaining strategies had a relatively high motivation for control and a low motivation for pleasure. People who used rational compliance-gaining strategies had a relatively high motivation for control and a low motivation for affection. In this study, the motive of control was very significant in discriminating between people that would, or would not, use a particular type of compliance-gaining strategy. Control seems to be a primary motive.

Myers, Zhong, and Mitchell (1995) investigated the relation between motives and conflict in romantic relationships. People were asked to recall a conflict episode and to report on the content of the conflict, the strategies used in resolving the conflict, and the motives for resolving the conflict. Myers et al. found six motives for resolving conflict: concern for the relationship, avoidance, affection, control, inclusion, and situational factors. The authors concluded that their results support the proposition that certain motives might be context-related (in this case, a conflict setting; R. Rubin et al., 1988).

Another interest of communication researchers is how competent communicators differ in how and why they communicate. One way of looking at communication competence is to consider a person's assertiveness and responsiveness. The person high in both traits is considered competent. Anderson and Martin (1995a) found that competent communicators reported the motives of pleasure, affection, and inclusion more often than the other types of communicators. What was not tested in this study, and must be investigated further, is whether people who are competent communicate differently because they are competent or whether communicating for specific motives, such as affection, leads to competence. R. Rubin and Martin (1994) also investigated the relation between competence and motives. They found that interpersonal communication competence was positively related to the motives of pleasure and affection.

Martin and Rubin (1994) examined interpersonal communication motives in the affinity-seeking process in initial interactions. People who reported communicating for control also reported using rewarding affinity-seeking strategies. People who reported communicating for affection and pleasure, but not for control, reported using other-involvement and positive self-image affinity-seeking strategies. These people also scored higher in their interpersonal communication competence. Again, control affected behavior in predictable ways.

Hosman (1991) studied the relation among privacy, loneliness, conversation sensitivity, and interpersonal communication motives. People with a need for intimacy reported communicating more for pleasure and affection than people with a need for seclusion. Similar to the findings of Downs and Javidi (1990), Hosman also found that lonely people communicate less for affection and pleasure needs. Additionally, conversational sensitivity was positively related to the motives of pleasure, affection, and relaxation. In studying elders' loneliness and their use of the telephone, Holladay et al. (1992) reported that lonely elders used the telephone for escape and safety needs, whereas less lonely elders used the telephone for affection. Here, the need for inclusion resulted in primary need gratification.

Canary and Spitzberg (1993) distinguished between chronic and situational loneliness. They concluded that the chronically lonely become more habitual users of communication and are less instrumental in their motives. The media, in particular, were useful channels for situational loneliness.

Sense of humor is another variable related to interpersonal motives. Barbato, Graham, and Perse (1994) found that the use of positive humor in conversation was associated with the motives of pleasure, affection, and comfort. Negative use of humor, on the other hand, was associated with the motives of escape and control. These results indicate that interpersonal motives are connected to the types of humor used in conversation.

In their article introducing the Interpersonal Communication Motives Model, Graham, Barbato, and Perse (1993) studied the relation between motives and self-disclosure. They found that people who talk for pleasure or affection are willing to talk about many topics but do soon a less personal or intimate level. Although affection was unrelated to disclosure of high intimacy topics, affection was linked to greater disclosure of low intimacy topics. The motive of control was related to depth of selfdisclosure, but not breath. Again, self-disclosure regularities seem to be connected to different motives. Graham et al. concluded that communicating for control might be a form of conversational dominance and that the behavioral display of this motive might be context bound.

Motives in Contexts. As noted earlier, depending on the relationship, people differ in their motives for communicating with others. Graham et al. (1993) explained that the intimacy of family relationships is demonstrated in part in that people communicate more with family members for the motives of affection, pleasure, inclusion, and relaxation, in comparison to relationships where people have more formal relationships. In studying the role of motives in the father-young adult relationship, Martin and Anderson (1995) found that fathers and their children were similar in their motives for communicating with one another. Additionally, for both fathers and their children, when the person's motive for communicating was affection or pleasure, the person was more satisfied in the relationship. Anderson and Martin (1997) found similar results in the mother-young adult relationship. Additionally, when mothers or their children reported communicating with the other person for control, satisfaction with the other person was lower. This shows how others can affect interpersonal motives.

In the organizational setting, Anderson and Martin (1995c) found that when employees report communicating with their superiors and co-workers for the motives of pleasure, affection, inclusion, but not for the motive of escape, employees reported being more satisfied with their supervisors, jobs and also had greater organizational commitment. Although women communicated more with their bosses and co-workers for affection, men communicated more with their co-workers for control. Additionally, employees reported communicating more with their co-workers than with their superiors for every motive, except for a motive labeled *duty* (e.g., "I communicate with this person because it is part of my job"). Duty seems to be context-based.

The role of motives in group communication has also been investigated. As an exit questionnaire for a group project, Anderson and Martin (1995b) asked students to discuss why they talked to the members of their group, their interaction involvement during the group process, and their overall satisfaction with the group. Communicating for pleasure, affection, inclusion, and relaxation were all positively related to satisfaction, whereas communicating for control was negatively related to satisfaction. The motives of pleasure and affection were positively related to being attentive and responsive during the group interactions, whereas the motives of control and escape were negatively related.

In a later study of classroom groups, Martin and Anderson (1997) compared students' trait motives for communicating with others with their reported motives for communicating in a long-term task group in which they were participating. Students with the trait motives for communicating for pleasure, affection, but not control reported that in the group interactions, they communicated for pleasure, affection, but not for control. Additionally, people who reported a trait motive of control reported communicating for all six motives in their group interactions. In this task situation, it appears that people will act on their motive for control.

Several studies have looked at interpersonal communication motives in cultures other than the United States. R. Rubin, Fernandez-Collado, and Hernandez-Sampieri (1992) examined cultural differences between the United States and Mexico. People in Mexico reported communicating less for affection, pleasure, and affection than those in the United States. Using a Chinese sample,

Anderson, Martin, and Zhong (1996) found that people communicate with their friends for the motives of inclusion, helpfulness, solidarity, expressiveness, relational maintenance, and pleasure. However, because Geddes (1992) found no regional differences in interpersonal communication motives, we could also conclude that motives are consistent within cultures. Future research will need to further explore why people communicate with others in different cultures, as well as the motives for why people communicate cross-culturally.

GOALS, PLANS, AND BEHAVIOR

Although this chapter focuses mainly on interpersonal communication needs and motives, we cannot forget the remainder of the model sketched in Figure 12.1. Goals are objectives that inspire strategic (planned) interaction with others (McCann & Higgins, 1988). Dillard, Segrin, and Harden (1989) explained that goals are also primary and secondary. A primary goal, in a control situations, for example, might be "to bring about behavioral change in a target person" (Dillard et al., 1989, p. 20). Secondary goals, however, are "objectives of several sorts that derive directly from more general motivations that are recurrent in a person's life" (p. 20). These secondary goals might be socially appropriate interaction or arousal management. Thus, primary and secondary goals result from primary and secondary needs and motives.

Plans

Plans are predetermined sequences of actions designed to achieve goals (Berger, 1988). Plans involve a target of communication, the chosen channel, and how the anticipated behaviors might result in successful strategic actions. Regardless of whether motives are trait- or state-related, plans cannot be determined independent of context. Graham et al. (1993) took this into account when they suggested identifying not only why we communicate (motives), but also who we communicate with (receiver, target, or partner), and how we choose to communicate our motives (channel choice and strategic actions). *Why, who,* and *how* are equally significant, equally dependent, and equally represented in the communication interaction (Graham et al., 1993).

Who. Graham et al. (1993) suggested that as interpersonal needs change, so too does selection of conversational partners. In relating this to the U & G theory, Graham et al. explained that, just as certain media channels are thought to be satisfying for specific motives, different individuals are also thought to be more appropriate for fulfilling certain interpersonal communication needs. Graham et al. found that people talk to close friends, lovers, and family members more often than strangers and co-workers for the motives of pleasure, affection, inclusion, and relaxation. The degree of relational intimacy between conversational partners has a strong influence over topic choice, amount of disclosure, and number of interactions.

How. Relationship level also becomes an influential factor in determining the frequency and type of interpersonal interaction (Graham et al., 1993). If the interpersonal need is affected by the relationship between the sender and receiver, the context in which the need is conveyed may also be affected. The intensity of the relationship may have the capacity to influence the channels used to convey particular interpersonal communication needs. All channels do not satisfy all motives equally well. For example, personalized and intimate relationships may more frequently use face-to-face communication channels rather than mediated channels (Finucane & Step, 1994).

Graham et al. (1993) suggested that interpersonal communication needs should be compatible with the method of need fulfillment. The method for fulfilling the interpersonal need is adapted and modified as a result of the communicator's personal approach. What channel is used to fulfill the need may also reflect personal approach. For example, people seeking to fulfill a need for inclusion who use an indirect or inactive approach may choose a less interactive (e.g., written) channel to communicate the interpersonal need.

From this early work on interpersonal communication motives (Barbato, 1985; Graham et al., 1993; R. Rubin et al., 1988), we know that individual needs, manifested in the motives people express, influence the selection of interpersonal partners, communication strategies, channels, and expectations about the strategy's success. Strategies are employed in communication behavior, interpersonal outcomes, like interpersonal need fulfillment or media gratification, can be cognitive, affective, or behavioral. Outcomes influence people's social positions and reinforce behavioral predispositions and personality traits. Interpersonal needs and motives are then affected by these social and psychological conditions.

Functional Alternatives. People are motivated to fulfill communication needs and select channels to accomplish interpersonal goals (Perse & Courtright, 1993). With interpersonal needs, face-to-face channels seem more appropriate than mediated channels although U&G stresses that media channels are sometimes functional alternatives for face-to-face channels (Rosengren, 1974; A. Rubin & Rubin, 1985). Channel choice is determined by the communication motives, social structures, and communication predispositions. It precedes behavior.

According to U&G, active audience members are motivated to seek gratifications and they act strategically to do so. Part of a plan is the choice of a communication channel or medium. Typically, people choose the medium that can best provide immediate gratification, but should it not be available or should skills not be sufficient, alternative media might be chosen (Rosengren & Windahl, 1972). "If television use provides a viable means for satisfying an escapist motive, magazines and music may be functional alternative for gratifying that motive" (A. Rubin & Windahl, 1986, p. 193). Katz, Gurevitch, and Haas (1973) identified certain media that are better substitutes (e.g., television for radio, friends for lectures). Overall, they found that nonmedia channels resulted in higher gratification than media sources, even for escape and entertainment motives. This finding has been replicated repeatedly (Perse & Courtright, 1993; R. Rubin, Westmyer, & DiCioccio, 1996).

Rosengren and Windahl (1972) defined functional alternatives as optional methods of supplementing, complementing, or substituting for a preferred method of need satisfaction. They explained that if a person needs social interaction, the primary means of satisfying this need would be for face-to-face communication with another, but a functional alternative channel might be communicating via telephone (if environmental possibilities—living in a different state—prohibit face-to-face) or letter (if individual possibilities—CA—are lacking). Watching television might substitute, but would be less satisfying than communication with a human being.

As Rosengren and Windahl (1972) explained, having the preferred method of need gratification available will determine channel choice, such that functional alternatives might not be necessary. This seems to be a healthy, functional means of channel choice. If one needs weather information during a storm and the radio emergency channel broadcasts weather alerts (and the batteries are charged in the radio) and a radio is available, this channel is the most functional, and newspapers, books or people by not be; it doesn't matter if people are available because the primary means of safety need satisfaction (the radio) is available. However, if the primary channel is not available and alternatives are restricted, dependency can result. Telephoning a friend across town to inquire about tornado touchdowns might have to be a functional alternative if no others are available. Yet if personal channels are substitutes (instead of supplements or complements), the channel might be dysfunctional.

Dysfunction occurs when substitution is enacted when it shouldn't be. Interpersonal communication substituting for a more appropriate mediated channel might not provide accurate information. Likewise, substituting media contact to satisfy a need for inclusion (e.g., loneliness) might be just as dysfunctional. Yet should a person lack interpersonal communication skills or not have others available for interaction, the substitute provides incomplete need satisfaction by providing vicarious experiences. Thus, we could viably hypothesize that people with inclusion needs who live alone or do not have telephones would have higher levels of parasocial interaction with television characters than would those who live with others, use e-mail frequently, or have ready interpersonal contact via telephone. Alternatives, then, are functional when they supplement and complement primary need satisfaction channels, but dysfunctional when they substitute needlessly for those channels.

Behavior

Now that the plan is set, communicators can enact their plans and communicate as planned. Because we have already ventured beyond our initial goal of examining traitlike features of interpersonal communication motives, we do not move into descriptions of behaviors at this time that might accomplish goals and fulfill needs. Most of our communication literature examines such behaviors. We also acknowledge that this model is only a small part of a larger communication model that includes the same sorts of processes going on within communication partners and features of the actual interaction that also influences how plans are enacted. This needs-based model, however, can be used to identify primary and secondary needs, motives, and goals.

REFERENCES

Anderson, C. M., & Martin, M. M. (1995a). Communication motives of assertive and responsive communicators. *Communication Research Reports, 12*, 186-191.

Anderson, C. M., & Martin, M. M. (1995b). The effects of communication motives, interaction involvement, and loneliness on satisfaction: A model of small groups. *Small Group Research, 26*, 118-137.

Anderson, C. M., & Martin, M. M. (1995c). Why employees talk to coworkers and superiors: Motives, gender, and organizational satisfaction. *Journal of Business Communication, 32*, 249-266.

Anderson, C. M., & Martin, M. M. (1997). *Communication models of mothers and their adult children: The path from motives to self-disclosure to satisfaction.* Manuscript submitted for publication.

Anderson, C. M., Martin, M. M., & Zhong, M. (1996, November). *Communication motives: A Chinese study of mothers, fathers, and friends.* Paper presented at the annual meeting of the Speech Communication Association Convention, San Diego.

Atkinson, J. W. (1965). Some general implications of conceptual developments in the study of achievement-oriented behavior. In M. R. Jones (Ed.), *Human motivation: A symposium* (pp. 3-29). Lincoln: University of Nebraska Press.

Barbato, C. A. (1985, November). *Uses of interpersonal communication.* Paper presented at the annual meeting of the Speech Communication Association , Chicago.

Barbato, C. A. (1995, April). *Directions for future research in communication motivation.* Paper presented at the annual meeting of the Eastern Communication Association, Pittsburgh, PA.

Barbato, C. A., Graham, E. E., & Perse, E. M. (1994, November). *Uses of interpersonal communication motives and humor among elders.* Paper presented at the annual meeting of the Speech Communication Association, New Orleans.

Barbato, C. A., & Perse, E. M. (1992). Interpersonal communication motives and the life positions of elders. *Communication Research, 19*, 516-531.

Berger, C. R. (1988). Planning, affect, and social action generation. In L. Donohew, H. E. Sypher, & E. T. Higgins (Eds.), *Communication, social cognition, and affect* (pp. 93-116). Hillsdale, NJ: Lawrence Erlbaum Associates.

Brenders, D. A. (1987). Perceived control: Foundations and directions for communication research. *Communication Yearbook, 10*, 86-116.

Canary, D. J., Cunningham, E. M., & Cody, M. J. (1988). Goal types, gender, and locus of control in managing interpersonal conflict. *Communication Research, 15*, 426-446.

Canary, D. J., & Spitzberg, B. H. (1993). Loneliness and media gratifications. *Communication Research, 20*(6), 800-821.

Cattell, R. B. (1957) *Personality and motivation structure and measurement.* Yonkers-on-Hudson, NY: World Book Co.

DeCharms, R. (1968). *Personal causation: The internal effective determinants of behavior.* New York: Academic Press.

Dillard, J. P., Segrin, C., & Harden, J. M. (1989). Primary and secondary goals in the production of interpersonal influence messages. *Communication Monographs, 56,* 19-38.

Downs, V. C., & Javidi, M. (1990). Linking communication motives to loneliness in the lives of older adults: An empirical test of interpersonal needs. *Journal of Applied Communication Research, 19,* 32-48.

Finn, S., & Gorr, M. B. (1988). Social isolation and social support as correlates of television viewing motivations. *Communication Research, 15,* 135-158.

Finucane, M. E., & Step, M. M. (1994, April). *Understanding interpersonal motives on the telephone and in face-to-face conversation.* Paper presented at the annual meeting of the Eastern Communication Association, Washington DC.

Geddes, D. S. (1992). Comparison of regional interpersonal communication dispositions. *Pennsylvania Speech Journal, 48,* 67-93.

Graham, E. E. (1994). Interpersonal communication motives scale. In R. B. Rubin, P. Palmgreen, & H. E. Sypher (Eds.), *Communication research measures: A sourcebook* (pp. 211-216). New York: Guilford.

Graham, E. E., Barbato, C. A., & Perse, E. M. (1993). The interpersonal communication motives model. *Communication Quarterly, 41,* 172-186.

Holladay, S., Crutcher, K., Gustavson, K., Jones, J., Laughlin, L., & McKown, S. (1992, November.). *Elder's motives for mediated interpersonal communication: An examination of telephone communication and loneliness.* Paper presented at the annual meeting of the Speech Communication Association, Chicago.

Hosman, L. A. (1991). The relationship among need for privacy, loneliness, conversational sensitivity, and interpersonal communication motives. *Communication Reports, 4,* 73-80.

Javidi, M., Jordan, W. J., & Carlone, D. (1994). Situational influence on the selection or avoidance of compliance-gaining strategies: A test of motivation to communicate. *Communication Research Reports, 11,* 127-134.

Katz, E., Blumler, J. G., & Gurevitch, M. (1974). Utilization of mass communication by the individual. In J. G. Blumler & E. Katz (Eds.), *The uses of mass communications: Current perspectives on gratifications research* (pp. 19-32). Beverly Hills, CA: Sage.

Katz, E., Gurevitch, M., & Haas, H. (1973). On the use of the mass media for important things. *American Sociological Review, 38*(2), 164-186.

Kondo, D. S. (1994). A comparative analysis of interpersonal communication motives between high and low communication apprehensives. *Communication Research Reports, 11*, 53-58.

Lewin, K. (1951). *Field theory in social science: Selected theoretical papers*. New York: Haper.

Madsen, K. B. (1965) Theories of motivation: An overview and a synthesis. In M. R. Jones (Ed.), *Human motivation: A symposium* (pp. 49-68). Lincoln: University of Nebraska Press.

Martin, M. M., & Anderson, C. M. (1995). The father-young adult child relationship: Interpersonal motives, self-disclosure, and satisfaction. *Communication Quarterly, 43*, 119-130.

Martin, M. M., & Anderson, C. M. (1997). *Communication motives in task groups*. Manuscript submitted for review.

Martin, M. M., & Rubin, R. B. (1994, November). *The affinity-seeking process in initial interactions*. Paper presented at the annual meeting of the Speech Communication Association, New Orleans.

Maslow, A. H. (1954). *Motivation and personality*. New York: Harper.

McCann, C. D., & Higgins, E. T. (1988). Motivation and affect in interpersonal relations: The role of personal orientations and discrepancies. In L. Donohew, H. E. Sypher, & E. T. Higgins (Eds.), *Communication, social cognition, and affect* (pp. 53-79). Hillsdale, NJ: Lawrence Erlbaum Associates.

McClelland, D. C. (1960). *Personality*. New York: Holt, Rinehart & Winston.

Mead, G. H. (1934). *Mind, self and society from the standpoint of a social behaviorist*. Chicago: University of Chicago Press.

Murray, H. A. (1938). *Explorations in personality*. New York: Wiley.

Myers, S. A. (1996, April). *Interpersonal communication motives, communication apprehension, and student gender in the college classroom: Implications for the basic course*. Paper presented at the annual meeting of the Central States Communication Association, St. Paul, MN.

Myers, S. A., Zhong, M., & Mitchell, W. (1995). The use of interpersonal communication motives in conflict resolution among romantic partners. *Ohio Speech Journal, 33*, 1-21.

Palmgreen, P., & Rayburn, J. D. (1982). Gratifications sought and media exposure: An expectancy value model. *Communication Research, 9*, 561-580.

Pasmore, W. A. (1979). Turning people on to work. In D. A. Kolb, I. M. Rubin, & J. M. McIntyre (Eds.) *Organizational psychology: A book of readings* (pp. 101-115). Englewood Cliffs, NJ: Prentice-Hall.

Perse, E. M., & Courtright, J. A. (1993). Normative images of communication media: Mass and interpersonal channels in the new media environment. *Human Communication Research, 19*, 485-503.

Rosengren, K. E. (1974). Uses and gratifications: A paradigm outline. In J. G. Blumler & E. Katz (Eds.), *The uses of mass communications: Current perspectives on gratifications research* (pp. 269-286). Beverly Hills: Sage.

Rosengren, K. E., & Windahl, S. (1972). Mass media consumption as a functional alternative. In D. McQuail (Ed.), *Sociology of mass communications* (pp. 166-194). Middlesex, UK: Penguin.

Rubin, A. M. (1981). An examination of television viewing motivations. *Communication Research, 8*, 141-165.

Rubin, A. M. (1983). Television uses and gratifications: The interactions of viewing patterns and motivations. *Journal of Broadcasting, 27*, 37-51.

Rubin, A. M. (1984). Ritualized and instrumental television viewing. *Journal of Communication, 34*(3), 67-77.

Rubin, A. M. (1993). The effect of locus of control on communication motivation, anxiety, and satisfaction. *Communication Quarterly, 41*, 161-171.

Rubin, A. M., & Bantz, C. R. (1987). Utility of videocassette recorders. *American Behavioral Scientist, 30*, 471-485.

Rubin, A. M., & Rubin, R. B. (1985). Interface of personal and mediated communication: A research agenda. *Critical Studies in Mass Communication, 2*, 36-53.

Rubin, A. M., & Rubin, R. B. (1989). Social psychological antecedents of VCR use. In M. R. Levy (Ed.), *The VCR age: Home video and mass communication* (pp. 92-111). Newbury Park, CA: Sage.

Rubin, A. M., & Windahl, S. (1986). The uses and dependency model of mass communication. *Critical Studies in Mass Communication, 3*, 184-199.

Rubin, R. B., Fernandez-Collado, C., & Hernandez-Sampieri, R. (1992). A cross-cultural examination of interpersonal communication motives in Mexico and the United States. *International Journal of Intercultural Relations, 16*, 145-157.

Rubin, R. B., & Martin, M. M. (1994). Development of a measure of interpersonal communication competence. *Communication Research Reports, 11*, 33-44.

Rubin, R. B., Perse, E. M., & Barbato, C. A. (1988). Conceptualization and measurement of interpersonal communication motives. *Human Communication Research, 14*, 602-628.

Rubin, R. B., & Rubin, A. M. (1992). Antecedents of interpersonal communication motivation. *Communication Quarterly, 40*, 305-317.

Rubin, R. B., Westmyer, S. A., & DiCioccio, R. L. (1996, November.). *Competent interpersonal communication: Appropriateness and effectiveness of communication channels and motives.* Paper presented at the annual meeting of the Speech Communication Association, San Diego.

Schutz, W. C. (1966). *The interpersonal underworld.* Palo Alto, CA: Science and Behavior Books.

Shaver, P., & Hazan, C. (1987). Being lonely, falling in love: Perspectives from attachment theory. *Journal of Social Behavior and Personality, 2,* 105-124.

Steinfatt, T. M. (1987). Personality and communication: Classical approaches. In J. C. McCroskey & J. A. Daly (Eds.), *Personality and interpersonal communication* (pp. 42-126). Newbury Park, CA: Sage.

13

Future Directions in Communication Trait Theory and Research

Michael J. Beatty
Cleveland State University

Plotting the course for future research and theory development from a trait perspective is a relatively straightforward task in light of the history of trait-oriented scholarship in our field and the criteria for good theory. First, trait perspectives of interpersonal communication have a rich tradition in the conceptualization of interpersonal communication. Until the mid-1980s socially significant interpersonal behaviors were commonly viewed as manifestations of individual predispositions. However, challenges to trait conceptualizations were briefly popular in psychology and a few communication scholars followed suit. Since the mid 1980s, personality theorists have begun returning to trait models of human behavior for three principal reasons. First, vast differences exist among people and models that ignore these differences are doomed to low predictive power. Second, sufficient evidence has accumulated to validate personality traits at the neurobiological level. Finally, the major objections to trait conceptualizations can be seen not as fatal flaws but as a need for further research. Part of the rationale for this chapter is to propose a needed research agenda.

Developing theory is a long-term process, requiring attentiveness to details of particular studies, familiarity with the breadth of related research, conceptual and methodological competence, creativity, the patience to draft manuscripts, and courage to risk being wrong and/or rejection. Criticizing others' theories is easier, which perhaps explains why there are so many critics, but so few theories. A compilation of the criteria appearing in the literature about theory construction in general (e.g., Blalock, 1969; Reynolds 1971; Rudner, 1966) as well as in communication (e.g., Infante, Rancer, & Womack, 1993; Littlejohn, 1983) suggests that theories can be evaluated according to their internal consistency, testability, predictive power, explanatory scope, parsimony and elegance, empirical relevance (i.e., consistency with known facts), and the degree to which they provide a sense of understanding about the phenomenon of interest. Despite the accumulation of a huge corpus of empirical research conducted from trait perspectives (much of which is cited in this volume), an integrated and comprehensive trait-based theory of interpersonal communication has not materialized. As the work contained in this volume illustrates, clusters of scholars have persistently forged ahead, making considerable progress researching particular traits. At the same time, however, the overall body of trait-focused literature is fragmented. The rationale for this chapter, therefore, also includes laying out the conceptual and empirical work needed to facilitate theoretical development.

Although far from exhaustive, the major thrust of future theory and research regarding communicator traits can be organized into five broad categories.

1. Reducing the current, very large number of communicator traits into a smaller, more parsimonious set.
2. Establishing the connection between communicator traits and neurobiological functioning.
3. Identifying the origin of communicator traits.
4. Enhancing the accuracy of predictions of behavior from communicator traits.
5. Exploring the consequences of suppressing trait-driven responses.

DEVELOPING A PARSIMONIOUS SET OF COMMUNICATOR TRAITS

This volume and other literature reviews (Giles & Street, 1994; McCroskey & Daly, 1987), even when limited in scope, document the existence of numerous measures of supposed unique communicator traits. The sheer number of trait constructs that have appeared in the communication literature since the 1960s is enough to thwart scholars' attempts to develop cohesive, parsimonious models of interpersonal interaction. The current state of affairs is problematic for scholars seriously interested in developing theory for two reasons. First, there is much overlap between many traits. For instance, a researcher employing measures of selfmonitoring, rhetorical sensitivity, adaptability, and other measures of competence (of which there are several), and interaction involvement as predictors in a regression model will undoubtedly face multicolinearity problems and a complicated interpretation of results. Statistical complexities aside, scholars interested in the just mentioned domain of research are faced with a fragmented literature. Second, there are too many communicator traits. Even if all of the constructs contained in the trait literature were unique traits and necessary to explain human interaction, any subsequent model would not fare well on the parsimony criterion.

Personality theorists faced a similar problem regarding the number of basic dimensions of personality. In recent years, however, personality scholars have reduced the number of major dimensions of personality to between three and seven. Although consensus has not yet been reached concerning the final set of basic personality dimensions, factor-analytic studies have reduced the available items to a manageable number of factors (Cloninger, 1987; Costa & McCrae, 1992; Eysenck, 1991; Tellegen, 1985; Zuckerman, 1994). Some of the major personality dimensions discussed by personality theorists seem inherently related to the study of interpersonal communication (e.g., agreeableness and cooperativeness), which should not be surprising given the central role traditionally assigned to interpersonal relations in many personality theories. However, it may be that data-reduction studies of measures of communicator traits produce additional dimensions to those extracted from analyses of personality measures. Regardless of the outcome, communication scholars should attempt to reduce the number of basic communicator traits to a more parsimonious set.

Part of the proliferation of trait constructs stems from the mode of scholarship that was in vogue when many of the constructs were proposed. In addition to a strong individual difference orientation, the notion that communication scholars should be concerned about theory in any strict sense was somewhat foreign to most active researchers. However, much of the problem resides in methodological practices surrounding factor analysis. Generally, few scale development studies provide compelling evidence to differentiate the proposed new measure from similar existing ones. In many cases, unrotated matrices that indicated unidimensionality and strong interfactor correlations are ignored. Instead, new factors are often artifacts of forced rotations. Such practices are tolerable and even encouraged during early stages of empirical investigation of phenomena. At some point, however, increased methodological rigor is justified.

For trait-oriented scholars, the ramifications of underemphasizing unrotated matrices and interfactor correlations and overinterpreting rotated matrices are two-fold: First, we accept a set of questionnaire items as measuring a unique trait when it probably represents a parallel measure of an existing trait, and second, we accept a newly proposed trait as multidimensional when it probably is unidimensional. Although "complex" is often considered superior to "simple" when it comes to evaluating colleagues' ideas, parsimony and elegance remain the ideal when evaluating theory. Rather than raising arguments in favor of complicated interpretation of results, we should now lean toward parsimony. When unrotated matrices indicate unidimensionality, especially when rotations produce factors that are correlated, unidimensional interpretations should be preferred.

Studies designed to reduce the overall number of measures to the basic communicator traits should be given high priority. In addition to producing a more parsimonious set of constructs, narrowing the range of what are considered basic communicator traits is likely to produce superior, robust measures of the traits by merging the best items from each related measure. It is difficult to anticipate what traits will emerge from such an analysis. Anyone who has conducted many factor analyses has witnessed the profound impact adding or deleting a few items can have on the overall analysis. However, the task needs to be undertaken.

GROUNDING COMMUNICATOR TRAITS IN BIOLOGY

Since the late 1980s psychobiologists have made considerable progress describing the neurobiological structures that underlie personality traits. Chapter 2 (this volume) discusses the principles of communibiology, a paradigm that requires consistency between theoretical speculation about communicative traits and neurobiological functioning. Observations that neurobiological operations do not function as hypothesized within the conceptualization of a particular trait constitutes strong evidence against the construct validity of the trait. If we posit the existence of particular cognitive processes, we must specify the neurological activity responsible for those processes or relay on scholars from other disciplines to do it for us. Doing the work for ourselves, of course, will be a tedious process, probably requiring considerable work for most of us. Even a cursory examination of the neurobiological complexity involved in describing a single trait amply demonstrates that explicating the neurobiology of traits is no simple task. Still, taking the responsibility to show the neurobiological foundation of communicator traits is preferable to leaving the work up to other fields for two reasons. First, constructs that originate in our field are not likely to attract the attention of other fields. If communication scholars abdicate the responsibility to explicate the neurobiology of communicator traits, the work probably will not be done. Second, scholars within any strong vital discipline should take responsibility for explaining the roots of its constructs.

Within the fields of psychology, sociology, and anthropology numerous scholars actively work at discovery focused on linkages between aspects of human functioning and biology. Why should communication scholars remain inattentive to the central role of biology, especially brain operations, in interpersonal functioning? What excuse can we offer for communication theories uninformed by facts regarding brain functioning when other social sciences are infusing a rapidly accumulation of biological evidence concerning human behavior? To argue that we understand cognitive processes such as encoding, message construction, strategic thinking, planning, listening, perspective-taking and affective responses such as anxiety, anger, and embarrassment without understanding the role and operation of the brain in regard to our research specializations weakens the intellectual status of our field

On the other hand, we could take the initiative and explicate the neurobiological processes that produce the observable phenomena we recognize as communicator traits. Indeed, communication scholars should view neurobiological explication as laudable scholarly work in its own right. Although a tedious task, such an undertaking produces four sizable yields for theory development from a communicator trait paradigm. First, linking neurobiological operations to specific traits establishes that traits are more than mere theorists' attributions about human behavior. Second, because most traits in our field are measured through self-report data, connections between neurobiological functioning and traits establishes that traits represent something more than persons' subjective perceptions. Third, linking neurobiology and traits establishes internal consistency, a necessary feature of theory, of trait conceptualizations. Finally, neurobiological explication of traits establishes empirical relevance, a consistency between knowledge generated independently through two separate analytic realms, in this case neuroscience and communication.

IDENTIFYING THE ORIGINS OF COMMUNICATOR TRAITS

The validity of a trait can be substantially supported by evidence regarding its origin and development. When scholars can point to antecedent conditions that effectively sort people into various trait categories, much is accomplished in the way of establishing the validity of the trait conceptualization. For nearly three decades, trait theorists have either made no claims about the origin and development of communicator traits or have attributed their source to social learning processes (Bandura, 1971). However, the assumption that traits represent schema resulting from personal experience needs serious rethinking for several reasons. First, a review of the communication literature shows that very few studies have tested the assumption that predispositions are learned. Rather, such claims have merely extended Bandura's (1971) thinking to communicator traits. Second, the few studies that have appeared in the literature are exclusively based on college students' retrospective self-reports of childhood experiences. Although this research paradigm is often the only practical means for glimpsing family dynamics, advocates of learning theory must yield to findings based on more direct research designs. Third, the published studies regarding the development of communicator traits have demonstrated comparatively little predictive power. For example, three studies of social learning and communication apprehension development (Ayres, 1988; Beatty, Plax, & Kearney, 1985; Daly & Friedrich, 1981) and one study focused on social learning and assertiveness (Plax, Kearney, & Beatty, 1985) accounted for between 4% and 15% of the variance, depending on the number of predictors used. In contrast, studies based on identical twins (reviewed in chapter 2, this volume) show that between 30% and 60% of the variance is attributable to genetics. It has been shown that the single best predictor of many traits is the twins' level on the trait, whether the twins are raised together or apart. The traits that have already been shown to be heavily influenced by genetics include assertiveness, aggressiveness, nurturance, and empathy. Similarly powerful genetic effects for some dimensions of communicator style are reported by Horvath (1995, also discussed in chapter 2 of this volume). Compared to social learning accounts, the extant research clearly supports a communibiological theory of communicator trait development on the criterion of predictive power. Fourth, the upper levels of predictive power for the social learning studies required seven predictor variables, whereas the strong effects for genetic models require one predictor—genetic inheritance. Thus, in terms of communicator trait development, the communibiological approach is more parsimonious than social learning. Finally, in addition to the twins studies, social learning theory does not account for the mountain of research evidence from psychobiologists (reviewed in chapter 2 in this volume) which shows that many trait characteristics are observable soon after birth prior to social experience. Thus, social learning theory perspectives burden scholars with much knowledge that is not easily explained within its principles.

Trait-oriented communication scholars can significantly advance theoretical development by following the psychobiologists' lead and conducting studies of identical twins and separate the effects of genetics and other variables concerning the development of communicator traits. Horvath's (1995) study is nothing short of ground-breaking in this respect. This is not to suggest that only genetic models should be assumed, but they need to be tested. It may be that communicator traits turn out to represent genetic and experiential blends. However, we must remember that variance not explained in such studies may be due to methodological error and not necessarily to social forces. Our trait measures are imperfect in their reliability and validity. Sample distributions, scaling complexities, and many other methodological imperfections place a ceiling on the maximum degree of association between any two variables. In any case, although all prospective theories of trait origins should be tested, existing research findings strongly encourages the pursuit of genetically based accounts of communicator trait development.

ACCOUNTING FOR BEHAVIOR

Regardless of one's position regarding trait conceptualizations of communication, predicting behavior in social contexts remains a formidable challenge. Although communication scholars have discussed and tested alternative conceptual and methodological approaches to measuring behavioral manifestations of traits (e.g., Beatty, 1987; Jaccard & Daly, 1980), improvement regarding the treatment of communicator traits is also warranted. Critics of the trait perspective point to the residual and/or behaviors not accounted for in trait studies as evidence of the inadequacy of individual difference models of communication. Much can be done to discover whether the proportion of unexplained variation in studies using communication trait predictors is due to situational factors or whether it is due to imperfections in measurement, sampling, or additional traits not included in the study.

Scholars relying on communicator traits in the prediction of social behavior have operated from one of three perspectives: (a) single trait perspective in which one trait is employed as a predictor of some index of behavior (e.g., Beatty, 1987), (b) interactionist perspective in which behavior is seen as an interaction between a trait and situational factors (e.g., Infante, 1987), and (c) multiple trait perspective in which behavior is viewed as a function of more than one trait (e.g., Sampter & Burleson, 1984). A related alternative to the multiple trait perspective, which has been used productively in the study of temperament, employs *types* of people based on trait scores. For instance, Chess and Thomas (1989) used various combinations of consistently observed features of behavior (persistence, adaptability, attention span, threshold of reaction, etc.) to categorize children in easy, difficult, and slow-to-warm types. The 30-year research program presented by Chess and Thomas (1989) indicates that the validity, reliability, and usefulness of their typology has been quite impressive. In the event that we are unsuccessful at reducing the number of communicator traits, theories could be simplified by creating types or profiles of communicators based on conceptually guided combinations of various trait scores. For instance, a person low in verbal aggressiveness but high in general hostility might be seen as a passive aggressive type.

Although more research is needed to establish which of the three should be considered the dominant perspective, the predictive power of both the interactionist and multiple trait models are generally superior to the single trait approach. The multiple trait perspective is potentially more parsimonious because dependence on situational factors is eliminated. Regardless of the perspective adopted, scholars should conduct studies that provide estimates of the impact on predictive power when traits are removed from statistical analyses.

DETERMINING THE CONSEQUENCES OF SUPPRESSING
PREDISPOSITIONS

In addition to continued interest in the prediction of behavior, trait-oriented scholars should turn their attention to the short- and long-term effects of suppressing an individual's natural trait responses. Critics of trait perspectives point to instances when people do not behave in a manner consistent with trait assessments as evidence against the validity of the trait. However, such thinking is flawed. For example, the predisposition of individuals categorized as apprehensive about communication is to avoid communication. At times, however, either because of coercion or more salient traits communication apprehensive individuals do communicate even though they are strongly predisposed to avoid the activity. Does their behavior invalidate the trait assessment? Absolutely not. Research shows that compared to people low in the trait, highly apprehensive communicators experience high levels of anxiety (Beatty, 1987). Thus, although the apprehensive participants in the study did not act according to their trait, they experienced consequences for the behavioral incongruity. Because communication apprehension was initially defined as the predisposition to "avoid communication, if possible, or suffer a variety of anxiety-type feelings when forced to communicate" (McCroskey, Daly, & Sorensen, 1976, p. 376), the consequences of incongruous behavior were embedded in the conceptualization of the construct and guided researchers.

Most traits, however, do not specify the consequences to suppressing trait-generated urges. Future research focused on both short-and long-term effects of behaving inconsistently with trait orientations would provide considerable insight into the dynamics of interpersonal relationships. We understand the ramifications of forcing a communication apprehensive person to present a public speech but what are the consequences of forcing verbally aggressive persons to remain passive during conflict or insisting on simplistic analyses from cognitively complex individuals? In communibiological analysis (chapter 2), we argue that because traits are biologically based any misfit between environmental demands and communicator traits produces stress. However, we might also inquire as to the effects of acting against predispositions at times subsequent to the social episode in which traits were suppressed. Studies that confirm these theoretical expectations will fortify the validity of trait conceptualizations by establishing the existence of significant latent features of traits that remain despite manifest behavior.

FINAL COMMENTS

The preceding discussion is not intended to be restrictive to trait scholarship in any way. Clearly, numerous lines of research can and should be initiated that do not fall neatly into any of the categories just listed. Moreover, not all trait scholars in our field will agree with every idea presented in this chapter. Regardless of our specific perspective about communicator traits, however, we all can agree that they represent major dimensions of interpersonal functioning. We can also agree that interpersonal communication theories that omit consideration of communicator traits are hopelessly incomplete and can never accurately describe, explain, or predict human interaction.

REFERENCES

Ayres, J. (1988). Antecedents of communication apprehension. *Communication Research Reports, 5,* 58-63.

Bandura, A. (1971). *Social learning theory.* Morristown, NJ: General Learning Press.

Beatty, M. J. (1987). Communication apprehension as a determinant of avoidance, withdrawal, and performance anxiety. *Communication Quarterly, 35,* 202-217.

Beatty, M. J., Plax, T, G., & Kearney, P. (1985). Reinforcement versus modeling in the development of communication apprehension. *Communication Research Reports, 2,* 80-85.

Blalock, H. M. (1969). *Theory construction: From verbal to mathematical formulations.* Englewood Cliffs, NJ: Prentice-Hall.

Chess, S. & Thomas, A. (1989). Temperament and its functional significance. In S. I. Greenspan & G. H. Pollock (Eds.), *The course of life: Early childhood* (Vol. 2, pp. 163-228). Madison, CT: International Universities Press.

Cloninger, C, R, (1987). A systematic method of clinical description and classification of personality. *Archives of General Psychiatry, 44,* 573-588.

Costa, P. T., & McCrae, R. R. (1992). *NEO-PI-R: Revised personality inventory.* Odessa, FL: Psychological Assessment Resources.

Daly, J. A., & Friedrich, G. (1981). The development of communication apprehension: A retrospective analysis of contributory correlates. *Communication Quarterly, 29,* 243-255.

Eysenck, H. J. (1991). Dimensions of personality: The biosocial approach to personality. In J. Strelau & A. Angleitner (Eds.),

Explorations in temperament (pp. 87-103). London: Plenum Press.

Giles, H. & Street, R. L., Jr. (1994). Communicator characteristics and behavior. In M. L. Knapp & G. R. Miller (Eds.). *Handbook of interpersonal communication* (2nd ed., pp. 103-161). Thousand Oaks, CA: Sage.

Horvath, C. W. (1995). Biological origins of communicator style. *Communication Quarterly, 43*, 394-407.

Infante, D. A. (1987). Enhancing the prediction of response to a communication situation from communication traits. *Communication Quarterly, 35,* 305-316.

Infante, D. A., Rancer, A. S., & Womack, D. F. (1993). *Building communication theory* (2nd ed.). Prospect Heights, IL: Waveland.

Jaccard, J., & Daly, J. (1980). Personality traits and multiple-act criteria. *Human Communication Research, 6*, 367-377.

Littlejohn, S. W. (1983). *Theories of human communication* (3rd ed.). Belmont, CA: Wadsworth.

McCroskey, J. C., & Daly, J. A. (Eds.).(1987). *Personality and interpersonal communication.* Newbury Park, CA: Sage.

McCroskey, J. C., Daly, J. A., & Sorensen, G. A. (1976). Personality correlates of communication apprehension. *Human Communication Research, 2*, 376-380.

Plax, T. G., Kearney, P., & Beatty, M. J. (1985). Modeling parents' assertiveness: A retrospective analysis. *Journal of Genetic Psychology, 146*, 449-458.

Reynolds, P. D. (1971). *A primer in theory construction.* Indianapolis: Bobbs-Merrill.

Rudner, R. S. (1966). *Philosophy of social science.* Englewood Cliffs, NJ: Prentice-Hall.

Sampter, W., & Burleson, B. R. (1984). Cognitive and motivational influences on spontaneous comforting behavior. *Human Communication Research, ll*, 231-260.

Tellegen, A. (1985). Structures of mood and personality and their relevance to assessing anxiety with an emphasis on self-report. In A. H. Tuma & J. D. Maser (Eds.), *Anxiety and anxiety disorders* (pp. 681-706). Hillsdale, NJ: Lawrence Erlbaum Associates.

Zuckerman, M. (1994). An alternative five factor model for personality. In C. F. Halverson, G. A. Kohnstamm, & R. P. Martin (Eds.), *The developing structure of temperament from infancy to adulthood* (pp. 53-68). Hillsdale, NJ: Lawrence Erlbaum Associates.

Author Index

Subject Index

A

act frequency, 19-21
affective orientation, 171-179
  correlates of, 172-175
  measures of, 178-180, 186
  tobacco and, 181-185
aggressive communication, 150-152
aggressiveness, 45, 48, 315
agreeableness, 3, 195
altruism, 48
amiables, 134
analyticals, 134-135
argumentativeness, 141, 149-
  170, 194-197, 208-210
  beliefs about, 153-154
  defined, 152
  effects of, 156-164
  enhancing, 161-164
  measuring, 155
assertiveness, 45, 48, 133-145,
  151, 315

B

behavior activation system
  (BAS), 52-53
behavior inhibition system (BIS),
  52-53

C

cognitive complexity, 233-286
  defined, 233
  management of social
    interactions, 260-263
  measuring, 241-244
  message production, 249-256
  message reception, 256-260
  social perception skills, 244-249
communibiology, 21, 41-67, 69-
  94, 120, 144-145, 196, 218-220,
  309-319
  implications of, 57-60
  physics of, 54-57
  propositions of, 46-54